Once Upon a City

Once Upon a City

Greensboro, North Carolina's Second Century

HOWARD E. COVINGTON JR.

Greensboro Historical Museum, Inc. | GREENSBORO, NORTH CAROLINA

Designed by Barbara E. Williams
Set in Scala and Diskus types
by BW&A Books, Inc., Durham, N.C.

The paper in this book meets the guidelines for permanence
and durability of the Committee on Production Guidelines
for Book Longevity of the Council on Library Resources.

ISBN-13: 978-0-9747456-1-9
Library of Congress Control Number: 2007942465

cloth   12 11 10 09 08   5 4 3 2 1

Contents

Illustrations

A gallery illustrating Greensboro 1900–1959 follows page 44 (Figs. 1–25)

1900–1945

FIG. 1. Greensboro's Elm Street was the retail marketplace for customers from throughout the northern Piedmont region of North Carolina. *(Courtesy Greensboro Historical Museum)*

FIG. 2. The Cone brothers, Moses and Ceasar, opened mills and started marketing fabric from Greensboro in the decade before the twentieth century. Their Cone Export and Commission Company marketed southern-made cloth. *(Courtesy Greensboro Historical Museum)*

FIG. 3. The Cones created an entire community of homes, retail stores, and churches in the area around their textile plants on Greensboro's north side. A trolley connected the city-within-a-city to downtown. *(Courtesy Greensboro Historical Museum)*

FIG. 4. Greensboro's Dudley High School, named for James B. Dudley, a president of Agricultural and Technical College (now NC A&T State University). It was one of the first fully accredited high schools for African American students in the state. This is the graduating class of 1930. *(Courtesy Greensboro Historical Museum)*

FIG. 5. Julian Price built the Jefferson Standard Life Insurance Company into a major force within the industry. He also played a significant role in the development of the community prior to his untimely death in 1946. *(Courtesy Greensboro Historical Museum)*

FIG. 6. Greensboro's location made it a central spot along the rail lines that crossed the South. Southern Railway Company, using the credit of the city of Greensboro to underwrite its effort, opened a new passenger station in 1930. *(Courtesy Greensboro Historical Museum)*

FIG. 7. The largest military post opened within a U.S. city during World War II was the basic training camp in Greensboro. It also served as the jumping-off point for servicemen headed to Europe as one of three overseas replacement depots. *(Courtesy Greensboro Historical Museum)*

FIG. 8. During World War II, schoolchildren collected scrap metal and rubber for the war effort. *(Courtesy Greensboro Historical Museum)*

FIG. 9. The military encampment on Greensboro's north side was built in record time and included training facilities, housing, hospitals, and entertainment for thousands of service personnel. It was decommissioned shortly after the war, and some buildings continue to be used for private businesses. *(Courtesy Greensboro Historical Museum)*

FIG. 10. Spencer Love built Burlington Industries into a worldwide enterprise by adapting new techniques and new fibers to an old industry. *(Courtesy Greensboro Historical Museum)*

FIG. 11. Burlington Industries would grow into the largest textile operation in the world. Its early headquarters opened in the mid-1930s on the edge of downtown Greensboro. The building later became the home of the county's social services department until it was razed to make way for construction of a new minor-league baseball park. *(Courtesy Greensboro Historical Museum)*

1946–1959

FIG. 12. The Greater Greensboro Open golf tournament resumed following the war. One of the perennial favorites was golfer Sam Snead. He often came in early to catch up on some fishing with his Greensboro friends. *(Courtesy* Greensboro News & Record*)*

FIG. 13. Grimsley High School, formerly known as Greensboro High School, opened in the 1930s and was expanded with a football stadium that was under construction by 1948. *(Photograph by Carol W. Martin, Greensboro Historical Museum Collection)*

FIG. 14. Ben Cone was an energetic mayor of Greensboro in the early 1950s. He was a leader among the mayors of North Carolina cities and helped direct some state highway funds to pay for urban street and highway needs. *(Courtesy Greensboro Historical Museum)*

FIG. 15. World War II delayed the opening of a regional catalog sales fulfillment center for Sears, Roebuck and Company until 1947. *(Courtesy Greensboro Historical Museum)*

FIG. 16. The nationwide polio epidemic hit North Carolina particularly hard, and Guilford County experienced more cases than most. A hospital to care for children and adults was built by volunteers with materials contributed by donors from across the country. *(Photograph by Carol W. Martin, Greensboro Historical Museum Collection)*

FIG. 17. Mayor C. M. Vanstory pressured the military to leave ORD as soon as possible after World War II. He managed the opening of Moses Cone Memorial Hospital and went on to head Security National Bank, one of the predecessor banks of Bank of America. *(Courtesy Greensboro Historical Museum)*

FIG. 18. Summit Shopping Center was Greensboro's first large retail concentration outside of downtown. It opened in 1950 on property at the edge of the former military installation. *(Courtesy Greensboro Historical Museum)*

FIG. 19. William Hampton, a physician, was the first African American elected to the city council. His election in 1951 was the result of a concerted effort by the Greensboro Men's Club, whose members included leading African American businessmen, teachers, doctors, and lawyers. Hampton is seated at the far right. *(Courtesy Greensboro Historical Museum)*

FIG. 20. Greensboro's city manager in the 1950s was James R. Townsend, a retired general. He laid the groundwork for improvements and changes to the city's infrastructure—especially water and traffic—and became a model for efficient municipal management around the state. One of his greatest concerns was an adequate water supply. The city's Lake Townsend was named in his honor. *(Courtesy Greensboro Historical Museum)*

FIG. 21. Moses H. Cone Memorial Hospital opened in 1953. The hospital had been a bequest in the will of the benefactor, who died in 1908, but money for construction did not become available until the death of his widow, Bertha, in 1947. *(Photograph by Carol W. Martin, Greensboro Historical Museum Collection)*

FIG. 22. To ease the postwar housing shortage, Greensboro builder Herman Weaver, who had helped erect military installations in the Carolinas, began building affordable homes in Greensboro to house returning war veterans. He was one of the first to build apartments, and his planned housing units won national recognition. He is pictured here with his wife, Edith, and son, Michael. *(Photograph by Carol W. Martin)*

FIG. 23. Elm Street in downtown Greensboro continued to be the retail center for the northern Piedmont into the 1950s. *(Photograph by Carol W. Martin, Greensboro Historical Museum Collection)*

FIG. 24. Cigarette manufacturing moved to Greensboro in 1954 when construction began on P. Lorillard's $13 million plant on the city's east side. It was the largest project of its kind in the state at the time. *(Photograph by Carol W. Martin, Greensboro Historical Museum Collection)*

FIG. 25. The Greensboro Coliseum was more than a decade in the making. When it opened in 1959, it had a seating capacity of nearly 11,000 for athletic events, the circus, and public concerts. *(Courtesy Greensboro News & Record)*

A gallery illustrating Greensboro 1960–1999 follows page 204 (Figs. 26–51)

1960s

FIG. 26. Ceasar Cone II was president of Cone Mills Corporation, the consolidated company that emerged after World War II, until he turned the company over to its first non-family chief executive, Lewis Morris, in 1965. *(Courtesy Greensboro Historical Museum)*

Fig. 27. Vance Chavis had a legendary following of his former students at Dudley High School when he was elected to the Greensboro City Council in the 1960s. *(Courtesy Greensboro Historical Museum)*

Fig. 28. The Jaycee leadership of the Greater Greensboro Open golf tournament broke ranks with leading tournament organizers and invited golfer Charlie Sifford, the first African American to become an approved tournament player through the Professional Golfers' Association, to participate in the 1961 tournament. Sifford returned for other tournaments. He is pictured here in 1967 with Bud Allin, a former GGO champion. *(Courtesy* Greensboro News & Record*)*

Fig. 29. Investment broker Oscar Burnett (center, flanked by GGO chairman Jim Melvin, left, and 1963 GGO champion Doug Sanders) turned the former military training base into one of the state's first industrial parks. In the 1960s, he helped negotiate racial tensions at the height of the civil rights movement. He was honorary chair of the GGO in 1963. *(Courtesy* Greensboro News & Record*)*

Fig. 30. Greensboro dentist George Simkins Jr. challenged the segregated world with determination and perseverance. His legal challenge to the racial segregation of Greensboro hospitals resulted in the removal of racial discrimination in medical facilities throughout the country. He later led the effort for district election of members of the city council. *(Courtesy* Greensboro News & Record*)*

Figs. 31 and 32. The sit-in demonstrations at Greensboro's Woolworth store in February 1960 sparked a movement that led to similar demonstrations around the country. Later, African American demonstrators filled downtown in demonstrations that led to mass arrests. *(Courtesy* Greensboro News & Record*)*

Fig. 33. Television's leading variety show host, Ed Sullivan, and South African golfer Gary Player played a round together at the 1965 GGO, where Sullivan hosted the tournament's annual banquet. *(Courtesy* Greensboro News & Record*)*

Fig. 34. Greensboro was selected as an All-America City by the National Civic League in 1966. Seated between L. Richardson Preyer (right) and his wife, Emily (left), at the celebratory dinner is businessman and civic leader Marion Follin. *(Photograph by Carol W. Martin)*

Fig. 35. Greensboro and Jim Melvin received nationwide attention in the late 1960s when a newspaper syndicate featured Melvin and the work of the state Jaycees' Partners of the Alliance project in Bolivia. Melvin traveled to South America with Greensboro businessman Hargrove "Skipper" Bowles, a major booster of the project. *(Courtesy Jim Melvin)*

Fig. 36. Jim Melvin watched returns on an early election with his wife, Susan. He was elected to a seat on the Greensboro City Council and, when reelected two years later, was chosen by council members as the mayor. He ran successfully for mayor four more times. *(Courtesy Jim Melvin)*

FIG. 37. Joseph M. Bryan adopted Greensboro as his hometown as if he had been born here. One of his favorite pastimes was hunting with his English spaniel, Jason. Jason's ashes are buried with those of his master at Bryan Park. *(Courtesy* Joseph M. Bryan Foundation)

FIG. 38. Gifts to the community from Joseph M. Bryan made possible the development of the award-winning park named in his honor on the banks of Lake Townsend north of the city. At the dedication with Bryan are his wife, Kathleen (seated left), and U.S. representative L. Richardson Preyer (at the podium). Behind and to the right is Greensboro mayor Jack Elam. *(Courtesy* Greensboro News & Record*)*

FIG. 39. Builder Joe Koury opened up new sections of residential development and then built the city's largest shopping mall, Four Seasons, which opened in 1975. He went on to develop the Grandover Resort and Conference Center. *(Courtesy* Greensboro News & Record*)*

FIG. 40. Greensboro's civic and business interests struggled to revive the center city after the major retail stores left Elm Street for the suburban shopping malls in the mid-1970s. The first major residential project was Greensborough Court, a joint development spearheaded by Jim Melvin of First Home Federal (left). With Melvin is Hugh North of Jefferson-Pilot Corporation, a partner in the venture that received a major setback when a fire destroyed a portion of the historic buildings included in the project. *(Courtesy Jim Melvin)*

FIG. 41. The city council elected in 1983 included members elected from districts as well as from the community at large. The new method ended more than a decade of contentious debate. The new council included (left to right) council members Dorothy Bardolph, Jim Kirkpatrick, Earl Jones, and Joanne Bowie; mayor John Forbis, city manager Tom Osborne; and council members Lois McManus, Lonnie Revels, Katie Dorsett, and Cameron Cooke. *(Photograph by Carol W. Martin, Greensboro Historical Museum Collection)*

FIG. 42. Mayor Jim Melvin's first campaign was powered by the slogan "Greensboro stinks." He and city manager Tom Osborne (center) worked for more than ten years to see the opening of a new sewage treatment plant that relieved south Greensboro of odors from an overworked facility. The groundbreaking celebrated by Melvin, Osborne, and Richard Howard preceded the 1984 dedication of the facility in Osborne's honor. *(Courtesy Jim Melvin)*

FIG. 43. On the morning of November 3, 1979, five demonstrators were killed after Ku Klux Klansmen and neo-Nazis descended on a group of communist labor organizers preparing for an anti-Klan march. A week later, marchers under heavy guard wound their way through Greensboro streets as the incident became embedded in the city's national reputation. *(Courtesy* Greensboro News & Record*)*

FIG. 44. Greensboro business leaders got behind a campaign to raise the level of sports competition at UNC Greensboro to Division I status. Leading the effort were (left to right) Stanley Frank, Michael Weaver, Charles Reid, Charles Hayes, and Jim Melvin. *(Courtesy Jim Melvin)*

FIG. 45. Sports became a major interest on the UNC Greensboro campus as the school's soccer team rolled up national championships under coach Michael Parker. The team celebrated its third NCAA Division III National Championship in Saint Louis in 1985. The Spartans won their third national title in four years with a 5-0 win over Washington University. *(Courtesy UNC Greensboro Sports Information)*

1990–1999

FIG. 46. Greensboro honored the contributions of Joseph M. Bryan to the city with the naming of a major thoroughfare in his honor following his death in 1995. At the unveiling of the signage for the new road were (left to right) Jim Melvin, Joseph M. Bryan Jr., N.C. secretary of transportation Garland Garrett, and the chairman of the state board of transportation, Douglas Galyon of Greensboro. *(Courtesy Jim Melvin)*

FIG. 47. One of the additions to downtown Greensboro came through the work of Action Greensboro, which spearheaded the development of Center City Park that formally opened in fall 2006. A signature of the park is a fountain with generous sprays of water. *(Courtesy Greensboro News & Record)*

FIG. 48. First Horizon Park replaced the city's aging War Memorial Stadium, which opened in 1927, as the home of the city's minor-league baseball team. In its first two years, the Greensboro team led the league with record-breaking attendance. *(Courtesy Greensboro News & Record)*

FIG. 49. Nothing symbolized the collapse of the textile manufacturing operations in Greensboro more than the demolition of the Burlington Industries headquarters building in 2005. *(Courtesy Greensboro News & Record)*

FIG. 50. The additions to the Greensboro Coliseum in the decades following its opening in 1959 created a facility capable of seating 23,500 in the arena and 2,400 in the adjoining auditorium. *(Courtesy Greensboro News & Record)*

FIG. 51. Downtown Greensboro began to enjoy a revival of businesses and entertainment venues. Elm Street is home to Triad Stage, a regional center for life performances; new eating establishments; and boutique businesses that took space in renovated buildings, some of which dated to the late nineteenth century. *(Courtesy Greensboro News & Record)*

Foreword

$\mathscr{I}$ you love Greensboro, this book is for you. It is a twentieth-century history of our city that was researched and written over a five-year period by Howard Covington Jr., who is a splendid storyteller who makes our leaders, our crises, our successes, our disappointments, our accomplishments all come alive.

When China's Mao Tse-tung was asked to evaluate the effects of the French Revolution that so closely followed our own (and Greensboro's founding) in the late eighteenth century, he responded, "It is too soon to tell." This book does not attempt to analyze or evaluate what unfolded in just half of that time. The writer presents the developments, the crises, the problems, giving all sides a chance to be heard. The challenge of having a city council that truly represents our population is dealt with. The tragedy of the Klan/Nazi disaster is faced. The tensions between our African American population and the white community are expressed, showing the emerging leadership from neighborhoods that had been left out of the decision making for much of the city's history.

You will enjoy reading about Moses and Ceasar Cone, Julian Price, Spencer Love, and many others who contributed to our economic life and gave leadership to the community.

This book is also the story of Jim Melvin and his incredible leadership in our city for nearly half of the twentieth century, beginning with his leading role in the Jaycees, later as a member of the city council and mayor for five terms, and culminating as the president of the Joseph M. Bryan Foundation. I have known Jim as a friend for more than three decades and have had an opportunity to observe him up close. He is a person with a strong religious faith, a true love for this city, and a deep desire to make Greensboro a great place to live. I am sure he has made mistakes along the way, but they are of the mind and not of the heart. God has given him boundless energy, enthusiasm, vision, and determination, and the city is better because he has lived among us.

It is intriguing that almost every project he undertook met with controversy. People often questioned his motives, criticized his methods, and doubted his integrity. I am reminded of the experience of the Israelites rebuilding the temple in Jerusalem after their return from their Babylonian captivity. The Book of Ezra vividly records their difficulties determining who would rebuild the city, allowing us to picture these builders at work with a trowel in one hand and a sword in the other. That seems to describe many of Jim's efforts.

As Greensboro celebrates its two-hundredth anniversary, it has much to be proud of, especially as it has been busy rebuilding itself in recent decades. When I arrived in Greensboro in the early 1970s, the downtown was quickly becoming deserted. I saw so many empty storefronts. Two hotels were imploded. It all looked so discouraging. Now, the downtown is becoming a vibrant, thriving area. The Depot looked so pathetic back then. Now, it is refurbished to the architectural gem it was meant to be, as rail and bus passengers move in and out throughout the day. We now see the economic results of extending Wendover Avenue out to I-40. We now have a boulevard to the airport and surrounding suburbs. Over these decades, the public parks have become showplaces, and our environmental concern has heightened. We have lost the industries that made us economically strong forty years ago, but they are being replaced by job training for new technologies that were unimaginable when I arrived.

I have seen the leadership of the city change, too. No longer do we depend on the chieftains of industry to be our only leaders. There is broad and diverse participation of residents from throughout the city who want to be a part of the decision making. Sometimes, this has created tension and disagreement. This is a by-product of a democratic society. If we can keep our civility and respect the opinions of others, we will win the day.

Once Upon a City is a splendid read. If you love Greensboro, as I do, this book is for you.

Joseph B. Mullin, Pastor Emeritus
First Presbyterian Church
Greensboro, North Carolina

W HEN THE last history of Greensboro was published in 1955, the city was a husky textile manufacturing center with mills producing staggering quantities of denim and other fabrics. Tobacco was king, not only for the farmers in the Piedmont who hauled their leaf to markets but also for workers who were just beginning to learn their jobs at the city's new cigarette manufacturing plant that was about to open on East Market Street. Elm Street, Greensboro's main north-south thoroughfare, was the retail center of the area, and its stores drew customers from all the surrounding counties. Every Saturday, the crush of shoppers made Elm Street look like the Christmas shopping season in most towns. Higher education was a pleasant by-product of the investment of the state of North Carolina in two state institutions that was augmented by colleges supported by Methodists and the Society of Friends. Greensboro was a pleasant city to raise a family, and those who thought about the future saw nothing but fair skies ahead.

A half-century later, none of the above was true. Textile manufacturing had disappeared. It was illegal to light up a cigarette in public buildings and restaurants, and one-time tobacco farmers had taken to producing crops of strawberries and other more benign crops. Some had begun cultivating vineyards. Downtown Greensboro was no longer central North Carolina's shopping destination. The suburban shopping malls had killed it off in the 1970s. Higher education, long taken for granted, had become one of the city's most important economic components, as had health care. The Moses Cone complex of hospitals employed more workers than any other nongovernmental business.

It is my hope that this book will help readers better understand the changes that transformed Greensboro in its second century. This city's story reflects much of what happened in other communities across the Carolinas, as traditional industries and businesses took flight and reshaped a world many had found comfortable and secure.

After the city's founding in the first decade of the nineteenth century, Greensboro became an agricultural center, with railroads linking it to markets across the land. Late in that era, entrepreneurs like the Cone brothers led the way into the twentieth century as the northern textile industry moved to the South to take advantage of lower wages and other advantages of being closer to the fields that produced the raw materials for their mills. Later, other entrepreneurs, including the irrepressible Spencer Love, created even larger enterprises. Love's Burlington Industries became the world leader in the textile industry. Its position looked unassailable, and its power and prestige helped make Greensboro the home of other industry giants. Much of this history is chronicled in *Greensboro, North Carolina*, a thorough study by Ethel Stephens Arnett and William C. Jackson published by the University of North Carolina Press in 1955. The Arnett-Jackson book tells Greensboro's story in solid academic fashion. Each compartment of the community's history, from religion to industry, is carefully recorded there. I recommend *Greensboro, North Carolina* to anyone interested in the city's first century and a half.

This book takes a different approach to Greensboro's story since the Second World War. It is a narrative that weaves together the lives of those who shaped Greensboro in the twentieth century. It is an account of those who wrestled with the challenges as all the accepted truths of commerce and industry began to unravel, leaving Greensboro to enter the twenty-first century with uncertainty.

One who figured most prominently during this period was Jim Melvin. He followed in the footsteps of other steady civic builders, but no other individual equaled Melvin's half-century of devotion to his hometown. He began in the early 1960s as a volunteer with the Greensboro Jaycees and continued as a council member and later mayor of the city during some of its most troubled days. After leaving public office, Melvin resumed his efforts on behalf of Greensboro from the private sector. Most recently, as the head of the Joseph M. Bryan Foundation, he led a rebirth of spirit and energy that continues to affect the appearance and future of Greensboro.

This book would not have been possible without the support of the Bryan Foundation and the willingness of dozens of people who helped me gather the story as it is presented here. They include the staff of city hall, who made space for me to review more than sixty years worth of newspaper clippings that are preserved there. Stephen Catlett of the Greensboro Historical Museum helped me find manuscripts in the museum's collection, as well as photographs to illustrate this period. These were combined with additional images provided the *Greensboro News & Record*. Helen Snow of the Greensboro Public Library also assisted in walking me through the oral history collection that is available there. Most importantly, I extend my thanks to the Bryan Foundation for underwriting this project.

I also appreciate the willingness of the Greensboro Historical Museum to adopt this book as publisher and usher it into public view just as Greensboro opens its bicentennial celebration. There could not have been a more fitting introduction.

Once Upon a City

Old Roots

It WAS ONE OF THOSE bright, glorious days in late fall 2002. The morning chill was sharpened by a brisk wind that cut through the small crowd gathered for a groundbreaking on a hillside northeast of the center of Greensboro, North Carolina. Those in coats pulled them tighter as gusts lifted the architect's rendering of a proposed new public building off a tripod and dropped it to the ground. Before long, the wind also had toppled a cluster of short-handled shovels that had been polished to a ceremonial shine and propped against a shaky podium. The clatter of the falling tools distracted the dignitaries from their prepared remarks.

None of these inconveniences seemed to matter greatly to the collection of city and county officials who had interrupted their morning routine to attend the ceremony, which some later described as a "tipping point" in Greensboro's history. Most were eager for a few minutes of encouraging words after weeks of public wrangling that had aroused emotions and sent official meetings into overtime. One city council session had not adjourned until well past midnight.

The day was particularly satisfying to Jim Melvin, the guiding presence of the Joseph M. Bryan Foundation and the man at the center of much of the storm. A former mayor, Melvin had given up public office so long ago that the current chair of the county's board of commissioners, attorney Mike Barber, was a teenager attending a city youth meeting when he heard then-mayor Melvin utter words that inspired him to pursue public service. Melvin had long since passed the mantle to others, but he had never set aside his determination to do what he could for his hometown, and he believed his current mission was as important as any of those he had undertaken in his years at Greensboro's city hall.

Greensboro was in deep trouble at the beginning of the twenty-first century, Melvin said when his turn came to speak. The region's industrial base was disappearing. Young people were choosing to begin their careers in larger and livelier communities. Once second only to Charlotte in size and economic promise, Greensboro had been bypassed in the 1990s by Raleigh and the economic blessings of the booming Research Triangle Park that had made even Durham a metropolitan contender. The structure Melvin could envision rising on the land where the ceremony took place would be more than just an office building for the agencies that delivered health and human services to Greensboro, he predicted. It would be the beginning of the renaissance of a city that would be far different from the Greensboro he had known as a young man. This $10 million structure was just one part of a much larger package that could renew Greensboro, especially the center city, whose skyline was visible in the distance.

And therein lay the rub in a scenario that was so routine yet so full of contradiction. None disputed the numbers Melvin and others had compiled in taking the measure of Greensboro's flagging economic and civic health. Yet as the shovels turned the dirt on that hillside, there were some in the precincts working just as hard as Melvin to stall the momentum behind a principal element of the plan for a renewed city offered by Action Greensboro, a community-based effort that Melvin had helped create. Critics believed something had to be wrong with the swap that Melvin had engineered to give the county a new building on ten acres of land in exchange for a plot of county property downtown where a subsidiary of the Bryan Foundation planned to build a minor-league baseball stadium.

Deep skepticism threatened a deal that would produce a gleaming new building local government could not otherwise afford in exchange for a few acres of land and a deteriorating structure downtown. While many praised Melvin's continued public interest in the city, there were others who wished he had faded into retirement long ago. His style of doing business was the wrong style for modern Greensboro, they said, and it represented the city's old establishment crowd once again deciding what was best for the people. Lost in the debate about personalities, however, was the notion that in many ways Greensboro was a city searching for its future.

Greensboro had begun the twentieth century with enthusiasm. In 1903, the Cone brothers, Moses and Ceasar, employed more than twenty-five hundred workers in their mills. Like other textile men of their day, the Cones constructed not only mills but entire communities for their employees that included houses, schools, stores, and churches. The Cones did not build Greensboro by themselves, but they certainly shaped what it would become in the twentieth century. In time, they were joined by other entrepreneurs, who expanded the manufacturing base that turned out work clothes and jeans with the popular names of Blue Bell and Wrangler. In the second half of the century, local firms would produce fabrics to line the interiors of automobiles and upholster sofas and chairs built by area furniture plants. None of the Greensboro-based textile enterprises would equal the work of J. Spencer Love, whose Burlington Mills Corporation, later Burlington Industries, set all manner of records for size and ingenuity as it became the largest textile manufacturer in the world.

Manufacturing *was* Greensboro, but the city also took pride in its appearance and good works. Local citizens turned out in 1948 to create, in less than a hundred days, a convalescent hospital for polio victims—a heroic effort that captured national attention. When the Greensboro Coliseum opened in 1959, it was a monument to civic vision, and it remained one of the largest venues in the South for a generation. The city's parks and recreational areas achieved national recognition. Good government was a hallmark, too, under a succession of proficient, professional civic engineers. If there was one thing for which Greensboro always received high marks, it was its neatly structured thoroughfares. "You can get anywhere in town in twenty minutes" became a popular mantra. For decades, a 1950s traffic engineer named Babcock was remembered for his contributions to the construction of the city's roadways as if he were a war hero.

In the 1960s and even into the 1970s, there were some who said this city, so well situated between the mountains and the coast, had become the rival of Charlotte, the state's leading metropolis that lay ninety miles south. "Let's make Charlotte a suburb of Greensboro" exhorted brickmaker Orton Boren, one of the good old boys who invigorated the local chamber of commerce in the late 1950s. Some tried to make good on Boren's bold challenge, but that was not to be. The old hands said the competition was over in the spring of 1960, when Charlotte bankers stole a march on competitors in Greensboro with the creation of North Carolina National Bank, which by 1998 had morphed into the huge Bank of America, one of the nation's largest. The 1960 merger closed Greensboro's largest banks, the reliable Security National and Guilford National, and dashed any hopes that Greensboro would be a financial center. Forty years later, with Charlotte's towering skyline carrying the names of the leading banks in the nation, some still talked about what might have been, like disconsolate southerners recalling Pickett's charge at the battle of Gettysburg.

The city's future may not have been in banking and high finance, but there were always textiles, furniture, and tobacco to fatten local payrolls. When Lorillard opened its $13 million plant in Greensboro in the mid-1950s, one writer at the *Greensboro Daily News* noted that the smell of tobacco was the smell of money. Greensboro remained a city of some heft. In 1970, it ranked second in the state with a population of 145,000. It was the headquarters of three insurance companies, including Jefferson Standard, which had regional holdings in broadcasting and other ventures. Five Fortune 500 companies had Greensboro addresses. That base seemed sound enough even into the 1980s, when Lorillard consolidated its operations and brought new folks into the city. The textile industry was in for a bumpy ride, however. Cone Mills weathered a financial raiding party in the early 1980s, as did Burlington Industries, which in 1987 fended off an attack that leveraged billions of dollars on the company's future. But Greensboro still seemed satisfied with its economic health. Upstart Guilford Mills, specializing in warp-knitted products for the auto industry, surged ahead.

The problems were not seen for what they were: early signs of the decline of American textile manufacturing. New employers moved in, and the city appeared to weather the rough times as textile plant jobs began to decline. Greensboro remained such a darn good place to live that some outsiders said the city suffered from "terminal smug."

Greensboro was chosen for the prestigious All-America City award by *Look* magazine in 1966. Millions in federal dollars poured in during the 1970s while Melvin was mayor. The city council used much of the money to build a first-class parks and recreation complex. There was just no better place to be, and locals were downright myopic. After Melvin bragged about Greensboro's quality of life to a group of Volvo employees due to be relocated from Portland, Oregon, one of the visitors noted that Portland was ranked even higher than Greensboro by Rand McNally. Melvin had not noticed.

By the mid-1990s, as cities around the Carolinas experienced booming growth, especially Charlotte and Raleigh, Greensboro's numbers paled in comparison. Greensboro had landed a blue-chip corporate citizen in 1985 when American Express opened a regional center on the outskirts of town, but that success was followed by a number of missed opportunities. The city was plagued by uncertainty over an inadequate water supply. Corporate mergers and acquisitions moved headquarters and home-office executives to other cities. The city retained its reputation as a twenty-minute town, but some wished for more than a "rush minute" on their way to and from work. If there were no cars on the streets, that meant the people were somewhere else, too. Those who could read the signs issued warnings about Greensboro's future. One of them was retired businessman William Hemphill.

Hemphill had grown up on the city's blue-collar south side in a neighborhood bordered by textile mills. His father waited tables in a hotel restaurant; his mother clerked in a dime store. During the Depression, young Bill sold copies of the weekly newspaper *Grit*, and Jim Melvin's father, Joe, always bought his first copy when Hemphill stopped by Melvin's Texaco station on South Asheboro Street. During World War II, Hemphill went to England with the air corps and returned to get his education under the GI Bill. His native ability with numbers, his clear head for analysis, and his steady business sense eventually made him a millionaire. Hemphill caught the attention of Ceasar Cone II, who had enlisted Hemphill's help with various civic assignments. Then, before Cone's death, he asked Hemphill to help manage a foundation that he planned to establish in the names of his children, Ceasar III, Martha, and Lawrence. In the early summer of 1999, Hemphill was due to meet with Ceasar's children during the foundation's annual meeting, but at the last minute found he could not attend. He sent a taped message instead.

It was time for new and bolder initiatives, Hemphill told the heirs. "There are forces working on Greensboro that are going to make this a terrible place to live in five, ten, or twenty years from now. The problems are going to be huge. Five years from now, the textile industry may not be in Greensboro. That is harsh to say. I don't know anybody who says that publicly, especially somebody like me."

Indeed, the dire pronouncement was all the more profound because of the man who delivered it. A quiet, studious businessman, thorough in every detail, Hemphill was not given to hyperbole or surprises. He had grown up in the worst of times and enjoyed the best of times. Moreover, he was well-schooled in the etiquette of the boardroom and for years helped manage the affairs of United Guaranty Corporation, which became a subsidiary of AIG, a worldwide financial enterprise. He knew the value of a dollar, as they say, but he was also familiar with nickels and pennies. Ceasar II once told him he picked him for one assignment because Hemphill, like himself, was a "cold-blooded son of a bitch." Actually, Hemphill's unflappable demeanor and bottom-line thinking belied an underlying warmth and liberal persuasion that often irritated his neighbors in well-to-do Irving Park. He had never thought of himself as an SOB.

"Textiles are gone as a place to provide employment. Tobacco is on the way out. Furniture is on the way out," Hemphill continued in his description of the changing economic landscape. "My grandchildren are going to have a terrible time making a living in Greensboro. What I am coming to with this pitch is that we ought to start thinking bigger in the foundation."

Hemphill prepared his assessment for only a handful of people, including Ceasar III and Martha, two of Ceasar II's surviving children, who were all members of the board of the Cemala Foundation. (The name of the foundation was created from the first two letters of the names of the three Cone children.) But word of Hemphill's videotaped remarks spread like a virus. Cemala's president, Priscilla Taylor, passed the tape to Melvin, who showed it to the members of the board of the Bryan Foundation, one of whom was his close friend, Mike Weaver, who then arranged for the members of his family's foundation to hear Hemphill's analysis. In time, copies made their way into the hands of many more.

Hemphill's predictions were all too accurate. By 2003, Cone Mills Corporation and the once-proud Burlington Industries were in bankruptcy, as was Guilford Mills. The city was on its way to having lost twelve thousand jobs in just three years. New jobs were being created in the service sector, but these replacement positions paid only half as much as those being lost in manufacturing. Moreover, the chamber of commerce was broke, and the city remained years away from finding a reliable source of water to sustain future growth.

The challenge offered by Hemphill was far different from anything Taylor or Melvin had ever brought to their board members, and they struggled with how to respond. Community building, especially economic development, was an entirely new area of enterprise. Where to begin? What was the goal? Who would provide the labor? There was no handy nonprofit standing ready with a grant proposal in hand. There were no models, no patterns, and only a few suggestions. At first, Melvin and Taylor just talked about possibilities. Richard L. Moore, a former university development officer recently recruited as the chief executive at the Weaver Foundation, soon joined them.

The three decided the first step was to take a measure of Greensboro's economic condition. They hired the nationally recognized management firm McKinsey and Company to do the work, and when the McKinsey report arrived in the latter part of 2000, the results confirmed the story already told in familiar daily headlines: Greensboro's economy was stagnant at a time when the rest of the southeast was enjoying unprecedented growth. Equally shocking, especially to civic pride, was the realization that Greensboro's peer cities were no longer Raleigh or Charlotte, which were clearly leading performers in the southern constellation, but communities like Chattanooga and Knoxville in Tennessee and Columbia, Greenville, and Spartanburg in South Carolina. And even among this second tier, Greensboro was not a leader.

With the baseline data in hand, along with recommendations from McKinsey about future steps, Taylor, Moore, and Melvin took the findings to the community, especially to those in elective office who carried the responsibility for the area's future. The results were disappointing. Elected officials heard their presentation and congratulated the trio for bringing the report to the community. All agreed something must be done, but none accepted the challenge of doing the heavy lifting. At the close of a presentation to the Greensboro City Council, one council member said, "This is great. Now who's going to do this?" Melvin, Taylor, and Moore looked at one another with surprise and dismay.

If the city's political institutions were unresponsive, average citizens were not. As word of the McKinsey report spread, the list of volunteers eager to work on behalf of Greensboro grew in a matter of weeks to more than fifteen hundred names. The result was Action Greensboro, a community-based civic improvement movement supported by money from the Bryan, Cemala, and Weaver foundations, as well as four other local foundations. Melvin, Taylor, and Moore remained at the center of the action, guiding, prodding, and shepherding the process along. They had not chosen this role for themselves; it fell to them by default. "We didn't have a long history to know we weren't supposed to do it," Taylor would later say.

Urgency dogged their steps. The clock was ticking; the community had no time to waste. In the context of a robust regional economy, a stagnant Greensboro would decline quickly if the old assumptions were not replaced with new ideas to meet future challenges. Melvin even wondered from time to time if the patient was already beyond recovery. That was a possibility apparent to the volunteers, and others, to whom Taylor passed a copy of her favorite book, *Who Moved My Cheese?* The book is an allegorical tale about change and the response to new and unexpected conditions. Greensboro must adjust, Taylor argued. Survival required breaking the habitual pattern, as the characters in Dr. Spencer Johnson's little book taught.

The resulting plan called for a $37 million program that reached into many areas, including business development, public education, business retention, the development of an attractive atmosphere for young professionals, and, of course, polishing Greensboro's image. In the spring of 2002, Action Greensboro unveiled a plan for downtown development that presented a center city where people lived and enjoyed life more than they conducted business. Among the anchors of the proposed revived downtown were a minor-league ballpark to be built at the edge of the city's southern boundary on South Elm Street, where a century of use by service stations, auto repair shops, light industry, and coal yards had turned the land into an environmental brownfield. It was no Love Canal, but the site clearly would require rehabilitation before anything, even a ballpark, could safely occupy it again.

The ballpark idea was pure Melvin. He liked the excitement of a new venture and looked forward to the change that a new stadium could bring to the city. The facility would offer a more presentable home for the city's minor-league baseball team than the aging War Memorial Stadium, which had opened in 1927. It could also energize others to look to Greensboro for investment, especially in downtown. Melvin had seen the impact of such a project in Chattanooga, which, like Greensboro, had reshaped itself with the help of a local foundation that inspired new projects along a deteriorated riverfront.

The resulting headlines in Greensboro focused on the stadium, but for Melvin, the project was not about baseball. Rather, the ballpark would be a tangible first step in Greensboro's recovery that would produce affordable family entertainment. It also could arouse the city's cautious public officials, who seemed to be waiting for someone else to make the first move.

Melvin was ready to act. Ahead of a public announcement of his plans, in an effort to avoid inflated land prices, stadium backers had quietly secured options on virtually all the land that would be needed. A schematic was ready, and a straw poll of the city council indicated its solid support. Then the process began to unravel.

Critics howled that the deal smacked of conflict of interest because Melvin held a minority share of the local minor-league franchise. Melvin sold his portion of the team, which he had bought a few years before in an effort to bring ownership of the franchise back home, but the issue would not disappear. When Greensboro's city manager suggested using a portion of the city's share of federal economic development funds to clean up the brownfield that was the proposed site of the ballpark—a necessary municipal expense regardless of what was to be built there—the furor grew louder. One member of an advisory committee who was a longtime critic of the former mayor claimed the stadium project would deprive the city of low-cost housing. Council support evaporated overnight. There was no denying the personal edge to the controversy. A few weeks later, when the council apportioned some of the federal "housing" money to buy land for a barbecue restaurant in an inner-city strip mall, there was no similar outcry.

So how did everyone end up on the hillside in November, just four months after the stadium seemed doomed? Getting there was not easy, and the outcome clearly demonstrated Melvin's determination and political savvy. With the South Elm Street site off the table, an alternative location that had always been an option became more attractive. There were problems. This site was just west of downtown and smack in the middle of a district that the highly touted Action Greensboro plan had envisioned as residential. When word reached nearby neighborhoods that the ballpark would be moving in, a new opposition campaign arose, and again the rhetoric turned personal—even mean.

Melvin pushed on in the face of a petition campaign to foreclose the construction of any stadium anywhere downtown. He fashioned an exchange with the county commissioners for the land and the aging building sited on it. Finally, in a council meeting that continued well past midnight, Melvin won approval for the closing of a street that bisected the proposed infield. The council vote was barely recorded before Melvin had a phone call in to Mike Barber, the chair of the county commission, setting a date for the groundbreaking of the county's new health services building.

For a project that had begun with great excitement, the victory seemed hollow somehow. As a result of an effort to revive the city, residents now seemed more divided than ever. The grumbling from neighborhood groups suggested a level of resistance to change that Melvin and others in Action Greensboro found troubling, not for the drag it placed on their plans but for what it said about a community stuck in its tracks. Even some of Melvin's peers, particularly those comfortable in the old way of business, questioned his motives and the activist role that the foundations had cast for themselves. Greensboro was struggling with itself, and no one, even those with the well-financed plans and architects' renderings, really knew what lay ahead.

The chill wind crossing the hillside north of Greensboro discouraged lingering for small talk when the groundbreaking ceremony for the new county building came to an end. As people hurried for their cars, some of them passed a knee-high granite monument just across the street in front of a building that had once been the site of a YMCA built by the Cones. The brass plaque on the stone marked the introduction in 1903 of a social work and health care program financed by the Cones for the benefit of workers who lived in the village that at one time had spread across the surrounding acres.

In a few weeks, construction of the new building for the county's social services departments began. Barring any unforeseen delays, the building would open in the fall of 2003. Perhaps this modest event would be a "tipping point." It was too early to tell.

Chapter 1

The Pivot of the Piedmont

If TEXTILES WERE THE engine driving Greensboro into the twentieth century, then the Cone brothers, Moses and Ceasar, were the men at the controls. The Cones and their partners owned not only three huge mills on the city's northeastern perimeter but also the houses, the stores, and even the streets and schools that served the twenty-five hundred workers—men, women, and children—who answered work whistles at the Proximity, Revolution, and White Oak plants they opened between 1895 and 1905.

The Cones built a manufacturer's "utopia"—or at least, that's what the *New York Herald* called it in 1915 when a writer paid a call on a mill village that was virtually self-contained. Workers paid less than a dollar per room per week to live in small frame houses within walking distance of the mill gate. During their first two decades of business, Ceasar and Moses, who died in 1908, opened the first industrial YMCA in the country, introduced a health program with company-paid social workers and nurses, and sent the milk, beef, and pork produced on their Proximity Farm to the company store to be sold at cost. The milk was delivered so quickly from the cow to the table that it was bottled raw and unpasteurized.

By the 1920s, Greensboro was well more than Cone Mills, to be sure. The city had begun to exercise the muscle of an emerging industrial center with a population of forty thousand, a number that doubled after the 1923 annexation of the Cone mill community on the north side and the Pomona mill village on the west side, as well as assorted suburbs on the perimeter. The city's footprint expanded from four to eighteen square miles.

By the middle of the decade, more than a hundred manufacturers had plants or home offices in Greensboro. One of the largest was the Blue Bell Overall Company, which cut and sewed sturdy blue denim into more bib overalls than any competitor. Home-grown Vick Chemical Company had a national market. The 1918 flu epidemic had turned Vick's VapoRub, a remedy created by Greensboro pharmacist Lunsford Richardson, into one of the nation's most popular drugstore items. Even the El-Rees-So Cigar Company had to put on extra workers in 1926 just to meet demand. Five life insurance companies and five fire insurance companies had home offices in Greensboro. And between 1926 and 1928, Bernard Cone, who had succeeded to the presidency of Cone Mills Corporation following his brother Ceasar's death in 1917, spent $4 million renovating the White Oak and Proximity mills. Old machinery was replaced, and individual motors were installed to replace the old belt and shaft system that powered looms in the huge weave rooms. With individual motors in place, the laborers in the weave rooms could keep working even when a nearby machine went down.[1]

The pride of Greensboro was the seventeen-story Jefferson Standard Life Insurance Company Building that opened in 1923 on Elm Street, the city's main thoroughfare. The twin towers of the $2.5 million building prompted a visiting Will Rogers to compare it to a youngster with a gap-toothed grin. Architect Charles Hartmann was so certain that other tall buildings would join the Jefferson headquarters that he left unadorned the sides of the building that did not face main streets.[2] Actually, there was nothing quite like this building between Washington and Atlanta. Visitors flocked to the rooftop restaurant, where a multi-course meal could be purchased for less than a dollar. The building was the candle on Greensboro's cake. Radio station WBIG—"We Believe In Greensboro"—beamed its signal from a tower on top.

Local boosters liked to say that Greensboro was the "Pivot of the Piedmont." Indeed, every car and truck traveling north, south, east, or west in this section of North Carolina passed through the intersection of Elm and Market streets, right at the foot of the Jefferson Building. U.S. 70 was the main route from the mountains beyond Asheville to the coast at Morehead City. U.S. 29 connected Greensboro with Washington, D.C., to the north and Charlotte to the south. U.S. 421, another mountains-to-the-coast highway, carried travelers on to Wilmington. The city's location at this nexus of highways and rail lines had prompted a late-nineteenth-century newspaper editor to call Greensboro the "Gate City."

Trucks left daily for distant locations with deliveries from local wholesalers in groceries, hardware, and drugs and sundries. Fashionable department stores and national retail chains, including F. W. Woolworth and S. H. Kress, had stores on Elm Street, which became the destination of Saturday shoppers from surrounding counties. So many customers crowded the sidewalks during the 1920s that downtown looked like Christmas every weekend of the year.

Local leaders were so proud of Greensboro that they built a new city hall in 1924 and a few years later opened a central fire station with a salaried crew of firefighters. The city built playgrounds and tennis courts and an athletic stadium that seated nine thousand spectators dedicated in memory of those who lost their lives in World War I. The mayor and council thought big. After a water shortage in 1923, the city sold bonds to install new water lines and later invested a million dollars in schools for whites and blacks. Greensboro's Dudley High School became the only accredited high school for African Americans in the state. The city operated a modern health department, built sixteen railroad overpasses, and encouraged housing development by cheerfully paving streets in subdivisions opened by real estate speculators. Eight hundred and fifty homes went up in 1925, and some predicted that four thousand new homes a year would be needed to keep up with demand. A population of one hundred thousand was predicted by 1935. The city extended credit to the Southern Railway Company to facilitate the opening of a new railroad station in 1927, where dozens of passenger trains stopped each day.

The city's two newspapers proudly reprinted, day after day, the new population figures, which placed Greensboro behind only Charlotte and Wilmington. The boastful mood was captured by essayist Gerald R. Johnson, who took note of Greensboro's overweening pride in an article published in April 1924. "Greensboro is the Master Key to the South's Best Markets. If you don't believe it, ask the Chamber of Commerce," Johnson wrote. He described a striving, an envy, and an energy in Greensboro that would not be denied as the locals sought to make Greensboro the equal of bona fide cities of the South, regardless of the consequences. Greensboro was no longer a "somnolent little Southern town," as it had been described at the turn of the century by native son William Sydney Porter, better known as O. Henry. At quarter century, Johnson said, "Greensboro . . . is new, but it is not complete; and the only story connected with it that is worth the telling must be a story of aspiration, a story of hopes hardly formulated, of ideals dimly perceived."

The new railroad station on Washington Street was long overdue. Like the highways, the railroads gave Greensboro access to all compass points. The new station was near the King Cotton Hotel, which opened in 1927 with 225 rooms. This hotel joined the slightly older O. Henry on Elm Street, and both offered accommodations as fine as travelers could find anywhere. A third hotel was planned for the building on the corner of Washington and Elm, but at the last minute, as the rousing crescendo of real estate development was beginning to fade, the structure became the home of United Bank and Trust Company. Formerly the Greensboro Bank and Trust Company, the new bank put its offices and teller windows on the lower floors and rented offices in the upper stories to business and professional people.

If anyone was unconvinced of Greensboro's place in the new, modern world, then they had not been to the western edge of the county, where an air terminal was built on open land that had once been part of J. Van Lindley's thriving nursery business. Greensboro was added to the airmail route in 1926, and in October 1927 famed aviator Charles Lindbergh was one of the first to put his wheels down on the site, just five months after he landed in Paris at the end of the first transatlantic flight. By 1930, passengers were boarding flights by Eastern Air Transport—a forerunner of Eastern Airlines—when Eastern initiated service between Richmond and Atlanta, with stops in Greensboro and Charlotte.

Greensboro was a comfortable town in a comfortable era. The city's elite owned large, spacious homes in Fisher Park, which sat astride North Elm Street, or in Irving Park, a newer subdivision on the city's northern rim whose wooded lots hugged the perimeter of a golf course at the country club. The success of Irving Park had inspired others, and real estate speculators thrived on infectious optimism about growth and progress. Subdivisions pushed west from downtown, past the campus of the Methodists' Greensboro College and the recently renamed North Carolina College for Women, which produced teachers for classrooms all across the state.

Among the more ambitious was A. M. Scales, who had created Irving Park in 1911. In the early 1920s, Scales purchased four thousand acres beyond the western city limits, where, convinced he would have a success equal to that of Irving Park, he incorporated the town of Hamilton Lakes and subdivided the land into lots, including a seventeen-acre lakefront tract on which he built a thirty-six-room Georgian mansion. Greensboro was born of real estate speculation in 1808, when one man's land was laid out as the city proper by the legislature; land development was still and would continue to be a principal engine of commerce.

By the end of the decade, the hubris of the 1920s was beginning to take its toll. Scales began as a millionaire, but his vision outran his fortune, and he forfeited his new town to creditors when the real estate boom turned to bust in 1928. As other real estate ventures failed, the solvency of local banks that had supported the frenzied market was threatened. Speculators had poured nearly $500,000 into the development of the Sedgefield Inn, a country manor between Greensboro and High Point with a golf course and riding stables; it sold for $75,000 at public auction the day after United Bank and Trust Company failed on December 30, 1931. The bank's collapse stunned the city and sent shock waves into nearby Reidsville and Burlington and as far east as Sanford, where United operated branch offices. Six months later, the bank reopened, but only after depositors agreed to take sixty-five cents for each dollar of deposits. For the balance, they received stock in a company that held the real estate United had taken in collateral on failed loans.

Greensboro did its best to paste over the mounting economic problems. When the bank reopened in July 1932 as The United Bank and Trust Company, having changed its identity only by adding "The" to its name, boastful newspaper ads proclaimed confidence in the bank's new structure. Business leaders urged citizens to stop hoarding their cash and spend—wisely, of course—to bolster the local economy. The front page of the *Greensboro Daily News* carried a large picture of an armored truck delivering $1.1 million in cash that the new bank had borrowed from a federal relief agency in one the largest loans yet made in North Carolina. "We have restored confidence in ourselves and each other," said Claude Kiser, The United's vice president. State Commissioner of Banks Gurney P. Hood said, "A wonderful people, with renewed spiritual power, will lead this community as it has never been led before."[3]

The newspaper was more restrained on February 10, 1933, when it reported that The United had failed as well. By this time, bank runs had become more commonplace, and more frightening. The United's failure seriously undermined public confidence and deflated the city's spirit. Greensboro's leading businessmen had failed in their efforts at economic resurrection. A month later, the North Carolina Bank and Trust Company collapsed. Nearly ten times larger than The United and headed by former governor Angus McLean of Lumberton, the bank had been created just weeks before the stock market crash in 1929 out of a merger of banks from Wilmington to Greensboro. A subsequent infusion of more than $3 million from the federal government's Reconstruction Finance Corporation was not sufficient to save it.

After president Franklin Roosevelt's "bank holiday" in March 1933,

Greensboro became the largest city in the nation without full financial services. The normal affairs of business, from cashing a check to securing a modest loan, ground to a halt. Everyone felt the pinch; the city government's bank account was virtually frozen. Like other customers, city officials could draw out only 5 percent of the nearly $90,000 in cash it had on deposit at North Carolina Bank and Trust Company. By the middle of the month, Greensboro city manager Andrew Joyner Jr. was able to raise only half the money he needed to pay the wages of city employees. He was not optimistic a few days later when he told a reporter, "We'll just have to muddle along and pay them [payrolls and local debts] as we get the money."[4]

Equally troubling was the fact that Greensboro had more than $70,000 in interest payments due on $17 million in public works bonds that had been used to build schools and a water system in the good times, before the real estate market crashed. With hats in hand, Joyner and others traveled to New York and begged for leniency from creditors.

Greensboro's leading financial man was Julian Price, the head of Jefferson Standard Life Insurance Company. He did his best to shore up confidence and urged people to remain "cool and calm" when he was quoted in a front-page story in the *Greensboro Daily News* as banks closed their doors. "We are going to emerge from this troublous situation with a cleaner, sounder financial structure in the United States," Price declared.[5] He did not suggest that time would be soon, however. In the coming years, his company foreclosed on nearly one-third of the $18 to $20 million in mortgages it held in North Carolina and elsewhere, including a sixty-three-hundred-acre Mississippi plantation.[6]

Businesses already weakened by a sagging economy were brought to their knees. The El Moro Cigar Company put three hundred workers on the streets when it could not withdraw enough cash from the bank to meet its payroll. The company did what it could and made arrangements with local grocers to get food for employees. The city council formed an emergency committee to investigate the possibility of issuing scrip, a move applauded by the merchants on Elm Street, whose customers had no money to buy goods. Julius Cone, who ran the Cone Export and Commission Company, chaired a committee that promptly produced plans to implement a scrip program within forty-eight hours. The situation was eased and the immediate crisis passed, however, when Cone Mills and Vick Chemical, firms with accounts in banks outside of Greensboro, began paying employees in cash.

There was other good news. Ceasar Cone's family announced that they would make good on the losses of depositors in the Textile Bank, a Cone enterprise that had been absorbed into North Carolina Bank and Trust Company in 1929. According to Ceasar's son Herman, "Ceasar Cone organized the Textile Bank . . . in order to encourage his employees to save a part of their earnings and to provide a safe place where they could deposit their savings."[7] The bill for this act of generosity eventually came to $300,000.

Many in the city were in desperate straits. By April, 900 men had signed up for relief jobs; about 350 reported each day for duty that included improving public parks and streets. When these workers struck for wages better than the eighty cents a day they received, a local reporter quoted a bystander who said that the strikers should be happy to have something to take their minds off their problems. Local services provided help where they could. Twenty-eight families of the unemployed agreed to leave their homes in the city and relocate to farms, where they were hired on as tenant farmers. About thirteen hundred families in the city joined a program to grow table food. The city distributed two thousand free boxes of seeds for tomatoes, lettuce, cabbages, turnips, beets, and carrots, and three hundred acres went under cultivation.[8]

A hobo community on the city's western edge was growing in population. Dozens of men, women, and children took up temporary residence in the open spaces beside the freight yards at Pomona. Their numbers varied from day to day, but one sunny spring afternoon as many as five hundred were counted on a train headed west. The travelers came from all corners of the country. A black man and his wife were just back from California, where they had gone to find jobs as servants in the home of a movie star. "Out there you can't get no work," he told a reporter, explaining, "There's too many Mexicans and furriners." An eighteen-year-old said he had been to army recruiting offices in forty-eight states but was turned down everywhere. When he asked one recruiting sergeant why he had not removed a sign that read "Join the Army" from the office window, he was told that if the sign were removed, the sergeant would have to close the office.[9]

In early July 1933, Greensboro got to feel good about itself, if only for a day, when four thousand people turned out for the dedication of a new post office on West Market Street. U.S. Postmaster General James Farley attended, along with the state's U.S. senators, Josiah Bailey and the recently elected Robert Reynolds, who had defeated incumbent Cameron Morrison by campaigning for the repeal of prohibition. Farley, a tall man who stood a full head above Bailey, brought some hope that

Franklin Roosevelt's plans for recovery would change Greensboro and the rest of the country for the better.

A week later, the city turned out again, this time to mourn the death of Paul Lindley, Greensboro's mayor, who drowned when he fell overboard from a small fishing boat on his farm near the airport. It was a freak accident: Lindley drowned in water just seven feet deep. Once an excellent swimmer, he had recently dislocated his arm in a fall and could not help himself when he fell headfirst into the water as he stood to release a line. A thirteen-year-old companion who rowed Lindley's fishing boat for him brought rescuers. They found the mayor's body semi-upright underwater, resting against a log.

Lindley had been a mainstay of the city leadership. His father was one of the city's largest landowners and the creator of Lindley Park, a subdivision that featured an amusement park at the terminus of the western trolley line. The Lindley nursery business was known throughout the South, and the family had money in Pomona Terra Cotta, Jefferson Standard, Carolina Steel and Iron Company, and a host of other business enterprises. Mayor Lindley, too, had fallen on hard times and was unable to pay his property taxes at the time he drowned. His death was rumored to be a suicide.

Normal times remained a distant dream in the summer of 1933, but on August 28 there was an important development: the doors opened on a new bank. Called Security National Bank and Trust Company, it was created from the remains of North Carolina Bank and Trust, the failed Page Trust Company of Aberdeen, and Independence Trust of Charlotte. The official notice of the charter arrived from federal regulators on a Saturday with the stipulation that business begin immediately. Bank president N. S. Calhoun made a nominal deposit, and Security was in business. When the doors opened Monday, three tellers stood ready for the first customers. By the end of the day, two more tellers had been recruited to handle deposits of more than $800,000. Calhoun told a reporter that the day's business had all but depleted the bank's supply of deposit slips. After a lapse of nearly six months, Greensboro was finally reconnected to the nation's financial network.

––––––

The man behind the creation of Security National was Julian Price, whose Jefferson Standard Life Insurance Company had continued to grow and pay dividends despite the bad times. Price himself refused to publicly acknowledge the Depression; he referred to recent years as a "small boom."[10] As the new bank opened, the company was preparing to celebrate Price's birthday. The occasion was a gimmick Price had introduced in 1915 to boost sales of insurance policies. Each year, agents worked like demons throughout the fall and then cheerfully delivered stacks of new policies to the company headquarters on Price's birthday, November 25.

Price was not an imposing figure, but he was memorable. He was of average height and build and well-outfitted. He wore bespoke suits, sported a neatly trimmed mustache, and was never without a walking cane, and he insisted on wearing his hat indoors. Dimpled cheeks and soft, hooded, close-set eyes offered up a relaxed expression that hid an inner toughness and determination. He had risen through the ranks of the company he had joined in 1905 after a short turn as a snuff salesman and training as a telegraph operator. His own experience may have been the basis for Jefferson's reputation for loyalty to its agents and home-office employees. Promotions came from within the ranks, and the good feeling was returned: Price was a beloved corporate leader. He had an aversion to pay raises, but he opened a rooftop lounge for the 250 home-office employees and built a company playground with a clubhouse and a lake for swimming on several hundred acres of land near Guilford College west of town.

Price was well-known throughout the state, but only insiders were aware that he was the man responsible for the restoration of Greensboro's banks. Not long after he engineered the opening of Security National, The United was resurrected as Guilford National Bank in March 1934. The majority of the stock in the second bank was held by Pilot Life Insurance Company, which Jefferson Standard had acquired in 1930. Price preferred working behind the scenes. The harsh realties of the Depression had harmed public opinion of bankers, and he worried that such ill will could spill over to Jefferson if local citizens knew his company controlled local banking.[11]

Life in south Greensboro was a long way from the world of Julian Price. One of the main thoroughfares was Asheboro Street. It peeled off from Elm south of the railroad tracks, turned southeast, and became U.S. 421 by the time the two-lane highway passed over South Buffalo Creek at the city limits. Houses lined both sides of Asheboro Street for most of the distance. Some of them had been the grand homes of merchants, bankers, and businessmen in the horse-and-buggy age. Now the street offered a mixture of aging Victorians and tidy bungalows on small lots owned by a broad spectrum of the city's citizens.

On Asheboro Street proper, most were middle-class folk, the kind who ran retail stores and worked in offices on Elm Street. Just east of Asheboro Street was the edge of Greensboro's African American community, whose residents held a range of jobs, from domestic workers in the homes in Irving Park to faculty positions at Bennett College and the state agricultural and technical college on East Market Street. West of Asheboro Street were textile plants and a mill village. Farther south, along the banks of Buffalo Creek, were fertilizer mills, the city's sewage treatment facility, and a foul-smelling rendering plant where the carcasses of horses and cows were turned into usable tallow and glycerin. When the wind came out of the southeast on warm, humid summer nights, south Greensboro was definitely not Irving Park.

Joe Melvin's service station on Asheboro Street was a favorite last stop for travelers headed south out of Greensboro. Three streets intersected in front of his Texaco sign, and the nexus created a compact shopping center for a handful of merchants. Melvin's father had run a grocery and meat market in a building just behind the station before it failed in the early days of the Depression. It was said that S. O. Melvin would sort his mail each morning by throwing the bills in the trash can and pocketing the checks. Now his sons, Joe and Charles, who ran his own grocery near the Woman's College of the University of North Carolina (locals called it "the W.C."), each took money out of the tills of their own businesses to whittle away at the debts their father had left behind.

Joe Melvin knew a lot of people, and about a lot of people. Some of his civic intelligence had been collected during the years when he and his brother made deliveries from their father's grocery store to the homes of the wealthy out Summit Avenue or in Irving Park. The servants and cooks liked to talk about their employers. Mostly, though, he had gotten to know his neighbors because he liked to chat when they stopped by his station to buy gas or tires, to wait for minor repairs, or just to visit. He kept the station spotless and paid attention to every detail and every expense. Each day at noon, he put a nickel in the pay phone, dialed the number of his house just down the street, and let it ring one time. He then dropped the receiver back in the cradle and retrieved his nickel. That was the signal to his wife, Virgil, that he was on his way home for lunch.

Joe Melvin was nothing if not frugal and hardworking. He opened the station promptly at 6 AM and was on duty—except for lunch—until

7 PM. That made the difference with a young family to support. In the fall of 1933, he and Virgil already had one son, Joe's namesake, and she was expecting again. They made their home in the 1800 block of Asheboro Street in a small frame house six blocks south of the station.

Joe had deep roots in the area. His family was from the northeastern corner of the county, where his grandfather had been one of the founders of a Methodist church. Virgil was born in Knoxville, Tennessee, which was one of several cities her family had called home before her father, an engineer with the Southern Railway, landed a choice assignment as an engineer on the Southern Crescent, which passed through Greensboro twice a day. Their home was on Summit Avenue on the north side, where the Cones and other executives at the mills had large houses. She met Joe at the grocery store, and the two eloped to Asheville to be married in 1927.

Greensboro merchants were in an optimistic mood as the Christmas shopping season approached in 1933. "The attitude of fear, so prevalent last year, has disappeared," one businessman was quoted as saying in the *Greensboro Daily News*.[12] Public records seemed to bear out the claim: the number of marriage licenses issued had doubled from a year before. Two days before Christmas, Bernard Cone announced a cash bonus and free Christmas hams for employees—usually there were just hams.

There was also desperation, however. On Christmas Eve, as Virgil Melvin gave birth to a son, someone left an infant on the doorstep of the North Carolina Children's Home on Fairmont Drive. Fortunately, the weather was relatively mild, almost fall-like, the paper said. Both infants were reported to be healthy and hearty. Joe and Virgil chose Edwin Samuel as their son's name, but his older brother, Joe, thought the name Jim sounded better. In time, everyone would call him "Jim."

——

It would take years before Greensboro climbed out of the deep financial hole that the city fathers had dug for themselves in the 1920s during the period of unrestrained real estate development; in this, Greensboro was like most of the nation. By the mid-1930s, when the banking crisis had passed, the city settled into paying debts that would consume as much as half of the city's revenue for years to come.[13] As a result, many local institutions and programs, including the public schools, went without. When Bob Jamieson joined the faculty at Greensboro High School in 1933 to start a career in coaching two generations of Greensboro athletes, he found that the teams of Greensboro's proud new high school had no uniforms. The following spring, at the start of baseball season, his players were outfitted in dungarees. He solicited money for jerseys from Greensboro merchants in exchange for stitching the names of their stores on the back. It would be years before the coach found uniforms easier to come by. In the lower grades, football helmets were in such short supply that the coaches had to take players' head size into account when making substitutions during games.

Greensboro held as steady as it could, thanks largely to the production of Cone Mills's denim, part of the uniform of everyday working people, farmers and factory hands alike. The Greensboro plants kept running—though often with shortened workweeks and reduced payrolls —producing fabric for fifty-cent chambray shirts and two-dollar overalls. During the most difficult days of the Depression, the Greensboro mills remained open, even in the face of the nationwide textile strike in the late summer of 1934.

By the 1930s, the South was the home of the nation's textile industry, and the Carolinas were the living room. More cotton was consumed, more spindles turned, and more workers answered work whistles in North and South Carolina than anywhere else in the nation. The textile industry had forsaken its traditional home in New England in the first quarter of the century and moved south to take advantage of abundant, cheap electrical power and lower wages. At the start of the Depression, there were 1,292 mills in the cotton-producing states of the South, and 752 were in the Carolinas. Greensboro was not as large a textile center as Gastonia, just west of Charlotte, or some cities in South Carolina. Nonetheless, nearly ten thousand workers—one-fourth of the city's population—owed their livelihood to the local mills.

The Cone presence in Greensboro was commanding, and deeply beneficial. In May 1934, the family announced that it was building a $250,000 addition to its White Oak plant, where twenty-five hundred employees worked. The expansion would add another thousand jobs. Such news was rare in those times, and well-received.

The strike called by the United Textile Workers of America in the summer of 1934 was to begin on Labor Day, September 4. By flexing the collective muscle of their membership, union organizers hoped to force owners to raise wages and end so-called stretch-outs, which forced fewer workers to produce more yarn or cloth in less time. The 1934 strike threat followed years of unrest and mounting problems. The enthusiasm for a walkout gained momentum in some corners of the region as Labor Day approached, but in Greensboro, where the union had managed to develop only a modest toehold in the community, the call to strike went unheeded.

Management's position was well-known. Some workers believed that Ceasar Cone had left instructions in his will to close the mills rather than recognize a union. During an organizing drive in 1930, a union representative could not even find a landlord willing to rent him office space. The organizing effort continued nonetheless, and in August about a thousand workers attended a rally in an open field at McAdoo Heights, a neighborhood of mill workers at the edge of the Cone property. The rally followed a court hearing over the eviction of workers from mill houses whose union membership was known to their bosses. One Cone official admitted in open court that a man had been discharged and subsequently evicted because of his union activity.

Many workers nonetheless remained loyal to the Cones. The entire family had been generous, not only with Christmas turkeys and hams but also with cash to build churches and facilities such as the YMCA, where a man could pay a dime and take a shower, just like his overseer. Herman Cone, Ceasar's oldest son, built and supported Camp Herman, a camp on Cone land north of Greensboro operated for boys from the mill community. "The Cones is awful good," one worker told a visitor, "where big things is concerned. I've got nothin' to say against the Cones, and I'll have nothin' to do with no labor union."[14]

Labor Day, 1934, passed, and the mills in Guilford County operated as usual. Bernard Cone, speaking for management, told the newspaper that all four of the company's plants—Proximity, White Oak, Revolution, and Proximity Print Works—were operating. He told one reporter that workers seemed more concerned about baseball than about "distant labor troubles." He likened the labor agitation to a boil upon the industry that "needs lancing." This treatment, Cone explained, would "bring out the bad blood and refine the good."[15] A day later, roving groups of striking workers—known as "flying squadrons"—fanned out across the Carolinas to bring the strike home to large employers like Cannon Mills, where fifteen thousand employees reported to plants in Kannapolis, North Carolina, and Springs Mills, with its ten thousand workers in Fort Mill, South Carolina. Greensboro and the Cones' mills also were on the list.

Picketers closed mills in nearby High Point and Jamestown, but in Greensboro they were met by Sheriff J. S. Phipps and about three hundred "special officers" whom he had deputized to protect private property. National Guard troops also moved in and ordered forty men to leave Greensboro Weaving Company's plant on Arlington Street, not far from Joe Melvin's service station. Picketers were rousted from the villages around the Cone plants on the north side of town, as well. By week's end, "the Cone mills . . . presented the appearance of a miniature armed encampment as steel-helmeted Guardsmen patrolled the industrial areas with full field equipment." But every Greensboro plant was operating normally. That was in stark contrast to Gastonia, where only 3 of the city's 104 mills remained in operation. Elsewhere in the state, a total of 67,035 workers stayed off the job.[16]

After six workers were killed in Honea Path, South Carolina, confrontations closer to Greensboro threatened violence. As the strike moved into its second week, 150 National Guardsmen stood between a crowd of three thousand and the gates at the Adams-Millis hosiery mills in High Point as workers who had remained on the job tried to leave after their shifts. The uncertain atmosphere pervaded every corner of the surrounding area, and some workers gathered for outdoor rallies in support of the strike.

The mood was tense at one such rally in Gibsonville, just east of Greensboro, but Ben Cone, Ceasar Cone's second eldest son, dared to attend. He stood in the crowd and listened and then without invitation mounted the platform and commended the organizers for the sane tone of their rhetoric. All he asked before he stepped down was for voters to remember him in November in his campaign for the state legislature.[17] The strike was waning by the third week, just as an organizer for the Communist Party declared he planned to open a regional office to lend support to the Cone workers. By the end of the month, it was over. Workers who had walked out in other cities returned to their jobs, some with modest concessions from owners in their hands. The Cone plants continued on as usual.

J. Spencer Love's Burlington Mills Corporation avoided a direct hit from the nationwide strike. Unlike most companies whose operations were concentrated in one town with workers clustered nearby in the mill village, Love's company's plants were scattered across the Piedmont. As a result, organizers found it hard to focus their campaign against the company. Love had not planned it that way. Beginning in the mid-1920s, he had built a network of mills by buying bankrupt companies. He stripped the buildings of old machinery, installed new equipment, and by 1934 had mastered the production of fabrics from rayon, a synthetic fiber called "the poor man's silk" that old cotton men found hard to spin into usable yarn. Burlington Mills quickly became a world leader, and Love's plants turned out vast quantities of shiny, hard-wearing bedspreads that sold out as soon as they arrived in stock, despite having an unattractive seam down the middle—necessary because Love's early looms were not wide enough to produce a full-sized product.

At the beginning of the Depression, Love's company was headquartered just east of Greensboro in Burlington, the town that had bid for his interest when he was first starting in business in 1924. Known originally for its railroad shops, Burlington had been transformed by Love into a textile town. The early arrangement proved so successful that he adopted Burlington as the name of his company and repeated the strategy of combining money from local investors with his own borrowed cash to quickly organize more than thirty textile companies around the state.

Love was a New Englander who was trained at Harvard and had come south to make his fortune after World War I. He made his home in Burlington, where he rented a large, stately old dwelling for $300 a month, an astonishing sum to his neighbors. Burlington was a small town, and Love's home was not far from a mill community with a rough reputation. Fights were common on weekend nights. Drinking and hard living was the norm. If Love knew of the problems on the streets, he paid them little heed. He was constantly on the road and seldom in one place long enough to invest himself in Burlington's local affairs.[18]

In 1935, the year after the nationwide textile strike, Love moved his company's headquarters to Greensboro and began construction on a twelve-thousand-square-foot mansion on Country Club Drive in Irving Park that was finished in 1936. Work on his home and on another for Herman Cone produced welcome jobs for unemployed carpenters, masons, and laborers. In 1937, the same year Burlington Mills Corporation joined the New York Stock Exchange, the company moved into a new headquarters building on Eugene Street at the western edge of downtown Greensboro. Burlington's national exposure added considerable luster to Greensboro's reputation as a textile center.

Other businesses enjoyed a lift as work returned to the mills. In 1939, a new Belk department store opened at Greensboro's busiest intersection, Market and Elm. It was the first air-conditioned store in the Belk organization that had spread across the Carolinas. The Meyer's department store, a locally owned business, also expanded its space. Traffic returned to Elm Street, where a series of neon signs shaped like arrows directed drivers around a circle near the railroad. A year earlier, a group of young businessmen called the Junior Chamber of Commerce, or Jaycees, had produced the Greater Greensboro Open golf tournament, which attracted virtually every leading professional golfer in the country, with a total purse of $5,000. Six thousand spectators crowded around the greens at the course at Starmount Country Club for the first round on March 26, 1938. Two days later, Sam Snead walked away with the top prize of $1,200.

By the summer of 1941, Greensboro was calling itself the "City of Charm." The slogan appeared on lighted fifteen-by-thirty-five-foot billboards that the chamber of commerce placed along major routes forty to fifty miles from downtown. Indeed, Greensboro was as comfortable a place as could be found in the state at the time. Retail sales were growing, and the city offered many advantages as a place to live. Professional baseball was back with the arrival of the Boston Red Sox farm team, which had formerly played out of Rocky Mount in eastern North Carolina. It had been absent from Memorial Stadium since 1934, when the team moved to Asheville after Greensboro voters prohibited professional baseball, along with movie houses, as unsuitable Sunday entertainment.

Thirty-two passenger trains arrived daily. Air passengers now had access to an east-west service aboard Pennsylvania Central Airlines Transport. Six Eastern Airlines flights left daily from an airport with improved runways, thanks in large part to Ceasar Cone's youngest son, Ceasar II, who offered to put up the entire $60,000 the city needed to qualify for a federal grant for airport expansion.

Greensboro had more than a hundred churches, five colleges with a total of four thousand students, five hospitals, and five fire stations with thirteen pieces of equipment between them. There were nineteen parks covering 425 acres. The White Oak plant was the world's largest denim mill, and Blue Bell was the world's largest manufacturer of overalls. The Richardson family's Vick Chemical Company had moved its headquarters out of the city at the start of the Depression following a short-lived merger with four other companies, but its popular remedies, VapoRub and Vick's Cough Drops, were manufactured locally and known across the country. The chamber of commerce mounted an aggressive campaign for Greensboro citizens to promote the city and pledge allegiance. "This Is Your Greensboro," a full-page newspaper ad proclaimed, demanding, "Make Its Problems Your Own!"

Indeed, the city was beginning to shake off some of the scales of the past. But behind the hyperbole was the raw fact that in 1940 the municipal budget was 10 percent less than what the city council had spent in 1936. Real estate sales had fallen far short of expectations, and many of the city's 138 miles of paved streets passed vacant lots. Greensboro was still paying off notes for money used to provide services to neighborhoods that would not have homes for another decade or more. "My predecessors in office had just about paved everything," recalled Huger King, a young attorney who won his first city council term in 1939. He said the new fire hydrants standing sentry on empty streets were only useful to "woodpeckers [that] were using them to sharpen their bills."[19]

Yet it appeared that Greensboro might be heading in the right direction. On the day after the municipal elections in the spring of 1941, the city council—all of whose members had been easily reelected—took up a controversial zoning change to permit construction of a regional distribution center for a major retailer. Nothing was official, but it was said that Sears, Roebuck and Company wanted to put a regional mail-order center on a forty-acre site alongside Lawndale Drive on Greensboro's northwest side. The $2.5 million project would produce the largest structure in town, with three times the floor space of the White Oak plant. City leaders were thrilled; this was the biggest economic development plum Greensboro had seen in years. Eight hundred to a thousand jobs were on the line.

Neighbors along Lawndale and in the nearby well-to-do precincts were horrified, however. Voters in Kirkwood and Irving Park packed the council chambers and leaned heavily on council members such as King, who had married into the Richardson family and himself had an Irving Park address. "It was just a few scattered houses," King said some years later, "but they saw it as great threat. I knew what I was going to do and knew what most of the council was going to do. We couldn't afford to lose something like this."

King had only recently become mayor. He let the meeting run long, as more than fifty people asked for time to be heard, but he did not doubt the outcome. The council was a homogenous group. They were all businessmen and on the side of the chamber of commerce, which had heavily courted Sears. Sitting with King on the council were Kemp Clendenin, one of the leading real estate men in town, and W. H. Sullivan, a building contractor. They all knew what the project would do for local business. Edgar Weaver, the representative from the Cone Mills district, could be counted on to approve the change. Just before the vote, however, T. A. Glascock, whose company manufactured cast-iron stoves, leaned over to King and said he had taken account of the protesters and changed his mind. "I can't vote against my daughter," he told King before casting the lone dissenting ballot.

It would take six years for the Sears building to open, but it was a war, not opposition from the neighbors, that delayed the project.

Chapter 2

Army Town

$\mathcal{G}$ REENSBORO'S BLUE laws forbade business on Sundays. That was fine with Joe Melvin, whose family could always be found attending the Sunday school and worship services of West Market Street United Methodist Church, an established congregation whose distinctive brick Romanesque building stood just across from the courthouse. In the afternoons, it was not unusual for Joe and his boys to head out in the family's 1939 Chevrolet to spend a few hours on the farm. Melvin had modest investments in real estate, and one of his holdings was fifty acres of rolling farmland that fronted on Alamance Church Road a few miles south of the city limits. Elements of the farm often found their way to the Melvin home on Asheboro Street; a goat was sheltered in the family garage at one time, ponies at another.

On the afternoon of December 7, 1941, Joe Melvin and his son Jim were on their way to the farm to check on a new calf when they heard the news about the Japanese surprise attack on Pearl Harbor on the car radio. Joe Melvin pulled the car to the side of the road, and the two listened carefully.

Elsewhere across the city, others stopped and absorbed radio reports of life-changing events that had occurred half a world away. Even as the broadcast continued, men in uniform were moving through the city. On that Sunday, more than twelve hundred army vehicles carrying eight thousand men of the Pennsylvania National Guard were en route home through Greensboro after three months of maneuvers in the North Carolina sandhills near Fayetteville. Mayor King and other city officials urged folks to remain calm. Residents were assured that the one Japanese national known to be in Greensboro had been accounted for. "He has been examined," said police chief L. L. Jarvis, "and will be examined again." Within days, men and boys flocked to the recruiting offices.

America's defensive preparations for the growing war in Europe already had taken Greensboro men into active duty. In September 1940, the local National Guard contingent, a coast artillery unit nicknamed the Guilford Grays, reported for service. They shipped out to Trinidad under the command of Major Ralph L. Lewis, the city's popular mayor, who resigned from office in favor of Huger King. The original assignment was for one year, and when the men had not returned by the summer of 1941, mothers, wives, and sweethearts sent a delegation to Washington to complain. Some of the wives and families of the officers had even begun to prepare to join their men in Trinidad when the unit was ordered back to the states. At the time of the Pearl Harbor attack, the Grays were stationed at Fort Bragg, near Fayetteville, and a welcome-home dance was scheduled for the night of December 13.

The war would change all of America before it concluded in 1945, but it would have a particularly profound effect on Greensboro, a city of almost sixty thousand residents in 1941. Before it was over, the largest military post built entirely inside municipal boundaries would open just south of the Cones' Proximity mill village. Between early 1943, when the post opened, and 1946, when it was decommissioned, more than 302,000 members of the Army Air Corps would pass through Greensboro for basic training or final preparation before shipping out to assignments overseas. Everything turned on the outcome of the war; big building projects like the Sears mail-order center would just have to wait.

Greensboro industry became part of the war effort, and forty factories eventually were involved in some form of war work. Textile mills produced tents and garments. The Vick Corporation contributed rocket fuel. A struggling dairy cooperative run by an enterprising manager named Mose Kiser grew to regional prominence supplying milk to the mess halls at the new army installation. The glycerin produced at the rendering plant south of Joe Melvin's service station turned Carolina By-products Company into an "essential industry." The northern terminus of an interstate petroleum pipeline opened just west of Greensboro in February 1942, and within a year, a hundred trucks were loading there each day for distribution throughout the region.

As these companies began to serve new markets, their success trickled down to smaller businesses like Melvin's Texaco station. The man who ran Carolina By-products, Stanley Frank, had met Joe Melvin on his first day in town in 1936, when Frank stopped in the station to change clothes before reporting to work. Carolina By-products now had first call on tires, oil, and gasoline. Frank collected the ration points at the

Office of War Production in the Southeastern Building downtown and then headed to Melvin's Texaco to make his purchases. In the years to come, Frank's company would become one of the city's leading businesses, and Frank would prove instrumental in the development of air transportation.

Joe Melvin had been too young for the first war and was too old for this one, but he shouldered his local obligations. He became an air raid warden and was issued an official white helmet and sash. His assignment was to direct traffic rushing from Greensboro in the highly unlikely event of an air attack. It was not clear where people were supposed to go as they fled the city, but he and others were assigned their posts nonetheless. The wardens took the job seriously, enforcing blackouts with authority, even though it would have been next to impossible for an enemy bomber to make its way to Greensboro. The warden who covered Walker Avenue on the west side of town carried a pellet gun that he used to shoot out offending porch lights left burning after dark.[1]

Everyone, young and old, pitched in, including nine-year-old Jim Melvin and the other children at Gillespie Park Elementary School. Gillespie's 504 students collected 71,037 pounds of scrap metal, or about 141 pounds each. The youngsters climbed atop the mound created on the school's front lawn for a photograph. Across town, a twelve-year-old at Lindley Elementary School donated a cannonball he had found on James Island, South Carolina. It had been identified as one fired from federal guns at Fort Sumter at the outbreak of the Civil War. For weeks before it was hauled away, the pile of rubble at Gillespie School sat in the middle of the lawn, a daily reminder of local efforts to conserve, to volunteer, and to sacrifice for the war effort.

Downtown stores closed on Wednesday afternoons, when business was slow, and encouraged their customers to spend the time working in "victory" gardens, small plots cultivated to produce vegetables for the dinner table.

——

Certainly the single most transformative wartime event for the city was the army's decision to open Basic Training Camp Number 10 there and outfit it to serve five thousand trainees. Most military installations were located outside of cities, well beyond civilian residences and businesses that might be disturbed by such things as grenade practice, shooting ranges, and aerial target practice. Greensboro competed with cities across the South for the base, although it might have had a slight edge over other locations. Before the outbreak of hostilities, the Army Air Corps had a modest contingent based at Sedgefield, where the First District of the Technical Training Command occupied offices in the Pilot Life Insurance Company Building. Most of the officers, including a brigadier general, lived at the Sedgefield Inn, the once-promising golf and riding resort. Their presence was nothing at all to compare to the huge, olive drab complex that began to rise within the northeast boundary of Greensboro in November 1942.

Not everyone was excited about the prospect. One of the conditions the army required of Greensboro was the suspension of the city's Sunday blue laws, which closed movie houses, bowling allies, skating rinks, pool halls, and other entertainment venues. The council readily complied. Even before the formal announcement of the arrangement with the military, when rumors were running their course, Mayor King was concerned about the city's ability to provide for the installation's basic needs, such as adequate water and sewer service. Before he left to serve in the navy in April 1942, the mayor paid a call on the commanding general in Atlanta whose approval was required in the selection process for the camp's location. King told the general Greensboro was not interested.

"You know we don't want to be unpatriotic," King said. "If you need it and this happens to be logical spot for the camp, we will be glad to see you. But to gratuitously put it in there because you think we want it, no thank you."

"What did you say?" the general replied. "I have had mayors from all over the Southeast banging on this door asking me for a camp. My staff is not going to believe me when I report your visit."

King explained that he was not sure Greensboro could handle the demands of a military post. Plus, he said later, "I didn't see what we were going to get out of it."[2]

King was in a decided minority. After he left for active duty, his successor, W. H. Sullivan, and a host of business leaders began a vigorous lobbying effort to get Greensboro into the war. Sullivan and others believed that a military post would restart Greensboro's economic engine. They needed no more evidence than what they had seen in Durham, which the army's Camp Butner had turned into a boomtown. While Greensboro had issued building permits in 1942 for structures worth less than $5,000, Durham builders were busy on $235,000 worth of projects. Wilmington was awash in military folk, as was Fayetteville, which had swelled from a town with less than twenty thousand people to a military center with more than sixty thousand soldiers.

Urged on by the daily newspaper, which worried that Greensboro's bid might arrive too late, Sullivan, the chamber of commerce, and councilman Kemp Clendenin worked closely with the contingent at Sedgefield and assembled several possible locations for the camp, including one in Starmount Forest. They argued that Greensboro had sufficient housing for officers and men who would be permanently stationed at the post, that there were seats in local schools for their children, and that Greensboro had something no other North Carolina city could offer: Sunday beer sales.

The army settled on 652 acres on the city's northeastern corner. Most of the property belonged to the Cone family, but when the amount of land held by the Cones came up short, Clendenin purchased more and made it available. In November 1942, Sixth District congressman Carl Durham announced that the army would build a $2 million basic training camp for air corps inductees. Before it was over, the government's investment would exceed $8 million.[3]

Site preparation began even before the formal announcement, sparking a flurry of rumors as equipment and men began removing trees and clearing land. Altogether, the army would erect barracks to house five thousand soldiers, open multiple mess halls to feed them, and provide chapels for religious services, two libraries, ten post exchanges, and theaters for training sessions—all within about four months. Altogether, 994 buildings would be erected. Soon after the initial announcement, the army announced plans for a seven-hundred-bed hospital as well. It had more capacity than anything available on the civilian side of the gates, which stood near the corner of Summit and Bessemer avenues.

In the early negotiations, the Cones responded to the army's offer to rent the land for the base at the proposed rate of one dollar a year with the condition the property be returned at the end of the war with all improvements—including buildings, water and sewer lines, and streets —intact. The army balked and said the owners would have to pay for the improvements. In the end, the Cones put the land into a holding company called Summit Avenue Building Company and negotiated a lease of fifteen hundred dollars a year, with the stipulation that the Cones would have first opportunity to buy the improvements when they went up for sale.[4] The family also arranged for the army to use Herman Cone's boys' camp for aquatic training.

The army beat its construction deadline of April 1, 1943, by a month, with some help from the Guilford County sheriff. Men who signed up for construction jobs but failed to report for work were hauled into court, where the judge told them, "Work, fight, or serve time." In the final days of construction, the project's contractor, J. A. Jones Construction Company of Charlotte, had five hundred men on the job, including students from the nearby agricultural and technical college.

The first of the trainees arrived in Greensboro in March, while the construction work was still under way. The 943 early arrivals were shipped from an overcrowded camp in New Jersey. Men who had been civilians less than three weeks earlier hoisted mattresses and blankets onto their shoulders and slogged through muddy streets into barracks that were little more than one-story, single-ply wooden barns. The frame buildings were not built to last, although some would still be standing fifty years later. As the construction was completed on these and other buildings, Greensboro and the army settled into a close—and usually profitable—relationship for the duration of the war. Unhappiness about the suspension of the blue laws spilled over into the 1943 municipal elections, but incumbents who were reelected held the course. Only pool halls remained closed on Sundays.

King had been right in at least one respect: Greensboro was not prepared to support a military installation that eventually increased the city's population by more than half. With housing in short supply, the army's occupation presented a challenge for virtually every family. Some homeowners responded gladly and profitably, making spare rooms available to boarders. Such spaces were quickly absorbed by officers and enlisted men assigned to permanent duty. After the camp was converted to the Overseas Replacement Depot (ORD) a year later, making it the last stop for men and women headed overseas, the housing shortage became even more acute, as wives and sweethearts followed their men to the city for their last few days together. Hotels and boardinghouses were packed. Those who could not find shelter slept in the parks and on benches at the bus and railway terminals. Restaurants were busy day and night. The overcrowding was compounded from time to time by the arrival of troop trains. If they pulled in at mealtime, uniformed men marched up Elm Street to eat at Boyd Morris's Mayfair Cafeteria. "The city, in a sense, was under siege," recalled Julia Burnett Davis, whose husband, Oscar Burnett, would later own ORD.[5]

Greensboro took on a decidedly olive hue. Servicemen who rode the bus to town to attend Sunday worship services could always find an invite to Sunday dinner, with families often bringing home one or two soldiers for a meal. The Melvins invited soldiers into their home on Sundays and on other occasions. If, as he closed his station at night, Joe Melvin saw a soldier hitchhiking south to Fort Bragg, the young man often ended up at the Melvins' for a meal and an overnight stay before setting out early the next morning. Another Sunday feature at the Melvins' was preparing ration books. Melvin's sons spent part of the day pasting ration stamps their father's customers had turned in the week before into books that he submitted to maintain his fuel allotment.

Through the rough buildings at ORD passed the Army Air Corps's future pilots, crewmen, armorers, weathermen, mechanics, and clerks. They were processed on a rigid thirty-five-day schedule before being shipped on to other training. The camp reached such a state of efficiency that a troop train could be loaded in three minutes.[6]

The army's presence gave Greensboro a feeling of being in the war, especially after a mock battle was played out downtown. The army's financial contribution was more substantial, however, providing jobs for about twelve hundred civilians, around two-thirds of them women. Government contracts for food, milk, and perishable items that could not be shipped in aided local farmers and businesses. One study showed that between 1942 and 1946, the army paid out $300 million in payroll and bought $42 million in wholesale purchases. Nothing could compare with the boost its spending gave the local economy, even when a large percentage of the payroll was wired out of the city to families elsewhere in the country.

Greensboro gave the nation its share of local heroes. Second Lieutenant Sarah Johnson was among the first contingent of African American nurses to land in England in August 1944. Major George E. Preddy, who had gone into service with the Guilford Grays in 1940, became an air ace, shooting down nearly two dozen enemy planes, including six German fighters within five minutes on one occasion. He was killed in December 1944 when his plane was hit by friendly antiaircraft fire while in pursuit of a German plane over Belgium. His brother, William, shot down three enemy planes before he was downed himself in 1945 over Czechoslovakia.[7] Altogether, nearly ten thousand men and women from Guilford County served in the war; another fifteen thousand were involved in jobs in war industries.

ORD was preparing men for assignments in the fight against Japan when the war ended in August 1945. Greensboro celebrated with the rest of the world. When word reached the Mayfair Cafeteria, an evangelist, the Reverend F. M. Detweiler, grabbed a microphone and announced the surrender over the restaurant's public address system. He then offered a prayer for peace. Jefferson Square filled with people who snatched extra editions of the newspaper out of the hands of newsboys. The crush of excited people was so great that store windows were broken as the crowd pressed against them. That evening, baseball fans got a free game and watched the Greensboro Patriots beat the Danville Leafs 11–10. The Quakers were at Guilford College concluding their 248th annual session on August 10, the day news reached the United States of the bombing of Hiroshima and Nagasaki. Errol T. Elliott, secretary of the Five Years Meeting of Friends and a Quaker journalist, called upon the assembled Friends to rejoice at the end of the conflict and to "weep over thousands that are dead."[8]

Although the shooting stopped, the army remained a very visible part of Greensboro. Just as ORD had become the last stop before assignment overseas during the war, it now became the first stop for thousands of soldiers being processed out of the service. In the months immediately following the end of the war, ORD discharged an average of five hundred soldiers a day.

Greensboro was ready to return to peacetime long before the army was ready to leave the city. In May 1946, a year after the end of the war in Europe, mayor C. M. Vanstory wired the district's congressman, Carl Durham, and asked him to do what he could to move the army out of town. It was a surprising request, since the army was continuing to provide Greensboro with a handsome payroll—more than $21 million in the first six months of that year—and was buying another $368,000 in food and supplies. Vanstory did not wish to be inhospitable to the nearly two thousand servicemen in Greensboro. Rather, he said, the land and buildings on the army post were needed to accommodate returning veterans who were looking for homes. To help satisfy the mayor, the post commander announced that sixty-three of the barracks buildings would be converted into two-family apartments.

The *Greensboro Daily News* argued that the army should stay. Greensboro was running against the tide, the paper said. Many communities that had enjoyed a steady military payroll were eager to have Congress make wartime installations permanent. The paper said the inconveniences to the city had been minor and that Greensboro should be proud to have served thousands of men who "got their last taste of American life and American living here." The city would get back to normal, an editorial in the paper explained, "but there are other things than normalcy which carry their significance and their compensation."[9]

Finally, on August 1, 1946, thirteen hundred men paraded down Elm Street while a flight of P-51 Mustang fighters passed overhead in the last Air Forces Day parade of the war. The same day, ORD's commanding officer, Colonel H. K. Mooney, announced that the post would be closed and consolidated with a discharge facility in New York.

Greensboro was poised at the start of an impressive burst of growth and prosperity, and the urgency of people's desire to get on with life was apparent throughout the community. Construction on the promised Sears, Roebuck and Company catalog facility was about to begin. By the end of the year, bulldozers would begin preparing the forty acres that had been zoned for a building put on hold for five years. Everything—car sales, bank deposits, and even voter registration—was on the increase. The Greensboro envisioned by Mayor Vanstory was one with popular appeal. He and others like him in the inner councils of government and business would make sure it prevailed.

Chapter 3

Building a City

THUNDERSHOWERS threatened a Greensboro that was warm and humid under overcast skies on May 20, 1947, when newly elected mayor Fielding Frye clipped a ribbon to formally open the Sears, Roebuck and Company mail-order center on the city's northern boundary. It was the largest building in Greensboro—and most of North Carolina, for that matter. Thirteen acres of roof covered a multistory structure large enough to service nineteen freight cars at one time while thirty more sat parked on a special siding. Inside, day-and-night shifts of fifteen hundred workers tended ten miles of conveyor belts where customer orders were filled, boxed, and made ready to ship in three hours. When Sears's legendary chief executive officer, General Robert E. Wood, landed at the Greensboro–High Point airport, he was greeted like royalty.

The addition of Sears to Greensboro's corporate registry boosted civic pride and evoked relief. The building had been a long time coming. As if to compensate for the six-year delay, Wood and his entourage of corporate vice presidents announced that Greensboro also would be getting a new $1.7 million retail store on the edge of downtown, and perhaps a paint factory. Wood declared at a chamber of commerce banquet that the South offered Sears its greatest opportunity for expansion and that one-fourth of its $20 million investment in the region would be spent in Greensboro. Wood projected a scenario of trickle-down economics. In addition to a fat new payroll for the community, the Sears center—the company's eleventh—would benefit the local economy by purchasing furniture and other goods from manufacturers in the area, as well as increasing postal and freight shipments. Orders processed in Greensboro were shipped to customers from Wheeling, West Virginia, to Columbia, South Carolina.

Those taking the pulse of Greensboro would have seen a simple truth behind the hyperbole: an invigorating spirit was alive in some quarters, and the setbacks from the speculative misadventures of the 1920s were now history. The city was getting a fresh start with young men whose lives had been interrupted by the war and who were eager to realize dreams that had been nurtured in foxholes and on distant beaches during the past five years. Walter W. King Jr., for example, came home and started a construction company that he and partner Robert Hunter of Charlotte had begun planning on an island in the South Pacific, where the two were serving with the Seabees. King-Hunter Construction Company began building houses and soon expanded to schools, factories, and commercial buildings.

The business tickers showed Greensboro's financial health was strong. The city was in the midst of a surge in home building in a market in which demand seemed to have no end. Security National Bank and Guilford National Bank, the two institutions that had been opened with federal aid during the Depression, now were strong and processing more loans and checks than ever before. Meyer's department store on Elm Street, which offered fine fashions to its Irving Park customers, was preparing a major expansion and renovation. Downtown traffic was so heavy that city officials were making plans for a bypass across the city's northern boundary. They had chosen the name "Memorial Drive" because the route passed near the proposed site of a new auditorium to be built in honor of the war dead.

There was some hope that the University of North Carolina would locate a new four-year medical school in Greensboro in connection with the opening of a new hospital—a memorial to benefactor Moses Cone that had been promised the city thirty-five years earlier following Cone's death.

Prewar leaders had been right: the army's occupation of Greensboro had been a boon for local business. Companies large and small had benefited from the millions in government spending. When the Cone plants were presented their wartime E pennants for on-time production and high performance, the government's procurement chief had declared that "cotton is with every soldier and sailor or flier 24 hours a day, every day, wherever he may be." Carter Fabrics, which began operations in 1937, had become part of an $81 million merger that created J. P. Stevens and Company, an emerging textile giant in the South. Guilford Dairy, a farmers' cooperative that had supplied milk to ORD, was planning to expand. During the Depression, money had been so tight that Guilford's manager, Mose Kiser, had to wait for deliverymen to return with daily collections before employees could be paid. In 1946, by contrast, Kiser announced that the co-op would build a new plant to produce milk, ice cream, and other dairy products on Greensboro's west side. It opened in August 1948 at a cost of $400,000.

Greensboro's future had not looked this promising in twenty years.

———

As in the years before the war, a cadre of businessmen, deeply rooted in local traditions, presided over civic affairs and made decisions about the city's future. The city council was composed of businessmen and lawyers, most of whom were handpicked to perform their civic duties. As a result, local political contests usually were mild affairs with predictable outcomes. During the war, there was a minor uprising against the city's relaxation of the blue laws—essential to the continued satisfaction of the army—but the opposition failed to elect a single candidate. Surprises were not entirely out of the question, however. In 1947, Thomas E. Brown, a furniture store owner, jumped from tenth in the primary to number three in the general election with the placement of one ad. It was published the day before the election, and it questioned the wisdom of the city's having a council on which five of the seven members lived in the same neighborhood, Irving Park. It was a political refrain that would be repeated in the future, with far greater consequences.

The council members picked the members of the city school board and all other boards and commissions, including zoning and planning boards with the power to determine the value of real estate. These were the same men (some women were appointed to city boards and commissions) who ran the chamber of commerce, whose plan for the city's development consumed a full page in the newspaper in May 1947. The plan was the result of a heroic effort on the part of the chamber, which held public meetings around the city and sent the Jaycees door to door to solicit suggestions and measure citizen concerns. The plan touched on every aspect of public life—industrial development, schools, sanitation, traffic, housing, and civic affairs—and came complete with detailed recommendations. The chamber suggested, for example, that downtown policemen carry change for parking meters as a convenience to shoppers. It also encouraged the adoption of yet another city slogan.

Greensboro's mayors, who were selected by fellow city council members, were largely ceremonial leaders, and the office was shaped by the personality of the man in it. W. H. Sullivan, who had been a commanding leader during the war, was succeeded in 1945 by C. M. Vanstory, who asserted his own forceful presence. Vanstory customarily used the formal, public council meetings to endorse what council members had already decided in private. After the unexpected death of Julian Price, who was killed in an automobile accident in the fall of 1946, Vanstory became one of the leading members of a group that filled the civic leadership vacuum, recruiting local leaders as Price once had. In 1947, Vanstory personally paid the filing fee for Ben Cone, who happened to be traveling outside of the country when the deadline arrived, so Cone could become a candidate for city council. Cone placed third in the primary. He would be reelected in 1949 and named mayor.

Vanstory was a tall, imposing man with a solid, square jaw and distinguished bearing. After guiding the resurrection of Security National Bank in the 1930s, he had joined Burlington Mills Corporation as assistant treasurer, but he left to supervise the construction of the new Moses H. Cone Memorial Hospital.

Vanstory's two years in the mayor's office proved to be stormy. When Sears, Roebuck decided it wanted to put a new store downtown, Vanstory engineered the availability of a prime corner lot that the city was holding in reserve for the proposed war memorial auditorium. Business interests were paramount for Vanstory, who bulldozed the opposition and weathered a referendum challenging the council's decision to sell the land to private interests. Midway through his term, he mounted the campaign to get the army out of town, saying the city needed ORD as a site for veterans' housing. He was also the backbone of the city council throughout a contentious period created by the closing of a major thoroughfare, Walker Avenue, which ran through the campus of Woman's College. Vanstory was not shy about defending his positions and was impatient with those who challenged his authority. He once dared an angry caller to meet him outside of his house, where the two could settle their differences man to man.

———

When Vanstory stepped down as mayor in 1947 in favor of Fielding Frye, Greensboro was growing into the ambitions that developers had harbored two decades earlier. Vanstory was right to predict returning veterans' desperate need for homes. In a period of declining family size, the number of inhabitants in each home in Greensboro had risen by 20 percent. In 1947, over eleven hundred homes and apartments were added to the city's inventory—more than had been built in the previous four years—but even this building boom could not match demand. The city planning commission reported in June 1948 that Greensboro's population was eighty-two thousand, with another twenty-two thousand people living in the suburban perimeter.

Most of the expansion in housing was in one direction: to the northwest, beyond the leafy, well-ordered neighborhoods like Sunset Hills, Westerwood, and Lake Daniel that were within easy reach of Greensboro Senior High School. Ed Benjamin's Starmount Company, whose holdings included the incorporated bedroom community of Hamilton Lakes and virtually everything else in the city's northwest quadrant, announced in the summer of 1946 that Starmount would open four new tracts for development, including some with houses priced to attract veterans buying their first homes using GI benefits. A six-room model in Starmount's Guilford Hills could be had for payments of $68.86 a month. Meanwhile, Benjamin renewed his promotion of his higher-priced development, Starmount Forest, where, in the fall of 1948, a sturdy, two-story brick home was outfitted with electric appliances and a fully stocked library, along with other amenities, and was billed as "Mr. Blandings's Dream Home" in an effort to capitalize on a popular motion picture of the time. In Starmount Forest, the company rationed new developments, opening lots to builders slowly to keep demand, and prices, high. To maintain his vision of what the neighborhood should look like, Benjamin stipulated that he would approve all house plans personally.

New homes also were being built in the undeveloped lots in Sunset Hills, one of the boom-time developments of the 1920s, and in Irving Park, which remained the neighborhood of choice for the wealthy. Especially popular was Kirkwood, a development on Irving Park's western flank. It had gone into default during the Depression before a single house could be built.

The demand for housing turned home builders like Herman Weaver into some of the busiest men in town. Weaver had started a modest building concern during the Depression and had honed his skills erecting housing at military posts all across North Carolina during the war. With open land hard to come by in Greensboro after the war, Weaver eagerly bought about a hundred lots in Kirkwood for around one hundred dollars apiece. The lots were among more than three thousand land parcels that local government had taken in lieu of back taxes during the Depression. Weaver put his crews to work building two- and three-bedroom homes that sold for between eight and nine thousand dollars.

He could not get them finished fast enough to meet demand. One day, a woman arrived at Weaver's office downtown and demanded to see him. Weaver's wife, who managed the financial side of the business, showed the woman into her husband's office and left the room. When the door closed, the woman pleaded for special consideration and suggested she would do whatever was necessary for the favor. Weaver, an exceedingly modest man, panicked. He called his wife into the office, told the anxious woman she would have to talk to her, and quickly left.[1]

Builder John R. Taylor, another creative army veteran, showed he could produce a house literally overnight. Taylor's customers ordered houses sight unseen from a veteran-owned business in Marietta, Georgia, that fabricated each home's walls, floors, and roof in the factory and then shipped the parts to the building site. In September 1946, the first of Taylor's "factory engineered" houses, a two-bedroom model, arrived on two trucks at 2104 Brice Street on the west side of town, a site prepared by King-Hunter Construction Company. The house was "in the dry," under its roof, by nightfall. Taylor also experimented with building houses of steel and concrete. Another company constructed unfinished houses and financed buyers, who completed the interiors on their own.

During this same period, the Cone mill community was expanded to supply housing for workers. Caught in a tight labor market, with the city's housing shortage only aggravating conditions, the Cones invested $2 million in building 65 new homes and renovating 363 older ones between 1946 and 1948. About 150 structures, mostly two- and three-room houses dating to the turn of the century, were demolished.[2]

Lying northeast of downtown, the 450-acre mill community was second in size only to Cannon Mills' Kannapolis. Fifteen hundred houses, some of them as small as three rooms, were home to 2,675 workers, about half the total number employed in the nearby mills. The community had been incorporated into the city in 1923 but was not entirely of the city. Due to custom and convenience, the mill workers remained apart from the general population and patronized their own stores, churches, community centers, and schools. Until 1946, a child could finish formal schooling at the Cone-built schools without ever sitting next to someone whose parents were not on the Cone payroll.

Changes in the mill villages' arrangements with the city were part of a much larger reorganization of the Cone manufacturing interests. In September 1945, all the Cone corporations were combined into the Proximity Manufacturing Company, which would later become Cone Mills Corporation. A year earlier, in late 1944, Herman Cone had notified the city council that it was time that the mill village received the same services as other Greensboro neighborhoods. Negotiations led to the end of a 1923 arrangement that had guaranteed the Cone interests a seat on the Greensboro City Council. The separate election district for the Cone property was eliminated, and the city assumed responsibility for garbage collection, police protection, and the maintenance of twenty-six miles of streets. Water meters were installed on mill houses that previously had none, and streetlights were erected. The community's schools, which were housed in some of the finest school buildings in the county, were given to the city and became part of the city school district.

The former army camp and the campus of the Negro Agricultural and Technical College of North Carolina, known throughout the state as "A&T," separated the Cone mill village's northeastern quadrant from southeast Greensboro, where virtually all of Greensboro's African American citizens lived. The life of the community revolved around a host of churches and Dudley High School, which was one of the leading black schools in the state. The faculty that served A&T and nearby Bennett College, a Methodist college for black women, enhanced the size of the black middle class, whose homes on Benbow Road were as nice as any in the city.

Most African Americans were not so fortunate, and the urgency of decent housing was felt most keenly in this part of Greensboro. With few exceptions, houses in southeast Greensboro were small and in poor repair. Most neighborhood streets were unpaved, and the neighborhoods had no representation at city hall to make the case for improvement. As local builders scrambled for materials to expand the white suburbs, a city-funded study found that the shortcomings of inner-city housing for the poor and near-poor were "as severe, if not more severe, than elsewhere in the nation." The postwar effort to erect temporary housing for veterans included a small number of homes—about one-fourth of the total—for African Americans, but the thirty-four units that eventually became available were no match for the need.

South Greensboro also was home to working-class whites, especially in the neighborhoods around the hosiery and cotton mills along South Elm Street and in the industrial sections near the railroad tracks. There was one black enclave. It was a unique neighborhood called Warnersville that had been created after the Civil War to provide homes for former slaves. A Quaker preacher bought the land, divided it into lots, and sold them at modest prices to the freedmen.[3] Otherwise, south Greens-

FIG. I. Greensboro's Elm Street was the retail marketplace for customers from throughout the northern Piedmont region of North Carolina. *(Courtesy Greensboro Historical Museum)*

FIG. 2. The Cone brothers, Moses and Ceasar, opened mills and started marketing fabric from Greensboro in the decade before the twentieth century. Their Cone Export and Commission Company marketed southern-made cloth. *(Courtesy Greensboro Historical Museum)*

FIG. 3. The Cones created an entire community of homes, retail stores, and churches in the area around their textile plants on Greensboro's north side. A trolley connected the city-within-a-city to downtown. *(Courtesy Greensboro Historical Museum)*

FIG. 4. Greensboro's Dudley High School, named for James B. Dudley, a president of Agricultural and Technical College (now NC A&T State University). It was one of the first fully accredited high schools for African American students in the state. This is the graduating class of 1930. *(Courtesy Greensboro Historical Museum)*

FIG. 5. Julian Price built the Jefferson Standard Life Insurance Company into a major force within the industry. He also played a significant role in the development of the community prior to his untimely death in 1946. *(Courtesy Greensboro Historical Museum)*

FIG. 6. Greensboro's location made it a central spot along the rail lines that crossed the South. Southern Railway Company, using the credit of the city of Greensboro to underwrite its effort, opened a new passenger station in 1930. *(Courtesy Greensboro Historical Museum)*

FIG. 7. The largest military post opened within a U.S. city during World War II was the basic training camp in Greensboro. It also served as the jumping-off point for servicemen headed to Europe as one of three overseas replacement depots. *(Courtesy Greensboro Historical Museum)*

FIG. 8. During World War II, schoolchildren collected scrap metal and rubber for the war effort. *(Courtesy Greensboro Historical Museum)*

FIG. 9. The military encampment on Greensboro's north side was built in record time and included training facilities, housing, hospitals, and entertainment for thousands of service personnel. It was decommissioned shortly after the war, and some buildings continue to be used for private businesses. *(Courtesy Greensboro Historical Museum)*

FIG. 10. Spencer Love built
Burlington Industries into
a worldwide enterprise by
adapting new techniques and
new fibers to an old industry.
*(Courtesy Greensboro Historical
Museum)*

FIG. 11. Burlington Industries would grow into the largest textile operation in the
world. Its early headquarters opened in the mid-1930s on the edge of downtown
Greensboro. The building later became the home of the county's social services
department until it was razed to make way for construction of a new minor-league
baseball park. *(Courtesy Greensboro Historical Museum)*

FIG. 16. The nationwide polio epidemic hit North Carolina particularly hard, and Guilford County experienced more cases than most. A hospital to care for children and adults was built by volunteers with materials contributed by donors from across the country. *(Photograph by Carol W. Martin, Greensboro Historical Museum Collection)*

Fig. 17. Mayor C. M. Vanstory pressured the military to leave ORD as soon as possible after World War II. He managed the opening of Moses Cone Memorial Hospital and went on to head Security National Bank, one of the predecessor banks of Bank of America. *(Courtesy Greensboro Historical Museum)*

Summit Shopping Center
PARK ONCE
AND CHECK OFF YOUR SHOPPING LIST
EACH STORE A SPECIALTY SHOP
WHERE YOU CAN BUY ANYTHING YOU NEED

Fig. 18. Summit Shopping Center was Greensboro's first large retail concentration outside of downtown. It opened in 1950 on property at the edge of the former military installation. *(Courtesy Greensboro Historical Museum)*

FIG. 19. William Hampton, a physician, was the first African American elected to the city council. His election in 1951 was the result of a concerted effort by the Greensboro Men's Club, whose members included leading African American businessmen, teachers, doctors, and lawyers. Hampton is seated at the far right. *(Courtesy Greensboro Historical Museum)*

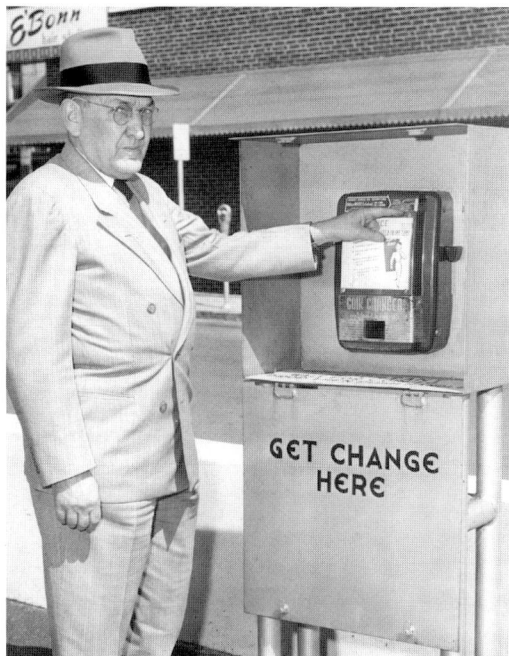

FIG. 20. Greensboro's city manager in the 1950s was James R. Townsend, a retired general. He laid the groundwork for improvements and changes to the city's infrastructure—especially water and traffic—and became a model for efficient municipal management around the state. One of his greatest concerns was an adequate water supply. The city's Lake Townsend was named in his honor. *(Courtesy Greensboro Historical Museum)*

FIG. 21. Moses H. Cone Memorial Hospital opened in 1953. The hospital had been a bequest in the will of the benefactor, who died in 1908, but money for construction did not become available until the death of his widow, Bertha, in 1947. *(Photograph by Carol W. Martin, Greensboro Historical Museum Collection)*

FIG. 22. To ease the postwar housing shortage, Greensboro builder Herman Weaver, who had helped erect military installations in the Carolinas, began building affordable homes in Greensboro to house returning war veterans. He was one of the first to build apartments, and his planned housing units won national recognition. He is pictured here with his wife, Edith, and son, Michael. *(Photograph by Carol W. Martin)*

FIG. 23. Elm Street in downtown Greensboro continued to be the retail center for the northern Piedmont into the 1950s. *(Photograph by Carol W. Martin, Greensboro Historical Museum Collection)*

FIG. 24. Cigarette manufacturing moved to Greensboro in 1954 when construction began on P. Lorillard's $13 million plant on the city's east side. It was the largest project of its kind in the state at the time. *(Photograph by Carol W. Martin, Greensboro Historical Museum Collection)*

FIG. 25. The Greensboro Coliseum was more than a decade in the making. When it opened in 1959, it had a seating capacity of nearly 11,000 for athletic events, the circus, and public concerts. *(Courtesy* Greensboro News & Record*)*

boro was a sprawling area with a mixture of homes, factories, and warehouses that followed the south side of the tracks from Asheboro Street west to the fairgrounds on Lee Street. Many of the homes in south Greensboro had been built well before the Depression. Along Asheboro Street, some dated to the nineteenth century.

Downtown remained the retail center for shoppers in Greensboro and surrounding counties. Stores of every description filled nearly a dozen blocks of Elm Street from the O. Henry Hotel north of the Jefferson Building south to Lee Street. Variety stores that were part of national chains operated beside locally owned shops that sold shoes, men's clothing, ladies' fashions, groceries, and jewelry. Just off Elm Street were supermarkets and car dealers and acres and acres of parking lots to accommodate shoppers, as well as office workers and others who made their living downtown.

Small retail clusters had grown up at strategic locations around the city. For the most part, they served a walk-in trade from the nearby neighborhoods. Most included a locally owned grocery, variety store, bakery, shoe shop, beauty parlor, and drugstore. One of the more robust centers was adjacent to the campus at Woman's College at the intersection of Walker and Tate streets, where Joe Melvin's brother, Charlie, ran a grocery store. The center even had a small department store. Nearly all of these local retail clusters had at least one service station like Melvin's Texaco at Asheboro Street and Randolph Avenue.

Some called Joe Melvin the mayor of south Greensboro. He chaired the neighborhood war bond campaign and organized a businessmen's club. He was such a dependable customer at Security National Bank that the bank's president gave him a key to the back door so he could slip in before regular hours to make deposits and conduct business. Since he often cashed checks for customers at the station, Melvin's deposits were usually large, and he did not like to stand in line.

The family lived comfortably, but without frills. The station required attention six days a week. The Melvins preferred to vacation at a lake in southeastern North Carolina after a venture into New York City turned into a disturbing experience: they had settled into their hotel room for the night when a brawl broke out in a bar just one floor below. Trips to the lake were adventure enough.

Joe Melvin's youngest son, Jim, was a lively youngster and part of a troop of friends from the neighborhood. There were usually enough boys on hand to organize a football game on the front lawn of Gillespie Park Elementary School. In the summer, South Buffalo Creek was their swimming hole. Years later, after Jim discovered that the creek was little more than a drainage ditch for area industries, including an abattoir and nearby fertilizer plants, he marveled that neither he nor his buddies got sick as a result of the time they spent in the polluted waters.

Joe Melvin's station was a gathering place for customers and others who stopped by for conversation or to take the pulse of the community. He kept newspapers and a checkerboard on hand to occupy customers waiting on minor repairs, a change of tires, or for full service with a gas sale, which included sweeping a car's interior. Melvin's wash pit was usually busy; as many as thirty to thirty-five cars went through it in a weekend. Among young Jim's chores, in addition to keeping the brass shiny and the restrooms clean, was slathering the sides of washed cars' tires with an indelible blacking compound that remained in the crevices of his hands and fingernails for days.

Postwar changes turned Greensboro Senior High School into a social mixing bowl for white teenagers, some of whom had never explored beyond their own part of town. Students from the mill villages joined kids like the Melvin brothers who lived on the south side with the well-to-do from Irving Park at the classically designed school set on a sprawling campus just northwest of downtown. School superintendent Ben L. Smith put a priority on academics, especially libraries, while coach Bob Jamieson regularly produced strong, competitive, athletic teams. Jamieson scouted the lower grades for promising talent for his basketball, football, and baseball teams, just like music director Herbert Hazelman courted musicians for his marching band. Herman Cone Jr., the son of the head of Cone Mills, was one of Hazelman's best clarinetists.

Playing on a Jamieson team involved more than athletic competition: it was a way of life. Jamieson imposed strict rules regarding dress and behavior and made sure his players knew "a little about living and not just playing," as he once put it.[4] His teams practiced hard and stayed in shape. Soft drinks were forbidden during the season. He did not tolerate profanity. Once asked if he had ever uttered a cuss word, Jamieson said, "No, I never had to." On road trips, the team members wore white shirts and ties, and youngsters minded their manners. Many Greensboro teenagers spent their first overnight in a hotel and ate their first restaurant meal without their parents on one of Jamieson's athletic road trips.

Coach Jamieson's word was law. When his top five performers showed up late for the bus that was to take them to one out-of-town game during the 1950 season, he stopped the bus to bring them aboard, but they spent the evening on the bench while lesser players took a beating on the field. Jamieson's decision cost the team a victory but taught the unforgettable lesson that in life there were more important things than winning.

Jamieson had come to Greensboro High School in 1933 and was midway through his career when Jim Melvin followed his brother, Joe, onto the football team. Jim was strong and determined. One day, he caught a glimpse of a scouting report on him that had been prepared by an opposing team. "Big, fast, but dumb," it said. Jim never matched his brother's aptitude for academic achievement, but he was his equal on the field, in part because of his use of a set of weights Joe fashioned for his brother from concrete blocks. Jim played guard and set at least one record during his senior year, when he was a team cocaptain. His selection for the state all-star team in 1951 made him the only Greensboro Senior High School student to perform in two postseason all-star football contests. He appeared once as a freshman, when he was a member of the school band, in which he played clarinet, and later as a member of the West All-Star football team.

In the spring of 1948, families living on the dirt streets of southeast Greensboro and in the new suburbs along Battleground Avenue found a reason to ignore the class and racial separations that partitioned their community. Poliomyelitis had no respect for where a father worked, where a child attended school, or where a family observed Sunday services. The growing frequency with which ambulances arrived at all hours in neighborhoods across the city terrified everyone equally.

North Carolina had seen its first serious outbreak of the crippling and sometimes fatal disease called polio in 1937. Another followed in 1944. Like most communities that had firsthand experience, Greensboro had an active chapter of the March of Dimes, the national fund-raising organization that was pumping millions into the search for a cure. The local campaign usually concluded with the annual president's birthday ball; this had become almost routine when, in the fall of 1947, medical doctors and chapter leaders grew increasingly concerned about the rising number of cases.

Much of the money raised locally supported the care of patients at a special hospital in Hickory, North Carolina. With the Hickory center reaching its capacity and beds hard to find in local hospitals, however, Greensboro March of Dimes worker John R. Foster and others knew they had to find additional space. They soon were looking over an abandoned ORD building that the army had used as a theater and recreation hall. It was a mess. The roof leaked, and birds were roosting in the rafters. There was no central heating, and the high windows offered modest ventilation but little natural light. However, it could be used at no cost and was the largest space available that could serve as an isolation ward for new victims. Volunteers went to work. They cleaned the building and installed plain white cotton curtains that provided some privacy in a makeshift ward that soon held more than forty patients.

"There was great fear," Foster later recalled. The city was in a "calm panic."[5] The disease had no cure and struck children and young adults without warning according to no established pattern. This time, most of the victims were children under the age of fourteen, more often white than black. By June 1948, schools were closed for the summer, and fearful parents kept their children confined indoors. Public swimming pools closed. Churches cancelled vacation Bible school. Movie theaters shut their doors. The nearby town of Gibsonville prohibited any public or private gatherings of children under fourteen. To help relieve anxious parents coping with impatient, bored youngsters, the Greensboro recreation department aired radio quizzes, games, and contests. "We'll promote the handicrafts by radio instruction," the city's recreation director, Oka T. Hester, announced, "and follow up with a contest when the outbreak is ceased."[6]

When a case was diagnosed as contagious, patients were quarantined, even from family members. One father circled the hospital in his car at night just to be close to a son lying on a bed inside.[7] Fear so infected the city that Foster had difficulty hiring nurses for the makeshift ORD facility because he could not find them a place to live: landlords were afraid they would bring the disease back to their rooms. Foster finally called on Dr. Horace Strickland of the medical staff at Southern Railway, who arranged for Pullman sleepers to be parked on a nearby siding. The nurses balked at this idea, and space was found for them in the empty dormitories at Woman's College.

By the middle of June, it was clear North Carolina was in the midst of a major outbreak, and, for unknown reasons, Greensboro was affected most of all. Of the more than 650 cases reported statewide since the first of the year, 123 were in Guilford County. The ORD center, which held 50 patients by summer, was becoming dangerously overcrowded, and more patients were arriving daily. Greensboro fire chief C. W. Wyrick was particularly alarmed. He told a meeting at city hall that the wooden structure was so prone to fire that it was a disaster waiting to happen. As a precaution, he kept a fire truck standing by.

It was clear to doctors and health officials meeting in late June that a larger, semipermanent facility capable of treating more than a hundred patients would be needed, and soon. In the meantime, patients not in isolation were to be moved from ORD into other temporary, and safer, quarters. A city-owned building downtown, once the offices of the *Greensboro Record*, was chosen, and the current tenants, the county's employment security workers, were relocated to space at the city farmer's market amid some grumbling that farmers would be displaced from their usual stalls. Samuel Ravenel, a member of the Guilford polio medical board and a doctor who had delivered hundreds of babies, declared that he had had enough of remarks such as that. "What's more important," he asked, "saving vegetables or saving lives?"[8]

It seemed there would be no end to the epidemic. Four new cases were reported as the health officials were meeting to determine what to do next. They decided to build a temporary hospital with a hundred convalescent beds to replace the temporary space at the *Record* building and ORD, but two weeks later the health professionals upped the ante. The new facility should be permanent, they advised, and nearly twice as large to accommodate 134 beds for convalescing victims, therapy rooms, and isolation wards for the most contagious diseases, including polio. What had been estimated to cost $60,000 now was projected at $175,000.

Organizers of the effort had been doubtful that they could raise $60,000; the idea of more than doubling the expense was overwhelming. Nonetheless, construction plans moved ahead, based largely on the faith of volunteers and promises of in-kind support from architects and engineers. Building supplies were promised free or at cost. On July 12, less than three weeks after the decision was made to build the larger facility, a bulldozer with three young polio survivors riding alongside the operator crawled across a former cane field owned by the county on the east side of Greensboro as work commenced on the Central Carolina Convalescent Hospital. Earlier that morning, Guilford County's twelfth polio death was reported. Foster recalled, "We said, 'Damn the torpedoes, full speed ahead.'"[9]

Construction and fund-raising united the Greensboro community and produced astonishing results. Three weeks after the campaign began and a week after construction commenced, the newspaper announced that $140,000 had been pledged. (The paper also carried news of four new polio cases.) Contributions had climbed to more than $200,000 by the end of August, and in mid-September more than $325,000 had been paid or promised. Bob Poole, a familiar voice on WBIG radio, alone raised $50,000 from his appeals. And more than dollars came in from the community and beyond. Union and nonunion tradesmen—electricians, carpenters, plumbers, painters, and masons—worked without pay. Lights were strung around the building as it rose from the ground to allow construction to continue after sundown. Local restaurants provided free meals to workers. The Jaycees collected and sold a hundred and twenty thousand pounds of scrap paper in aid of the cause. Volunteers gathered at the Red Cross office to cut and sew four thousand hospital gowns, loincloths, ice cap covers, and other items needed in the treatment of patients. Equipment arrived from other hospitals around the state. Altogether, more than eleven thousand hours of volunteer skilled and unskilled labor went into the building.

Foster, an executive at a wholesale hardware company, took on the task of locating building materials and securing equipment to outfit the center. It was not easy with lumber, steel, windows, doors, and concrete all in short supply due to the postwar housing boom. Roofing timbers were found in Kentucky, and Blue Bell, the overall manufacturer, diverted company trucks to haul them to Greensboro. Cement came from Maryland over Southern Railway's tracks thanks to Dr. Strickland. Heating and air conditioning units were built at the Trane factory in Wisconsin, where workers gave up a day's pay to the project. Foster prevailed upon U.S. secretary of war Kenneth Royall, a North Carolinian, to expedite delivery, and Royall arranged for a military air transport to bring the heavy units to the city.

The effort captured the attention of *Life* magazine, which featured Greensboro's volunteers in a photo story in late August. Hollywood moviemaker RKO produced a twenty-five-minute short feature on Greensboro as part of a March of Dimes campaign that ran in sixteen thousand theaters across the nation. Taking advantage of all the publicity, Foster sent an appeal to Ford Motor Company and asked for a Ford station wagon to ferry nurses to their lodgings and retrieve medications from drugstores. Ford executives gave him little encouragement. They argued that if Ford gave Greensboro a car, it would be obliged to do the same for every hospital in the country. Foster told them there was no other hospital like this one and sent along the evidence to prove it. The hospital got the car, complete with tags and a tank of gas.

The builders had set an impossible completion deadline of September 1—about six weeks from start to finish. That date passed with the buildings incomplete, and appeals went out for more volunteers. Meanwhile, more than a hundred patients remained in the old newspaper building and at ORD, which was reserved for those who required the most attention.

In late September, a shortage of painters and roofers pushed the opening day back another week. Finally, ninety-five days after work began, the Central Carolina Convalescent Hospital was ready for patients. On October 11, policemen, firemen, and the Jaycees helped move sixty-one patients from the newspaper offices. Two days later, another fifty-six were moved into the facility. The new one-story hospital was set up with wings for children and adults, for males and females. Whites and blacks, rich and poor shared common wards, an arrangement that was brought to the attention of North Carolina governor Greg Cherry, who sent a Greensboro attorney to see Foster.

Race was a delicate issue. Just a few weeks before, presidential candidate Henry Wallace, whose Progressive Party ticket included black and white candidates, had been hit with eggs and rotten peaches when he stepped out of his car for an appearance on the courthouse steps in Greensboro. People called him a communist.[10] The race had already been distinguished by racist campaigning when South Carolina's governor, Strom Thurmond, launched his campaign for president under the banner of states' rights and racial segregation.

Foster did not flinch at the questions put to him by the governor's representative: "I said, 'You go back to the governor and ask him to bring that up as an issue and he will be crucified for doing it,'" Foster recalled. "No one was concerned about integration or segregation. The problem was too serious."[11]

When the polio hospital opened, one bystander, a gray-haired man of some age, told a writer, "Yep, it seems that it ain't rightly just a building at all. . . . It's more like a kind of monument. A buildin's got to belong to somebody. That there building don't belong to nobody, and at the same time it belongs to everybody. If you started to take it apart and give a piece of it to everybody that owns a piece there just wouldn't be enough to go around."[12]

Some years later, Foster was asked how such a project could be completed so quickly largely using donations of money, labor, and goods from local people. Aside from the property given by the county and the assist from the military in the delivery of supplies, no government money was involved in the project. It was simple, Foster said: "People realized that only they could solve it in time."

Chapter 4

Honor City of America

*T*HE MAN WHO MADE the ORD building available as a temporary ward for polio victims was Oscar Burnett, a tall, likeable Georgian with an open face and a ready smile. He had moved to Greensboro from Atlanta in 1930, where he was in charge of the southern offices of New York's Guaranty National Bank and had made a market for the Bank of North Carolina's bonds with a number of wealthy Greensboro investors.

Traveling to and from Greensboro, Burnett liked what he saw of the city and subsequently left Atlanta to open his own brokerage firm there. He later expanded his business with an office in Winston-Salem, where tobacco wealth was as plentiful as Greensboro's textile dollars. Among his clients were members of the Cone family, with whom he was especially close. During the early days of the war, Burnett had used his connections in Washington to help Ben Cone secure a commission in the navy, a branch of the military that admitted few Jews to the officer ranks. As Mayor Vanstory's campaign to evict the army was reaching a crescendo in the summer of 1946, Burnett got a call from Ben's older brother, Herman, who ran the family business.[1]

The Cones, and especially Herman, had carefully avoided public controversy over the years. Most of the Cones lived well, but without pretension. As Jews in a decidedly Protestant South, they worked hard at becoming a part of the community, and the family was proud of its reputation for generosity and good works. The low rent offered to the army on the ORD property was just one example of the family's public spirit, but now the return of that same property brought with it the potential for embarrassment.

Herman Cone was sensitive to accusations of profiteering, and rumors to that effect were circulating. In early August 1946, just before the army announced the closing of ORD, the *Greensboro Record* published a letter that laid out in print what many in the community were thinking. The writer, who was only identified as "M. O.," accused Vanstory of serving as a foil for the Cones "so that they may 'save face' and still regain their property with all those costly improvements while it will bring the highest price." The response was swift. Two days later, the paper noted that the opinions of letter writers were their own. A week later, the paper published a groveling retraction and apology that said, in part, "The *Record* states that it is its honest belief that the conduct of the Cone family . . . have in all instances been free from any illegal or improper motives."[2]

As the army's plans became clear during the summer, Cone listed the property with a real estate salesman, but the man could not find a buyer. Finally, Cone talked to Burnett and Greensboro attorney Herbert Falk, who handled legal matters for the Cone companies, and the two agreed to pay six hundred thousand dollars for most of the real estate —about 433 acres—held by the Cones' Summit Avenue Building Company. Cone left Burnett and Falk to negotiate with the government for the buildings and other improvements, which they purchased for another two hundred thousand dollars with the help of Raleigh attorney Fred Williams, who had managed government real estate during the war for the army's Corps of Engineers.

After completing negotiations with the army, Williams returned to his Raleigh law practice, but he remained interested in the ORD project. After a few weeks, he called Burnett and asked if he needed someone to help dispose of all that property. The result was General Enterprises Incorporated, a company Williams, Burnett, and Falk formed to handle what Williams called "the wrecking of ORD." Williams set up temporary housekeeping in the quarters of the former camp commander and went to work finding customers. He advertised two-thousand-square-foot buildings that had been the temporary home of thousands of transient soldiers for sale at prices below four hundred dollars. Sinks and commodes went for ten dollars each, as did a warehouse full of the Warm Morning coal stoves that had heated the buildings.

Williams attracted such a variety of buyers that he nicknamed the company "General Surprises." Some of the buildings ended up on farms in the mountain foothills, where they were converted to chicken houses. Builders salvaged the sturdy oak and pine flooring, rafters, and two-by-fours for use in other construction. For a short time, some of the barracks became temporary rental housing for veterans and their families. Before the army turned over the property in the latter months of 1946, forty to fifty of the buildings had been partitioned and converted into two-family apartments. Arrangements were made with a volunteer group to continue offering some housing, but the leases were short-term. Williams and Burnett were not in the housing business. When Burnett opened the office of his new venture, Bessemer Improvement Company, he envisioned ORD as Greensboro's first industrial park.[3]

———

Industrial development was a novel concept in the late 1940s. Prior to the war, local communities largely left recruitment of new business and industry to the utility companies and the railroads, which had the most to gain from new industrial customers. After the war, American industry was ready to expand and meet consumer demands for goods denied for half a decade. As companies in the Northeast looked for alternatives to union labor and outdated facilities, the available land and plentiful workforce in the South appeared attractive.

In the first decade after the war, one of the South's most creative salesmen for the development of industrial sites was Romeo Guest of Greensboro. His company, Romeo Guest and Associates, created a name for itself by locating suitable building sites and then erecting new factories on them. A lasting landmark to Guest's vision was the Research Triangle Park between Raleigh, Durham, and Chapel Hill, an idea Guest first promoted to North Carolina governor Luther Hodges in 1954.

Guest's energetic promotion of Research Triangle Park—what would later be called "the selling of the South"—was still five years away when Bessemer Improvement Company went into business. Early ORD development was guided by neither vision nor range; it was strictly opportunistic. Burnett was happy for any customer willing to pay cash for land and buildings. A plumbing company took a building, as did a machine shop. Cotton broker Pierce Rucker purchased the refrigeration units and launched a commercial cold storage business. Kraft Foods Company put in a one-hundred-thousand-dollar distribution warehouse on the eastern end of the property, further enhancing Greensboro's reputation as a regional distribution center. Burnett and Falk took ten buildings along the eastern boundary and opened a commercial warehouse. Home builders Herman Weaver and John R. Taylor bought parcels on the fringes. Taylor built about a hundred tract homes, while Weaver built both houses and apartments and a neighborhood of duplexes with more than two hundred units that won an award for its design.

Burnett controlled what the city's planning staff said was urgently needed in Greensboro—a large tract of land open for industrial development. Much of the real estate in Greensboro and on the perimeter of the city was held by a handful of landowners. Among the largest were the Cones, who owned thousands of acres north of the city, and Ed Benjamin, who held land to the west and northwest. The Richardson family, whose Vick Chemical Company was a major employer, also owned large tracts.

Such concentration of ownership made ORD a rare gem. Among the state's largest cities, only Charlotte had such a site already outfitted with streets and utilities and ready for the industrial market. Yet when Burnett applied to the Greensboro planning and zoning commission for approval of plans to develop his property, he ran into a brick wall. Objections to his proposal were never fully aired in public; that was not the way things were done in Greensboro. The commission's chairman, Stark S. Dillard, an outspoken and blustery stalwart of the status quo, simply told Burnett—after he had made numerous adjustments to his plan to accommodate the city's objections—that the commission would not approve it even "if [he brought] all the plans and charts in the world before them."[4]

The objections apparently were not about the land Burnett had earmarked for industrial development but about a shopping center he intended to build on a corner of the property. Such a project, albeit small, went well beyond what the Greensboro Merchants Association, which was controlled by the downtown business interests, was willing to tolerate. Summit Shopping Center would not only have a larger complement of stores than most of the pocket shopping areas that had emerged in Greensboro neighborhoods but also plenty of free, at-the-door parking. Such convenience gave the prospective Summit merchants an advantage over their competitors downtown. The project's challenge to the downtown retail market kept Burnett from getting the zoning he needed to move ahead until he finally prevailed at a special session of the city council in September 1948.

The Summit center was perfectly suited for success. It was a located within an easy drive from the major residential areas. The long side of the center fronted on Summit Avenue, or U.S. 29, which was the northern entrance to downtown less than a mile south. The shorter arm fronted on Bessemer Avenue, a major east-west route that was a tree-lined boulevard to the center's front door. There were plenty of potential customers nearby. Weaver's Forest Grove Homes, the award-winning cluster of duplexes, was immediately behind the new center. His Rosewood Homes, which had been completed the year before, was just beyond. The center was only a few blocks away from the Cone mill village.

Despite these advantages, Burnett and Fred Williams literally had to beg merchants to become tenants. Elm Street merchants, who controlled most of the clothing stores in town, turned him down. So did Greensboro's druggists. Williams finally placed an ad in various North Carolina papers offering space for a new drugstore, and he heard from a mother in Asheville. She said her sons, two young pharmacists, would call soon to ask about the opportunity. Marion and George Edmonds were just starting their careers and had no credit, but Burnett signed them on anyhow. Bessemer Improvement Company guaranteed the first shipment of merchandise for the shelves of Edmonds Drug Store, which became the first of five stores the brothers would open over the years. Williams finally signed up a bakery in Reidsville that was looking to expand and a beautician with a west side address who was eager to increase business. Guilford Dairy agreed to put in a dairy bar, a dry cleaner took space, and a new Esso service station was built on the corner.

Summit Shopping Center had only seven of its anticipated sixteen stores when it opened February 7, 1950, with an A&P grocery store as the main attraction. Like the center itself, the new grocery was modest in size at seventy-five hundred square feet, but that was half again as large as the store A&P had offered to build in the first place. The chain agreed to expand the size of the space only after urging from Williams, who negotiated the lease. Nonetheless, Summit had a "supermarket" that was completely "self-service," and Greensboro had its first bona fide shopping center. If the downtown merchants had not stalled Burnett's plans, the city might have had the first planned shopping center in the state. As it was, Raleigh's Cameron Village opened in early 1949.

The Summit Center barely put a dent in the retail sales of stores on Elm Street, although A&P discovered that its small store was one of the most profitable in the region. Seven years would pass before another shopping center would open in Greensboro on Benjamin property on Friendly Road west of downtown—and this only after a competitor's plans for a similar project were turned down by city hall.

At mid-century, Greensboro appeared comfortable, with its growing neighborhoods, strong downtown churches, and the familiar merchants on Elm Street. And it was all girded by the unassailable economic strength of the textile industry. Work was proceeding on a major hospital, the one that had been promised in Moses Cone's will. A major crosstown thoroughfare, Cone Boulevard, was in the planning stages. It would offer a more direct connection between the city's northeast, where the Cone interests were adding new homes, to the rest of the city.

Life was good. Bankers and professional men, along with business tycoons like Spencer Love, had large, fine homes in Irving Park. Unescorted youngsters rode the city bus downtown to the dentist's office in the Jefferson Building or took in double features at the movies on Saturdays. On weekends, Jim Melvin and his brother, Joe, were at their father's service station washing cars. Teenagers like the Melvin boys and hundreds of others had their own hangout in the former USO club on North Elm Street, where manager Weddie Huffman, one of the coaches at Greensboro Senior High, booked popular entertainers who were often touring college campuses around the South.

God-fearing southern Protestantism remained strong, and when the army vacated ORD, the suspension of the Sunday blue laws came to an end. "Let's make Sunday a Holy day, not a holiday," a minister exhorted city council in the summer of 1946. Travelers could not even buy a gallon of gas between 10 AM and 1:30 PM on a Sunday. When the thirty-three-year-old evangelist Billy Graham ended a five-week revival campaign in Greensboro in 1951, he observed, "The spirit of God has fallen like a mighty blanket on this city." A crowd of twelve hundred heard him on November 24 in a temporary building erected at the fairgrounds with sixty thousand dollars in donations.[5]

Ted Mack, the popular radio and television impresario, singled out Greensboro as an "Honor City of America." The Cone Mills Quartet was invited to audition in New York for his *Amateur Hour,* and forty pictures of Greensboro were broadcast nationwide on the television show.

There were some disquieting notes, however. After the entire community bonded together to build a unique hospital for the care of polio victims, no one seemed to be able to decide where to build the war memorial auditorium, a project already five years in the works. The city's large public debt—a remnant of the 1920s—remained a concern. Greensboro's obligations were more than twice those of Charlotte residents, a condition that made the city fathers stingy. The League of Women Voters guidebook to Greensboro published in 1949 noted that Greensboro was the only city of its size in the state without a fully equipped playground. With large tracts of land held by only a few owners, moreover, housing prices were among the highest in the state. A decided bias against apartments in favor of single-family homes sometimes made finding a place to live difficult.

If Greensboro was to grow—and there seemed no doubt of that— then it would need an adequate water supply and streets designed for automobiles, not horses and buggies. Though he had yet to prove himself, a retired general named James R. Townsend was about to leave as indelible a mark on the city as any industrialist.

Chapter 5

The General

W HEN JAMES R. TOWNSEND returned to Greensboro in 1947, he had seen much of the world since he was a lad on South Elm Street working in his father's harness shop. His army postings with the coast artillery included duty in Hawaii and Panama, as well as commands in North Carolina and California. During World War II, he was a combat commander in northern Italy and southern France before joining General Douglas MacArthur's staff to plan the invasion of Japan. With the war over, he retired as a brigadier general and was hired as the city manager of Greensboro, which was looking for a man with broad experience. He would be remembered for many things, but none as important as his efforts on behalf of a simple drink of water.

Townsend was the city's third manager in almost as many years when he arrived. He succeeded another retired general, sixty-one-year-old James L. Frink, who had stayed less than a year. Frink had followed a manager who left after about two years with a parting shot to the council members, whom he said had blocked his program for improvement of local services.

Townsend was more attuned to the city than Frink, an Iowan who had never lived in the South. Ten years younger, Townsend was thin, with a long face and a strong, square jaw. With his head of thick, unruly hair, he looked more like an itinerant preacher than a soldier, but everyone called him "General" out of deep respect. He was a quiet, curious man who had learned to ask questions, watch, listen, and learn. After a record fourteen years on the job at Greensboro's city hall, his name would linger longer than those of the mayors or council members under whom he served.

He was a peripatetic manager, not one to sit at his desk and issue orders. He hired trained professionals in the public works and planning departments, and they routed the latest information on population, land use, zoning, traffic patterns, and water needs to his office. Townsend transformed their work into solutions for the orderly growth of city services. He began with an overhaul of zoning laws untouched since the 1920s and proceeded on to promote the need for more open space and public parks. He weathered a police scandal in 1952 that sent four officers to jail for taking bribes from a gambler and worked toward a solution to downtown parking problems. He left his imprint on the city's roads, water and sewer systems, and even finances—the basic elements of municipal operations. One of his most enduring contributions was a thoroughfare plan that would guide city traffic planning for the next fifty years.

———

Greensboro roadways had changed little since the turn of the century, when all major thoroughfares intersected at Market and Elm. By the early 1950s, it was clear that the city's streets simply were not designed for the volume of cars that rolled out of Detroit after the war into the possession of an eager buying public. In just three years after 1945, Greensboro's car registrations had doubled to twenty thousand. Townsend and his staff tinkered with a tentative solution and in 1950 convinced the city council that one-way streets would improve traffic flow. The changes helped, but Ben Cone would never forget the complaints he received when he was mayor from angry drivers irritated at being forced to change their old habits.[1]

Townsend believed Greensboro's traffic needs went well beyond one-way streets, so he hired Willard F. Babcock of North Carolina State College to design a complete thoroughfare system. Babcock, one of the few traffic engineering specialists in the country, studied the streets and traffic arrangements in the summer of 1953 and produced a plan that was adopted by the city council in the following year.

The plan was deliciously simple, Babcock said years later, because Greensboro had an existing network of east-west, north-south streets. What Greensboro needed most was wider thoroughfares, which Babcock envisioned connecting in a series of circumnavigational routes that bypassed congested areas, such as the bottleneck at Market and Elm. His plan took advantage of existing streets and some county roads, which would be widened, extended, and, in some cases, substantially rebuilt.

The first ring took advantage of the one-way streets around the central business district. A second loop was about two miles out and used as its northern radius the proposed Memorial Drive, or Wendover Avenue as it came to be called, that had been envisioned soon after the war. A third loop was farther out and included a new east-west corridor along the latter-day Cone Boulevard that connected with a country byway called Holden Road to carry traffic south along the western boundary. The fourth and final ring was so far from downtown that it seemed preposterous excess to Greensboro in 1955, but it would be under construction in 2003.

Babcock's idea of major traffic arteries was advanced for the time. These were multilane, limited-access roads, some of which were divided in the center with grassy medians. They were designed to carry traffic at steady, moderate speeds through commercial and residential areas. As the road system was completed over the years, the exact routes were adjusted, but the basic plan remained in place. The completion of Wendover Avenue took more than twenty years, but it enhanced Greensboro's a reputation as a model of sound municipal planning.

The Babcock plan produced more than new and improved ribbons of concrete: the designation of the new routes gave city planners, home builders, and commercial developers guidance for the orderly expansion of Greensboro. By indicating where roadways would be in the future, moreover, the plan also made it possible for Townsend to make the most of the city money available for work on roads, even if it meant enduring some criticism. In the mid-1950s, for example, Townsend discovered a little extra money in the budget and ordered the construction of a bridge across North Buffalo Creek near Grimsley (formerly Greensboro) High School, even though the connecting roadways had not been built. The bridge sat unconnected to a roadway for nearly a decade, with the stark concrete in white relief against a field of weeds. It even became the object of scorn. Some called it Fool's Folly, but Townsend was unmoved. He knew that roads were cheaper to build than bridges and that the roads would get there in due time.

———

Developing a reliable and adequate supply of water for the city was Townsend's most vexing problem. If Greensboro were to remain viable and grow to accommodate new businesses, industries, and homes, it needed a steady, dependable flow of water. Located at the headwaters of the Cape Fear River on a ridge between two major river basins, Greensboro had no water source to compare with the Catawba River that supplied Charlotte, the French Broad that flowed through Asheville, the Neuse near Raleigh, or even the Yadkin, from which Winston-Salem could drink to its satisfaction. Greensboro was dependent on a creek that fed a reservoir, Lake Brandt, which had only been built after a major water shortage in 1923. With Lake Brandt at capacity by the 1950s, Townsend's public works department produced plans for a second pond upstream, but he knew that even this new reservoir would be insufficient to meet the city's long-term needs.

Greensboro was not entirely alone in its water situation. Many of the cities in the northern Piedmont section of the state depended on reservoirs for their water supply. In the early 1950s, it appeared to Townsend and others that a possible solution for all would be to dip into the Yadkin River as it made a turn west of Winston-Salem and headed south across the state into South Carolina. In late 1952, municipal professionals from Greensboro, Winston-Salem, and High Point announced a proposal for a multicounty, multicity system that would dam the Yadkin River and create a reservoir large enough to quench the thirst of the entire region. The dam was to be built on a site that the city of High Point had planned to use for a hydroelectric plant in the 1930s. The reservoir would occupy a portion of seventeen thousand acres of land upstream that had been set aside for the power project. The amount of water available from this new source would be simply staggering. Planners estimated nine hundred million gallons of water a day would flow over the reservoir dam. That amount was nearly fifty times the usage of all the cities combined.

The joint venture required new state law, and enabling legislation was requested from the General Assembly in the spring of 1953. The proposal died aborning, however. It ran into fierce opposition in Raleigh, mainly from the electric power companies that had come to regard the state's rivers as their private domain. Duke Power controlled the flow of the Catawba River with a series of dams and lakes, and it also eyed generation sites on the Yadkin. The company, which had defeated the High Point power project in 1939, renewed its opposition. Also weighing in against the measure was the Carolina Aluminum Company, which harnessed the Yadkin with its Baden and High Rock lakes to produce power for its smelting operations. The cities' bold proposal never received a full public airing, although it had the full support of former governor Kerr Scott, who was an early advocate for water conservation and regional projects.

Twelve months later, in the summer of 1954, the need for the cooperative water project became alarmingly clear as the entire state was parched by the worst drought in fifteen years. Rainfall in July was only a fourth of what had fallen by July of the previous year. Each day, temperatures climbed to one hundred degrees or more, baking the land and shrinking the reservoirs. All across the Piedmont, brown stalks filled the cornfields. Pastures were dry, and tobacco, the region's main cash crop, stood stunted in the fields. Occasional thunderstorms brought some relief to isolated locations, but Greensboro did not receive the steady, soaking coverage that was essential for the serious conditions to be relieved.

In late August, Townsend was working on emergency measures. The public works staff built a temporary dam on North Buffalo Creek as it flowed through Latham Park, a low-lying area surrounded on the north side by the homes of Irving Park, and pumped the water to the city's nearby filter plant. Townsend also began negotiations with the city of High Point, whose supply had been dwindling until a heavy local thunderstorm refreshed its reservoir watershed. These steps were not sufficient, however. "We face a water catastrophe," Townsend told the *Greensboro Daily News*.[2] He informed the council that the city's water supply would be gone in thirty days.

The council imposed water-use restrictions on homes and factories with the goal of cutting consumption by one-fourth. Members of the National Guard and the Jaycees were trained to read water meters and dispatched to neighborhoods to see that residents were not exceeding their fifteen-gallon-per-week ration. "It was as officious as it could be," recalled former congressman Horace Kornegay, who was an active club member at the time. "We would read the meters and tell them, 'Madam, you can't take but one bath this week.'"[3] Those found in violation were given a warning, along with information on where they could obtain water by the bucket if the infraction was repeated.

Everyone pitched in. Mrs. J. Spencer Love, the wife of the city's leading industrialist, reported that she served meals on paper plates and advised out-of-town guests they were limited to an inch of water in their baths. "I went to a cocktail party at the country club . . . and they served cocktails in paper cups," she said.[4] Residents wishing to wash cars drove to the emergency pond at Latham Park and worked at the water's edge. In a break with the usual decorum at Woman's College, the campus newspaper facetiously recommended that the students carry their share of the load by refraining from water entirely and drinking only beer. The restrictions did their work. Water usage was cut by half, down to 5.5 million gallons a day.

By October 10, five miles of eight-inch pipe laid in twin lines completed the emergency connection to the High Point reservoir. When the pumps were turned on, they began feeding two million gallons a day into a ditch on the western edge of Greensboro. The ditch fed a small stream that finally reached Horsepen Creek, which emptied into Lake Brandt. At the same time, water was being pumped out of Lake Hamilton in Starmount Forest, and the city began eyeing any large body of water that could be drained. In what appeared to be a desperate measure, the city council hired a Denver, Colorado, rainmaker, who said that seeding clouds with iodide crystals could produce up to four hundred million gallons of rain in sixty days.

On Friday, October 15, at 2 AM, the rainmaker's crystals were sent aloft into the outer rim of clouds associated with an approaching hurricane named Hazel. Five hours later, the downpour began, and the results were overwhelming. During the next six hours, Greensboro received between six and eight inches of rain. Streets flooded and lowlands turned into swamps, but there was no severe damage. Most threats to life and property were confined to the coast, where homeowners at Wrightsville Beach would remember Hurricane Hazel for years. The rain brought an end to the crisis. The pumps from High Point were shut off. Residents returned their paper plates and cups to the cupboard. When asked about the cloud seeding, Townsend said he had no comment. He clearly had more faith in Mother Nature than in Father Science. The cloud seeder was paid and sent back to Colorado.

The water shortage had a residual political effect: when the General Assembly met in 1955, the once-parched Piedmont cities succeeded in securing the enabling legislation for the Yadkin project that had failed to pass two years before. But even with the new authority, the water project proceeded slowly. A committee representing seven interested cities— Greensboro, Kernersville, Winston-Salem, High Point, Burlington, Lexington, and Thomasville—eventually was organized, and Greensboro city councilman Victor Higgins was elected chairman. An engineer by training, Higgins had led the council's efforts to secure additional water for the city in 1954. In April 1957, he convened a meeting of fifty municipal leaders at the Robert E. Lee Hotel in Winston-Salem to talk about a $23 million project that promised to provide sufficient water for the entire region for decades. Then, five months later, before anything substantive could happen, Higgins died unexpectedly, and the project all but died with him.

Talk about the seven-city project continued for another year, but the planning group never chose a replacement for Higgins. In time, Winston-Salem withdrew from the program. Leaders there said the city could expand its own water system more cheaply than it could under the regional plan. The project continued to wither under questions from South Carolina interests who objected to the proposed changes to the Yadkin, a river they called the Pee Dee after it crossed the state line.

Townsend held out some hope that Greensboro could benefit from a federal flood control project that included a reservoir farther upstream on the Yadkin near Wilkesboro. When this lake was completed in 1963, it was named for Kerr Scott, who had chided regional leaders for failing to be more aggressive in their pursuit of a common solution. None of the Scott reservoir water would ever fill a glass in Greensboro, however. It was too far away. Townsend settled for improvements to Lake Brandt.

—————

For the most part, Townsend maintained a city that ran smoothly, without any major embarrassments or scandals. There was an incident in the early 1950s, when four police officers were charged with taking bribes from a numbers racket (a form of lottery), but the corruption was not systemic, and Townsend rode out the bad news. In fact, the man seemed to have a knack for staying clear of trouble, even when his decisions created a furor. In 1952, for example, he put his own job on the line when mayor Robert H. Frazier took exception to the plan of public works director Hugh Medford to widen Lee Street. The mayor told Townsend to fire Medford. Townsend stood his ground and informed the council that he would resign before he let Medford go. The mayor backed down.

Townsend also survived the storm over fluoridation of the city's water supply, an issue that aroused emotions to such a state that it overshadowed concern about the 1954 drought and the U.S. Supreme Court decision desegregating public schools. It all began quietly enough. A newspaper article that appeared after fluoride was introduced to the water in October 1952 reported that not a single complaint had been received at city hall.[5] By the summer of 1954, however, Mayor Frazier and three other council members announced they would vote to suspend fluoride treatment in the face of a public uprising that included newspaper ads declaring that sodium fluoride affected the brain, hardened arteries,

credit for a decision that was important to the economic advancement of many in southeast Greensboro.[6]

———

Townsend's command of civic affairs was enhanced in the 1950s by a coterie of leading businessmen who had complete confidence in his performance at city hall. Their stomping ground was the chamber of commerce office on Greene Street, which became a convenient meeting place for work on all manner of civic projects, such as the development of the Greensboro Tobacco Warehouse. Rather than have farmers take their crops to other towns, where they might spend their sale profits in local stores, the chamber and the Greensboro Merchants Association organized a warehouse for the sale of tobacco, selling shares in the venture to businessmen all over the city.

Generally speaking, chamber leaders welcomed new businesses to town—at least if they were not unionized. Most said Greensboro fostered a more welcome atmosphere than that found in some textile communities, where employers actively discouraged new business for fear it would upset the stable, and often low, wages.

The chamber also was a clearinghouse for local politics. Chamber leaders, often with Townsend on hand, recruited members for public boards and commissions and picked a slate of nominees for the city council. They raised money for charitable causes and recruited new industry to the city. "The team was made up of people who knew each other, of impeccable reputations, no questions about motivations, performing civic duty," recalled William Little, who came to the chamber in 1955 from Memphis and took over the top chamber job in 1956.[7] Said businessman Stanley Frank, who was busy with his own growing business and not a member of the clique: "The good old boys were running the city. I hate to say that, but it was true."[8]

Greensboro was no different from most cities of the day, where the influence of the chamber of commerce was an accepted fact. The *Charlotte Observer* wrote: "Charlotte is run, primarily and well, by its Chamber of Commerce. We are pleased to acknowledge its bossism and wish it continued health."[9]

Greensboro's top executives were called on to do their share. Howard Holderness, who had succeeded Julian Price's son, Ralph, as the president of Jefferson Standard Life Insurance Company, was a member of the city school board. Ben Cone, whose brother, Herman, ran Cone Mills, served two terms as mayor, while his younger brother, Ceasar

II, was the driving force behind the building of the airport. Stark Dillard, whose Dillard Paper Company distributed to customers across the Southeast, was on the city's planning and zoning board. After two terms on the city council, Orton Boren shifted his interest to the chamber, where he served an unprecedented three one-year terms. He succeeded Huger King, the former mayor and leading local representative of the Richardson family, which maintained a quiet but impressive presence in the city. Nat Hayes, the head of Carolina Steel Corporation, the leading steel fabricator in the Southeast, was another active member of the group. These were strong-willed men whose positions at the top of their professions or businesses gave them the freedom to spend their time, and their money, as they chose. Their common bond was an abiding interest in the city. "When you had to get up money for something, all you had to do was make a half-dozen phone calls and you'd have what you needed," said William Jones, whose father-in-law, Orton Boren, brought him into the power set.[10]

Ceasar II and Ben Cone were perhaps the best known of the crowd. The balding and bespectacled Ben was the eldest. He was soft-spoken, thoughtful, and approachable. Like his brothers, he had gone to the public schools in Greensboro and then on to the university in Chapel Hill, where he became the close friend of a young writer named Thomas Wolfe. Cone remained active with the university after graduation, especially through the work of Albert Coates, a classmate who later taught law and created the Institute of Government. During the institute's early years, when it was supported almost single-handedly by Coates and his wife, Gladys, Cone's periodic contributions saved it from extinction. It was later adopted by the state and became a research center and training ground for local and state officials from all across North Carolina.

Of all the family, Ben was the most active in elective politics. He was elected to the state legislature during the Depression and the Greensboro City Council in 1947 in the first election after the Cone mill community election district was abolished. When he was elected to a second term in 1949, he was chosen to serve as mayor and seemed to thrive in the job. In addition to rerouting streets downtown, he led the campaign to bring state-controlled liquor stores to the city—doing so would produce needed local revenue, he argued—and he rose in the ranks of the statewide League of Municipalities.

Cone was president of the league in 1951 when municipal leaders went to the legislature to ask the state to provide a half-cent of state gas tax collections for use in the construction and upkeep of city streets. Governor Kerr Scott, whose loyalties were to a rural constituency, fought Cone and the mayors at every step to keep all the gas tax money for state road construction. The governor even convinced members of the Greensboro City Council to repudiate Cone's position. Publicly embarrassed by the action of his colleagues, Cone took the podium at a meeting in Raleigh and declared his intention to resign from office.

Council members immediately backpedaled and in an unusual joint statement denied they had been strong-armed by the governor or conspired against Cone. They begged Cone to remain in office, but they never rescinded the resolution that undercut the league's position, which eventually prevailed over the governor's objections. Cone remained for the balance of his term and was reelected to a third term on the council, although he was not chosen as mayor. He said later he stayed on "to see how Greensboro spent the revenue that I had gotten for them," explaining, "Each time I ran for council I had lost a few votes, and I decided to quit while I was ahead."[11]

Ceasar II was Ben's opposite. Blustery and often profane, he had a bulldog's chin as well as its bark. He never seemed to worry about the waves that swirled in his wake. Ten years younger than Ben, he was born in the Saint Andrews Hotel in New York City but grew up in Greensboro and attended public schools. His parents wanted him to finish his secondary education at the prestigious Woodberry Forest, a prep school in Virginia favored by wealthy families in the South, but the school turned him down. "[Woodberry Forest] said I wouldn't be happy up there because I was Jewish," Ceasar said some time later.[12] He enrolled instead at Oak Ridge Military Academy on the outskirts of Greensboro and then entered the University of North Carolina, where he graduated before going on to Harvard for graduate studies in business. Ceasar began his career with the mills as a salesman traveling to clients in Ohio, Indiana, and Michigan. After he developed tuberculosis in 1936, he moved to Arizona, where he bought a cattle ranch, before returning to Greensboro before the war.

Ceasar's passion was flying. He had learned to fly at Lindley Field in Greensboro in 1929, and he owned a plane for a few years before he let his license expire. His desire to fly and his interest in aviation never waned, however, and he was instrumental in the creation of the airport authority in 1941, of which he became a charter member. He leaned on his friend Captain Eddie Rickenbacker, the founder of Eastern Airlines, to increase flights into the Greensboro–High Point airport as easily as he did his brother Ben to obtain favors from city hall. On one occasion,

Ceasar convinced the council to change the city's health regulations to satisfy a dairy farmer who refused to cut a tree in the flight path unless he could sell his milk inside the city limits.

There was nothing subtle about Ceasar. He made that plain when he became chief executive officer at Cone Mills following the death of his brother Herman in 1955. Ceasar II acknowledged that he had inherited his job but declared that nepotism was over. Nepotism "meant probably you were missing one or two real good people," he once said, "but on the other hand you were upsetting a heck of a lot of people and you were stuck with a lot of folks that weren't worth a damn."[13] A decade later, his successor as CEO was Lewis Morris, who was the first non–family member to hold that job.

———

Missing from the ranks of the corporate leaders who gave the chamber of commerce its energy in the mid-1950s was the city's leading business-man, J. Spencer Love. It was not that Love did not care about Greens-boro, the chamber's top professional, William Little, discovered. It was simply that Love had his hands full running the world's largest textile concern. Burlington had plants in thirteen states and four foreign coun-tries, with enough workers—about forty-nine thousand—to populate a small city. Love was constantly on the move, and he owned residences in New York, Palm Beach, and Linville, a resort in the North Carolina mountains, in addition to his home in Greensboro. If Love had any free time, he was more likely to be found on the tennis court or play-ing bridge than to be engaged in civic affairs. But mostly, he worked. He communicated through brief, terse memos typed by secretaries who traveled with him. It was his way of keeping those around him informed of what he was thinking, what he was doing, and what he expected of his subordinates.

Love remained current on Greensboro affairs through various surro-gates. One was Ed Zane, a financial wizard who negotiated many of the deals that built Burlington Industries. Zane joined the city council in 1957 when the Hamilton Lakes community, where he was mayor, was incorporated into the city. Another contact was one of Love's attorneys, Ed Hudgins, who chaired the city school board. Love's lines also ran into the city's African American community. From time to time, he met with David Morehead, a creative young executive who ran the Hayes-Taylor branch of the YMCA that served African Americans in east Greensboro. When Morehead paid a call on Love, he usually left with a check that he used to pay for various projects.[14] These investments were very practical for Love: maintaining racial peace in Greensboro was important for a company that reached a worldwide market and recruited management from outside of the region.

Love's world was one of power and influence. While he was responsible to a board of directors, he ran Burlington Industries as he wanted. An associate once asked Love how he justified Burlington's fleet of airplanes to his shareholders, to which he responded that he did not justify anything to his shareholders.[15] He regularly called on Washington policymakers whose decisions affected the wages he paid and the tariffs that protected Burlington goods from foreign competition.

Love was an important player in the textile industry, but he did not always run with the crowd. In 1958, he shocked his peers when he advocated an increase in the minimum wage. He argued the industry would benefit from a strong economy that encouraged consumer spending. At the same time, he said that higher wages should come with more protection from foreign competition.

Like most southerners, Love was a registered Democrat, but his letters to vice president Richard Nixon, a Republican, were addressed "Dear Dick." President Dwight Eisenhower's treasury secretary, Douglas Dillon, was another close acquaintance. At the same time, he stunned Nixon, and many in the textile community, when he endorsed Democrat John F. Kennedy rather than Nixon in the 1960 presidential campaign. It was a decision Love felt the need to explain to those closest to him. In a lengthy letter to his second wife, Martha, Love said that while he held Nixon in higher regard than Kennedy, Nixon was so bound to "reactionary groups" that Love did not believe "he could fully implement a very much more progressive policy if he tried to."[16]

Love pushed himself hard, just as he did those around him. He gained the reputation of being a demanding and unforgiving boss. When Weddie Huffman went to work for the company in the early 1950s, a friend described Burlington as the "pink-slip" company. Its reputation for frequent firings came in part from the fact that executives at companies that Love acquired often did not stay long. They were expendable, especially if they did not accept Love's accelerated pace of work. (One casualty was C. M. Vanstory, who left Burlington after a few years as assistant treasurer with a case of bleeding ulcers.) At the same time, Love hired eager young management recruits, paid them well, and pushed them to excel. When they did not perform to expectations, they too were gone, quickly.[17] Love could be intimidating. He declared in a memo to junior officers that one requirement of a successful executive at Burlington was that he have someone ready to fill his job. Yet he conceded he had failed to do that himself—he believed he was irreplaceable.[18]

Love once defended his reputation as a workaholic to his wife. He told her that while he often left the office on Thursdays for long weekends at Palm Beach, he did not loll about in the sunshine or simply play tennis or bridge. In a three-page memorandum on his lifestyle that he sent to Martha in 1960, he said he worked even harder while in the lap of luxury to indicate to others that he was "on the job even when there." He told her that Burlington required a driven leader who set a ferocious pace and could stay abreast of world economic conditions, shifts in the national political mood, and various and sundry causes, such as Davidson College, where he nudged the administration into accepting its first students of color in the early 1960s.

"Since I have accomplished at least something with my life," he wrote to Martha, "and since the Company so far has been successful, mainly as a result of my efforts, it does irk me for people not to appreciate that such results have necessitated many sacrifices, but instead merely charge that I am peculiar in loving work for work's sake and always actually preferring it to many other things I would actually like to do with a larger percentage of my time if I felt I could with an even half-way clear conscience."[19]

The chamber's William Little identified Love as just the man he wanted to lead the chamber's growing industrial recruiting efforts, which Little was hired to organize in 1955. Prospective industry leaders would have to be impressed with a courtship that included the Burlington founder, especially in a region known for discouraging new industry. In time, Little got an appointment with the man himself, who agreed to lend a hand.

In January 1958, Little mailed a personal invitation from Love to eighty Greensboro businessmen asking them to join Love for dinner to talk about expanding Greensboro's economic base.[20] The evening proved to be nothing less than a command performance. To his surprise, Little discovered that many of Greensboro's business leaders did not know Love or did not know him well. Little stood at Love's elbow to prompt him with the names of his guests. Nonetheless, Love proved an alluring leader for what was called the Ambassadors Club. Club members made trips to Cleveland, Detroit, and Philadelphia armed with the names of companies that supplied local businesses and attempted to lure them to Greensboro.

Little's early years at the helm of the chamber were productive. National companies like glassmaker Dow Corning and Gilbarco, the Standard Oil subsidiary that manufactured gasoline pumps, opened regional operations in Greensboro. These national names joined AT&T, the nation's telephone monopoly, whose subsidiary Western Electric had turned a former textile mill at Pomona into an electronics plant. AT&T found that the dexterity of textile workers complemented the intricate demands of its assembly line, and more than twelve hundred workers found jobs there. Gladiola Biscuit and Edgecomb Steel also added to the diversification of the Greensboro workforce. In 1947, more than half of the city's workers were in textiles. That number was down to 45 percent ten years later, when the city's population was pushing one hundred thousand.

Retail businesses expanded. In August 1957, Ed Benjamin's Starmount Company opened Friendly Shopping Center. It was built on a rolling expanse of Benjamin land just outside the city's western edge. With twenty-four tenants, including national retailers F. W. Woolworth (the variety store) and Colonial Stores (the grocery chain), as well as acres of free parking at the door, Friendly was the suburban shopping location whose arrival the downtown merchants had been fearing for more than a decade.

Most notable among the Friendly tenants was the Belk department store. John Belk of Charlotte, the son of company founder William Henry Belk, had overruled his Greensboro manager and personally directed the opening of the store at Friendly, which became the company's first suburban location in the Carolinas. The store was smaller than the downtown store at the corner of Market and Elm, but with twenty-four thousand square feet, it was a significant step into the suburban marketplace. On opening day, about two hundred company managers and executives joined John Belk to greet customers. One senior executive who remained loyal to downtown locations told Belk the company ought to sell shotguns if it was going to have stores so far out in the country.[21]

When Orton Boren addressed the chamber of commerce in November 1958, he asked, "Why did these things happen?" He answered his own question: "Because people wanted them to happen. The change that has come about in Greensboro . . . [is the result] of the new outlook of citizens of Greensboro. We had the reputation of being a very conservative community, and maybe a little self-satisfied.

"There has been a change," he continued, "A very definite change, and this, I think, is the reason that Greensboro today is on the verge of a period of growth and prosperity greater than any we have ever known before."[22]

Chapter 6

Elephants with Ears Flapping

*P*ERHAPS GREENSBORO did have the resolve in 1958 to make the transition from a textile town to a modern, diversified city. Out on Lee Street, on a flat tract of land where for half a century the Greensboro Agricultural Fair had set up its midway and local farmers had brought in livestock and produce for their annual show, construction was finally under way on the Greensboro War Memorial auditorium and coliseum.

The twin buildings included seating for 2,500 for concerts, public meetings, or revivals, while the accompanying 10,800-seat coliseum offered one of the top arenas for sporting events in the region. The project had bedeviled the city since 1944 with disputes that at times had broken into open warfare between the city council and the commission created in 1947 to build a memorial to the World War II dead. The project had been before the voters four times, once in a referendum challenging a council decision, before supporters finally won approval of construction bonds. Twice, the state supreme court had been required to sort out the details. The tangled story of the coliseum—just like that of the General Townsend's Fool's Folly bridge—had helped reward Greensboro with a reputation for being unable to finish what it started.

W. H. Sullivan was mayor in 1944 when John L. Voehringer was killed in France and the soldier's father, John K. Voehringer Jr., offered the city $25,000 toward the construction of a memorial to those who had fallen in World War II.[1] The auditorium proposal that W. H. Sullivan came up with was received with lusty enthusiasm, and a public subscription campaign raised $265,000 within eighteen months. Generous contributors included the Cones' Revolution and Proximity mills, as well as Burlington Mills, Carter Fabric Company, and Jefferson Standard Life Insurance Company. As envisioned in plans produced in 1946, the memorial hall was to have a 4,000-seat auditorium that would be accompanied by assembly rooms, an exhibition hall, a swimming pool, and an eight-lane bowling alley. This oversized community center was to be built three blocks west of downtown on land adjacent to the Burlington headquarters on Eugene Street, where the Charles L. Van Noppen house had stood for nearly a century.

The Van Noppen house and its surrounding grounds were a city landmark. One of a handful of eighteenth-century homes that remained on the boundary of downtown into the 1950s, the house was a stout two-story structure with exterior and interior walls of solid brick. It had simple lines and tall, graceful windows upstairs and down. A spacious porch spanned the entire front, while gardens and an orchard occupied grounds fenced by boxwoods that spread out behind the house toward the Burlington building. The grandeur of the place had begun to fade in 1936, when Van Noppen forfeited his house and land to the city in lieu of taxes. During the war, it had housed the offices of the American Red Cross. Garden Club members had plans to restore the gardens to their original splendor.

It was generally understood that the property would be the site of the new auditorium, or some public park, until the city's business interests, led by C. M. Vanstory, convinced the council the land was more suitable for a tax-paying commercial development. In 1946, the council accepted a bid of $200,000 for the property from Pilot Life Insurance Company amid talk the company might move its headquarters there from Sedgefield. The sale was delayed, however, when opponents eager to save the property for public use challenged the decision and demanded a referendum. The vote was held almost immediately, and fewer than twenty-five hundred voters—about half the number required to fill the proposed auditorium—affirmed the council's decision. Six months later, Pilot Life executives changed their minds and sold the property to Sears, Roebuck, which removed the house and built a $1.5 million retail store on the corner.

With the Van Noppen property out of the picture, the city purchased an alternate site on North Elm Street across from the proposed site of Moses H. Cone Memorial Hospital. The War Memorial Building Commission established by the legislature in 1947 launched a fund-raising campaign that brought the total contributions to nearly $900,000. Then the project fell victim to conflicting interests. It would take another ten years for the commission, the city council, and assorted civic groups to agree on what kind of building was needed and where to put it.

There was no consensus on what should go in the building. After first considering an auditorium, the commission began to lean toward a sports facility, a change that drew the ire of arts groups, especially the Euterpe Club, which had taken on its share of the fund-raising to build a hall for musicales. Meanwhile, those favoring an auditorium over a sports arena said the new gymnasium at Greensboro Senior High was large enough for sporting events.

Location also was an issue. Downtown interests objected to the North Elm Street site, which would put the memorial well beyond the reach of existing stores, hotels, and restaurants. They argued that a center-city location would prove most useful for out-of-town guests attending trade shows or patrons attracted to a concert. The entire project was stalemated in 1952 when the city council forced the issue by purchasing more land downtown and presented an architectural rendering for an auditorium and exhibition hall. The council set a date for a $1.9 million bond referendum to pay for the new hall, which prompted the building commission's chairman, McDaniel Lewis, to angrily resign his position. A leader in the state's burgeoning preservation movement, Lewis had been unhappy with the council's interference since the sale of the Van Noppen property and the destruction of the old home. Six months later, the bond referendum failed to win approval.

The dispute was approaching the absurd. Even the old lions gathered around the chamber of commerce could not agree. A chamber poll showed half the membership favored an auditorium, while the other half wanted a sports arena. A healthy majority said that the memorial should not be located downtown. Ceasar Cone II was so disgusted with the state of affairs that he wrote the commission and asked for the return of $10,000 he had given during the subscription campaign after the war. No money was refunded, but Cone's point was made. Finally, in 1956, after two lawsuits finally established the commission's authority to design and locate the building without interference from the city council, a second bond referendum to pay for a redesigned arena and auditorium combination at the Elm Street location was put to the voters. Once again, voters rejected the plan. Most of those reading the returns said the problem was the site: such a facility jammed in beside the hospital and at the edge of the city's finest residential neighborhood would not work.

Charles T. Hagan Jr. was in the midst of it all. He had left his law practice in Greensboro for military service in World War II and on his return was appointed to the building commission. After ten years of haggling, he was as eager as Sullivan to bring the project to completion. "Greensboro has a very large negative group of citizens," he said some years later. "They are 'aginners.' I always thought we had a little bit more than [the] normal number. There was always somebody who was not pleased with where we tried to go."[2] After the defeat of the bond proposal in 1956, Hagan joined former mayor W. H. Sullivan, William York, and W. C. Boren on a commission subcommittee to find a solution. Sullivan took the lead and one day called Hagan to ask his opinion about the fairgrounds property on Lee Street on the city's southeast side.

The fairgrounds was a familiar landmark known for an obelisk at the entrance that featured drinking fountains on four sides. The land was owned by George Hamid, a fair promoter in New Jersey who had gotten his start working for Annie Oakley in Wild West shows. His holdings included Atlantic City's famous Steel Pier, and he had been producing Greensboro's annual agricultural fair for nearly fifty years. In addition to the annual fair, the site was known for hosting regular motorcycle races on a dirt track behind the main fairgrounds. Sullivan and York paid a call on Hamid, who agreed to sell his land as long as he could use the property once a year to stage the fair.

In short order, Sullivan had the plans for the building that had been designed for North Elm Street adjusted to accommodate the new location. As before, the complex was to include an auditorium that would be connected by covered walkway to a sports arena whose main floor could accommodate ice-skating. The complex also would feature a smaller three-hundred-seat auditorium for community events. The cost was projected to be considerably more than the $900,000 on hand—less the $220,000 paid for the property—but at the commission's request the council put a $3 million bond referendum on the ballot for November 1956. It passed five-to-one with surprising ease.

Construction began immediately. Sullivan, an experienced heating and plumbing contractor, stayed with the project each step of the way. The main arena was not particularly stylish; the curved roofline gave it the appearance of a large airplane hangar. But the building was versatile. It could seat a large crowd for a basketball game and the next day play host to the circus. The auditorium was a full-dress affair and more accommodating than what the council had planned for the downtown location. Inscribed on the walls would be the names of not only the World War II dead but those who had fallen in the Korean conflict as well. The connecting walkway was more than a convenience, Hagan later recalled: it was necessary to meet the obligations of the original statute that called for the erection of an "auditorium" and said nothing about a sports area, which in the long haul would prove more useful to the city.

On October 29, 1959, the War Memorial complex that would later be known as the Greensboro Coliseum opened with a preview production of the 1960 "Holiday on Ice" show. Fifteen years had passed since Sullivan had proposed an auditorium on behalf of the Voehringer family. A half-dozen mayors and a host of council members had come and gone since he had accepted the first $25,000 contribution. Sadly, when the doors opened for dedication ceremonies on October 25, Sullivan was not present. He had died the previous June from complications related to surgery. Before his death, he checked on construction almost daily and would stand on the unfinished floor and imagine the days ahead, when the circus elephants would come through the huge doorways with their ears flapping.[3]

A few months before the gala opening of the coliseum, C. M. Vanstory stopped by Joe Melvin's service station on South Asheboro Street to buy a tank of gas. He happened to see Melvin's son Jim and asked if he had recently finished college. No, Jim told him, he had graduated in 1956 from the University of North Carolina and after volunteering for the draft had spent the last two years pushing papers as a personnel specialist in a peacetime army, only recently returning to Greensboro.

What were his plans? Vanstory asked. Melvin said he had taken a job with Texaco, the company that supplied his father's gasoline, and was due to report to Norfolk, Virginia, in a few weeks. Would he like to stay in Greensboro? "Yes," Melvin said. "Then come in to see me next Monday," Vanstory told him: "We need some good, young people."[4]

The neighborhood that Jim Melvin returned to in 1959 was different from what he had known in the early 1950s, when he drove his father's 1939 Chevrolet home from Greensboro High School after football practice. One by one, the white families who lived along Asheboro Street had moved away. Once Jim had finished high school, Joe and Virgil Melvin also departed in favor of a house on their farm south of town. The street was well into its transition from white to black by 1957 when the city school board picked Gillespie School, which stood across from the Melvins' former home, to receive five of the first six African American children in the city to be assigned to desegregate a formerly all-white school.

Greensboro's school board had captured national attention in 1954 when it become one of the first in the South to pledge compliance with the U.S. Supreme Court's school decision. "Integration is as inevitable as the sunrise," school superintendent Ben L. Smith told reporters as he led the board in the admission of the first black children to formerly all-white schools.

Jim Melvin had grown up in a segregated society, although Asheboro Street was already something of a racial twilight zone where, on some levels at least, the worlds of whites and blacks blended rather than collided. White boys and black boys played pickup games of football together on the lawn at Gillespie School. And the black employees at Joe Melvin's station were not only workmates but also occasional guests for supper. After two years in the army, Jim Melvin's mind was not on race but on a lesson learned from his father: that hard work brought reward, and it now was time to go to work. On February 1, 1959, he set out to become a banker.

Melvin arrived at Security National Bank early on a Monday and was on his way to the bank's back offices, where trainees learned the rudiments of banking by sorting and processing thousands of checks, when he was met by Hugh Beal, Security's crusty executive vice president. It was said that Beal's abrupt and callous manner could drive customers away almost as fast as Vanstory could bring them in. Beal stopped Melvin and coldly asked his business. Melvin explained he was a new hire; Beal was not impressed. Melvin's military haircut and thick-rimmed, army-issue glasses were presentable enough. It was his tweed sport coat, blue shirt, and khaki trousers that offended Beal. "Get out of here until you have a white shirt and suit," Beal growled.

Melvin withdrew to the service station, where he told his father of his first appearance at work. Jim sat around the station until just before 10 AM, when the downtown stores opened and Joe Melvin bought his son a new suit, two shirts, and a couple of ties. The store made alternations on the spot, and although Melvin reported for work before noon, his boss was not impressed. Melvin said later, "I thought that was an interesting way to start a career."[5]

In 1959, Security National Bank was Greensboro's leading financial institution. With nineteen branches across the state, including offices in Durham and Raleigh, it dominated the local market from its headquarters on the ground floor of the Jefferson Building. Security's closest competitor was Guilford National, which had its own ties to the Jefferson Standard Life Insurance Company.

Guilford's president, W. L. Burns, had nursed the bank through tough times in the Depression and still fought for every customer who came in the doors. He dogged Security's every move and picked up no small portion of new business from those who had been insulted by Hugh Beal. Burns had stepped aside to make way for a younger man, Patrick N. Calhoun, not long after Winston-Salem's Wachovia Bank and Trust Company, at the time the state's largest financial institution, entered the Greensboro market in 1957. Wachovia's share of local business was small but growing, and its statewide reach and national standing were sufficient to make Security nervous.

Wachovia's move into Greensboro, where it had acquired the Industrial Bank to gain a toehold, was an example of the awakening that was taking place in the banking business. Security had expanded to Durham by buying a local bank in the same way. Likewise, Charlotte's American Commercial Trust Company had leaped across the state to acquire a Raleigh bank. Unlike most states, which restricted branch-banking options, North Carolina presented no statutory obstacles to such expansion. The new opportunities for developing a statewide banking business were not lost on John Van Lindley (known as "Jack"), a Security board member and influential member of the Jefferson hierarchy.

Jack Lindley came from one of Greensboro's oldest families. His grandfather and namesake had been in on the founding of substantial Greensboro businesses, including Jefferson Standard and the Pomona Terra Cotta Company. In its heyday, the Lindley wholesale nursery on Greensboro's west side supplied customers all across the Southeast and was given credit for establishing North Carolina as a leading producer of peaches. Before the Depression, Lindley land stretched from the city limits well into the further reaches of the county from the city's western edge. Lindley Park, one of Greensboro's first subdivisions, featured trolley service to downtown and an amusement park. Lindley Field, the city's airport, was on what had once been Lindley land. The family's fortune had taken a hit during the Depression, when much of its property was forfeited to tax liens. During and after World War II, Jack Lindley had resurrected a portion of the family's holdings when he managed to recover some of the tax-defaulted property, often at less than market value, before and during a term as a city councilman.[6] His real leverage in business and politics, however, came from his control of a large amount of Jefferson Standard stock.

With the exception of his stint on the city council, Lindley preferred to operate in the shadows, which compounded his reputation for mischief. Jefferson Standard maintained an unmarked office for his use, but he was seldom there. In the course of a day, he might visit several cities in pursuit of some business deal or political favor that usually involved his substantial real estate holdings. His lifeline was the telephone, especially pay phones, whose location on familiar highways he knew by heart. He produced results for his friends and anger among his enemies.

Some of his projects showed real vision. In 1958, for example, four years after the drought, Lindley and Orton Boren bought four hundred acres of land along the Mayo River in adjoining Rockingham County with a plan to dam the river, create a reservoir, and produce a supply of water for Greensboro and other Piedmont communities, including Chapel Hill. Forty years later, at the time of Lindley's death, the venture remained wrapped in public and private controversy, and the land was just as Lindley found it.

Perhaps Lindley's greatest coup was in banking. In 1959, Lindley was set on merging Security National with another bank to create a competitor for Wachovia. He had called on several large institutions around the state by the time he got to the office of Addison Reese, the head of American Commercial Trust Company in Charlotte, who, Lindley discovered, was interested in Security's network of branches, which Reese believed would allow American Commercial to increase its statewide presence. Combined, Security and American Commercial would have both the size and the range necessary to compete with Wachovia.

Lindley's furtive ways were well-suited to the conspiratorial atmosphere that pervaded state banking circles. He could slip in and out of bank offices without notice, while the sight of two bank presidents with their heads together was enough to provoke speculation. That's what happened when Reese and Guilford National's president, Pat Calhoun, were spotted in Charlotte. But this leak was one that may have been arranged by Reese: when news of Reese's meeting with Calhoun made the papers, Fielding Frye, an influential Guilford director, discovered that Calhoun had met Reese without the knowledge of anyone on the Guilford board. Thinking they could head off American Commercial, Frye and others hastily arranged a merger of Guilford and Security National. Actually, Lindley and Reese were a step ahead. A week after the Guilford–Security National union was complete on March 31, a proposed merger of the new Security National with American Commercial was announced. The final deal was enhanced by the combination of the two Greensboro banks, both of which had substantial investment from Jefferson Standard, Lindley's sponsor.

The resulting new bank, which federal regulators approved in late May 1960, was North Carolina National Bank, or NCNB, as it was later known. In time, NCNB would become NationsBank as it expanded first to Florida, then across the Southeast, and into Texas, Georgia, and Missouri before a final merger in 1999 with Bank of America made it one of the largest banks in the nation. At the outset, the new NCNB claimed only forty-one branches and $500 million in assets, putting it at about half the size of Wachovia. In ten years, however, before Reese's retirement and after a host of other mergers, he and Lindley would achieve their goal of parity.

The new bank was no victory for Greensboro, although it was arranged to look like one. Security National's Vanstory was elected chairman of the board, and it was agreed that the bank would have dual headquarters, with board meetings alternating between Greensboro and Charlotte. Clearly, however, the power resided in Charlotte, where Reese served as president and the Charlotte interests maintained a one-vote margin on the new bank's board of directors.

Vanstory was a man very much caught in the middle. He had lost his bank, and there was little he could do about it. Perhaps even more galling was the realization that the deal had been engineered by Lindley, who installed a private telephone line to Vanstory's desk so that he could reach the chairman whenever he needed him. Troubling, too, was the handling of the directors of the Security and Guilford banks, who had been played like pawns in this high-stakes financial shuffle. Many of Vanstory's friends, Greensboro's top businessmen, had been tantalized with a bank directorship only to have the appointment, and the bank, dissolve within sixty days.

Stark Dillard, an important member of the Guilford board, was one of those shunted aside. He closed all his accounts and took his business to Wachovia. Ceasar Cone II kept the Cone Mills corporate accounts in place but was never reconciled to Greensboro's loss. For years, he lobbied unsuccessfully to have the Cone Mills stock certificates processed through NCNB carry a Greensboro, not a Charlotte, address.

Forty years later, those reviewing Greensboro's history never failed to mention the loss of the bank shuffle as a major turning point in the city's destiny. Certainly, the merger put Greensboro on a different course, but the destiny of Charlotte, rather than Greensboro, as the state's financial center was set in 1927, when Charlotte was chosen as the location of the

Federal Reserve branch office in North Carolina. In the age before high-speed electronic transfers, when paper rather than bytes carried financial data, banks clustered around reserve city offices.

Nonetheless, the merger was an ignominious end to the 1950s. It had been an impressive decade of progress and growth. As census takers began their work in 1960, it appeared Greensboro would hold on to its ranking as the second largest city in the state, with about a hundred and twenty thousand residents compared to Charlotte's estimated two hundred thousand. Cone Hospital was one of North Carolina's finest medical facilities. The Lorillard plant had added to the city's industrial base. The city had just constructed a performance hall and coliseum that was home to a new professional hockey team, the Greensboro Generals. James R. Townsend had created a city administration that was considered a model of efficiency.

In February 1961, Townsend announced his retirement as Greensboro's city manager at the age of sixty-seven. He moved to Durham, but he maintained his interest in Greensboro's water needs as a member of the state's water resources board. Ten years later, in 1971, Greensboro's newest reservoir was dedicated in his name.

Chapter 7

The Best in the Nation

$\mathcal{G}$OLFER SAM SNEAD could not leave well enough alone. Each time he opened his mouth, he only made things worse after his initial biting comments about the sorry condition of the Starmount Country Club course at the close of the 1960 Greater Greensboro Open (GGO) tournament. Now the tournament sponsors, the Greensboro Jaycees, were on the outs with course owner Ed Benjamin, and their prize project, the GGO, was officially without a home.

Greensboro was the place Snead called his "second home."[1] The likeable West Virginian enjoyed the golf and especially the fishing and the partying with the Jaycees that proceeded his tee times. Greensboro had become a relaxing stop as he made his way through pro golf's winter tour. It was also rewarding. By his seventh GGO victory in 1960, his Greensboro winnings amounted to more than twenty-one thousand dollars. He had won the GGO so often that his competitors called it the "Sam Snead Open."

The 1960 tournament had opened on a sunny Thursday morning. The crowds were large and the field was strong, but the Starmount course was showing signs of Greensboro's growing pains. Two years earlier, the town of Hamilton Lakes, which included the country club, the Starmount and Hamilton Lakes neighborhoods, and much of Benjamin's undeveloped property on Greensboro's western side, had been annexed to the city. In the fall of 1959 and on through the winter, the city's public works department had scarred the landscape and some of the Starmount fairways while installing water and sewer lines. The course was not up to its usual standard of green beauty, prompting Snead, as well as other players, to grumble about its condition. What really galled Benjamin, however, were Snead's public comments. At the closing ceremonies, Snead told the tournament gallery and a sizeable radio audience that perhaps it was time for Benjamin to spend some of his money on the course. If something was not done, Snead said, professional golfers would bypass the Greensboro tournament due to the lousy playing conditions.

By the time Snead got to New Orleans, his next stop on the tour and Benjamin's second home for much of the year, Benjamin was making noises of his own. He said he would rather not see Snead back at Starmount—ever—and suggested that the Professional Golfers' Association (PGA) censure Snead for what he considered outrageous remarks. Benjamin defended his course by observing that three weeks of snow had hampered preparations for the tournament. He said if Mr. Snead knew how to grow grass in the winter, then he was a better man for it. Besides, Benjamin argued, he had recently rebuilt the two greens that Snead admitted gave him a winning edge.

Snead just kept talking. He told a reporter that he thought he was doing a good deed by letting folks know what was on the minds of tournament players, as well some local Starmount members too reticent to speak for themselves. "Everyone I talked with was concerned about the condition of the course and I simply tried to get some action," he said. He had not meant to offend, but "simply wanted to wake them up." "Of course," he continued, "if [Benjamin] doesn't want the tournament that is up to him. He can always make a housing project out of the course."[2]

By the time Snead's last remarks were in print, Benjamin had already called the Jaycees on the carpet, and the 1961 tournament chairman, Mose Kiser Jr., was looking for an alternative site where Snead could defend his title.

By 1960, when the fracas with Benjamin took place, the Jaycees was the leading civic club in Greensboro for young men on their way up. Members were as patriotic as the Fourth of July, as faithful as the Boy Scouts, and as industrious as any group of young lawyers, businessmen, and junior corporate executives. Limited to men between the ages of twenty-one and thirty-five, the club, for some, was an extension of their fraternity days, but with more serious intent. It was *the* place for energetic young men who cared about their community and wanted to make a difference. Certainly, the excitement of the annual golf tournament, Greensboro's leading sporting event, was an additional draw.

Civic concern had provided the spark for the formation of the club in

1935. A group of five men decided they would convince Ford Motor Company to put a plant in Greensboro after they heard talk that the city's major employers had discouraged the company out of fear of competition for their workforce. The plant went elsewhere, but the group remained together and became the nucleus for a new chapter of the Junior Chamber of Commerce, a service organization formed in 1920 in Saint Louis, Missouri, to help young men develop their organizational skills and enhance their reputation in the community. The Greensboro charter was issued in September 1936, and Alex Stanford was elected club president. The first project was the distribution of ten thousand highway safety pamphlets.

It was a modest start, but the founding of the GGO followed in 1938 and proved to be a substantial building block. In addition to the tournament, which the Jaycees hoped would help put Greensboro on the map, the club members created a Christmas fund for needy children and in the early days of World War II devoted countless hours to the collection of scrap paper, iron, and metal. Activity waned as military enlistments drained the membership. Like Jaycees elsewhere, the Greensboro men organized their own army unit, the 686 Ordinance Ammo Company, and they remained together throughout the war.

Jaycee ranks swelled all across the nation in the late 1940s and 1950s, when public spirit among returning veterans reached an all-time high. Out of the Greensboro chapter came district attorney and congressman Horace Kornegay, federal district judge Edwin M. Stanley, at least six mayors, and a fire chief, as well as a number of state legislators, city councilmen, and county commissioners.

One of the Greensboro chapter's best-known citizens of the postwar years was oil dealer Carson Bain. The son of an insurance man, Bain had grown up in Greensboro and got his first taste of the oil business as a teenager, when he rode his bike through city neighborhoods soliciting cooking oil customers for the A&P grocery store. After the war, he joined the Jaycees and worked his way up to golf tournament chairman in 1950. It was one of the GGO's most successful seasons. So many spectators turned out that the ticket chairman imposed on Cone Mills for a supply of computer punch cards to use as last-minute fairway passes. Profits amounted to more than $12,400, a record that stood for years.

Bain became club president the following year and led a contingent to the national Jaycees convention in Chicago, where Greensboro men handed out so many denim promotional items from Cone Mills and Blue Bell at the host hotel, the Sherman, that a local newspaper headlined a convention story, "South Marches through Sherman."[3] In the mid-1950s, Bain was elected to the board of county commissioners and became president of the state Jaycee association. He would later serve as Greensboro's mayor and an active civic leader.

Golf had come early to the Carolinas. The first rounds were played in the mid-1890s on a nine-hole course associated with the Eeseola Hotel at Linville, a burgeoning resort community at the foot of Grandfather Mountain. By the turn of the century, James Tufts's Pinehurst in the North Carolina sandhills was a popular mid-South resort, and golf was the main draw. Greensboro's first course was just off Summit Avenue. The clubhouse was a wooden shack where players hung their jackets on nails. It was later replaced by fancier digs at the Greensboro County Club, which was nestled among the lavish homes and oversized lots of the Irving Park development. Interest in the game was such that in the 1920s the same crowd that built Irving Park put in another course at their Sedgefield Country Club, a development laid out on lush pastureland near Jamestown. Ed Benjamin started talking about hosting a golf tournament in Greensboro not long after he opened the Starmount course, Greensboro's third, in 1930.

The early years of the Depression distracted folks from leisurely pursuits such as golf, so it was not until after the Masters Tournament was established in 1934 at the Augusta National Golf Club in Georgia that Benjamin raised the question of a Greensboro tournament again. George Corcoran, the Starmount golf pro, provided the introduction to the PGA, where his brother, Fred, was tournament director.

Greensboro Daily News sports editor Laurence Leonard urged the Jaycees to adopt the tournament as a civic project, but the challenge was daunting. Before the PGA would even talk about setting a date, the Jaycees had to raise a purse of $5,000. The chapter's board of directors trembled at the prospect of gathering a pot easily ten times the size of a Jaycee's annual wage. They voted and turned Leonard down. After the evening meeting adjourned, however, a handful of men remained behind and continued to talk. "Let's make some phone calls," they said, "and see what we can raise." Twenty-four hours later, they had small pledges totaling $800 from club members. The board reconvened and agreed to take on the tournament.

Benjamin offered to put up $1,000 of the purse if the Jaycees would do the rest. Within a few weeks, the members had $4,500 in hand, including $1,000 from local hotels. Corcoran agreed to add Greensboro to the program as the seventh PGA event in the nation and the second in the South. The PGA set the tournament to open March 26, 1938, so play would begin right after the close of the North-South Open at Pinehurst —one of the leading regional amateur tournaments—and conclude a week before the pros were due in Augusta for the Masters. The tournament would open at Starmount and conclude four days later at Sedgefield Country Club in a unique two-course arrangement that made the Greensboro competition distinctive.[4]

The $5,000 Greensboro purse, with the winner taking away $1,200, proved to be a strong draw for pro golfers struggling to make ends meet. By opening day, virtually every player with any national reputation had a tee time at Starmount. "There were champions falling over champions," Leonard wrote in his column. "Johnny Farrell, Tommy Armour, Sam Parks, Willie McFarland, Gene Sarazen and Ralph Guldah have held the National Open championship at one time or another." Starmount's Corcoran called it the largest championship field of the year.[5]

Greensboro loved it. More than six thousand spectators turned out on opening day, despite an ominous thunderstorm that passed through quickly just before play began. Fans swarmed over the Starmount course, with the largest gallery of about fifteen hundred people trailing a trio that included Sam Snead. Only in his second year on the pro circuit, Snead already was one of the most popular players in the field. Gene Sarazen told Leonard, "Sam's got the swing and he's getting everything else he needs."[6] Fourteen thousand people showed up for the first two days at Starmount before the play moved to Sedgefield for the final thirty-six holes of play on Monday. When the first tournament ended, Snead was eleven strokes under par and five ahead of his closest competitor.

Snead still had thirty-six holes to play on Monday morning when Fred Corcoran announced that a second GGO would be held in 1939. Then there was a third, and a fourth, until 1942, when the event was suspended, to resume at the end of the war in 1945. Snead's presence was a tremendous help in rebuilding the tournament in the postwar years. Timing was a factor, too. The date of the GGO always fell close to the Masters, giving the top names in the game a good reason to stop off in Greensboro on their way to or from Augusta.

During the 1950s, the size of the GGO purse grew slowly. Twenty years after the first event, in 1958, the total purse was only $15,000.

Nonetheless, the GGO remained a popular tournament that produced a respectable field. Play alternated between Starmount and Sedgefield until 1960, when Snead's remarks brought an end to the Jaycees' arrangement with Benjamin. (Years later, the Starmount club members would buy the course from Benjamin and rename the main entrance road "Sam Snead Drive.")

———

Jim Melvin was a prime candidate for the Jaycees. He was just getting used to his job at Security National Bank when two high school buddies, Mose Kiser Jr. and Jim Betts, talked to him about joining. The outfit's involvement with the GGO was particularly appealing. Melvin loved his hometown, and he loved golf. As a youngster, he had learned to play on the old Gillespie Park course, which he and his buddies called "Yellow Sulfur Springs" on account of the discharge plumes from the nearby fertilizer plants that drifted overhead. The Jaycees' reputation at the bank was such that even his boss urged him to join. "If you're young, that's where you ought to be," Melvin said he was told. "So I joined."

With more than 250 members, the Jaycees were the civic shock troops. They had canvassed neighborhoods in 1954 to remind residents to conserve water and had turned out to help during the polio epidemic. The group also was known for its progressive stand on community issues. The Jaycees were the first civic club to support the Greensboro Board of Education's decision to follow the U.S. Supreme Court's school desegregation pronouncement. Members also collected signatures to support fluoridation of the city water supply. Jaycees formed the nucleus of a merchant group that organized the Better Business Bureau and were instrumental in getting a Junior Achievement chapter under way. They did nothing by half measure. Their monthly paper drives put hundreds of volunteers—some of them with their children in tow—on the streets in borrowed trucks to collect scrap paper that was sold to raise money for community project coffers.

This was serious business for a new generation of community leaders. Campaigns for the chapter presidency were as organized as any for public office. In 1957, Bill Burns Jr. was running for chapter president when he asked the advertising agency that worked for his father's bank, Guilford National, to create a catchy tune that borrowed heavily from the Pepsodent toothpaste jingle. "If you were going to be a leader in Greensboro, you had to be a member of the Jaycees," Burns said many years later after he retired as chief executive officer of Central Carolina Bank. "There's no question about it. All the leaders were members of the Jaycees."[7]

Club rules winnowed out the fainthearted. Members had to devote forty hours a year to volunteer service in order to remain in good standing. The real go-getters who logged a thousand hours or more during their Jaycee careers had their names added to a plaque at the Jaycee headquarters. The rewards for this high-energy crowd were the top assignments at the GGO, where scratch golfers got a chance to rub elbows with the likes of Arnold Palmer and other golf greats.

In his first year, Melvin was appointed tournament rules chairman, a title that implied lofty responsibilities. As the tournament approached, he discovered that his most important task was to see that the lime markings designating spectator areas were put in place by opening day. In 1961, with Kiser as chairman, Melvin got another "good" job: he was named grounds procurement chairman, which meant he was the man to see about parking, garbage pickup, and urinals.

After the flap with Benjamin, the Jaycees relocated the tournament to Sedgefield Country Club, which had been the host course for six tournaments since 1945. In truth, the Sedgefield layout worked to the tournament's advantage. The handsome Tudor-style inn at Sedgefield was larger and better equipped to accommodate out-of-town VIPs than the Starmount clubhouse. Moreover, there was ample parking space for spectators on the campus of nearby Pilot Life Insurance Company. A shuttle from the company lots to the clubhouse kept congestion to a minimum. In addition, Sedgefield's Donald Ross course was considered one of the state's golfing gems.

Melvin discovered on the eve of the 1961 tournament that Sedgefield's charm included a few flaws, however. To accommodate the crowd, the Jaycees had converted a former stable—Sedgefield was famous for its hunts as well as golf—into a men's room and installed a specially designed, and substantial, trough urinal. The plan looked good until the club reopened the water line to the barn. When the water pressure reached its maximum, the old pipes burst, sending a geyser of water into the sky. A plumbing firm was called, but each time one repair was completed, the line broke at another spot. The thought of several thousand beer-drinking golf fans relieving themselves behind Sedgefield's oaks and flowering cherry trees was sufficient motivation for Melvin to recruit twenty to thirty helpers, who worked through the night with the plumbing crew to install a new line.

The nation's golfing community had reason to pay close attention to the GGO in 1961. Two months before the Snead-Benjamin flap at Starmount Country Club the prior year, four students from A&T had sparked the national sit-in movement when they took seats at the segregated lunch counter of the Woolworth store on South Elm Street and refused to leave until they were served. The sit-ins galvanized the civil rights movement, especially among young people, who expanded the demonstrations to Kress and other stores in Greensboro until color barriers came down. The sit-ins invigorated an older generation of blacks as well, including George Simkins Jr., the leader of the Greensboro chapter of the NAACP. As the GGO approached in April 1961, Simkins telephoned Kiser and challenged the Jaycees to invite the PGA's first black professional, Charlie Sifford of Los Angeles, to play in their tournament.

Sifford had grown up during the Depression in Charlotte, North Carolina, where he learned the game as a caddy at the Charlotte Country Club. By the time he was a teenager, he was earning as much toting golf bags for rich white men as his father did as a laborer at a fertilizer plant. At seventeen, the young Sifford's scores in the low seventies were better than those of most of the golfers he saw on the course on Saturday and Sunday. By the early 1950s, Sifford was the leading black golfer in the nation, but the PGA stubbornly held to a whites-only clause in its membership until 1960, when Sifford finally secured a PGA designation as an approved tournament player. The card made him eligible—at age thirty-eight the PGA's oldest "rookie"—to join the winter tour. Local sponsors had the last word, however, and in 1961 his requests to enter tournaments in New Orleans, Palm Beach, and Wilmington, North Carolina, were all refused, despite his close finishes in PGA events in Tucson and San Francisco.

Simkins's challenge created some immediate concerns for Kiser, not the least of which was reaction from within the chapter. The Greensboro Jaycees had no African American members, although this segregation was the result of custom rather than organizational fiat. Kiser ran the idea by his executive committee, and they agreed that inviting Sifford was the thing to do. Next, Kiser had to clear Sifford's invitation with Sedgefield, an all-white private club.

He also was concerned about the community reaction. Greensboro remained unsettled following the protracted picketing that finally desegregated the dime-store lunch counters as well as the Guilford Dairy

Bars run by Kiser's company. Kiser was willing to give it a go, however. Guilford Dairy's ice cream counters had integrated without incident; so could the GGO.

The Sedgefield management would not stand in the way, but it did impose some conditions: Sifford could participate as long as he ate and slept somewhere other than on the Sedgefield property. Kiser called Simkins and told him Sifford would be welcome on those conditions. He also called Dugan Aycock, the pro at the Lexington Country Club, who had known Sifford from his days as a caddy in Charlotte. Dugan, the president of the Carolinas section of the PGA, eagerly reaffirmed the invitation to Sifford a week before the tournament was due to open.

In his own account, Sifford said he was uncertain about whether to go to Greensboro until his wife convinced him he should play. "Nothing's going to happen that you can't handle," she told him. Driving east from Los Angeles to North Carolina, a state he had left twenty years before in a time of the rawest form of discrimination, Sifford was overwhelmed with emotions: "I was alone on this trip, and there is no lonelier feeling than crossing into the Deep South and heading for an all-white country club."[8]

Some sportswriters called Sifford the Jackie Robinson of golf, a comparison that Sifford never appreciated. In professional baseball, Robinson had been followed into the major league by a succession of black players after he joined the Brooklyn Dodgers in 1947. The professional golf community remained all-white and even supported the PGA's all-white membership policy. Robinson also had a team behind him, while a golfer performs alone. "Golf is a little too intimate a game for many white people's tastes," Sifford later wrote. "They'd prefer their black sports heroes to maintain a respectable distance."[9]

Kiser met Sifford on his arrival at Sedgefield and walked him into the clubhouse to register for the tournament. Sifford recalled a "cool but cordial welcome" but was more impressed that no one seemed to make a fuss over his presence. Other golfers who knew him from the PGA's western tour treated him just like another pro. Simkins had arranged a room for Sifford in a dormitory at A&T, but Sifford moved out after his first night. The late-night antics of college students did not agree with a man preparing for an athletic event. He finally found a room in the home of a friend and ate where he got invitations. Simkins had wanted to do something more elaborate, but plans for a reception fell through, largely because of Sifford's own reluctance to use his presence for the movement.[10]

At the pro-am outing on the tournament's first day, Sifford played with Willard Gourley Jr., a former GGO chairman and an officer of the Sedgefield Country Club. Sifford pocketed $163 in bet money and discovered that the Sedgefield course, nursed into its best appearance since Ross had laid it out forty years before, was one that he could master. As he walked the fairways with his white companions, he heard whispers— "There's that black golfer"—but nothing more.

The weather on the day of the opening round was cold, wet, and windy. Sifford seemed to thrive in the challenging conditions and pushed through the course, chewing and smoking five cigars by the time he had finished his round with a three-under-par sixty-eight that made him the leader. While the first day went without incident, that night Sifford got a threatening telephone call that ended, "We don't allow no niggers on our golf course." Sifford told the caller he was to tee off at 10:15 the next morning and that he planned to be on time. During the night, he was uneasy, and his bravado faded to doubt. He considered withdrawing and phoned his wife in California, who told him, "Just keep going."

Kiser also received threats. One letter writer warned that if the Jaycees allowed Sifford to participate, Kiser had better not let his children play in his front yard. The Jaycees had extra uniformed officers on duty, and some undercover men mingled in the crowd.

As Sifford took his first shot on the second day, he recognized a voice from the gallery as the one he had heard on the phone the night before. He ignored a taunt, but a group of about a dozen whites dogged his steps throughout fourteen holes of play. He once found his ball in the rough covered with a pile of beer cans. Police finally removed the hecklers from the course, but the delay in their response left Sifford steaming. He later said it was the longest round of golf he ever played. Yet with all the harassment, he ended the day with a seventy-two.

"Even with that pack of wolves a few feet away from me," he later wrote, "I managed to save par on nearly every hole. I'd like to see any other golfer play under those circumstances."[11] The gang of toughs did not show again, but there were reminders of them throughout the next two days that made him uncomfortable. Nonetheless, Sifford finished fourth behind leader Mike Souchak and took home a check from the Greensboro Jaycees for thirteen hundred dollars.

A week later in Houston, it was as if nothing had changed. Sifford was denied admission to the Houston Classic. Even four years later, he would be refused service in country club dining rooms. Yet before the end of 1961, the PGA had removed the all-white membership clause from its bylaws in response to Sifford's demand. The GGO, Sifford later wrote, was a "kind of bizarre initiation that I had had to withstand in order to play on the tour."[12]

The Jaycees tapped into Melvin's high energy and unwavering determination, traits he had been known for since he was a teenager at Greensboro Senior High. Jim's forte was not scholarship—his brother, Joe, brought home the high grades—but he played clarinet in the band, was a member of the Key Club, and became one of coach Bob Jamieson's best guards on a scrappy, although hapless, football team. His senior year, the team only won three games after losing their opener to Wilmington 40–0. Jamieson trained his players hard, and they helped break in the school's new football field, where a stadium was still under construction. Melvin often went home with cinders ground into his knees and elbows.

Perhaps the only down time in Melvin's life had been when he left Greensboro for college and military service. He was offered a modest football scholarship at the University of North Carolina, but he turned it down after an illness left him short of playing weight. By his own account, Melvin floated through college earning average marks. Most of his spare time was spent at the Sigma Chi fraternity house in Chapel Hill, where he was known for clean living. Melvin and two others in the house were the only teetotalers.

Two years in the army had been largely uneventful. Most of that time, he sat behind a desk at Fort Jackson, South Carolina, interviewing trainees finishing boot camp before they shipped out for assignment in a military specialty. The one time he emerged from the blur of soldiers performing routine duties in peacetime remained etched in his mind for years. Midway through his tour, he was called before the post commander, who was red-faced over a Melvin gaffe that had caused quite a stir. The young sergeant had mistakenly assigned twenty-five uneducated, Spanish-speaking Puerto Rican recruits to the prestigious White House guard detail, even though assignment to the detail required some college training and fluency in English. Melvin explained that the army's specialty numbers—051 for truck driver and 015 for honor guards—were the root of the problem. He had reversed the numbers on the paperwork. The general was unmoved and threatened disciplinary action. Melvin was saved from a serious reprimand by his own commanding officer, who reminded the sputtering general that all of Melvin's superiors, including the general, had approved the orders making the assignment. Melvin never forgot the lesson in loyalty he learned from his commanding officer, who put his own position on the line on behalf of his sergeant.

The serendipitous job offer from C. M. Vanstory reconnected Melvin to Greensboro and eventually the Jaycees. "Where I caught the spark was in the Jaycees," Melvin said some years later. "The Jaycees proved to me that if you are ever going to make any progress or do any good, you are going to work hard. So I started working hard. You get into it for whatever reasons, and all of a sudden you get a sense that you really are doing something worthwhile."[13]

Bank customers got the benefit of Melvin's enthusiasm. After completing his training in the bank's transit department, Melvin put in a short time at a branch office near Guilford College before he was named manager of a branch on Bessemer Avenue. It was a territory full of businesses and retail shops that had grown up around Oscar Burnett's ORD property. After the teller windows closed each day at 2 PM, Melvin hit the pavement, making cold calls on businesses, new and old. Melvin's work paid off, and his branch became one of the bank's fastest-growing operations. His success was rewarded at NCNB, which was just beginning to develop a corporate culture that put a premium on bankers who established themselves as competitive. The job also introduced Melvin to businessmen of a much higher caliber than most young executives would get to know.

One of his early contacts was Oscar Burnett. With the branch's operations growing and the branch in need of additional space, Melvin's boss told him to contact Burnett and offer to purchase a piece of land adjacent to the Bessemer branch. Melvin made the appointment and arrived in Burnett's office to find him seated at his desk, which was set in the middle of a huge office under a bright overhead light. Melvin took a seat directly in front of Burnett and immediately noticed that the combination of the bright light and Burnett's thick glasses made Burnett's eyes appear larger than normal. Nervous and self-conscious at being introduced to one of Greensboro's most successful entrepreneurs, Melvin quickly came to the point. Burnett said he was not interested in selling. Melvin rose to leave and had nearly reached the door when Burnett called him back.

Burnett's demeanor softened, and he told the confused Melvin that their business was not done. While he was not interested in selling, he would consider a trade. In time, Melvin worked out a real estate exchange that suited all parties, and Melvin won a friend who would become an ally in the future.

Melvin held an advantage in business, and in the Jaycees, over many of his peers: he was still a bachelor. While most men his age were tending to responsibilities at home, Melvin was working, either at the bank or for the Jaycees. The only competition for his time came from a few cows he kept at the farm, where he lived with his parents. He harbored a romantic notion of becoming a farmer but disabused himself of that idea when he was called on to help deliver a calf on the opening day of the GGO.

By the time Melvin was named to chair the GGO in 1963, he had received the chapter's annual award for outstanding performance, which he earned largely through his tournament work in 1960, 1961, and 1962, when he was tournament vice chairman. He also had been instrumental in the creation of a junior Jaycee program at Page High School, which had just opened on the north side of the city and whose leader went on to become state president of the junior Jaycee movement. In addition, Melvin had helped to organize new chapters of the Jaycees in communities in Guilford County. He was a regular at the chapter's biweekly luncheon meetings at the Mayfair Cafeteria, which generally drew as many as 150 of the chapter's more than 300 members.

By the early 1960s, automakers and other corporations with a national market had discovered the promotional advantages of tournament golf, but the GGO remained a homegrown affair dependent on community spirit and backbreaking volunteer labor. The tournament leaders struggled every year to sell enough tickets to keep the prize money competitive. And the only way to draw a crowd was with a field of the top names in the sport.

Like his predecessors, Melvin's courtship of a stellar lineup of players continued right up to opening day. Unlike the chairmen of old, however, Melvin and the Jaycees could no longer count on the proximity in time and place of the GGO to the Masters in Augusta to draw top professional golfers. Changing habits and larger purses at competing events were offsetting the benefit of proximity that the GGO once enjoyed. Of late, golfers who placed well in the Masters had taken to staying in Augusta to hobnob with some of the club's well-known members, such as former president Dwight Eisenhower, rather than moving on to Greensboro. Some simply skipped the GGO to prepare for the Houston tournament, which offered a larger purse.

Melvin had hoped that a television broadcast of the GGO would boost its appeal. Prior to the 1963 tournament, he had offered exclusive broadcast rights to Greensboro's WFMY-TV, a CBS affiliate. The station declined, however, after its advertising salesmen were unable to find enough sponsors to cover basic production costs. (A year later, under chairman Bradley Faircloth, promoter C. D. Chesley did take on the tournament. Chesley's initial outing was a money loser, however, because the tournament went into an unexpected playoff between golfers Julius Boros and Doug Sanders. Boros won, but Chesley lost, as he was unexpectedly forced to pay for additional broadcast time. In subsequent years, the broadcasting of the tournament was a success for the station and the Jaycees alike.)

The field for Melvin's tournament was still thin two weeks out from opening day. In an effort to broaden the lineup, Melvin and a couple of volunteers climbed aboard a plane owned by Greensboro businessman Stanley Frank. This was the same Stanley Frank who had changed into work clothes at Joe Melvin's service station on his first day of work in Greensboro in the 1930s. He now ran the business, Carolina Byproducts, and had become one of the leading boosters of improved air service for Greensboro after he succeeded Ceasar Cone II as chair of the airport authority.

Frank flew Melvin and the Jaycees to tournaments in Miami and Wilmington, where they courted golfers with the lure of generous hospitality as well as a chance at the winner's share of a $35,000 purse. Golfers were promised the use of a new car along with a driver during the tournament week. They could count on free meals and, if their families were traveling with them, daytime child care and activities for their wives. The last-minute hustle paid off. Snead agreed to return, and so did Charlie Sifford. Gary Player signed on, as did the 1962 champion, Billy Casper. Among the remaining field were Tommy Aaron, Kel Nagle, Art Wall, Dave Marr, Doug Sanders, and a little-known newcomer named Chi Chi Rodriguez, who had just begun to make a name for himself with a win at the Doral Tournament in Miami.

Moving in the circles of professional golf was a heady experience for the young boosters from Greensboro, many of whom, like Melvin, had yet to reach their thirtieth birthdays. The GGO work gave confidence to these young men—sometimes more than was good for them. A few weeks before the GGO opened, Melvin put in a telephone call to Clifford Roberts, the crusty cofounder of the Masters Tournament at Augusta. After Roberts came on the line, Melvin introduced himself and suggested that as peers, perhaps they could share some of their experiences. Roberts hung up on him. (Some years later, Melvin saw Roberts at Grandfather Golf and Country Club, where he reminded Roberts about his call. The crusty Augustan's attitude had not changed. He said nothing, turned, and walked off.)

In an effort to build interest in the GGO among players, Melvin and his committee decided that the winner would share in the profits from the tournament, which they figured could add another $5,000 in prize money. The plan looked sound. Profits in 1962 had been $13,000, and as the tournament opened, it looked like the 1963 receipts would be as good. The crowds for play on Wednesday, Thursday, and Friday were so large that an excited Jim Melvin ordered the printing of additional tickets to cover anticipated sales on Saturday and the tournament's final day, Easter Sunday.

To his chagrin, the resupply was not needed. Saturday was chilly and cloudy. Spectators stayed home or—it finally occurred to the chairman—left town for the Easter holiday. To make matters worse, Doug Sanders finished Saturday with a five-stroke lead, a margin that eliminated any chance of a close finish. The shrinking size of the gallery turned Melvin's enthusiasm into deep concern. The check presentation ceremonies were only minutes away when Melvin and Jaycee president Neil B. Glenn stepped behind the headquarters trailer and flipped a coin to decide if the bonus check would be $1,250 or $2,500. The toss favored the larger amount, and the GGO's profits for the year were reduced to $1,947, one-sixth of those of the year before. It was the least profitable tournament ever. It also was a number that Melvin would never forget.

Despite the failure of the GGO to earn a handsome profit under Melvin's direction, his management of the tournament attracted notice. A few months after the GGO, he was asked if he would consider moving to Florida to take on another tournament. It was a job that would have required him to leave Greensboro, and the future of the position was uncertain. The rising popularity of tournament golf was not yet evident in the mid-1960s. Melvin declined the offer. If he had taken the job, his life would have taken a different turn. So would Greensboro's.

Melvin's spirits were revived a few weeks after the close of the tournament when he got a visit from W. Y. Preyer, the aging president of Vick Chemical Company. Preyer's father-in-law, Lunsford Richardson, had concocted the company's famous VapoRub, a product that had helped put Greensboro on the map. As Preyer neared retirement, the company had slipped from prominence in the city. The family owned considerable real estate in Guilford County, but most of the corporate decisions were made in New York City.

Melvin was not sure what to expect from Preyer's visit. Preyer told him, "Let me tell you something. Don't be too hard on yourself. You all did the best you could. A lot of good things happened, and out of this will come some good."[14]

Chapter 8

Changing Times

𝓙IM MELVIN'S DISAPPOINTING return for the GGO was just the
beginning of Greensboro's problems in 1963. That summer, the
city became known around the nation for civil rights demonstrations
that ended with more people in jail than protests in any other city, including Birmingham, Alabama. Later that year, voters turned down a
bond referendum that the city administration said was needed to repair
aging infrastructure and guarantee a plentiful supply of water for the
future. Once again, the city's campaign for the United Way fell short.
Seven of the last eight efforts had failed to reach their goal.

Columnist Roy Thompson from the *Winston-Salem Journal* took some
delight in Greensboro's run of bad news and repeated a quote from governor Terry Sanford, who wondered aloud about the quality of the city's
leadership. Thompson wrote that those he talked to publicly discounted
the governor's opinion; "privately, however, some will concede that he's
got something there," he continued. "They say that it's difficult to get
top-echelon men to lend a hand in city projects. You hear often, as you
roam the city, that Greensboro lacks leadership nowadays.

"'The people who used to run Greensboro aren't running it any more,'
they'll say.

"Ask, 'Who is?' and a surprising number of them will say, 'nobody.'"

Indeed, the city's leadership was in transition. In 1962, voters angry
over the legislature's extension of the state sales tax to include grocery
items swept virtually every elected Democrat in the county out of office
and replaced them with Republicans, most of them political unknowns.
The landslide ended the career of the city's most influential leader on
the state front. Before he lost his bid for reelection, Joe Hunt, a former
Speaker of the state House, was making plans to run for governor. It
was a bitter defeat, and Hunt never forgave Governor Sanford, who had

proposed the tax to pay for expansion of the state's public school program. The governor's words about Greensboro's leadership were salt to fresh wounds.

More important, perhaps, were changes on the civic front. Men who had shouldered the community projects and held nonpartisan city positions since World War II were dead or entering retirement. C. M. Vanstory, the city's forceful postwar mayor, was about to step down as chairman of NCNB's board of directors. Ben Cone and his brother Ceasar II were less involved in local affairs than they once had been. Howard Holderness, who had run Jefferson Standard Life Insurance since the early 1950s, was close to the end of his career. Oscar Burnett, the creator of the city's leading industrial park, was past sixty. Mose Kiser, the man who had turned Guilford Dairy into one of the state's largest milk processors, closed his civic career with a campaign in 1961 to build the new, 220-bed, $3.5 million Wesley Long Hospital. Orton Boren had capped his civic commitment at the chamber of commerce with election to the national chamber board. Burlington Industries founder J. Spencer Love was dead. He had collapsed from a heart attack in January 1962 while playing tennis at his home in Florida.

The failure of the fall bond campaign to pay for civic improvements was a shock. Chamber of commerce president John Harden said Greensboro was on the verge of either becoming one of the South's great cities or slipping into second-class status in North Carolina. "Through our apathy at the polls," Harden said, speaking of the rejection of the bond proposal, "we as much as turned to face backwards."[1]

The shine was off of downtown. Greensboro's share of retail sales had been in steady decline since the mid-1950s. According to a community survey conducted by the Jaycees, shoppers believed downtown was inadequate and that Greensboro's stores paled in comparison to what they found elsewhere.

The decline of downtown had continued despite persistent warnings from Boren, who had first focused attention on the problem during his extended tour as head of the chamber of commerce in the late 1950s. Greensboro had been his family's home since the mid-nineteenth century, when his grandfather, then a teenager, had carried handmade bricks to the masons raising Founders Hall at Guilford College. During his own time, Boren had pushed Greensboro and North Carolina into the mainstream of change. In the early 1950s, he convinced governor Kerr Scott to grab onto the federal government's plans for building interstate highways. As a result, Greensboro was not forgotten when interstate routes were laid out.

Boren's real passion, however, was downtown. "He just believed in the future of the community," recalled William Little, the chamber's top professional during Boren's three terms as president. "He thought we were just a jumble. We needed some identity as a community."[2]

Boren was a hard man to ignore. He had a commanding presence, with a strong jaw, bushy eyebrows, and the build of a farmhand. A gregarious and a plainspoken manner belied an inner sophistication. He was the only person from Greensboro ever to serve on the board of the U.S. Chamber of Commerce. "He was the world's greatest country boy," said Little, whom Boren always greeted by asking him what was going on. "He would just dumb you to death. He only knew what he heard, and he heard everything."

In 1958, Boren said that Greensboro was losing ground because the city's downtown business district has lost its aesthetic appeal. Elm Street was marked by dingy storefronts and unpainted brick walls exposed by demolished buildings. Boren said the broken windows and overhanging store signs gave downtown Greensboro "the hodge-podge look of a honky-tonk on Saturday night."[3]

He might have added that from a distance, the area was even less appealing. Viewed from above, downtown looked like a long strip center surrounded by acres of asphalt and concrete parking lots. Upwards of five thousand cars filled virtually any open space because the city had been slow to erect multilevel parking garages. One observer called Greensboro "the parking lot city,"[4] and a photograph of Greensboro's downtown appeared in a scholarly study above the caption "Urban Devastation."[5] Boren himself once said the best thing for Greensboro would be "a tornado or about fifty bulldozers."[6] If the future was the orderly, sheltered, broad sidewalks of suburban shopping centers, with their convenient front-door parking, then Greensboro was little more than a ragged monument to the past.

Boren's efforts generated talk and study but few substantive changes. In March 1959, the large sign that hung over the sidewalk in front of Southside Hardware Company was removed, but it would be more than a dozen years before the city council would ban all overhanging signage. Boren led chamber members and city officials on tours to Knoxville, Tennessee; Hartford and New Haven, Connecticut; Norfolk, Virginia; Binghamton, New York; and Baltimore, Maryland. On a tour abroad, the group covered sixteen cities in Western Europe. Travelers returned abuzz with ideas. The city hired an economist to take the city's pulse, and the Ford Foundation paid for seminars for local officials and community leaders at the Institute of Government at Chapel Hill. The chamber even brought in a French man who had been responsible for the rebuilding of Paris following World War II. He took a plane ride over Greensboro, and his report upon landing was that he had not seen anything worth saving.

This stunning appraisal was no worse than one issued by J. Spencer Love. In a letter to the *Greensboro Daily News* written only a few weeks before his death in 1962, Love said Greensboro had deteriorated to the point "where it could be one of the worst in the country for a city of our size."[7] Downtown buildings were "ugly, outmoded and lacking modern conveniences," he wrote. The center city needed "massive and radical changes." He complained of streets that went from "nowhere to nowhere" and said national retail chains were avoiding the city because of traffic congestion and inadequate parking.

Love's interest in downtown was based on more than appearances. He wanted to build new corporate headquarters on a site three blocks south of the Jefferson Building on Elm Street. His vision included twin towers straddling Elm Street, one of them topped by a landing pad for his helicopter, which would ferry him from the airport twelve miles west of town.

Unfortunately, Love's vision died with him. Had he lived, the Burlington building might have become an anchor for bold, innovative changes of the sort recommended by Archibald Rogers, a Baltimore designer hired by downtown merchants and others to forecast the future for Greensboro. When Rogers unveiled his plan in late 1963, he presented a vision of tall buildings that concentrated shopping, business, and retail in a center city friendly to pedestrian traffic. He proposed a performing arts center, fountains, and sculpture to enhance a residential feature that included fifty luxury apartments and another five hundred efficiency apartments. The most eye-popping option was a two-level thoroughfare that would send crosstown traffic on Elm and Market streets underground. Only local traffic would be allowed on a promenade designed primarily for pedestrians. This core city would be surrounded by a "green frame" created by the campuses of the nearby colleges and universities.

Some of Rogers's ideas would return forty years later in a plan developed by Action Greensboro. Certain elements would be discounted within a few years, however. Rogers dismissed the import of suburban shopping centers as "a place to buy convenience goods," for example. But American retail was already on the march away from downtowns, and it would never return to Main Street, especially in medium-sized cities like Greensboro. Rogers was right when he said that if Greensboro did not become the regional retail center, another city would.[8] The cost for the changes Rogers proposed: $40 million in private investment, $15 million from local government.

Other ideas came from within the community. Poet Randall Jarrell, perhaps the best-known faculty member at Woman's College, suggested the addition of trees and monuments to make downtown more livable. Councilman Ed Zane advised the city to purchase contiguous parcels of real estate as they became available, consolidate them into large tracts, and offer them for development. Zane knew the problem well. He had tried to consolidate enough property for Burlington's new corporate headquarters building but gave up in desperation because of the dispersed ownership of downtown real estate. It would later take First Citizens Bank sixteen years to round up signatures from two hundred heirs, most of them nonresidents, before it could build an office on one block of Elm Street.[9]

The plans were imaginative and bold, perhaps too much so for conservative Greensboro. The excitement over a new downtown Greensboro lingered for a time and then disappeared in the wake of the civil rights demonstrations. The moment seemed to have passed.

In 1964, Melvin was elected president of the Greensboro Jaycees. He succeeded Frank L. Hood III, a dynamic leader for a chapter that was the largest in the state, with a membership of nearly three hundred fifty men. Some companies, such as NCNB, had more Jaycees among their employees than there were members in entire chapters elsewhere in the state. "We took being a Jaycee very seriously," Melvin recalled. "We felt there were plenty of social outlets and that people were craving meaningful outlets where they could get involved in something that would make a difference."[10]

The chapter was also recovering from the thin profits Melvin had managed to squeeze from the 1963 GGO. The 1964 tournament was better, but with the bank account depleted, the club became even more active. Its activity paid off. A year later, Melvin and a contingent of Greensboro Jaycees were in Buffalo, New York, when the Greensboro chapter was named the best in the nation. Melvin picked up the trophy wearing a peaked cap in Carolina blue, looking like Robin Hood and sounding just as wholesome. He accepted the award on behalf of "three hundred seventy-nine of the best dad-burned Jaycees in America."[11]

A banquet at the Greensboro Coliseum celebrating the honor drew

U.S. senator B. Everett Jordan, lieutenant governor Bob Scott, Sixth District congressman Horace Kornegay, and a number of other dignitaries. A year later, the club was named the best in the world at the international convention in Sydney, Australia. The report on the club's activities justifying the honor created a stack of paperwork nearly three feet tall. In addition to organizing golf and tennis tournaments for teenagers, the Soap Box Derby, and a safe driving campaign for teens, as well as sponsoring a host of sports teams, the Jaycees had moved two hundred fifty thousand books into the city's new library, built a playground and park at a neighborhood community center, and hosted the state Jaycee convention.

No initiative was too bold for Melvin. Early in his presidential year, he wrote the city of Savannah and suggested that the remains of Nathaniel Greene, a Quaker general and Revolutionary War hero, be removed to Greensboro. After all, Melvin wrote, it was Greene for whom the city was named, in honor of his leadership at the battle of Guilford Courthouse. He received a terse reply from the Savannah Chamber of Commerce noting that the general and his son were buried under a very large monument in one of the city's most prominent squares. Disinterment was a preposterous idea, Melvin was told.

Melvin and the Jaycees also helped convince the city council to reintroduce sodium fluoride to the city water system, a proposal which, despite its contentious history, was approved on a simple majority vote. Melvin and attorney Henry Isaacson, another up-and-coming Jaycee leader, sat with mayor William L. Trotter Jr. at his home the night after the vote to offer moral support as he fielded phone calls from citizens angry about the changes to the water supply.

The project that most captured the attention of the judges, and the community, however, was the effort that the Jaycees put behind passage of a municipal bond referendum. Melvin and a delegation of Jaycees told the mayor and the city council in 1963 that if they would put the bond referendum for improving city services on the ballot again, the Jaycees would see that it passed. The council agreed, and in 1964 it offered a $19 million bond package to voters. Included was money for the repair of the water and sewer system, construction of a new reservoir, and further work on the road plan that Babcock had laid out a decade before. One of the proposed thoroughfares would finally connect up to the so-called Fool's Folly bridge. The Jaycees mounted a precinct-by-precinct effort and got out the vote. The bonds passed by a margin of four to one.

It was a remarkable turnaround for Greensboro and an eye-opening achievement for the Jaycees, whose golf tournament also had begun to attract national attention. The modest return of the 1963 GGO was quickly forgotten. In 1965, the tournament became part of the PGA's television broadcast package, and the purse grew to $70,000. In 1966, Allied Chemical Company, a supplier to major textile operations such as Burlington Industries, became the GGO's participating sponsor and pushed the program into the big leagues. Allied agreed to pay the winner's share of the total prize money, which the Jaycees increased to $100,000. The arrival of network television coverage and larger purses drew the top golfers in the field. In addition, well-known entertainers came to play in the pro-am segment and became attractions at the new champions' banquet.

Jaycee Doug Galyon, who later served on the city council and chaired the state board of transportation under two governors, was an Allied sales representative when his company became a major underwriter of the tournament. Allied used the GGO to showcase the company's hospitality for textile clients throughout the South and in New York. "We had planes shuttling customers down every morning from New York," Galyon remembered. "The first plane out picked up hamburgers and hot dogs from Knickerbocker Meats in New York City. Of course, we had an open bar. It was a nice place to be."[12]

By the time Allied joined the program, a champions' banquet had replaced the traditional pretournament stag night, which had become a raucous drunk that often lasted into the wee hours over cards at a private nightclub on the edge of the Sedgefield course. The drunken revelry did little to enhance the Jaycees' image. Melvin, known by some of his peers as "Mother Melvin," had never tasted hard liquor. He tried beer once and disliked it. He began lobbying for an event fitting for grown-ups rather than fraternity pledges. He envisioned something to which members could bring their wives and dates, and the result was the banquet introduced during his year as chairman.

The new program proved to be a successful addition, especially when well-known guests such as golfer Arnold Palmer headlined it. At the Palmer event, Melvin had to keep the bar open longer than he preferred, because Palmer's arrival was delayed when bad weather diverted his flight to Charlotte. Desperate but resourceful, Melvin called the father of a high school classmate who was a captain in the State Highway Patrol. Melvin explained his problem, and the officer arranged for Palmer to be ferried by patrol car from Charlotte to Greensboro in record time.

Melvin had better luck in 1965, when television impresario Ed Sullivan, whose popular Sunday night variety show was sponsored by Burlington Industries, agreed to serve as the main attraction for the banquet. Sullivan's plane arrived right on schedule, and Melvin and three other Jaycees—Bradley Faircloth, Jim Dixon, and Jim Betts—ushered him into a long black limousine. When Sullivan asked about the car, Melvin deadpanned, "Yes, sir, we had to cancel every funeral in town today to pick you up."

Sullivan appreciated the humor but got his best line of the evening after the four showed him to his room at the Sedgefield Inn and asked if he wanted a drink. Sullivan called out his pleasure, which sent the Jaycees into a huddle behind the bar. None of them were drinkers, and none knew how to mix Sullivan's selection. They finally told the toast of Broadway that he would have to fix his own drink. Later that night, Sullivan thanked the Jaycees for sending the "four Sunday school teachers" to welcome him to Greensboro.

The banquet quickly became the largest social event in the city. Growing attendance forced a move from the Plantation Supper Club on High Point Road to the Greensboro Coliseum. Tickets became hard to come by. Comedian Bob Newhart was the honored guest in 1966. Bob Hope came in 1967, and in later years he was followed by singers Pat Boone and Perry Como.

Other good things followed for the city. An important section of Wendover Avenue, a major crosstown thoroughfare, was completed. At the time, the $12.5 million project was the most expensive roadway in the state. Wachovia Bank and Trust Company moved into a fifteen-story office building downtown, and a new parking garage relieved some of the angst of downtown retailers. After years of discouraging losses, the United Way campaigns started surpassing goals and producing the highest per capita contributions of any city in the state. The city's Human Relations Commission, formed in the wake of the 1963 civil rights demonstrations, hired a full-time director, one of only two such staff positions in the South. The city and county governments began making plans to build a governmental center designed by one of the nation's leading architects, Eduardo Catalano of Boston. Jaycee membership pushed past 450 and included the chapter's first black members. So many members attended the biweekly luncheon meetings that they had to be moved to the O. Henry Hotel.

The inventory of success inspired a steering committee led by Melvin to produce a nomination for Greensboro as one of *Look* magazine's

All-America Cities in 1966. The last time *Look* had featured Greensboro was in February 1952, when the magazine cited the high incidence of vice crimes in the city. After that issue went on sale, the city council had tried to ban copies from the newsstands. On this happier occasion, Greensboro's presentation to the selection committee was made by Thomas I. Storrs, the second in command at NCNB who had made his home in Greensboro under the bank's dual management arrangement that had been conceived in 1960.

"Greensboro," Storrs said in the presentation, "is a city that responds to challenge with accomplishment." He capped his remarks with a quotation from Sidney Low, the head of Gilbert and Barker Incorporated (later Gilbarco), a subsidiary of Standard Oil of New Jersey that had recently selected Greensboro for its headquarters. After feeding all the factors that bear on business relocation into its computers, Low had said, "The answer was Greensboro, North Carolina."

The selection committee that chose Greensboro for the honor noted that Greensboro was not the state's largest city, an honor easily conceded to Charlotte. In truth, Charlotte's growth and development was outpacing Greensboro's. Charlotte's population now topped two hundred twenty thousand compared to Greensboro's one hundred forty thousand. In its application for All-America City status, Melvin's committee wrote, "Greensboro is well on its way toward realizing a goal—to become not North Carolina's largest city, but its finest."

In the early months of 1965, the city elections were approaching when Melvin and Bradley Faircloth, who was the chairman of the 1964 GGO, got an invitation to a meeting in the boardroom of Jefferson Standard Life Insurance Company. When they arrived, the two were clearly the youngest in the room, and they took their seats near the back. After settling in, Melvin surveyed those on hand. Seated at a big table were attorney Huger King, the Richardson family's man in Greensboro; Jack Lindley, who had arranged the bank merger creating NCNB; Howard Holderness, the head of Jefferson Standard; Nat Hayes, the CEO of Carolina Steel; Ed Zane, a top leader at Burlington Industries; and others known to have an inside track in local politics.

"Good golly," Melvin whispered to Faircloth, "look at who is in this room. I feel out of place here." Oscar Burnett, who was sitting nearby, overheard the whispered chatter. He leaned over to Melvin and quietly told him, "If you keep your mouth shut, nobody will know it."[13]

Melvin did as he was told, but those in the room took note of his presence. One of them was Hargrove "Skipper" Bowles, a wealthy businessman who had helped Terry Sanford get elected governor in 1960 and then stayed on to play an important role in his administration. Bowles was ten years older than Melvin and a terminally optimistic booster of any project he took on. His participation in the Sanford administration had whet his appetite for politics, and he was just about to begin a campaign for the state Senate that would lead, eventually, to a campaign for governor in 1972.

Bowles liked what he saw in the city's leading Jaycee. After Melvin passed on an opportunity to run for state president of the Jaycees, a likely jumping-off point for his own political career, Bowles asked him if he would like to take on a project with an international flavor. Melvin said yes.

Bowles had become interested in a State Department program called Partners of Alliance. It was an effort to connect communities in the United States with those in Latin America. North Carolina's adopted city was Cochabamba, Bolivia, a commercial center located midway up the Andes Mountains. Once a colonial outpost of the Spanish, Cochabamba was Bolivia's second-largest city. For Melvin, Cochabamba might as well have been on the moon. He had made few trips outside of Greensboro and certainly was unfamiliar with Latin America. "I still thought the world was flat and ended around the end of Asheboro Street," Melvin said some years later. With Bowles as his guide, Melvin headed south.

The two spent hours and hours in the air before the plane carrying them finally landed in the Bolivian capital of La Paz high in the Andes, where the rarefied atmosphere at fourteen thousand feet quite literally leaves visitors breathless. After a change of planes, the two flew on to Cochabamba. When the prop-driven DC-3 carrying Bowles and Melvin landed on Cochabamba's dirt runway, dust flew everywhere, and the sight startled Melvin. "I thought we had exploded," he remembers.

State Department officials met Melvin and Bowles and introduced them to people in the neighborhoods and communities of Cochabamba where the need was greatest. The poverty Melvin saw was unforgettable. Streets were packed dirt, and most houses lacked basic sanitation and running water. Poorly clothed children were the norm. The two took simple meals with families; Melvin choked down strange foods that Bowles consumed with gusto. After making their contacts and getting a sense of the need in the city, they returned to the states, where Melvin began working with the Jaycees and other civic groups to raise a million dollars for community development projects in Cochabamba.

Some of the money went to modest projects designed to meet basic needs. A grant of four or five hundred dollars was enough to build a well that could provide clean drinking water for a number of families. Larger amounts were used to help underwrite a monthlong visit by a medical team that tended patients and distributed ten thousand dollars in medical supplies.

Most of the projects were more successful than Melvin's experience with Pedro the bull. Melvin encouraged a North Carolina club to raise a thousand dollars or so for the purchase of a prize bull to be given to a community that wanted to improve its local herd. After the money arrived in Bolivia and the bull—nicknamed Pedro—was purchased, the man entrusted with Pedro's care disappeared before the bull could impregnate a single cow.

Melvin made a half dozen trips to South America, most of them to Bolivia, including one that left him sick and confined to a hotel room in La Paz. He was returning from a Partners meeting in Rio de Janeiro, Brazil, and planned a stopover in La Paz before heading home to Greensboro. By the time he reached La Paz, however, he was seriously ill. He checked into a hotel, and the manager called the American embassy, where a duty officer found him a doctor who put him under an oxygen tent and fed him penicillin while the State Department searched for the earliest flight home. Unfortunately, the next flight was not due to leave for two days, and Melvin depended on the care of two bellhops to keep him supplied with juice and water until he could be taken to the airport. After his flight was in the air, Melvin discovered the plane made an all-day layover in Lima, Peru. He got off the plane and sought out a movie house, where he spent the day watching *Doctor Zhivago*, a movie about the Russian revolution that was dubbed into Spanish.

Partners was an intense two-year experience that was capped with a remarkable event that literally changed the lives of those with whom Melvin was working in Latin America. One evening, Melvin was at the home of Sixth District congressman Richardson Preyer when he got a telephone call from a ham radio operator in Boston. The man said he had a message from a Father Leo in Cochabamba who was desperate for help in the wake of a polio outbreak that already had claimed three lives. Melvin told Preyer about the call, who then contacted a friend with connections to drug companies that immediately shipped ten thousand free doses of polio vaccine to Greensboro. Preyer also called North Carolina's junior senator, B. Everett Jordan, who arranged for the vaccine to be flown to Bolivia at no charge. Within five days of the radio message, the vaccine was being administered to children in Cochabamba, a week before the Bolivian government formally asked U.S. officials for help.

One civic assignment rolled into another as community leaders tapped into Melvin's boundless energy. He successfully chaired the 1968 United Way drive, which surpassed its $1.2 million goal. He followed that as cochair of a successful bond campaign to pay for a $5.2 million expansion of the coliseum, a $1 million exhibition hall, and a new city hall and county office building downtown that would cost more than $17 million. "It's kind of like getting your cruising speed up to ninety [during the GGO], because in that six- to twelve-month period you're running a big business and having to make a lot of quick decisions," Melvin said. "Once you've done that, your cruising speed never goes back down. Things that bother other people don't bother you."[14]

When Melvin moved into community projects, he usually brought along fellow Jaycees and chapter alumni who came to be known as the Melvin Mafia. Among his recruits was Susan Thomas, who had been the chapter's full-time secretary since 1963. She was a petite, attractive brunette with a mischievous grin, penetrating eyes, a ready smile, and enthusiasm to match that of any Jaycee. A friend had urged her to come to Greensboro from her home in Charleston, West Virginia, after she finished junior college in Boston. She had been offered a job at NCNB when she learned the Jaycees were looking for someone to run their office. It seemed like an ideal job, she said later: "All these guys and being involved in the heartbeat of the community."

Jim and Susan began dating in 1967 when he was thirty-four years old, a senior loan officer at NCNB, and living at home with his parents—an arrangement that caused some concern to his mother, who wondered if her son was ever going to marry. It was not that Melvin was without an active social life. He flirted with beauty queens he met through Jaycee-sponsored pageants, and a Miss North Carolina was a regular companion for a time. Susan frequently teased him about his taste in women, as he was usually seen with well-endowed, full-figured women who looked like Jayne Mansfield, whom Melvin once escorted to a Jaycee meeting to boost GGO ticket sales.

Mansfield was in Greensboro for an appearance at the Plantation Supper Club a few months before her death in 1967. At the request of the club owner, she had volunteered to help the Jaycees. When Melvin arrived at Mansfield's hotel, his knock on her door awakened the actress, who had forgotten about the event. She greeted Melvin in a robe, without makeup or her wig of flowing blonde hair. She apologized and asked for fifteen minutes to get ready. To Melvin's astonishment, she reappeared a few minutes later looking exactly as she did in her publicity photos. Melvin ushered her into a Buick convertible and drove her around town before introducing her at the well-attended Jaycee meeting.

"I wasn't the marrying kind," Melvin said some years later, "because I was always doing something, like chairing the GGO, chair of the United Way, doing this, doing that." One of Melvin's friends finally pulled him aside and said, "You've been dating Susan over a year now, and she is a wonderful girl. You aren't going to do any better, and you ought to decide whether you're going to get married or tell her you aren't going to get married." Melvin promptly went to the jewelry store and bought a ring. Five months later, on January 18, 1969, they were married in Charleston, West Virginia.

By his own admission, Melvin had seldom planned a day ahead in his life. He was headed to the oil business when Vanstory gave him a job in banking in Greensboro. His buddies had drafted him into the Jaycees. Put up a project and he would tackle it with the same enthusiasm he had given Bob Jamieson on the football field. "I assumed that if you worked hard and did good, then at some point it would pay off," he said.

Such advice had produced rewards. He had moved from novice Jaycee to the city's best-known alumnus. The Partners program had introduced him to a part of the world he had never expected to see. He had helped Greensboro become an All-America City and had chaired successful campaigns for the community. Most recently, the city's political leaders rewarded him with a seat on the committee planning the new governmental center, the largest public works project in Greensboro's history. One step had fallen easily after the other.

The appointment to the planning committee for the new municipal building was a plum assignment. Melvin was the junior member of an elite group that included city councilman Mack Arnold, an experienced city hall insider since the 1950s; Ed Zane, a former councilman and business leader; and Oscar Burnett. Together, the group assessed the city's needs for a building to replace an aging structure that had long been inadequate. The new building was modern and accommodating, part of a major investment in the center city.

Perhaps it is not surprising that Melvin's wedding and honeymoon proved to be only an interlude. Six weeks after Jim and Susan moved into a house in one of Ed Benjamin's new subdivisions on the developing west side of Greensboro, he became a candidate for the Greensboro City Council. What did surprise the public was Melvin's campaign slogan: "Greensboro stinks."

Chapter 9

Greensboro Stinks

$\mathcal{W}$HEN THE MEMBERS of the newly elected city council that included Jim Melvin took office in May 1969, Greensboro had 144,000 residents, many of whom would have called the city comfortable, even beautiful, although not many would have called it exciting. The author of an economic study produced for the chamber of commerce pointed out, "It is hard to imagine a resident or visitor advising a friend to 'Go to Greensboro; that's where the action is!'"[1] Indeed, the city's virtues were its stability, its solid middle class, and its wholesome atmosphere. It was a city that clung to traditions such as resting on the Sabbath. Under the city's blue laws, drivers could not even buy a gallon of gas until Sunday services had concluded.

Greensboro was by no means stagnant. New suburbs were pushing the community into the surrounding farms and woodlands. Cone Mills Corporation was making plans to develop nearly a thousand acres north of Irving Park into lots for expensive homes. Joe Koury and Bill Kirkman, two of the city's most aggressive home builders, were expanding their offerings on the southwest side with homes in a more affordable price range. The houses were going up within sight of a long-promised shopping mall that Koury said would be a regional attraction—as soon as he made up his mind just how big he wanted it to be.

Greensboro was a college town, with more than thirteen thousand students attending Bennett, Greensboro, and Guilford colleges or one of two state universities, the former agricultural and technical college that had recently been elevated to university status as North Carolina Agricultural and Technical State University, or NC A&T, and UNC Greensboro, which some still called "W.C.," or Woman's College. (Men had been on campus for less than a decade.) Higher education added a level of prestige and plenty of hard cash. In addition to the money students dropped at clothing and record stores, 15 percent of the city's annual construction was on local campuses. The institutions' presence was largely taken for granted, however, since the big Atlantic Coast Conference teams were in Chapel Hill, Raleigh, Durham, and Winston-Salem. Only A&T generated any measure of community enthusiasm, and that was largely among African Americans, for whom A&T's homecoming was the year's top social event.

City leaders were more likely to brag about Greensboro as a manufacturing center and the headquarters of some of the largest concerns in the nation's textile industry, whose position in the national economy appeared unassailable. Burlington Industries, the world's largest textile operation, was about to erect a new headquarters building on a wooded campus west of downtown. The city's factories and mills turned out yarn, denim, hosiery, blue jeans, overalls, cigarettes, steel, terra cotta pipe, and sophisticated electronic circuits for the nation's telephone network and defense systems. Jobs were plentiful.

City hall was a model of efficiency and the envy of other cities. When budding municipal administrators went to the Institute of Government in Chapel Hill to find out how to deal with problems, they often were sent to Greensboro to watch and learn. Tom Bradshaw, Raleigh's new mayor and a Jaycees alumnus, looked west to Greensboro for inspiration. The city had much that Raleigh was lacking—a strong corporate base to support local projects, a busy downtown, and a new reservoir at Lake Townsend that was soon to come on line. Bradshaw felt stranded without an interstate connection to Raleigh—one of two state capitals in the nation outside the network—while Greensboro sat at the intersection of two routes, Interstates 85 and 40.

Indeed, the city's strategic location made the Greensboro Coliseum one of the most attractive sports and entertainment venues in the Southeast. It was home to a new professional basketball club called the Carolina Cougars that planned to rotate its home games between Greensboro and Charlotte. Greensboro's professional hockey team, the Generals, was entering its second decade on the coliseum ice. Sports and appearances by big-name entertainers had pushed the coliseum's annual revenue to more than $1 million. After renovations paid for by the 1968 bond were completed, the coliseum would be the largest arena in the region, with seating for 15,500 spectators at a basketball game, 16,000 for a concert. The new arrangement would put fans sitting in the top row just 120 feet from center court, a better vantage point than they would have in New York's Madison Square Garden.

――――

So why had Jim Melvin built a political campaign around the slogan "Greensboro stinks?"

Mainly because it was true. For all the good that Melvin saw in his hometown, he was impatient with unfinished projects and unmet municipal needs, particularly the renovation of the city's aging waste treatment plant, which produced noxious plumes that infected a large portion of the city on foggy, damp mornings and disturbed the sleep of his former neighbors in south Greensboro. "Greensboro won't really be an All-America City," read a campaign reference to Melvin's work on behalf of the *Look* magazine honors, "until a lot of good projects that have been mentioned or started or worked on, are finished. Jim Melvin can help make Greensboro a better city to live in. You can, too. By electing him to City Council."

In February 1969, Jim and Susan Melvin had barely settled into their comfortable three-bedroom brick ranch just off Benjamin Parkway when Jim got a call from Oscar Burnett, who encouraged him to consider running for city council. Burnett assured Melvin he would get the support he needed. On Burnett's recommendation, Melvin called on accountant George Perrin, another political insider, who gave him a list of those who would be willing to contribute to his campaign. Perrin also offered a bit of advice. "If you stay on the council long enough and make the right decisions," Perrin told Melvin, "you'll make everybody in Greensboro mad at you. I can tell you right now, friends come and go, but your enemies are forever." Melvin would recall those words thirty years later, when he was still a political lightning rod.

Burnett's offer fell on fertile ground. Melvin had toyed with getting into politics, but the Preyer campaign had convinced him he really did not enjoy partisan battles. Far more satisfying were nonpartisan efforts, such as the bond campaign and work for United Way, where he had discovered what he called "the real Greensboro." Those experiences whet his appetite for public service, and a nonpartisan city council bid was the logical place to start.

After receiving Burnett's call, Melvin cleared his plans with his betters at the bank, who gave their blessing. Before he could make it to the board of elections office, however, he succumbed to the flu. Susan and her mother paid Jim's filing fee.

Melvin joined a herd of thirty-one contenders that was winnowed to fourteen two weeks later in the primary election, in which Melvin came in second. The race for a seat on the council was largely a popularity contest in which the seven candidates with the most votes became the choice of the electorate. This at-large system of election had been in place since the early 1920s, with the exception of a twenty-year hiatus when a special district existed for the benefit of Cone Mills. The Cone district was discarded after World War II, and since that time council members had been elected by all the voters, with the members themselves choosing the mayor.

Melvin's catchy slogan gave his campaign a nice boost. When the ballots were tallied in the first round in the municipal elections in late April, the thirty-six-year-old Melvin found himself within two dozen votes of leading the ticket. He was behind only Harper J. Elam III, Cone Mills Corporation's legal counsel and a council member since 1965. His success was all the more remarkable considering that five months before the election Melvin was not even eligible to hold a city office. Before he and Susan married in January and moved into their new home inside the city limits, Jim's legal residence was in the county, at his parents' home on Alamance Church Road.

Of course, Melvin's success at the polls was the result of more than a slogan. His service on behalf of numerous civic projects had given him a reputation among the city's elders, and the public at large, as a hard worker and conscientious contributor to the city's welfare. He had not reached the pinnacle of Jaycee achievement just to impress the political insiders who helped newcomers get elected to office, but they took notice just the same. When it became apparent that two incumbents—Forrest Campbell and mayor Carson Bain—were not going to seek reelection, Melvin's name rose to the top of the list as a potential replacement.

He was well-known within the local Democratic Party establishment, which at that time channeled young men into the political process. In 1968, Melvin had managed the successful campaign of Richardson Preyer, keeping the state's Sixth Congressional District safely in Democratic Party hands. Some later credited Melvin with Preyer's victory, as Melvin helped Preyer overcome his image as a son of the privileged class. Preyer's grandfather was Lunsford Richardson, the creator of VapoRub, and Preyer had grown up in the comfort of wealth. The candidate's polished manners and soft voice, along with an accent shaped by his years at Princeton University, was fine for Irving Park, but Melvin worried about how Preyer was being received at the mill gates. Riding home from an early campaign outing at the Alamance County Courthouse in Graham, where Preyer had come off as aloof and distant to a crowd composed mostly of textile workers, Melvin asked Preyer if he ever just got mad and cussed out loud. "No," Preyer replied, "but I had better learn how." Preyer won in 1968 and was reelected in 1970 and 1972 with Melvin as his campaign chairman.

In the runoff election on May 6, Melvin again placed second, this time 230 votes behind Elam. The two ran almost neck and neck, with Elam proving more popular in the black precincts, including the area surrounding Gillespie Park Elementary School, just down the street from Joe Melvin's service station. Most of the Gillespie Park votes went to two African American candidates, A&T faculty member Jimmie I. Barber, who placed seventh, and Vance Chavis, a retired school principal, who placed eighth.

The new council was a moderate-to-conservative group of four incumbents and, besides Melvin, included two other newcomers, Charles W. Phillips Jr. and Barber, the first African American elected to that office in six years. The members brought a mixture of backgrounds and interests to the job. Barber was director of student housing at A&T, while Phillips was an insurance man. Among the incumbents were Elam, whom everyone called Jack; Mary P. Seymour, a legal secretary and the leading female voice in local politics; William Trotter Jr., a hardware store owner and former mayor; and William Folk, a salesman for Westinghouse Electric Company. Like Melvin, Folk was a product of the Jaycees and had once chaired the GGO. In the postelection negotiating among the members over who would be chosen mayor, Melvin made a presumptuous and short-lived bid for the office, but Elam was the favorite.

It was just as well that Melvin was not chosen. The next two years proved to be a grueling test for Elam, a two-term incumbent and former city attorney who was well-schooled in the workings of city government. Three days after the new council's first meeting, Greensboro came under its second dusk-to-dawn curfew in about a year, with National Guardsmen surrounding the A&T campus, where police said snipers were active. The night after a student was shot and killed under mysterious circumstances, police intercepted a carload of black men they said were headed to Elam's house to set it on fire. In addition to the killing of A&T sophomore Willie Grimes, who by all accounts was an innocent victim, the violence left nine others injured, including a student hit by stray gunfire and five police officers ambushed on a dead-end street.

That was Elam's first two weeks. A month later, a summer deluge drowned the city under a hundred-year flood that disrupted the water supply. Before he finished his two years as mayor, Elam would also have to deal with a rent strike that further heightened racial tensions, garbage workers who walked out and shut down the city's sanitation department, labor disputes that boiled among police officers and firemen, and the emerging issue of proposals to create a ward, or district, system for the election of the city council. These challenges were just the start of a decade of profound change in Greensboro that would shape the city for years to come.

———

Jack Elam's roots went deep in Greensboro. His grandfather had founded the *Greensboro Record* before the turn of the century. He worked his way through the University of North Carolina, where he also earned a law degree and became Albert Coates's traffic specialist at the Institute of Government. He had learned the rudiments of city administration under former city manager James Townsend, who hired Elam in 1954 to succeed city attorney Herman Wilson, who was due to retire within the year.

The city needed a good lawyer in the 1950s. First came the controversy over the fluoridation of the water supply. A year later, Elam was called on to defend the council's attempts to dodge the racial integration of the city-owned golf course. Elam believed segregation was wrong, and he told council members they would lose a legal contest to defend their decision to turn the golf course over to a private operator. He was right, but he dutifully pleaded the city's position to a federal judge. He headed off further embarrassment in 1960, when the Greensboro Country Club was hosting a city-sponsored tennis tournament and threatened to bar a black doubles team led by George Simkins Jr. Elam called the club manager and told him that either Simkins played or the tournament would go elsewhere. Simkins's team won its division on the country club courts.

Councilman Ed Zane courted Elam to join the legal department at Burlington Industries, but in 1961 he accepted a job offer from Cone Mills in spite of his previous run-ins with Ceasar Cone II, who had frequently called the city attorney's office to voice complaints. Cone later told Elam that he decided to hire him after Elam hung up the phone in the middle of one of Cone's abusive tirades against city policy.[2]

Elam had decided on his own to run for the council in 1965, but he could never shake the popular perception that he was Ceasar's "nanny boy."[3] He proved to be an independent voter on council matters and something of a loner on issues. He occasionally fell out with his peers over the perks of public office, such as the use of free parking spaces at the coliseum and reimbursement for travel expenses. A more serious disagreement, with repercussions, arose in 1966 when he bucked the council majority that chose Carson Bain to fill a vacant seat. Elam's choice was Henry Frye, a young black attorney and promising political newcomer whose appointment would have restored black representation at city hall.

Elam ran for reelection in 1967 and led the ticket by nearly a thousand votes, but the new council elected Bain as mayor and Forrest Campbell as mayor pro tem, a clear snub of Elam, who, along with Trotter, an ally on the Frye nomination, was excluded from some of the council majority's private sessions. It was a chilly two years, Elam later recalled. "Billy and I just sat at the end of the table and an appointment to the zoning commission would be announced and Billy and I would look at each other and say, 'Well, gosh, we didn't know about that.'"[4]

When Elam was sworn in on May 12, 1969, he told Melvin, who was elected mayor pro tem, that he would turn over many ceremonial duties to him because of his workload at Cone Mills. Elam said he had one goal during his term: he hoped to settle the issue of how Greensboro voters elected the city council. That ambition would quickly be overrun by events. Ten days later, he was on the phone to the governor asking for help from the National Guard.

One explosive issue seemed to follow another. The rent strike took six months to resolve. Elam and Melvin helped negotiate a settlement after weeks of dangerous rhetoric and street marches in which children carried signs that read, "We're tired of sleeping with rats." On the heels of the rent strike in the spring of 1970 came the report from the state advisory committee for the U.S. Commission on Civil Rights that said the death and disorder at A&T was the result of "unequal treatment of citizens of Greensboro because of race."[5]

Elam had barely digested the advisory committee's advice about how to heal Greensboro when city sanitation workers walked out in a strike that cost many of them their jobs. Until the garbage trucks began to roll again, the city supplied local banks with plastic trash bags for residents. At the same time, city police officers called in with "blue flu," and firemen talked about slowdowns. By the end of his first term, Elam had experienced the most trying two years that any mayor had seen since the Depression.

He underscored the challenges facing city leaders when he spoke at the annual chamber of commerce meeting. He reminded the city's corporate leaders:

> Many of you have told me that you . . . fondly recall the past—a past based on memories of convenience—peopled by youths who were seen but not heard, poor but happy blacks who "knew how to keep their place," by preachers who sermonized about heaven and hell and stayed the hell out of anything in between, and by God-fearing Christians who prayed together on the Sabbath and counted their blessings.
>
> Today, the young who form a greater portion of our population each year are demanding a voice in the affairs of "our" city, blacks not only refuse to stay in their place, but seem to be forming some unflattering ideas about a "place" for whites, preachers hold dances, show movies, talk politics and prick the congregational conscience—at least some do. And God-fearing Christians now shop together and discount their blessings on Sundays.[6]

By the time his term as mayor came to an end, Elam had not made any progress in settling the issue of district representation. The mayor invited NAACP leader George Simkins Jr. to lunch at his home one day, but it was a meeting that only affirmed their differences. Elam's plan for a modified district system that combined at-large with district representation was left on the table as Simkins held out for a pure ward system.

Black representation in city government did improve while Elam was mayor. Businessman Alexander Parker was appointed to the city alcoholic beverage control board, and in September 1969, following the death of councilman William Folk, Elam successfully nominated Vance Chavis as a replacement. Not long afterward, Chavis urged the council to appoint twenty-nine-year-old attorney Walter Johnson Jr., a Greensboro native, air force veteran, and the first black law student at Duke University, to the Greensboro Board of Education.

———

In 1971, Elam stood for reelection, as did Melvin. The May election looked like a rerun of 1969; the two ended up within about three hundred votes of one another, but this time Melvin was in the lead. Both had broad support within the community, including the predominantly black precincts, where Elam gathered more votes than Melvin did by a slim margin. The newly elected council, which included all of the incumbents, chose Melvin as mayor, with former mayor William Trotter, who had backed Elam in 1969, casting the deciding vote. Elam was elected mayor pro tem.

Melvin was better prepared to campaign in 1971. He and his campaign team, most of them former Jaycees like Jim Betts, Bradley Faircloth, and Mose Kiser, organized three hundred volunteers, and in one night they distributed three thousand brochures door to door. The candidate canvassed precincts with a message that highlighted his efforts to get $12.5 million out of the State Highway Commission to complete construction of Wendover Avenue through to Interstate 40 and money from the federal government for downtown development. His pitch was thoughtful, clever, and coupled with a flurry of legwork and the posting of women in sashes that read "Melvin Again" outside the polling places.

The voters responded to Melvin and the rest of the incumbents, re-electing the entire council for the first time since World War II. Melvin beamed with pride after his selection as mayor. "Ten years from now," Melvin told a reporter, "the big jobs are going to be in the local offices, not in Raleigh or Washington. If we are going to solve our problems it must be done by local people."[7]

It appeared that at least one of Greensboro's problems had been solved as Melvin took office. In April 1971, the city dedicated a new reservoir. The huge lake on the northeast side that could hold 6.5 billion gallons of water was named in honor of James Townsend, who was on hand for the ceremonies. Ever the pragmatist, Townsend warned that what appeared to be a generous supply of water was only a temporary solution. "Citizens should start today to use less water," he said, "to conserve every drop they can." Given Greensboro's location at the head of major streams, Townsend told the crowd, creativity and imagination would be required to find a long-term solution. He suggested recycling water from the treatment plant, an idea that was not well-received.[8]

A side benefit of Lake Townsend was three hundred acres of property that had been acquired as part of the construction of the reservoir. Melvin and Elam sought permission from Joseph and Kathleen Bryan to dedicate it in their name as Bryan Park.

Joseph M. Bryan was a New York City cotton broker when he married Julian Price's only daughter. They moved to Greensboro, where he worked his way into Jefferson Standard's senior management. He never succeeded to run the insurance business, but he did lead the Jefferson interests into other lucrative enterprises, including broadcasting. He was retired from Jefferson Standard by the time Melvin and Elam arrived at his doorstep and was on his way to becoming a generous underwriter of projects that enhanced life in his adopted home.

In late May 1971, the new mayor announced that a golf course would be built on the land. It would be designed by George Cobb to accommodate the weekend golfer, although Melvin remained hopeful that one day the GGO might relocate the tournament there. Dignitaries of every degree heaped praise on the Bryans at the dedication ceremony. Congressman Richardson Preyer closed, saying that after all that had been said, the couple knew "how a pancake feels when the syrup is poured over it."[9] Before he left public office, Melvin would help Bryan invest more than his name in the park.

The city's new reservoir was at least temporary relief from the increasing demand for water. The delay in construction due to the defeat of the 1963 bond campaign had already cost the city. If Lake Townsend had been available four years earlier, Greensboro might not have lost a hot industrial prospect whose arrival would have added spice to the city's reputation. In 1967, Anheuser-Busch, the nation's largest brewing company, announced plans to build a $40 million brewery just south of Greensboro near Jamestown. The chamber of commerce optioned four hundred acres of land, cheerfully made it available to Anheuser-Busch, and had begun to count the benefits of the three hundred new jobs the brewery was to bring to the area. A year later, however, the company opted instead for a site near Jacksonville, Florida. There was talk that while Greensboro had the right highway connections, it did not have the plentiful, reliable water supply necessary to produce millions of barrels of beer.

The loss of the brewery was but the first in a series of "what-if" events that would continue to disappoint those eager to see the city remain a leading contender in the state. At about the same time as the brewery decision, there had been a flicker of hope that one of the state's top banks would move its headquarters to town. After Roger Soles succeeded Howard Holderness as head of Jefferson Standard Life Insurance Company in 1967, he made a deal to acquire an up-and-coming bank in eastern North Carolina, as well as Edwin Duncan's Northwestern Bank, which was based in North Wilkesboro. Duncan, an earthy, rough-hewn sort known to haul calves from one pasture to another in the backseat of his

Cadillac, had built Northwestern into a regional financial player in western and northwestern North Carolina. By the late 1960s, he was ready to retire, and Soles's offer suited him fine. The two sealed their deal with a handshake. Before the merger details could be completed, however, Congress enacted the Bank Holding Act in 1968, which required insurance companies to divest themselves of bank ownership within five years. Under those conditions, Soles said the merger no longer made sense.[10]

Such near misses were beginning to create an air of uncertainty among those assessing the city's future. "Greensboro's failure to establish a firm reputation as a thriving, progressive and sizeable place creates a moderate but significant margin of disadvantage from a developmental standpoint," a 1970 economic study conducted for the chamber of commerce said. "Nobody quite says that each new industrial facility will be the last, that the decay of downtown is a permanent state, that Greensboro colleges and universities are forever doomed to third-class status, or that the city will always be upstaged by Charlotte, Raleigh, and Winston-Salem, but the feeling is there and its effects are real."[11]

If a city's front door is its central business district, then Greensboro's was hanging loosely on the hinges as merchants nervously eyed the growing number of competing stores opening in the suburbs. In the early 1970s, downtown Greensboro had changed little since the 1920s, when boom times transformed Elm Street with the erection of tall buildings and the bustle of commerce. Wachovia Bank and Trust Company's fifteen-story building had opened in 1966, and a ten-story building for First Union National Bank had been erected two years later, but most of the remaining structures predated World War II. Some dated to the nineteenth century. The King Cotton Hotel, once the pride of the city, was a flophouse and a public nuisance that police were eager to close. Its owner was twenty-three thousand dollars in arrears on property taxes. The O. Henry Hotel was empty and awaiting demolition. Classic buildings that some years later would be bought for their charm alone were now called "wretched obsolescence."[12] Dingy windows and faded paint advertised the vacant space in two- and three-story retail buildings where the owners once lived above their shops.

By the time Melvin became mayor, the city had adopted only one element of the Rogers plan that had generated some excitement nearly a decade before. South of the Guilford County Courthouse on West Market Street, construction was under way on a new $15 million governmental complex to house city and county offices. The new buildings were kept tightly within budget, although Melvin and those planning the municipal building knew that more space would be needed soon. Nonetheless, a committee of citizens worked with architects to produce a modern-looking structure with a low profile and easy access. Windows on the upper floors and a center atrium opened the space to the outdoors. Next door was the county's huskier high-rise building with new courtrooms and offices.

Other Rogers ideas were in play, such as the use of four blocks of Elm Street as a pedestrian mall. Work had begun on a second multilevel parking garage that included direct access to Meyer's department store on Elm Street. Merchants were not entirely pleased, however. They were still lobbying for free parking, which they hoped would allow them to compete with the acres of space at Friendly Shopping Center.

For the most part, however, there were few champions of downtown, where at least twenty storefronts were empty. Melvin, who struggled for the restoration of the city's center as long and hard as anyone, received little encouragement. When he was courting a developer who would eventually open Carolina Circle Mall on the northeast side of the city, Melvin asked his opinion about downtown as they surveyed the area from an upper story. The developer's suggestion: flood the entire area to create a lake.

Greensboro had missed out in the mid-1960s on the federal government's Model Cities program, which pumped billions into the renewal of cities all across the country. When Greensboro officials had made moves toward redevelopment in the center city, their projects were modest and received with skepticism, while next door in Winston-Salem, city hall was moving ahead with plans to build a downtown convention center. An even larger public hall was under construction in downtown Charlotte. Just before the 1969 municipal elections, Greensboro's redevelopment commission declined to purchase two parcels important to the overall development of downtown after Ceasar Cone II raised an objection. Cone said the commission's requirements would have forced property owners like him to upgrade their holdings. "Downtown building is done to meet needs and you can't tell a man he has to run a certain kind of business in such and such a block," Cone told the newspaper.[13]

The decision deflated redevelopment commission director Robert Barkley. "We're back where we were ten years ago," he said after the commission bowed to Cone's concern. Mayor Carson Bain finally rallied support behind the project, and three months later, the commission reversed its position and acquired the land.

Greensboro's downtown was not only losing businesses, it was losing the workers who would have spent their lunch hours in its stores and restaurants. Almost simultaneously in 1969, two of downtown's largest employers—Burlington Industries and AT&T's Western Electric—announced plans to relocate their offices. AT&T went east to a site on Interstate 85 about seven miles from downtown. Burlington went west, out Friendly Avenue, to a setting adjacent to Friendly Shopping Center. These two employers alone evacuated sixteen hundred workers from downtown.

If Greensboro, and downtown in particular, needed an enthusiastic cheerleader, one who was ready to push ahead, then Melvin was made to order. "This is a position where I think I can really make a difference," he said shortly after taking office. "I can't make a difference in the state legislature. I can't make a difference in Congress, even if I could get elected. But you can make a difference for Greensboro if you've got a group of people, a council, working together."[14]

Melvin was energetic and undaunted, a style that would carry him through an unprecedented six terms in office, five of them as mayor. City Hall saw far more of him than it had of Elam, or many of his predecessors for that matter. Melvin was an early riser, and he usually got to the mayor's office before eight, where he put in an hour's work before he reported for duty at the bank by nine. Assistants at both locations managed his daily schedule, enabling him to cover civic and professional assignments, some of which did not end until well after dark. On occasion, his supper was a grilled cheese sandwich and skim milk eaten well after Susan had put their two sons, Taylor and Jimbo, to bed.

It was a work ethic that he had learned from his father, who was clear about what he expected of his sons: if they ate at his table, they would work in the family business. Jim Melvin did not get relief from duty at Melvin's Texaco until he went to college. "I thought I had died and gone to heaven when I didn't have to work on Saturday," he later said.

Melvin received every delegation that sought an audience. That included a band of angry mothers from Alabama who arrived in 1971 wearing red, white, and blue tennis shoes and demanding he do something about school busing. Melvin had already staked himself out in favor of a desegregation plan for Greensboro that implemented busing, and the ladies took exception to his refusal to add his name to their petition, which carried the names of Georgia governors Lester Maddox and Jimmy Carter, as well as Alabama's George Wallace.

He enjoyed the pulpit provided him by the city's top job. Within his first few months in office, he declared his support for the school board's desegregation plan, called for a list of polluters who were fouling South Buffalo Creek, and criticized the local medical community for not making better use of L. Richardson Hospital, a facility opened in the twenties to provide medical care to African Americans. In the years ahead, he would become even more visible. During the height of the nation's energy crisis in 1974, Melvin parked his car and rode a bus to work. He climbed into a Piper Cub airplane to report on city traffic for radio station WBIG. He became a regular on Lee Kinard's *Good Morning Show* on WFMY-TV. Kinard invited Melvin on monthly to talk about what was happening in the city. "I guess there was a political agenda," said Kinard years later. "He was a politician, but he just said, 'Here is what I think we ought to do, here is how we can do it, and let's get together and do it.'"[15] About the only honor Melvin declined was igniting the explosives that brought down the King Cotton Hotel in nine seconds on a Sunday in late 1971. He joked that with his luck, the crumbling structure would fall the wrong way.

Melvin's style reflected his on-the-job training in the Jaycees. "He's just one of the guys," said Jim Betts, a close friend from their days in Sunday school at West Market Street United Methodist Church. "He just pushed himself. He saw things that needed to be done, and he could pull everybody together and get it done. He had that kind of following."[16]

On Melvin's bookshelf at home were such selections as *You Can Change the World: The Jaycee Story* as well as *Enthusiasm Makes the Difference* by Norman Vincent Peale and *Effective Psychology for Managers: Make Each Day Count*. He was buoyant in the face of challenges and had little patience for those who appeared to be obstructing progress. "I was one of those guys who said, 'Let's get it done, let's get it done,'" he said some years later. He chafed at the slow pace of government. Patience had never been among his virtues.[17]

When he became mayor, he believed that if the council did not form a plan of action within ninety days, then it would be lost for the next two years. After gaining his legs, he invited the entire council elected in 1973 to a room at the Greensboro Coliseum, where a management consultant helped the group build unity and focus attention on objectives and goals. NCNB's consultants had put Melvin through similar exercises as a young executive, and he left somewhat bemused. Counselors invited participants to talk about their childhoods, parents, and feelings. Melvin believed that his upbringing was downright ordinary. The underpinnings of his value system were lessons learned at the gas station and on Coach Jamieson's football field.

Melvin hoped to translate the benefits of goal setting and group dynamics to city hall. Not everyone appreciated his consensus-building and "management by objective" techniques. In 1975, when Mary Seymour challenged him in the mayoral race, one of her supporters, fellow council member Mack Arnold Jr., said the council members were like "rubber ducks" blithely following Melvin and rubber-stamping recommendations from the city staff.

One of Melvin's elders was bewildered by his strategy. Melvin would occasionally hear from C. M. Vanstory, his one-time boss and a former mayor who was now fully retired. Vanstory would open each call the same way: he called Melvin "Boy." Vanstory then proceeded to explain that in his day, decisions were always worked out in advance of the formal council meetings. "I said, 'Mr. Vanstory, you don't do that anymore,'" Melvin recalled. "These days, it's different."[18]

When citizens complained that they could not get to council meetings held during the hours when they were working, Melvin scheduled night meetings in neighborhoods around the city. The effort drew a mixed response. After Melvin and a contingent of nineteen council members and city staff outnumbered the seven citizens who bothered to turn out for one meeting, he delivered a sermon on citizen apathy.

The city's elite got the same speech from the mayor. Midway through his time in office, Melvin told the Greensboro Rotary Club that those who had the resources to make a difference in the city were pulling back and not doing their share. He noted that Greensboro was alone among the top three cities in North Carolina in failing to achieve its goal for the United Way campaign in recent years. Greensboro needed a revival of the same spirit that had made the city a national wonder in the polio epidemic of 1948, he said.

Melvin brought younger blood, such as former allies in the Jaycees, into the city's affairs. After Jim Betts, his old Sunday school chum and Jaycee colleague, tugged on his sleeve about problems in the schools, Melvin arranged for Betts's appointment to the city school board, where he later served as chairman. Another Jaycee ally, Bradley Faircloth, was put in charge of handling local arrangements for the 1974 NCAA basketball championship when it was played at the Greensboro Coliseum.

The NCAA tournament was a public relations coup. Greensboro was the smallest city to host the national event that year, but it had the right venue for North Carolina. The city's coliseum was the leading arena in the state and one of the most successful city operations. A new manager, James Oshust, proved to be an energetic booster, and as a result the coliseum was booked more than two hundred nights a year. The Carolina Cougars, one of the teams formed in the newly organized American Basketball Association (ABA), played some of their home games in Greensboro, as well as Charlotte and Raleigh. At one point, Carl Scheer, the Cougars' president, who had once practiced law in Greensboro, approached Melvin and city manager Tom Osborne to ask for a concession on the coliseum rental rate to help the struggling team. With the coliseum in demand for so many events, however, Melvin offered Scheer no encouragement to take the matter to the city council.

The Cougars later folded, and Scheer moved on to Denver, where he helped with the merger of the ABA and the National Basketball Association. In 1988, he returned to North Carolina as the first president and general manager of the Charlotte Hornets, whose average attendance was the highest in the league in their first year. Melvin would later wonder if a different decision on the Cougars might have landed Greensboro the team.

The mayor's office was a hub of activity. Melvin's involvement in municipal affairs extended beyond Greensboro to a state commission on local government to which he was appointed by governor Bob Scott. He represented Greensboro on the new regional councils of government and in the North Carolina League of Municipalities, of which Elam had been president. He also led an effort to bring together the mayors of North Carolina's largest cities to talk about common problems and solutions. Included were John Belk of Charlotte, Tom Bradshaw from Raleigh, M. C. Benton of Winston-Salem, and others from Durham, Fayetteville, Asheville, and Wilmington. "We would just meet in one of our cities," Melvin recalled, "and spend the day together and talk about things we were attempting to do."[19] The issues on the table included transportation, guiding urban growth, and knotty problems such as the rise of union organizations among municipal workers.

One local project that other cities borrowed from Greensboro was the establishment of a youth council. Melvin had pushed through the creation of a program that gave teenagers a stronger voice in programs designed for them after the Reverend Harold Hipps at West Market Street United Methodist Church shaped a sermon around the lack of opportunities for young people.

Melvin was envious of Charlotte, which seemed to be gaining ground in the fight against urban decay. There, downtown revival built upon the daily infusion of thousands of workers to new office buildings, including a forty-story headquarters for NCNB. It was a building many in Greensboro believed rightly belonged in their town. When NCNB put a new building in downtown Greensboro in 1974, it was only five stories tall.

Those like Melvin who were eager to revitalize the center city were working against decades of benign neglect. The Greensboro corporate leaders whose support counted most were mostly manufacturing men for whom growth meant higher taxes. They were happy with the way Greensboro was and were content for it to remain that way. Moreover, many remembered the city's history of bonded indebtedness created by the exuberance of the 1920s. Meanwhile, Charlotte was run by people who fortunes were linked to retail sales from a large customer base. Under the leadership of John Belk, the leading family member in the Belk department store group, and executives of the large statewide banks whose headquarters were on Tryon Street, Charlotte eagerly pushed ahead with the construction of a new convention center, office towers, and urban roadways to accommodate the growth that Belk and others anticipated would come.

When Melvin met with the mayors of the larger North Carolina cities in Greensboro, he invited Belk to join him on Kinard's *Good Morning Show* to talk about Charlotte's new convention center and office towers, which Belk said would one day be connected by overstreet walkways. "I was sitting there and thinking, 'Yes, and you're smoking something too,'" Melvin said, recalling Belk's plans for his city. Yet while he was skeptical of Belk's vision of what eventually came to pass in Charlotte, he realized that Belk and Charlotte had something that Greensboro did not: "What he was saying was they had a vision and they had a commitment."

Greensboro's victories came in modest packages. The city's redevelopment commission purchased the King Cotton Hotel in 1971 and reduced it to 960 loads of rubble with a dynamite blast. After the site was cleared, the city had some hope that twin towers to include apartments and office space would rise on the same spot. The deal fell through in 1973, however, when the city failed to get its asking price for the land. The site sat empty, just another vacant space downtown, until Melvin convinced the Greensboro News Company, owned by Landmark Communications of Norfolk, Virginia, to shelve its plans to build outside of downtown and to put its new offices for the morning *Greensboro Daily News* and the afternoon *Greensboro Record* there. The decision helped mollify some who were still smarting over the out-of-town ownership of the city's major dailies.

Melvin's enthusiasm for Greensboro was undeniable and indefatigable, even in the face of personal tragedy. One afternoon in the fall of 1972, he stopped by his father's service station on the city's south side for one of his regular visits. On this occasion, he and his father talked about retirement. Joe Melvin was sixty-nine, but he would hear nothing of it. What would he do with his time? he asked. Before Jim left that day, he warned his father against carrying the large wad of cash—sometimes as much as four or five thousand dollars—that he kept stuffed in his back pocket.

A few weeks later, on the afternoon of October 24, Jim planned to see his father at his son Taylor's third birthday party, but a busy schedule caught up with him, and he did not make it to the party. It was after five when his office phone rang and Jim heard his father's voice. "There are certain things in life that are important," Joe Melvin said without bothering to offer a hello, "and a three-year-old's birthday party is one of them. You should have been there." Then he hung up.

The next morning, Joe Melvin was found on the floor of the service station, dead from two gunshot wounds. Witnesses standing at a nearby bus stop said they heard the shots and saw two men run from the station. When police arrived, Melvin's body was lying on the black-and-white-checked tile floor just outside a doorway to the storage room in the back. A gun belonging to Melvin was under his body. He apparently had confronted his assailants, who shot him and then fled.

Police said the motive was robbery. A week later, Jim got a call from one of his father's employees, who said he did not believe his father's killers had gotten any money. Joe had taken his son's advice, Jim was told, and had begun to hide his cash in a storeroom box marked with a big X. Jim drove to the station, opened the storeroom, and found several thousand dollars where his father had put it only moments before he was killed.

The gun was a complete surprise. Jim did not know his father had begun carrying a pistol to work. In fact, Joe Melvin had not told his son about his growing concern for his safety, although he had spoken of it to his neighbors on Asheboro Street. Joe Melvin's barber, Leslie Davis, who ran a shop across the street, said Joe told him he "hated to work these days because things were getting so bad."[19] Police surmised that Melvin's routine of arriving an hour before the other station help reported for work, along with his reputation for carrying large amounts of cash, had attracted the two young men, who lived in a nearby public housing project. They were charged with and subsequently convicted of the crime.

Joe Melvin's funeral was held the day after his death at West Market Street United Methodist Church. His murder stunned and shocked the community. Word even reached those far from Greensboro. In the aftermath, the family received notes of condolence from some of the soldiers who remembered a kindly service station operator who had given them a few gallons of gas to make it back to Fort Bragg or offered them a bed for the night. Riding home from the cemetery, Virgil Melvin told her sons to see that the service station was open the next morning. "That's what your dad would want," she said. The station opened on schedule. Jim Melvin never missed another of his children's birthdays.

―――

Joe Melvin's death was seen by many as an example of what was wrong with Greensboro's center city: it was a dangerous place despite the window dressing that city hall had installed to make the area more appealing to shoppers. In the fall of 1972, Melvin and other city officials gathered in the middle of Elm Street to open the city's "semi-mall." High school bands performed while eighteen American flags flapped in the fall air. Small concrete planters held struggling new trees. The overhanging signs that had nagged Orton Boren in the 1950s were finally gone; the city had closed the street one full day to facilitate the removal of the largest of them. Altogether, four hundred were taken down, and overhead utility lines were buried.

Downtown boosters were excited about the changes. Elm Street traffic was funneled into two lanes to provide for wider sidewalks that merchants hoped would fill with shoppers during the upcoming holiday season. New lighting atop contemporary light poles gave the street a brighter hue. A few weeks after the festivities, restaurant business was up at Meyer's department store, and Sam Leonard at Griffin Shoe Company—which did business from the same location on Elm Street for thirty-five years—said sales were good. But the owners of Pep Boys auto store said their business was down. Before too long, so were the American flags. After being reminded of proper flag etiquette by the American Legion, the city manager said the city could not afford to raise and lower them daily.

About four hundred thousand dollars in federal funds went into the attempt to put a new face on downtown, a substantial sum for Greensboro, although a pittance in the nation's overall investment in reversing the flight to the suburbs. Merchants spent another eighty thousand dollars on amenities, including sprucing up their storefronts. All in all, it was too little too late: the era of downtown shopping was over for Greensboro and most other medium-sized American cities. A few weeks before the dedication, Melvin and others stood with ceremonial shovels in hand for the groundbreaking of a new Sears store to be built next to Friendly Shopping Center. The following year, the downtown holiday parade was cancelled in the face of declining attendance. Band directors also told the sponsors that marching bands could not navigate the confines of a two-lane thoroughfare.

The image of Elm Street as a street of familiar shops, genteel department stores, and a hometown atmosphere was all but gone. The new lights, wider sidewalks, and potted plants could not overcome the growing sense of city residents in Greensboro and across the country of downtowns as alien and dangerous, especially for whites. In Greensboro, Elm Street was perceived to be "a black street along which whites have retained an easement," as one writer put it.[21] The reputation was not yet entirely deserved, but it would grow as small shops with names like "Bad Rags" and "Soulful Strut" replaced Thalhimer's, Belk, and Meyer's.

Victories seemed hard to come by. A second parking garage opened on Davie Street early in 1976 and gained instant notoriety—for suicides. In the space of a week, two people, one of them a mental patient, dove off the top of the five-story structure onto the pavement below. Jordan Marsh, the national retail chain that purchased Meyer's department store, promised to make a stand downtown, but it hedged its bets by opening stores at suburban locations.

The evacuation of Greensboro's center city was gut-wrenching for Melvin because it happened so fast. Within a matter of months, between the spring of 1975 and the end of 1976, two shopping malls opened on the city's perimeter. One was Carolina Circle on the city's northeast shoulder along U.S. 29. The other was Four Seasons, the grand project that Joe Koury had been promising since the late 1950s. Both malls were huge, especially Four Seasons, which opened first in February 1975. With ninety-five stores and nine hundred thousand square feet of retail space, Four Seasons was more than twice the size of the full-service department store that Archibald Rogers said in 1963 was needed to make downtown viable. With two enclosed levels (built to expand to three), it was practically large enough to qualify as its own city.

Downtown was becoming the hole in the doughnut as suburban Greensboro continued to expand, especially to the north, northwest, and southwest, where builders had begun to convert farmland into subdivisions. Years later, such unrestrained growth would earn Greensboro dubious recognition as one of the nation's best examples of urban sprawl. Real estate developers won more often than they lost when planners or adjacent landowners questioned their plans. One prime example was the approval of a seven-hundred-acre development of fine homes and a golf course planned for an area just north of the airport. At public hearings for rezoning and construction approval, airport officials argued that homeowners would be unhappy when a future runway was built within fifteen hundred feet of the development's perimeter. Developers said they would work with the airport on the "noise problem" and even suggested that deeds would relieve the airport authority of any liability. Thirty years later, when Federal Express announced plans to use the airport as a regional hub, homeowners cried foul and fought the project in court.

More houses and more people added to the challenges of maintaining basic services, such as water, sewer, and police and fire protection. At the top of Melvin's list for civic improvement was finding a long-term solution to problems with the city's delivery of basic services, particularly the deficiencies of its sewage treatment facility. The blight on the city he had identified in his first campaign remained unresolved.

The answer appeared to be at hand in November 1972, when North Carolina voters approved $150 million in state water and sewer bonds to build water systems and treatment plants in cities and towns all across the state. Greensboro had its eye on a piece of this pot of gold to help pay for a new treatment plant to replace the aging facility that Melvin kept talking about in his reelection campaigns. Now the money was finally available, and the man to put the project together for Greensboro was Thomas Z. Osborne.

Chapter 10

From Camelot to Dodge City

No ONE KNEW GREENSBORO'S infrastructure better than Tom Osborne. A map of water and sewer lines was imprinted on his brain. Pick a road and he could tell you when it was built and where it went. Thumb the hundreds of pages in the city's budget, stop on any line, and he would recite how the money was spent. When city manager James Turner announced his retirement in 1973, Osborne was the council's first choice for his replacement.

Osborne was a man of easy manner and medium build who kept himself lean and trim with a challenging tennis game. He spoke with a mountain accent that marked him as the product of a farm in Alleghany County. He was barely out of his teens when the Marines sent him to the South Pacific, where he fought at Iwo Jima and on other distant beaches in World War II. North Carolina State trained him as an engineer, but it was city manager James Townsend who taught Osborne how to run a city. When Osborne followed Turner into the manager's office in 1973, he had been the director of public works for four years.

Osborne was involved and hands-on. His friends called him "T.Z.," and to many city workers he was just "Tom." He would show up at roll call at the police department late shift, and he knew the first names of the men who repaired city streets. His skill as an engineer was coupled with the instincts of a politician. Before he recommended to the city council that plastic sewer lines be substituted for terra cotta because the newer product was cheaper and easier to handle, he called in Melvin and warned him that he could expect a response from Pomona Terra Cotta. The company was one of Greensboro's oldest manufacturing operations and known around the Southeast as a manufacturer of clay pipe. At the same time, Osborne was uneasy with the citizen groups that were beginning to ask for a greater say in setting the municipal agenda. Dealing with them was not something that he had learned about from Townsend or in the classroom in college. Professionals were regarded for their expertise; amateurs should let them do what they did best.

Osborne was modest, frugal, and scrupulously honest. Once, Jim Melvin saw him crossing the street in the rain on his way to the YMCA on West Market Street. Later, he asked Osborne why he had not parked closer to the building. The city manager explained that as a city employee on twenty-four-hour call, he was entitled to a car. But since his Y visit was personal, he had pulled his car into a church parking lot that was along his route home rather than add more miles to the car's odometer by circling the block to park closer to the Y's door. During his tenure, the city never increased taxes, and on more than one occasion, Osborne left his own pay raise on the table rather than unbalance a finely tuned budget.

When he became city manager, Osborne was forty-five years old, and Melvin was thirty-nine. The two were close enough in age to form a relationship not unlike that of brothers. They trusted one another enough to openly disagree, and to benefit from and respect their differing points of view. Even when the votes were clearly stacked against him, Osborne pleaded his case. Before Melvin and the rest of the council voted to extend city services to the controversial housing development on the perimeter of the airport, Osborne publicly supported a study that opposed extending services so far from the city limits. If an idea he favored was rejected, he simply parked it away until a better opportunity came.

Osborne was the perfect complement to Melvin. He loved the details of municipal work, which Melvin was happy to leave to others. Actually, Melvin had trouble reading long documents. Also, Melvin's attention span was limited, especially once he figured out where a speaker was headed with a point. He absorbed it and was ready to move on. In Osborne, he had someone who appreciated the finer points and backstopped him on details.

In their years together, Melvin and Osborne—they came to be referred to as a team—pushed through the completion of major portions of the 1950s Babcock plan, with new thoroughfares that made Greensboro one of the easiest cities in the state to navigate. Osborne's creative use of federal funds also helped the city pay for new parks and recreation facilities, leaving local taxes to pay for essential services.

Before Melvin left office, Osborne also helped turn a citizen's complaint into one of the city's most important assets. In the early 1980s, the community's successful youth soccer program was strong enough for program leaders to consider building playing fields for the program's exclusive use rather than borrow space at schools and parks around the city. The Greensboro Youth Soccer Association (GYSA) had options on about thirty acres of land north of town, and plans were under way to build a number of playing fields when Melvin got a call from William Klopman, the head of Burlington Industries. Klopman argued that the complex would overload local streets, and he told the mayor to do something. Melvin looked into the objections from the city's leading businessman, who happened to have a home near the proposed soccer fields, and became convinced that Klopman's concern was legitimate. The mayor's alternative proposal was for the GYSA to use land at Bryan Park, where the soccer association used its money to develop eleven fields and a stadium with covered seating on land purchased for the purpose by Joseph M. Bryan. Twenty years later, the soccer program's annual weekend tournament was drawing hundreds of teams from around the southeast and had become a welcome off-season bonus for local hotels and restaurants.

Most important among the projects that occupied Melvin and Osborne was the new sewage treatment plant that Melvin had promised to do something about when he first ran for the office with the declaration, "Greensboro Stinks." The Metro Sewer Plant was an ambitious project with more than its share of problems when the city council finally approved it in 1974. The chosen site required the city to reach beyond its eastern boundaries for land near the confluence of the north and south forks of Buffalo Creek, the stream that for years had carried Greensboro's treated wastewater to the Haw River. The new location would give relief to thousands of residents in southeast Greensboro, who might finally breathe sweet air again. At the same time, it aroused the ire of residents of nearby McLeansville, a one-time textile mill town where landowners and others objected to Greensboro's leapfrogging into the county to treat its offal.

Standing in the way was an influential Republican, McLeansville's Odell Payne, whose family had a farm in the vicinity of the proposed site. Payne had sufficient pull with the new Republican administration in Raleigh to stall the project for four years. Study after study was required, and in 1976, Melvin told a civic club, "I am sorry to report that today we are no farther along than we were in 1968."[1] A year later, more than a thousand people turned out to oppose the project at a public hearing. By that time, the original price tag of $17 million had jumped to

$40 million, and any chance of using state clean water bonds had long since passed. That money had gone to cities that had projects ready to go following a statewide bond referendum in 1972. It would take another five years before construction on the Greensboro plant would begin.

There were multiple opportunities, and reasons, to abandon the project as lawsuits and foot-dragging in Raleigh postponed construction. Yet Melvin and Osborne pushed it forward inch by inch. "I bet there weren't many days that he didn't spend some significant time working on the plant," said Melvin of Osborne. "He knew that was the kind of thing needed. If you don't drive, drive, push, push, drive, drive, the bureaucracy will cause it never to happen. The bureaucracy delayed us."[2]

Looking back on that period, Melvin said that the Metro Sewer Plant was the crowning achievement of his years in office. For a politician, it was something of a curious victory. He fought for a dozen years for a building that most voters would never see—or even want to see—to provide a service that virtually everyone took for granted. Even those who no longer suffered the odors of the old plant were rarely aware of who had been responsible for improving their side of town. Yet Melvin knew the plant was an absolute necessity if Greensboro was to accommodate future growth.

When the plant was dedicated in 1984, it was named for Osborne, who quipped that unlike Melvin, for whom a public building had been named, at least he knew that the effluent from the structure bearing his name had been treated. The old plant was demolished and the property turned into a park that the city named in honor of Jimmie I. Barber.

It would take even longer to secure a reliable source of water for the city. City officials seemed to respond only when the problem reached a crisis, such as in the 1920s, when the first large reservoir was built, and in the 1950s, when Greensboro had to borrow water from surrounding communities and employ a rainmaker to keep the taps full. The opening of Lake Townsend had relieved some of the anxiety, but as Townsend himself had said at the dedication, it was not a long-term solution.

One option that looked very attractive but always seemed slightly out of reach was to tap into the Mayo River, which flowed into Rockingham County just north of Greensboro. The water in the Mayo was exceptionally clean, and the riverbed lay within easy reach just across the county line. In fact, two Greensboro businessmen, Orton Boren and Jack Lindley, had purchased a 400-acre tract alongside the Mayo in the 1950s with the thought of later selling it to the city as a site for a small impoundment from which water could be collected and piped south. Lindley believed the Mayo could supply Greensboro as well as other cities in the North Carolina Piedmont. At one point, he carried elaborate plans for a supply line from the Mayo to University of North Carolina president Bill Friday in the hope of gaining support for a water project to supply Chapel Hill.

Melvin was attracted to the Mayo as a solution. He believed it made good sense and was the most economical arrangement, but he also was aware of the complications, not the least of which were laws prohibiting the interbasin transfer of water. The Mayo was part of the Roanoke River Basin in southern Virginia, while Greensboro was in the Cape Fear River Basin in central North Carolina. Nonetheless, Melvin and Osborne talked about the possibilities. At one point, Osborne said the city should consider the Mayo as a reserve supply for when the reservoirs were low.

The two learned just how difficult it would be to get Rockingham County to agree to such a plan when they walked into a meeting in the neighboring county that they had called to talk about regional cooperation. The two were met by angry Rockingham residents who had heard a news report that day that Greensboro was looking to the Mayo to meet its future water needs. One of Lindley's allies on the Guilford County Board of Commissioners had speculated out loud about tapping into the Mayo but had not bothered to alert the mayor and city manager. Melvin and Osborne came close to needing police protection to get out of the county and return to Greensboro.

Melvin quickly disavowed any plans to explore the Mayo as a water source for Greensboro, drawing considerable heat from Lindley, whose influence at NCNB, Melvin's employer, was considerable. The city's attention shifted south to the community of Randleman in Randolph County, where the U.S. Army Corps of Engineers had long planned a large dam as part of a major flood control project for the Deep River, one of the tributaries of the Cape Fear. There was no way of telling in 1976, when the corps plans were announced, that it would take thirty years for the project to reach completion—and even then not as an federal project but one financed by residents of Greensboro, High Point, and other, smaller central North Carolina cities. And the cost would more than double to over $120 million.

By the spring of 1979, Jim Melvin had been part of city government for nearly ten years. He had won election as a council member twice and had been elected mayor three times after the city's charter was changed in 1972 to allow voters to choose the mayor. None of those contests had really given him any trouble. In 1973, in his first race as mayor, he collected 27,171 votes, while his opponent got 1,261. Council member Mary Seymour, who had served with Melvin, appeared to have the best chance of unseating Melvin with her challenge in 1975, but she only received 3,000 more votes than Melvin's 1973 opponent, while Melvin's vote total was nearly 15,000. In 1977, the outcome was the same.

As Melvin prepared for his last race, he had made a significant career change. In February 1978, after nearly twenty years with NCNB, the last six as the bank's top officer in Greensboro, Melvin had become CEO of Home Federal Savings and Loan, the state's leading thrift institution and one of the largest in the Southeast. It was a golden opportunity, Melvin believed. He could remain in Greensboro without pressure to move within the expanding NCNB field of operations, and he could run his own show.

Melvin had all the trappings of success. His new position promised job security and a handsome salary, as well as opportunities for a comfortable retirement. He and his family lived in a spacious brick home with a large yard and long driveway in New Irving Park on a lot that Jim had bought in partnership with a builder when lots in the development became available in 1972. He also was the best-known elected official in the city. Three-fourths of those questioned in a 1976 poll correctly identified him as mayor. Three-fourths of the same sample could not name another local public official.

Melvin's years at city hall had been scandal-free and relatively clear of the racial turmoil that had been a constant strain on his predecessor. The city was well along in completing a thoroughfare plan, while new fire stations, branch libraries, and parks had enhanced Greensboro's reputation as a comfortable place to live and raise a family. If anything, the city was too comfortable. It was said that Greensboro suffered from "terminal smug": change came slowly. One major bit of unfinished business was the extension of Benjamin Parkway, a major roadway that planners said was essential to accommodate expanding suburban growth. The northwest was up in arms over the boulevard that one day would be the city's main route to a new airport.

Melvin was ready to spend more time with his family. Jim and Susan's two sons, Taylor and Jimbo, had never known a time when their father was not involved at city hall. On occasion, he had taken Taylor with him to public meetings. One night, he looked over at his son, who was struggling to keep his eyes open, and decided that as good as his intentions might have been, this was cruel punishment for an eight-year-old. To make up for evenings away from the family, Melvin created "Super Saturdays," which were devoted to family activity, even if it was only raking the yard.

Yet he was not quite ready to leave city hall. Nagging at him was the still-dilapidated state of downtown Greensboro. In 1976, writing for the Jaycees' publication, *The Projector*, he said, "One of the things we're all going to have to get used to is . . . that downtown Greensboro ain't going to be the central retail center because the need has long since vanished. That battle was really lost in the early fifties, and I didn't recognize it 'til 18 months to two years ago. But that doesn't mean that our central city can't be a useful, helpful, positive place."

There was a stirring of new life downtown. A campaign led by Betty Cone, a determined civic volunteer, was under way to save the Carolina Theater, which had been a showplace in the era of the silver screen. Cone and others also were gathering the necessary details that would lead to the designation of downtown as a historic district. Some believed that the aging structures that so bothered Orton Boren were now worth saving. There were even a few sturdy pioneers eyeing the upper floors of empty storefronts as residences. In order to live in the buildings, city ordinances required their tenants to be certified as night watchmen.

In the summer of 1979, Melvin launched a last effort to revitalize downtown with a plan for a civic center, convention hotel, and matching office buildings to be constructed in the heart of the city. Armed with a consultant's report that showed the project was the answer to what ailed Greensboro, the mayor had the numbers and commitments from first-rate companies to build the hotel and office buildings if voters would pay for the construction of the public space that would be used as a civic center. First Citizens Bank planned two office buildings, while Roger Soles at Jefferson Standard said his company would take a position in the ownership of a hotel to be built by Loew's Corporation, whose P. Lorillard Company was one of Greensboro's leading employers.

The entire project was to fill two square blocks immediately southwest of Elm and Market streets with new buildings. The state of that area of downtown was desperate: weeds and gravel decorated the southwest corner, while across the street the four-story Belk store had stood vacant for four years. The Belk name, spelled out in art deco letters on the store's sign, stood out like scarlet letters of decay. On the northeast corner was the Southeastern Building, a structure of the same vintage as the Jefferson that had aged far less gracefully. First Citizens Bank's new buildings would replace the empty Meyer's department store and surround the aging F. W. Woolworth store, the last remaining retailer from Elm Street's golden days.

The pieces for his convention center had fallen into place nicely, Melvin believed. Private investors would raise office buildings and a hotel, while the city would pay for the meeting rooms, a restaurant, and a convention hall, all for a modest public investment of $7.5 million. "The way the thing was going to work was the city was going to have a common area—the meeting space—and it was going to be attached to a hotel tower which Loew's would own. We were so buoyed by that, and so encouraged. What we didn't know was that Joe Koury was planning what he was planning."[3]

When those in the city's economic and leadership establishment lamented the lack of vision in Greensboro, they made grudging exception for Joe Koury, a man more comfortable in sweaty T-shirts, scuffed work boots, and a pickup truck than in a boardroom. His favorite location was a job site; his recreation was planning the next grand project. By the late 1970s, he was on his way to becoming the county's largest landowner, but he had little to do with the downtown business crowd with whom Melvin was most familiar. Koury was reclusive, they said, and held to his own plans with stubborn determination. Years later, no less a corporate maverick than Guilford Mills's Charles Hayes would call Koury "the Howard Hughes of Greensboro."[4]

Koury was running a mail-order fabric shop in the early 1950s when Fred Williams, Oscar Burnett's partner in the liquidation of the ORD property, talked him into buying sections of the army's hospital buildings and converting them into housing. From that modest start, Koury got into home building, and by the end of the 1950s, he and his partner, William Kirkman, were the busiest home builders in Greensboro.

With land north and west of the city controlled by either Starmount or the Cones, Koury and Kirkman turned to the southwest along High Point Road, the major connector between Greensboro and High Point. They converted former dairy farms into subdivisions with hundreds of moderately priced, well-built homes. Among Koury's dreams was a shopping center that he wanted to put on ninety acres beside Interstate 40 at the High Point Road interchange. With Greensboro pushing steadily toward the northwest, Koury told a friend, "We can do something for the southwest side of town."[5]

Koury's shopping center remained a moving target for more than a decade. At first, he favored an open center along the lines of Raleigh's Cameron Village or Greensboro's Friendly Shopping Center. He even made a trip to Kansas City to see Country Club Plaza, the nation's first shop-ping center and the model for both Cameron Village and the Friendly center. His would be different, however, and for a designer he courted none other than Edward Durrell Stone, whose works included the Ken-nedy Center for the Performing Arts and the U.S. pavilion at the Brus-sels World's Fair. Stone was finally persuaded to accept the commission, but his design never left the drawing board. By the time it was ready, Koury had changed his mind. Now he wanted an enclosed mall, not a shopping center. He had seen the new megabox configurations where shoppers strolled air-conditioned indoor streets lined with shops, de-partment stores, and eateries. That was what he wanted to build.

The shifts in direction and other delays seemed to embolden Koury. At one point, an exasperated Fred Williams, who left Burnett to join Koury in the early 1960s, told Koury that each time he talked to a news-paper reporter, the project just got larger. By the time construction on the Four Seasons Mall finally began in 1972, what had started as a 275,000-square-foot center finally topped out at 900,000 square feet—with an option to grow by a million feet more.

The Four Seasons opening in 1975 was a great personal victory for the former mail-order merchant. Koury had overcome obstacles all along the way, including an ice- and snowstorm that threatened to disrupt open-ing day. He had met impossible leasing requirements from skeptical lenders who said the project was too big for Greensboro. He stood down advisors who told him he was wasting money by building a foundation sufficient to expand a building they believed was already too large. And he salvaged construction after his contractor went bust. Finally—and perhaps this was the sweetest victory of all—he had succeeded against the competition of that downtown crowd who had facilitated the build-ing of Carolina Circle Mall on the other side of town.

Melvin and city hall had literally paved the way for Alpert Investment Corporation of Atlanta, one of the nation's largest mall developers, to open the 600,000-square-foot Carolina Circle Mall on the city's north-east side. When the Alpert brothers came calling in 1972, Koury's proj-ect still existed only on paper. The only evidence of a future mall was some excavated earth and a lonesome bulldozer that Koury drove around the property from time to time. Melvin made no excuses about lobbying the state to pay for the extension of two major streets across U.S. 29 to allow easy access to Carolina Circle, a project that was real.

Encouraging Carolina Circle was simply good planning, the mayor said. Melvin and others believed that Carolina Circle would balance the growing concentration of development in the northwest. Moreover, Carolina Circle would strengthen Greensboro as a regional marketplace. The Alperts envisioned shoppers driving in from Reidsville twenty miles to the north and even from as far away as Danville, Virginia. Customers also would arrive from Burlington twenty miles to the east to shop Carolina Circle's stores and enjoy its ice-skating rink, a novelty addition that proved popular.

This was scant consolation to Koury, who gambled everything he owned on his vision. So when Melvin came around again in the summer of 1979 proposing a convention center for Elm Street, Koury was mad. The convention center and downtown hotel were going to be direct competition for his Holiday Inn–Four Seasons, a hotel and meeting complex that anchored a prime location beside the proposed Four Seasons Mall. With more than 200 rooms and 20,000 square feet of meeting space, it was spacious and well-appointed. The hotel's restaurant was first-class, and the lounge was one of the most popular nightspots in the city. A month after Melvin announced plans for a bond referendum for a downtown convention center, Koury called reporters out to show them that his engineers were laying the groundwork for an addition to the Holiday Inn. Construction on a 250-room tower would begin soon, and he planned to triple the size of the meeting rooms in the convention hall. Koury said he expected to spend $10.5 million.

Melvin believed the convention center was the kind of project that would continue the momentum that had begun to build downtown, where business and commercial investment seemed the alternative to retail. When Southern Life Insurance Company announced in late 1978 its plans to replace the aging O. Henry Hotel with a $30 million complex that was to include an office building, hotel, and enclosed mall, Melvin called it "a turning point in the history of downtown."[6] A few months later, the idea of the convention center began to take shape. In August, Melvin and the city council flew to Greenville, South Carolina, where they looked over a similar project. By the end of the month, a referendum on $7.5 million in bonds to build the center was scheduled for October, less than six weeks off.

Opposition to the downtown project arose quickly, especially from those who argued that public money should not be used to compete with private enterprise. Ceasar Cone II helped pay for a round of newspaper ads calling on voters to defeat the bonds. Others took exception to the underlying economics of Melvin's plans. Ten days before the election, a UNC–Greensboro economist characterized the city's feasibility study as "undocumented figures taken out of the air and projected into the future without any justification."[7] Melvin also found George Simkins Jr. lined up against the bonds after Melvin refused to trade support for the adoption of a ward system in exchange for Simkins's endorsement of the bonds. Even the usually solid ranks of the city council did not hold. Councilman Marion Follin III defected, saying he was being bulldozed into accepting the mayor's vision for downtown.

On October 9, voters rejected the bond proposal by a margin of two to one. The only winning precinct was in Irving Park, but even there the difference was small. Melvin's vision evaporated overnight. First Citizens announced the following day that it was revising its construction plans to include only one office building, not two, and the remaining structure would be a scaled-down version of what was initially planned. There would be no hotel. Empty buildings shabby with age would remain.

Years later, Melvin conceded that the project had not been right for the city. The public space would have been too small to make Greensboro a real competitor for major events. And, he acknowledged, his own impatience and eagerness to move along a project that had eluded Greensboro for years had blinded him to the necessity of building public support.

At the time, however, his thoughts ran in another direction. He was shaken by the drubbing his plan had taken at the polls and began to question his own effectiveness at city hall. He had been mayor longer than anyone in Greensboro's history. Perhaps he had stayed too long. One newspaper report asked whether the mayor had lost his magic touch with the voters. Even the *Greensboro Daily News* editorial endorsing Melvin's reelection noted the mayor's enthusiasm was tainted by impatience and a "hot temper and a sharp tongue"[8] for those who disagreed with him.

As Election Day approached, Melvin even grew anxious about the outcome of the mayoral contest—an outcome that everyone else took for granted. His opponent was Sol Jacobs, a retired delicatessen operator who had filed as a candidate only to prevent Melvin from taking the election by default. Jacobs was a civic gadfly who throughout the fall raised nagging issues such as the need for district elections and better mass transit. But he was no candidate. His son had to talk him into running a campaign ad; Jacobs did not think it was right to pay money to buy the attention of the public. Melvin may have been the only person in Greensboro who gave Jacobs much of a chance.

On November 2, the Friday before Election Day, Melvin and Osborne met over lunch. Among the items on Osborne's agenda in his weekly update for the mayor was a Saturday morning march and rally that had been organized by the Workers Viewpoint Organization (WVO), a small but noisy group of labor activists and communists who had been trying to enroll textile workers at Cone plants in their cause. During the summer, the WVO had won some notoriety when its members confronted a small group of Ku Klux Klansmen in China Grove, a textile town about fifty miles south of Greensboro.

The WVO now had a "Death to the Klan" march planned for Saturday, November 3, in Greensboro that was designed to capitalize on what organizers considered a major victory at China Grove. The event was to start before noon, with marchers winding their way through the city's African American community before ending at a meeting hall, where a rally was scheduled. Osborne outlined for Melvin the police arrangements that had been made and issued assurances that the city was prepared. He then left town for his farm in Alleghany County, about a hundred miles away in the northwest mountains.

Less than twenty-four hours later, Greensboro businessman Paul N. Howard was sitting in a bar in Moscow when he looked at a television and saw the image of his mayor, Jim Melvin, talking about a shooting in which five people had been killed in Greensboro during a violent confrontation between communists and Klansmen and self-styled Nazis.

Back home, at about the same hour, Melvin was trying to figure out how he had gone from being the mayor of Camelot to the mayor of Dodge City in eighty-eight seconds of deadly gunfire.

Chapter 11

They Don't Give a Thing

THE FACTS WERE INDISPUTABLE: Shortly before midday on Saturday, November 3, 1979, a dozen or more Ku Klux Klansmen and neo-Nazis confronted a group of communists gathering on a street corner in southeast Greensboro where a "Death to the Klan" march was about to begin. The fight that erupted was brief but deadly. In eighty-eight seconds of gunfire, with shots fired from both sides, five anti-Klan protesters were killed, and nine others were injured. The images that television news crews captured on videotape later failed to convince a jury that murder had been committed, but for many, the stunning visuals were enough to produce a devastating new signature for Greensboro.

News of the killings was broadcast around the world. By the end of the day, president Jimmy Carter was aware of the events in Greensboro, even as threats of a takeover of the United States embassy in Iran came across his desk. Jim Melvin first heard there was trouble within minutes of the shootings. He had just returned from a soccer game with his son Taylor and was raking leaves in his front yard when the police watch commander called him at home. Melvin left for police headquarters immediately, wearing his work clothes.

Less than two hours later, Melvin was surrounded by a growing phalanx of reporters, who fell upon Greensboro to consume facts and half-facts as they were revealed. Regrettably, what would later prove to be a very complex story lent itself too easily to being told in stereotypes about Klan violence, the legacy of southern racial conflict, and Greensboro's reputation as a textile town. Before the first press conference began, Melvin was standing at the back of the crowd when he heard one out-of-town journalist ask another for details on the mayor. "Oh," the other said, "he's some typical small-town redneck." Still wearing a day-old beard and the dirty blue corduroy trousers, work shoes, and rumpled plaid shirt that he had on when he got the call at home, Melvin tapped the speaker on the shoulder, introduced himself, and said, "I look forward to getting to know you and I hope you will me."[1]

For a Greensboro patriot like Melvin, what these extremists from the far right and far left had done to his city was unforgivable. They had turned his beloved hometown into a shooting gallery and smeared the city's respectable, progressive reputation, which he had spent his public career trying to expand and improve. At his first opportunity, Melvin denounced both sides in the conflict and tried to minimize Greensboro's role as circumstantial. This was something that could have happened anywhere, he said.

The full extent of his role in managing the fallout from the incident became apparent soon after Melvin arrived at the police command center, so he called his wife, Susan, and asked her to bring him a change of clothes and a razor. Because the municipal building was saving energy by limiting hot water on weekends, he opened several nicks on his neck shaving in cold water. Thus refreshed, Melvin stepped forward with police chief Ed Swing to issue news updates, but neither was prepared for the pummeling they took from reporters. The two were as stunned by the rush of events as anyone.

At the outset, Melvin believed that dealing with the violent conflict was purely a police matter, and he deferred to Swing to respond to reporters. Swing was unaccustomed to the pressing questions of reporters, however, and Melvin, who had more experience with the media, stepped in and became the principal spokesman as the story unfolded. "Look," Melvin said, "there is a lot we don't know about this, but you have got my pledge and the pledge of this city that you will get the information as soon as we get it."[2]

Melvin was mindful of the problems that had been created by the delay in the release of information following the 1969 shooting death of a student on the A&T campus. He was not going to make that mistake. At the same time, he offered a strong vote of confidence in the ability of the police to handle the matter—a vote that was premature. Later review of command decisions revealed a lapse in judgment by officers in the field, who had allowed the Klan caravan to arrive, and the confrontation to take place, without a patrolman in sight. Melvin's support for the police was not forgotten, however. More than twenty years later, an officer who was on duty that Saturday wrote the mayor and told him about the comfort she received from his support for the police department when everyone was looking for scapegoats.

Events over the next ten days would become a blur for the mayor. Day rolled into night as Melvin monitored developments at the police department and met with lawyers, ministers, and community leaders, especially African Americans, whose inherent suspicion of the police would prove to be the soft spot in the city's handling of the incident. Black churchmen were asked to call for calm on Sunday morning. This was a difficult task for those whose parishioners lived in the vicinity of the Morningside housing project where the shootings had occurred. Children, as well as their mothers and fathers, fully expected armed white men to return. To calm his flock, the Reverend George Brooks posted lookouts in the church parking lot, and services went on as scheduled.

Melvin presided over several difficult sessions with African American leaders who wanted to know why and how the city had allowed this to happen. It was inconceivable to them that police would not have uniformed officers on the ground where the marchers were gathering, particularly if they were aware of the potential for conflict. In any other part of town, they said, uniformed officers would have been put into position in just such a way. Later sessions with those planning a funeral march were especially frustrating for Melvin. Before the shootings, the taunts of march organizers, aimed at the police in general and Melvin in particular, had been merely an irritation; now Melvin considered their accusations of a police conspiracy and cover-up to be inflammatory.

After more than four days with little or no sleep, Melvin finally retreated from public view and drove his wife and sons out of town after threats against their safety had been called in to their home. Once they were situated in a familiar vacation spot at Myrtle Beach, he returned to Greensboro. Some of the relatives and friends of the victims noticed his absence and fed the rumor that the mayor had suffered a nervous breakdown. It was only concern for his family that kept Melvin from his day-in, day-out post at City Hall, however.

Almost ignored in the furious aftermath was Election Day, which arrived three days after the shootings. Melvin won reelection handily, but it was difficult for the mayor to take any satisfaction in winning an unprecedented fifth term in the midst of the tragedy that had fallen upon the dead, the wounded, and especially his city, his Camelot.

In fact, Greensboro was neither Melvin's gleaming city on the hill nor the communists' nest of bourgeois conspirators bent on destroying their work among the laboring poor in the textile mills. Rather, it was a city like many in the South that was struggling with unresolved issues between whites and blacks. At the same time, Greensboro seemed to carry a heavier burden than other communities in the state. From before the Woolworth sit-ins in 1960 and on through the contentious years of the civil rights movement and the student's death at A&T, racial tension had plagued Greensboro.

A number of episodes of race-related conflict had left scars and lingering resentment, as well as unanswered questions. Just a few months before this latest tragedy, in the summer of 1979, the *Carolina Peacemaker*, a newspaper written by and for Greensboro's African American community, had published reports blaming police for the unsolved murder of Willie Grimes, the A&T sophomore killed ten years earlier.

In the coming months, the resulting trial and acquittal of those accused of murder on November 3 would show that while police had made tactical mistakes in handling the confrontation, there was no evidence that city hall or private business interests had orchestrated the event or participated in any way, as some conspiracy theorists continued to claim. The outcome of the trial did exacerbate a gnawing sense of injustice and political impotence among African Americans, however. It was against this backdrop that NAACP leader George Simkins Jr. renewed his campaign for changes at city hall that would allow the black community to choose its own representatives and take a larger role in the running of the city.

———

The election system that Simkins had been working to overhaul for more than a decade had its roots in the post–World War I municipal reform movement, during which Greensboro exchanged the election of full-time city commissioners, who managed different departments of the city, for a paid city manager who was supervised by a part-time, seven-member city council. The idea was to put the management of city government in the hands of professionals, who would run the city much like a corporation.

Greensboro's plan was no different from many adopted in that day, with one exception. In 1923, the city created a separate voting district for the Cone interests after Greensboro annexed an area that included the mills, company houses, and company-owned shops and stores, as well as water reservoirs and acres of open land that belonged to the Cone family and its corporations. The Cones agreed to maintain many municipal services for a fee in lieu of normal taxation. For seventeen years, until his death in 1940, the District 1 councilman was Julius Cone, Moses and Ceasar's younger brother, who managed Cone Export and Commission. After World War II, this unique arrangement was abolished, and the city assumed responsibility for normal municipal services instead of paying Cone Mills to maintain the streets, as well as law and order.

The other six council members were elected at large, meaning each member represented the entire city, not a prescribed area. Theoretically, the seats were open to anyone who wished to run, and the arrangement was regarded as the epitome of democracy. As a practical matter, however, these six seats were usually occupied by those who had time, wealth, and a vested interest in civic duty. Most of the time, they were white, middle-aged men of comfortable means with personal and financial connections to the city's business interests. Before his death in 1946, one of those who recruited members for council seats was Julian Price, the head of Jefferson Standard Life Insurance Company. Price would tap a candidate and see that his campaign expenses were covered.[3]

There were occasional contests for the city council seats, but local elections were never very heated, and surprises were few. The cozy nature of the process and the racial and social attitudes of the day militated against the election of contenders from outside of a close political club. Perhaps the greatest obstacle to the election of a candidate from outside the clique was the lack of voting districts or wards that would ensure the election of candidates from places other than the affluent precincts in the city's north and northwest.

This virtually closed system frustrated repeated attempts by African Americans to win a seat on the council, both before and after World War II. It was not until 1951 that William Hampton became the first African American elected to the council, largely through the work of the Greensboro Citizens Association, a political action group created by the small but influential organization of politically astute black professionals known as the Greensboro Men's Club. While Hampton's election was groundbreaking, it had limited impact. From 1955 until 1979, only four other African Americans served on the council, and two of them owed their seats to the white majority that appointed them.

For Simkins, and many others in east Greensboro, the city's at-large system effectively disenfranchised African Americans, fully one-third of the city's population. Simkins believed that black votes counted for less as long as the African American community was beholden to a white majority for approval of its representatives. He found at-large elections to be as oppressive as any of the other inequities he had fought in numerous civil rights battles beginning in 1955 on Gillespie Park Golf Course, the city-owned course on Asheboro Street where Jim Melvin had once caddied and developed his own love of the game.

———

George Christopher Simkins Jr. had grown up in relative luxury, the son of a dentist who was as much a leading figure in the community as his son would become a generation later. At least one mark of his status was his role in 1935 as a founding member of the Greensboro Men's Club, which met monthly to socialize, enjoy a fine meal, and digest political issues. For years, formal dress was required for admission to dinner and an evening with special guests who included singer Paul Robeson, writer James Weldon Johnson, educator Mary McLeod Bethune, and the NAACP's Walter White. Over the years, the club members talked of the problems in the black community, and in 1939 they encouraged the elder Simkins to run for a seat on the city council. He lost. Usually, the group was left to use persuasion and direct appeals in an effort to nudge city hall for relief of some of the inequities in the segregated system that separated east Greensboro from the rest of the city.

George Simkins Jr. graduated from Greensboro public schools and attended a Chicago prep school before he entered Talladega College in Alabama. He received his medical degree from Meharry Medical College in Nashville, interned in New Jersey, and then returned home in 1949 and got married. His wife was Anna Atkins, the daughter of the founder of Winston-Salem State College, J. Alston Atkins, who was a graduate of Fisk University and Yale's law school. After marrying, Simkins did not immediately join his father's dental practice. Instead, he worked for the county health department treating indigent children in the segregated schools. Upon his father's retirement in 1954, he moved into the Simkins dental office on Benbow Road, where he would practice for the next forty-plus years.

In the early 1950s, Greensboro whites considered their town to be as progressive as any in the South, especially after African Americans began to take a role in government in 1951. Hampton's election to the city council led to the appointment of David Jones, the president of Bennett College, to the city school board in 1953. George Evans, a physician, leading member of the Men's Club, and head of the Greensboro Citizens Association, was a member of the Greensboro Housing Authority. It was Evans who had given a name to the housing project where the 1979 shootings occurred, calling it "Morningside" because its location on Greensboro's east side meant it was the first part of the city to receive the morning sun.

Whites talked about Greensboro's excellent race relations, an image enhanced in 1954 by the city school board's early endorsement of the U.S. Supreme Court's school desegregation decision. From another perspective, however, Greensboro's progressive image was illusory. African Americans had little control over their community and the delivery of public services, down to and including the board of trustees of A&T, an institution that was a source of immense pride within the black community. The legislature picked the board members, with no consultation from the campus.

Because of their prominence and token participation, Hampton, Jones, and Evans practiced the politics of accommodation and tried to maintain a balance between advocacy and supplication. They picked their battles carefully. A year after Hampton was elected to the city council, the Men's Club asked in a letter to the council whether the new coliseum that voters were being urged to support with a bond referendum would have segregated seating. After an awkward few days, Hampton beat a retreat, saying publicly that the club's request for the coliseum seating to be integrated was "regrettable." Local politicians sidestepped the issue, and the letter went unanswered. Yet Hampton later succeeded in securing Jones's appointment to the school board after Hampton publicly challenged mayor Robert Frazier, who he said reneged on a promise to appoint an African American.

Greensboro held tight to the old ways of life, which meant a city of two worlds, one white and one black. Whites seldom ventured into east Greensboro and saw the unpaved streets and slum housing or experienced the other ragged civic conditions that would have been intolerable in their own neighborhoods. Usually, their only contact with persons of color was with the domestic workers who cleaned their homes and cooked their meals for low wages. Black lawyers, doctors, and professionals like Simkins had little interaction with their white counterparts. The sick and injured from east Greensboro were treated at L. Richardson Hospital, which had opened in 1927 to provide treatment for African Americans. Only severe cases went to Moses H. Cone Memorial Hospital, where they were treated by white physicians, because black medical professionals were not admitted to the staff. Likewise, black attorneys were not invited to join the local bar association, though such invitations were virtually automatic for any white lawyer who hung out his shingle. The few black police officers were forbidden to arrest whites.

This separation of worlds cut both ways. The black schools—especially Dudley Senior High and Lincoln Junior High—were administered with little interference from whites, creating a level of stature and influence for teachers and school principals that extended far beyond their pay. Some black educators, like Vance Chavis, had legendary followings. In his classroom at Dudley, his students learned as much about the dignity of humankind as they did about physics. "Chavisology" included a strictly enforced dress code and lectures on motivation. He told the slackers seated in the back of the classroom that if they did not pay attention, then all they needed to learn was how to read a tape measure so they would be able to calculate the depth of the ditches they would be digging for the rest of their lives. Those who listened went on to study at the top black colleges and universities.

Black-owned businesses along East Market Street thrived in what amounted to a captive market created for them by the discrimination of businesses on Elm Street, where African Americans were only conditionally accepted in the white-owned stores. When he was a youngster, Walter Johnson Jr. heard his father telephone a shoe store downtown to ask about an advertised special on popular Buster Brown models. No, the elder Johnson was told, black customers were not admitted for that sale.[4]

That blacks and whites occupied separate worlds was just fine with many in the city, including leading citizens who resisted change. Reaction to the Supreme Court's 1954 school decision produced the Patriots of North Carolina, a group that enjoyed the support of leading Greensboro businessmen such as Stark Dillard, whose paper company was one of the largest in the Southeast, and Pierce Rucker, a descendant of the legendary nineteenth-century governor and master of Blandwood, John Motley Morehead. The Patriots publicly defended segregation before school boards around the state and privately leaned on public officials to hold the line. Such behind-the-scenes pressure caused the city council to stumble badly in 1957 when it tried to replace Hampton, whose term had expired. Council members named a white man, Montgomery Hill, as a successor without first asking Hill if he would serve. Hill subsequently declined the offer, and Hampton was reappointed by a vote of four to three.

There were clearly limits beyond which the city was not prepared to go. George Simkins Jr. discovered that truth in December 1955, when he and five friends showed up at Gillespie Park Golf Course, paid their seventy-five-cent green fee, and proceeded to play a round of golf over the protests of the management. A week earlier, another group of black players had been turned away with the promise that their applications for membership would be duly submitted, a requirement never imposed on white "guests," who played without any questions. Simkins was tired of such duplicity, but most of all he resented being relegated to playing the ragged nine-hole course at Nocho Park, which was well below his ability, when the city owned a fine eighteen-hole course at Gillespie. He and his friends finished nine holes before they succumbed to the demands of club pro Ernie Edwards that they leave immediately. When Edwards asked Simkins why he was there, the young dentist replied it was for a cause. "What cause?" Edwards demanded. "The cause of democracy," Simkins replied.[5] That night, police officers arrested Simkins and his friends on the charge of trespassing.

The treatment Simkins received in court changed his life. "During the trial," he later recalled, "the sheriff, the solicitor, and the judge, they were all grouped together, laughing, lying on the stand, and I just couldn't understand—of course, I was naive—why you couldn't get a fair trial. It was all made up that they were going to find us guilty."[6] The golfers were sentenced to thirty days in jail. Simkins's father posted his bond while the decision was appealed.

The golf course case dragged on for four years, and its curious turns further convinced Simkins of the city's resistance to equality. The original charge was thrown out on a technicality related to the drafting of the warrants. By that time, a federal judge had declared in a civil case brought against the city that Greensboro could not duck its obligations to equal treatment under the U.S. Constitution by leasing public facilities to a private operator. Even in the face of the federal court decision, however, new warrants on criminal trespass charges were filed. Simkins and the others were tried and convicted a second time. The convictions were upheld on all appeals, but Simkins never served a day in jail. Governor Luther Hodges commuted the sentences after reading the argument against conviction written by U.S. Supreme Court chief justice Earl Warren in his dissent to the decision upheld by the majority.

The city closed the golf course shortly after the federal court ruling in 1957, and it did not reopen until 1962, when it had only nine holes of play. During the interim, the city had consumed a portion of the course to build a maintenance facility for city vehicles. Nonetheless, Simkins was the first man off the tee.

By that time, the damage had been done as far as Simkins was concerned. His treatment in the courts and at the hands of the men who ran Greensboro was something he would never forget: "They got me involved. The way they were treating me in the courts, I said, 'I'm going to devote my life to civil rights.'"[7]

As Simkins's legal challenge to the segregation of the golf courses was playing out, the city also denied blacks the use of a new $220,000 Lindley Park swimming pool that had opened in 1955. Elbert Lewis, the parks and recreation chairman, warned that if blacks did not voluntarily stay on their side of town, the city would be forced to close the Lindley pool as well as one built for African Americans at Nocho Park. Lewis's response was reinforced by mayor George Roach, who announced that he could see "nothing but discord" if blacks and whites were permitted to swim together. When the NAACP persisted in its demands, the city sold the Lindley Park pool in 1957 for half its value to a white, nonprofit swim association that upheld the segregated tradition. The older pool at Nocho Park, built during the Depression with WPA funds, also was sold.

At the outset, Simkins did not think of himself as a reformer. He simply wanted to enjoy golf and tennis, his favorite pastimes, at venues that matched his level of skill. He all but stumbled into his role as the leading voice for African Americans in Greensboro. After Simkins was hauled into court, legendary NAACP legal counsel Thurgood Marshall chastised him, saying the cause of civil rights would have been better served if Simkins had asked a court to enjoin the city from barring admission to blacks rather than force his own arrest. Simkins told Marshall he did not even know what an injunction was.[8]

Indeed, Simkins was not a model civil rights activist. He was quiet, almost shy. He was available to news reporters, but usually only when they called him. He was not one to make bold announcements, and while his public comments were tough, they were never inflammatory. He preferred to work in the trenches. Even before the A&T students challenged convention at the lunch counter at F. W. Woolworth in downtown Greensboro, Simkins had begun an active letter-writing campaign to force employers to open jobs to blacks. His actions caused a stir among some in the black community who thought he was moving too fast. Later, he said he was relieved the students had acted. It took some of the pressure off him.[9]

It was the NAACP's legal clout, however, that helped Simkins succeed in his challenge to Greensboro's medical establishment, an accomplishment that changed medical care for African Americans all across America. Simkins had long chafed at the restrictions at Greensboro's white hospitals, Moses Cone Memorial and Wesley Long, that prohibited black physicians from entering their doors to treat patients. Unlike Cone, which admitted black patients under the care of white physicians, Wesley Long prohibited black physicians and patients outright.

In 1960, Simkins began putting his case together by applying with other black doctors for admission to the staffs of the two hospitals. After their applications were denied, they had NAACP lawyers file suit in federal court on their behalf. The doctors' case rested on the argument that both hospitals had been built with federal money—in this case Hill-Burton funds that had become available following World War II—and therefore should be open to all.

The lawsuit was a direct affront to Greensboro's white establishment. Both hospitals were the pride of the community. Cone was one of the largest and best-financed institutions in the state. Wesley Long was a private institution named for its founder, whose board of trustees included the city's leading businessmen, including Guilford Dairy's Mose Kiser; Carl Jeffress, whose family owned the Greensboro newspapers; W. C. Boren III of Pomona Terra Cotta; attorney Thornton Brooks; Blue Bell executive E. A. Morris; and businessman Stark Dillard. The hospital was located downtown before a new $3.5 million facility, built with Orton Boren's bricks, was dedicated with great fanfare on November 19, 1961, on a site near Friendly Shopping Center.

A year after Wesley Long opened, U.S. district judge Edwin M. Stanley ruled against Simkins, saying the hospitals were private corporations. Stanley's decision was overturned on appeal, however, and in March 1964, the U.S. Supreme Court ruled that since the hospitals had been built in part with federal funds—over half the cost of the new Wesley Long had been paid by the government—neither admission nor professional privileges could be denied on the basis of race. On May 7, 1964, Maggie Shaw became the first African American admitted to Moses Cone under the care of a black physician. She was treated and discharged two days later.

"One thing I found out is that this city is different from any city in North Carolina," Simkins said years later. "You've got to fight for every inch that you get in this city. They don't give a thing. I mean you either got to sue, or sit in, or wade in or whatever. This city doesn't give you a dime."[10]

Chapter 12

Casey at the Bat

On THE FALL OF 1963, John Parramore of the Greensboro Chamber of Commerce told a reporter that "the national press referred to Greensboro as a 'byword for racial conflict.'"[1] Indeed, the air was still clouded with mistrust, anger, and resentment following the mass arrests of street demonstrators that summer who had filled the county jail and drawn renewed attention to the state of race relations in Greensboro.

At the time of Parramore's comments, former mayor Boyd Morris, the owner of the Mayfair Cafeteria, remained steadfast in his refusal to serve black customers, despite the pleadings of members of a special human relations commission formed by mayor David Schenck following the demonstrations that had targeted the Mayfair. Even after the marches had ended and Morris's downtown competitor, the S&W Cafeteria, opened to all, Morris still refused to serve black customers. Sounding to all the world like Alabama governor George Wallace, Morris said, "I am not going to serve any Negro today, tomorrow or any day." He did not change his policy until passage of the Civil Rights Act a year later.

Morris was an affable chap, often ready with a free slice of pie for his regular customers. His cafeteria was a downtown institution, and Morris himself had shouldered his share of civic work in the 1950s as a councilman and later mayor. He had been influential in bringing Billy Graham's evangelical crusade to town in 1950. When the marchers turned on his business, his plea that he was a small businessman caught in the crunch of history resonated with the local business elite. He argued that an integrated cafeteria would be an empty cafeteria and said he was doomed to failure if he caved in to the demonstrators' demands. "Here I was a businessman," Morris said later, "and had served every facet of this community . . . wondering in my own little mind why is this happening to me."[2]

Morris's situation engendered more sympathy than had been offered in 1960 to the managers of the national chain stores like Woolworth's and Kress's who had refused lunch-counter service to African Americans. When Mayor Schenck called a summit of local corporate executives at the height of the troubles in early June 1963, only half of those he invited showed up. Missing was Jefferson Standard's Howard Holderness, who had personally lobbied Woolworth's top management in 1960 to open its counter service to all. Holderness was out of town for a meeting at a private woman's college in Virginia, while W. C. Boren III sent regrets in a letter signed by his secretary. Blue Bell's E. A. Morris also reported a conflict.[3]

Schenck managed nonetheless to pull together a hardworking committee of citizens who turned to the challenge of opening restaurants, motels, bowling alleys, and other establishments to black patrons. The group was composed of eight whites and eight blacks, among them George Simkins Jr., George Evans, attorneys Major High and Kenneth Lee, community activist William Thomas, and the Reverend Otis Hairston. The white members included Ed Zane, who brought experience from his negotiations during the 1960 sit-ins; former city attorney Jack Elam; mayor pro tem William Trotter Jr.; banker Bland Worley, who represented the chamber of commerce; businessman Oscar Burnett; and the Reverend Harold Hipps from West Market Street United Methodist Church, whose congregation included many of the city's business leaders.

At its first meeting, the group chose Evans as chairman and Burnett as vice chairman. Over the coming months, the two men worked closely together, sharing some modest successes in bringing change to the business establishments around the city. Along the way, they became fast friends. They were a good match. Both were soft-spoken, very low-key. Burnett had a quick sense of humor that could defuse tense situations; Evans had the easy bedside manner of an experienced physician. They worked quietly and out of the public eye, often meeting in Burnett's office near A&T to avoid drawing attention to their work. For months, Burnett carried on a shuttle diplomacy between Evans, A&T president Lewis Dowdy, and Burnett's contacts within the business community.

Meeting one-on-one with the owners of restaurants and other establishments, they began to change minds and convinced some to step into the unknown. Progress came slowly. Many owners felt the same as Fred Koury, who owned the Plantation Supper Club on High Point Road. He told the newspaper: "I feel like it's time to integrate. The only thing that is worrying the operators is the thought of white patrons walking out when colored patrons walk in."

Public spirit was low. Six months after the demonstrations ended, in the fall of 1963, a piddling handful of Greensboro's voters—less than nine thousand of forty-five thousand registered—bothered to turn out for municipal elections. Those who did were angry. An ambitious $14.5 million bond issue, which included money for a new reservoir to extend the city's water supply for the next century, was soundly defeated. So were requests for funds for road construction and a host of other projects. The heaviest voter turnout came from the west side of town—the Hamilton Lakes and Starmount neighborhoods that had been annexed in 1957. West side residents seemed to want no part of the city and were unconcerned about its needs.

The defeat of the bond referendum gave some pause to people like chamber of commerce president John Harden. In a lengthy analysis published in the *Greensboro Daily News*, Harden said: "Greensboro also is on the verge of slipping into second class status (or less) among North Carolina municipalities. Through our apathy at the polls, we as much as turned to face backwards."[4]

The consequences of postponing the building of the city's infrastructure were ominous. So were the results in the voting for city council. On the same day the bond referendum was defeated, the only black member of the city council, a bail bondsman named Waldo Falkener, failed to win election to a third term by 167 votes. There would not be another person of color on the city council for six years.

If there was ever a time when city hall needed a voice from the black community, it was in the late 1960s, as Greensboro struggled with changes far more substantial than determining whether blacks and whites could be seated together in a restaurant. Open housing, school desegregation, and the violence and civil disorder following the assassination of Dr. Martin Luther King Jr. all eventually found their way back to city hall, which resisted change. Mayor Carson Bain's attempt to block a memorial march following King's death bred deep resentment in the black community. Later, the council virtually ignored a study by the Human Relations Commission recommending that it end discrimination in housing and waited instead for federal open housing laws to take effect. Meanwhile, the city school board dug in its heels and prepared for a legal fight with the federal government rather than move beyond token integration of city schools.

The most progressive voice in Greensboro during this period became the chamber of commerce, where there was deep concern about the city's negative image. Chamber executive William Little said Greensboro was faced with a choice, much the same as Dallas, whose reputation suffered following the assassination of president John F. Kennedy Jr. Greensboro had to change or die. "I was a real pariah there for a while," Little said, "but to me it was a survival issue. The community had to change in some positive way or slide back into a morass."[5]

During the second half of the 1960s, Little effectively organized a campaign to improve the city's reputation. He first recruited white businessmen to demonstrate their support for opening public accommodations by lunching with black companions at the best restaurants in town. The chamber announced a drive to recruit black-owned businesses for membership and within a few years had more than 360 on its rolls. A&T's Dowdy was named to the chamber's board of directors and was joined later by entrepreneurs such as Joe Dudley, who was just beginning to develop a national line of black beauty products.

When executives at the leading bank downtown began pushing in the late 1960s for the establishment of a downtown private dining club, or city club, organizers talked to leading businessmen around town. The last such club, the old M&M in the O. Henry Hotel, had degenerated into a watering hole known for bad food and a midday gin rummy game. A new crop of business leaders was talking about something more upscale and inclusive.

One of those contacted early was Mike Weaver, who had assumed leadership of his father's construction company. Weaver was interested, but he was determined that the club would have black as well as white members. Relatively young, and a decided junior member of the club's proposed board of directors, Weaver sought out attorney Sidney Stern Jr. for advice on how to ensure that the club was integrated. Stern was supportive and agreed to second Weaver's motion for an integrated membership if Weaver, in turn, would support Stern's desire to include women. The young Weaver braced for a fight, but to his surprise, the charter members approved a racially integrated membership almost without discussion. The board got bogged down on the question of whether full membership would be offered to women, but Stern and others overcame objections.[6] Racial integration of the club had its consequences: similar clubs in Winston-Salem and Charlotte, which limited membership to whites, refused to offer reciprocal privileges.

Much of the chamber program was orchestrated by staff member Hal Seiber, who worked virtually full-time at opening a dialogue between blacks and whites. He called his discussion groups "cells," just to call attention to them. Seiber revived the chamber's magazine, *Greensboro Business*, and created an eye-catching logo of "Nat Greene," a cartoon character whose image alternated between a dark and light complexion from issue to issue. In the summer of 1968, *Greensboro Business* carried an article written by the director of the A&T Student Union, who said, "Today, Negro youth is angry—angry about the inequities of the past, angry about the inequalities of the present, and angry about the prospects for the future."[7]

The sight of the clenched black fist illustrating the article shocked and infuriated some chamber members who did not believe the chamber should be involved in social issues. A few dropped their memberships. Among those who left the organization over objections to its new course was Ceasar Cone II, whose withdrawal cost the chamber seventeen thousand dollars.

On the other hand, the chamber's new role as a force for change was supported by businessmen who were succeeding an older generation. Among them were Thomas I. Storrs, then second in command at NCNB, whose offices were in Greensboro; Wachovia Bank's rising new state-wide banking executive Bland Worley; Al Lineberry, a successful funeral director, active churchman, and community leader; broadcaster Allen Wannamaker, whose radio station, WBIG, was owned by Jefferson; Hargrove "Skipper" Bowles, who was beginning his political career; and Ted Sumner, First Union National Bank's local executive. Except for Bowles, whose family had been in Greensboro since the Depression, all were relative newcomers to the city and had been involved in public affairs for ten years or less. It was an impressive array of talent that was not intimidated by the old lions. In the early summer of 1968, chamber president Wannamaker pushed the chamber one step further when he named Worley to lead a study of the method for electing the Greensboro City Council.

Worley's committee recommended the adoption of a new system that included four members elected from districts, two at-large members, and a popularly elected mayor. When the chamber's board of directors endorsed the plan in the fall of 1968, the public argument for change could easily have been written by George Simkins Jr. Speaking for the study committee, Ed Zane said that continuation of the present system of at-large election would "not likely produce representative government of the type expected by contemporary democracy."[8] The chamber endorsed legislation proposed for the 1969 General Assembly that would permit the city to adjust its charter and adopt a new plan for city government.

The day of the chamber vote, Simkins and Greensboro attorney Norman Smith filed a petition of seventy-five hundred names with the board of elections calling for a referendum on another plan. Their choice was a twelve-district plan that could be adopted immediately without further legislative action. "We've grown out of an age of paternalism," said Smith, "and into an age of participation." The board of elections set the date for a referendum in mid-December.

The two plans created a muddle of politics. While Simkins and the chamber agreed that a district plan would be best for the city—an unlikely alignment to begin with—they disagreed on the details. Simkins dismissed the chamber's 4-2-1 arrangement as a half measure. He believed that the same crowd of middle- and upper-class whites who lived in the city's northwest would continue to dominate council decisions if such a measure were adopted. At the same time, not all of the supporters of the twelve-district plan were totally satisfied with it. A twelve-member council would be too big, many said, and the plan did not provide for a city manager. Smith and Simkins argued that while the twelve-district plan had its flaws, it was the only option that could be adopted immediately under current law and thus without further legislative action. Any imperfections could be remedied later, they said.

Many simply opposed both plans. Mayor Carson Bain mounted an aggressive campaign against them, distributing literature suggesting Greensboro was on its way to the devil if ward politics were permitted to corrupt city hall. Circulars depicting corrupt ward heelers showed up in the community. "I think you'd sacrifice service for politics," Bain told a civic club in a speech a week before the chamber directors' vote.

State election laws required that the referendum be held within ninety days of the submission of the petition. As a result, voters went to the polls in the midst of preparations for the Christmas holidays, but they turned out in greater numbers than they had for any election in years. On December 14, 1968, the 12-1 plan was rejected by more than a two-to-one margin. The first round was over, but the contest would continue for the next fourteen years, with voters returning to the polls five more times.

———

"I'm afraid it's the only way we will ever get a Negro on the city council," an unidentified black man said of the district system after the defeat of the 12-1 district plan. In fact, that was not the case. Six months after the referendum, in the spring of 1969, Jimmie I. Barber was elected to the council, running sixth among the seven winning candidates. Five months later, Vance Chavis, who had placed just out of the money in the May election, was named to fill the unexpired term of William Folk, who had died unexpectedly. For the first time in the city's history, black representation on the council—about one-third—came close to equaling the proportion of the black population.

Barber was affable, likeable, and was known as "Bow Tie" Barber because of his penchant for colorful neckwear. He campaigned as "the people's man." Barber had come to Greensboro during the Depression to attend A&T on a basketball scholarship, despite the fact that he was only five feet five inches tall. He never really left. Barber entered military service during World War II and later earned a master's degree in education from Columbia University before returning to work at his alma mater. When he won his council seat, he was fifty years old and director of student housing.

He had a round face, a beaming smile, and would prove to be popular with white voters during his more than ten years on the council. Because of his abiding good nature, many passed him off as a lightweight. Simkins discounted his participation because he believed Barber was in the pocket of the white majority. Those who served with him said that was not the case. Barber proved he could stand his ground when needed. During his first term, at the height of tensions during a garbage strike, a labor organizer towered over him and issued a direct threat. "Barber didn't blink," recalled Jim Melvin. He said Barber firmly told the man where he lived and when he would be at home.

Chavis was older and a veteran of the early battles for a black voice in city affairs. He had helped organize the Greensboro Citizens Association that elected Hampton to the city council in 1951. Well before the 1960 sit-ins, he had organized boycotts of downtown theaters to protest segregated seating. He preferred to walk rather than submit to sitting at the back of a city bus. In the 1950s, he quietly and successfully lobbied the county commission to not replace "white" and "colored" signs when the courthouse was being renovated. His experience bridged a time when black subservience was required to a day when he could enter any establishment in town—a state of affairs he had not expected to witness in his lifetime.[9]

Chavis's politics was based on pragmatism: Hampton, Evans, and others who preceded him in city appointments had compromised, he readily admitted, but their small victories were better than none at all. He did not share Simkins's enthusiasm for the district system, but he supported it nonetheless.[10] Not long after Chavis joined the council, he pushed through a resolution in support of open housing. It had little practical effect—new federal laws superceded any council action—but it was an important political statement for its sponsor.

The presence of Barber and Chavis on the council made a difference, said the two mayors—Jack Elam and Jim Melvin—who presided over the council in those years. Barber and Chavis spoke up for the needs of black Greensboro, and the council responded. Elam described how the white and black council members worked together: "We would meet at somebody's house and just talk about some things to help us get along better with each other. For example, Jimmie named a street down there and said, 'I wish you would go out there and look at that, it badly needs to be paved.' Two months later, the thing was paved. We put it right on through, put it high on the priority list, and there it went. Water and sewer problems, basic traditional municipal problems, they were invaluable in helping us work out. They will never get enough credit for it."

Elam tried to persuade Simkins that election of black candidates under the at-large system proved that the system worked well, but he failed. "I have a hunch he didn't want to see my point," said Elam. "He wanted to continue to pursue whatever plan he had for the city, and he didn't want me messing around with it."[11]

Melvin had no better luck in convincing Simkins that black Greensboro was not getting shortchanged. To counter the widespread belief among African Americans that northwest Greensboro was favored over other sections of the city, Melvin asked city manager Tom Osborne to prepare charts and financial analyses to show that, in fact, the northwest received less than its share. According to the mayor's numbers, the city was spending more money in the southeast than in any other quadrant. Melvin said the people who should be most upset with the present system were those who lived in the northeast, blue-collar whites mostly, who had less representation than blacks. Eventually, the southwest and northeast sections of the city would mobilize and join with Simkins in challenging the status quo.

Defenders of the traditional system like Melvin usually fell back on the argument that the most democratic council was one elected by all of the voters. They argued that a district plan would lead to a council caught up in horse trading and bickering over parochial issues rather than one that focused on what was best for the entire community.

Melvin seemed oblivious to the racial angles of the issue. There was nothing race-related about the need for a new sewer plant or adequate water supply for a growing city, the issues that concerned him most. He had grown up on the edge of the black community and had experienced more relationships with African Americans than most whites. While he had never joined a civil rights march, or even expressed much interest in the campaign that consumed the community in the 1960s, he had done his part as a council member to address issues that deeply concerned the black community, such as the problems with slum housing and inadequate medical care at Richardson Hospital. He stated with conviction that his father's death at the hands of two young black men never became a pivot in his thinking. In fact, the family did not oppose parole when that option became available to those convicted in Joe Melvin's death. (One of those convicted was ultimately released from prison and died soon after in an automobile accident. The second drew extended sentences due to infractions he committed as an inmate.)

"My debate with Simkins," recalled Melvin, "was that you spend the money where it is needed. You don't spend the money because it is allocated on a pro rata basis." He also argued that Osborne and his team at city hall were regarded as the best in the state and that city government was efficient and scandal-free. It did not make sense to Melvin to change something that worked so well.

"I said, 'Look, George, Greensboro has proven it will vote for qualified people.' I can show you in actual black and white facts where we take the four quadrants of the city, and there's one quadrant where we weren't spending money, the northwest," Melvin said. "He'd look at me and say, 'Yes, but black members are not making any decisions, and if black members aren't making any decisions, it is not a black folks' decision.' How are you going to argue with that?"[12]

For Simkins, the issue was not efficiency or financial parity. What was most important was how those who were making the decisions were chosen. "In order for any Negro to sit on the city council of Greensboro," Simkins once told a reporter, "he must now be subjected to the will of the double-standard people in other sections of the city. If it were not so tragic, it would be laughable to hear those who are now in power say that they represent the Negro ghettos as faithfully and well as they do the sections of the city where they live."[13]

For Simkins, it was wholly unacceptable for African Americans to be dependent on the whims of white voters. He had seen Greensboro go six years without a black council member in the 1960s, and in 1973, after the Reverend Prince Graves failed in an effort to replace the retiring Vance Chavis, African Americans had only Barber to speak for them. With the loss of one council member, they had gone from proportional to token representation.

––––––

After the first district system referendum failed, Simkins was philosophical about the outcome. He knew it had been a long shot but felt it was worth the effort. "We won't give up," he said. And he didn't. A year later, another plan was put to the ballot. This one—for eight districts and two at-large seats, with an elected mayor—was defeated by voters. In 1970, and again in 1972, two additional plans proposed for the city council to enact on its own failed to get a majority vote from the council, although voters approved the direct election of the mayor. Another effort arose in 1975, and it failed by a significant margin to win a majority.

The 1975 vote came on the same day as the mayoral election. After Melvin defeated councilwoman Mary Seymour in the most serious challenge of his political career, he said the outcome of the council reform plan was a signal that the people of Greensboro were happy with their government and that city hall therefore needed "to be very cautious in making any drastic changes."

Although reformers were stymied in Greensboro, changes were taking place elsewhere in the state. Raleigh exchanged an at-large system for district voting in 1973. In Charlotte, a groundswell of support for greater representation spearheaded by newly formed neighborhood organizations led to a referendum on that city's at-large system in 1977. Winston-Salem and Durham both had been governed by district governments for years.

When Simkins first proposed a district plan, he tried to cast it as an issue that cut across racial lines. "You can't tell me that the white people who live in the southwest section have been represented in anything," he said in 1968.[14] With each effort after 1968, his message penetrated a little deeper into other sections of the city that had not seen their residents elected to the council. In the fall of 1979, with the mayor and the downtown interests keen on building a civic center, Simkins tried to strike a bargain on behalf of the district system. He told Melvin he would throw his support behind the convention center in exchange for support for district elections. Melvin declined the offer, and the bonds failed. Melvin's only consolation was that support for the convention center was actually greater in the black precincts than in most of the white ones.

But the public mood was shifting. On November 9, 1979, with the city still on high alert in the wake of the Morningside shootings, a chamber of commerce survey of five hundred Greensboro households showed that nearly half favored a change in the election system. Among those most likely to support a change were voters who had moved to Greensboro from elsewhere. The only quadrant of the city where a majority remained in opposition was the northwest. Clearly, some change was going to be made. The question was when.

In the hours immediately following the Morningside shootings, Jim Melvin was concerned that the city would simply become unhinged. It had happened before. The A&T disturbance ten years earlier had led to three days of violence, with snipers firing at police and National Guardsmen patrolling the city in armored vehicles. That firestorm had risen from a spark far less threatening than what the city faced now. "This was an event that was not going to go away and had the possibility of changing the course of the history of the city," Melvin said. "At that point, we had visions of riots. We were really starting to prepare for what could be an all-out war."

Indeed, there were calls for vengeance the afternoon of the shootings from those whose neighborhood had been violated. As soon as he could, the mayor began making telephone calls to people around the city, starting with leading figures in the city's black community.

Reaching those he most wanted to see was not easy. The shootings occurred on the day of the homecoming festivities at A&T, one of the most important social events on the fall calendar for east Greensboro. As the marchers began gathering at Everett and Carver streets, many in the black community were preparing for the afternoon football game at the A&T stadium, where the Aggies were to play Tennessee State. The campus and its football stadium were only a few blocks from Morningside, but the news of the shootings took hours to penetrate the party atmosphere on campus. When Melvin did make contact, most of those he called came immediately. One of the last to arrive was Simkins, who stayed for the end of the game. He said later that the message he received did not convey the urgency of the mayor's call.

Melvin wanted everyone, especially those with a pulpit, to have all the available information. With few details yet available to him to explain how and why the tragic shooting had happened in Greensboro, he was in a tough position. At one point late Saturday afternoon, state representative Henry Frye asked why police had not intercepted the caravan of Klansmen they had under surveillance and whom they knew were armed. "Some guy got up and said any lawyer knows why [suggesting police had no cause to interfere]," recalled Frye, who later served as chief justice of the state supreme court. "I said, 'I am a lawyer, and a good one, and I don't know why.'"[15] The question would never be answered to his satisfaction.

The meetings produced at least some of what Melvin had hoped. The Reverend Otis Hairston, pastor of Shiloh Baptist Church, said, "I hope it won't go beyond this as far as violence is concerned and people keep their cool." Councilman Jimmie I. Barber asked those in Morningside to "allow cooler heads to prevail . . . and let justice prevail." At the same time, there was deep concern over the same question Frye had asked in the closed session. "We are very much concerned," said Simkins, "about the police department's failure to take more decisive action to prevent the senseless and brutal murders of innocent people."[16]

While Simkins, Frye, and others questioned the role of the police, they stopped short of embracing the conspiracy theories that soon came forth from Nelson Johnson, the community activist who had planned the anti-Klan march that provoked the incident, and others aligned with him in the Communist Workers Party (CWP), the new name of the Workers Viewpoint Organization. Johnson's movement into the radical politics troubled many of those who had known him since he was a student at A&T in the mid-1960s, when he had recruited students to register voters for Simkins and the NAACP. Early on, some leading black citizens had recognized his effective style and even encouraged him to run for public office. Johnson was not interested, and over the years he developed a disdain for politicians, whom he said were only persuaded by grassroots initiatives such as those he was most effective at organizing.[17]

Johnson preferred direct action. Some laid the troubles at A&T in 1969 to his interference in student elections at Dudley High School, which led to a dispute that spilled into the streets and onto the college campus. He had helped organize the Greensboro Association of Poor

People, and he had led a tenants' strike against the city's most notorious slum landlord. Johnson's early exposure as a demanding voice in the black community had served the traditional black leadership at one time. His confrontational style made Simkins's steady push seem almost benign.

By the late 1970s, Johnson had left mainstream politics and embraced a revolutionary approach espoused by the New Communist Movement and the radical labor movement. He now directed rhetoric he had once reserved for the white establishment at prominent leaders in east Greensboro. About a year before the shootings, Johnson accused wealthy African Americans who lived along Benbow Road of not being sympathetic with the needs of the poor. Johnson's words prompted the Reverend Howard Chubbs, the pastor at Providence Baptist Church and one of the leading religious voices in the community, to borrow a revolver he believed he might need to protect himself.[18]

Melvin did not know what to expect on Sunday, November 11, the day of the funeral for the slain demonstrators. CWP leaders had predicted as many as five thousand sympathizers would join in the procession that was scheduled to move through the black community on its way to a modest public cemetery on the city's east side. The negotiations between Johnson and Melvin over the terms for the march were unpleasant and tense. Johnson demanded that marchers be allowed to carry weapons. Melvin, his temper rising, flatly rejected such an idea. "No," Melvin said, "we're going to be the ones who have guns, and if you have any guns we're going to shoot you." It was finally agreed that those escorting the coffins could carry disabled firearms as a symbolic gesture and that the procession would follow a heavily guarded prescribed route.

Sunday, November 11, was cold and rainy. At best, about four hundred people showed up for the march that took place without incident along a corridor lined with police and National Guard troops. Most along the route stayed indoors or watched with curiosity from their front stoops. Ministers with churches near the scene adjusted the starting hour of services so their congregations could be clear of the area when the march began.

While the city appeared calm, more than seventeen hundred calls were received over a period of three days at a rumor control center set up by local government. Police made seventeen arrests on weapons charges after stopping two caravans of CWP sympathizers on their way into the city. Inside Greensboro, there was peace. "These three groups,"

Melvin said years later, referring to the communists, the Klan, and the neo-Nazis, "are against everything that this community officially and unofficially stands for. The reason that this community held together is because of that."[19]

Three months after the shootings almost to the day, Melvin and Tom Osborne were standing in the law library on the east side of the second floor of the city's municipal building. The day was windy, and the temperature was hovering around thirty. The large windows gave them a clear view of Greene Street, where a parade of marchers was headed south toward the Greensboro Coliseum. Greensboro was again under a state of emergency. This time, five thousand had turned out. The shootings of November 3 had become a rallying point for civil rights and leftist organizations of virtually every stripe, which laid aside their differences for a display of solidarity against the Klan. Melvin's lasting memory of that afternoon was the image of bright red banners carried by a handful of communists moving down Greene Street. He had never imagined such a sight in Greensboro.

The day before, on February 1, the bright lights of national television had also focused on Greensboro. National civil rights figures and others gathered to commemorate the twentieth anniversary of the sit-ins at the Woolworth lunch counter in a program that had risen from the ashes of November 3. After the shootings, Eugene Pfaff at the Greensboro Public Library had called Hal Seiber, who was then on the administrative staff at A&T. The former chamber executive had organized small February 1 events in previous years, and Pfaff said the twentieth anniversary should be something special. Seiber called community leader Shirley Frye, who signed on to help, and together they produced a weeklong series of commemorative events. It all began with "Equality Sunday," on which ministers all across the city preached on the theme, and it culminated February 1 with a day of speeches, reunions, national media attention, and a citywide pealing of church bells.

One of the focal points of the celebration was a breakfast at the Woolworth lunch counter, where the determination of four A&T freshmen had launched a nationwide movement. The four were middle-aged now and showing signs of gray. They ate a symbolic meal where once they had been denied a simple cup of coffee. Later in the day, U.S. ambassador Andrew Young spoke on the A&T campus, as did Mary Berry, a former U.S. assistant secretary of health, education, and welfare. The Greensboro four were shuttled from one venue to another before a closing reception at the end of the day. In mid-afternoon, a state historical marker was unveiled on Elm Street.

Melvin made an appearance on behalf of the city before the television cameras at Woolworth's. He had walked the two blocks from the municipal building with the city's public safety director, Hewitt Lovelace, and Osborne, who was looking a little bulkier than usual. Once Melvin's appearance on NBC's *Today* show concluded, the three returned to Osborne's office, where the city manager removed a bulletproof vest he was wearing beneath his shirt.

Melvin was surprised as Osborne peeled out of his body armor, even though he knew as well as anyone that the weeks since November 3 had been filled with potential danger. Police had delivered a protective vest to Melvin the night of the shootings, but he had never put it on. It lay unused on the floor of his car. He had taken precautions to protect his family following calls like the one taken by his son Taylor, then only ten, who was told that his father would never get home alive that day. For about a month, a police officer was stationed near the Melvins' home. Nonetheless, Osborne's precautions were both a surprise and a troubling reminder that the city remained in the whirlwind created by November 3.

From the beginning, Melvin's strategy had been to distance Greensboro from the tragedy that had unfolded on the city's streets. It was an effort doomed to fail. There was no way to remove the dateline from what was clearly an international news story. The only break that had come Greensboro's way was the shift in world attention on November 4, when Iranian students took over the U.S. embassy in Tehran. The Iranian hostage crisis dominated the world news in the coming year, along with the eruption of Mount Saint Helens in the state of Washington and summertime race riots in Miami.

Melvin tried to convince reporters that what had happened in Greensboro was not a racial incident, since four of the five killed were white. Rather, the incident was a clash of political ideologies. The *Carolina Peacemaker* endorsed the same theme in an editorial headlined "Greensboro Massacre." The paper said: "It was not a black-white issue. It was a red-white issue." Nelson Johnson and others would also later blame the characterization of the shootings as a race-based conflict for confusing the issue and diverting attention from what they considered to have been a conspiracy orchestrated by the textile interests to end their efforts to organize workers.

Melvin's attempts to deflect the story from Greensboro were frustrated by gaffes at city hall that further damaged the city's reputation. A federal judge delivered a humiliating defeat with an order to make the Greensboro Coliseum available for the February 2 anti-Klan rally after it became clear that coliseum manager James Oshust had attempted to prevent the march organizers from using the hall by scheduling a competing event of dubious authenticity. Oshust apparently acted on his own, but once his efforts were uncovered, city hall mounted a defense on his behalf. There were also red faces after police officers were discovered impersonating reporters to gain admittance to a march organization meeting. Public Safety Director Lovelace said such deceptions were not authorized.

November 3 and its aftermath was opening old wounds. A few days before the February 1 ceremonies, A. S. Webb, a black banker and former chair of the city's Human Relations Commission, said the denial of the coliseum for the anti-Klan rally was an "outrage" that showed "the urgent need for a change in the method of electing members of our city council."[20]

Years later, Melvin said he knew nothing of Oshust's shenanigans and recalled arguing vigorously that the coliseum should be open for use by the marchers. He said there was deep concern at city hall that the arrival of political activists from around the country could produce a politically volatile mix. "We were petrified," recalled Melvin. "There were a lot of people in this world who hated communists, who wanted no part of communism, and here we were going to have a big communist demonstration down our street. All you needed was to have someone set off one bomb, one stick of dynamite, one hand grenade."[21]

The night before the march began on Saturday morning, police checked every manhole and sewer drain along the 3.8-mile route that began at the city's aging War Memorial Stadium, passed by A&T, wove through downtown, and ended at the coliseum. Melvin and others worried about trouble there, and as a further precaution, police posted undercover officers as restroom attendants.

"It was not a real happy time," Melvin said. "But I didn't have time to lick my wounds, feel sorry for myself, or check my systems, because Tom and I felt that the very reputation of our town was at stake. For whatever reasons, maybe it was meant for me to be there when all this happened. I did have experience. I am not saying I deserve the credit for getting through this mess, but what if you had a brand new mayor? When they bring a bulletproof vest out and suggest you wear it, the job takes on a different light."[22]

The trial of six Klansmen and neo-Nazis who were accused of the murders of the five demonstrators killed on November 3 began in late summer 1980 with the selection of a jury chosen from the largest pool of prospects ever called. Susan Melvin, the mayor's wife, was stunned to find that she was on the list. She reported for duty but was excused. On the night of her first day in the jury selection process, the family received yet another threatening telephone call.

It took a month of jury selection before the trial opened on August 4. Testimony continued for more than two months. From the display of evidence and the compelling action captured on videotape by television news cameramen, the conviction of the defendants appeared a certainty. The prosecution labored through tedious testimony tracing lead fragments and bullets back to the weapons that had fired them. An FBI sound specialist analyzed the sequence of shots and their sources. The defense argued that their clients had simply fired to protect themselves (the twelfth shot was clearly identified as coming from a demonstrator's handgun), although under cross-examination their testimony generally fell apart. The defendants' descriptions of events failed to match the recorded evidence. The jury began deliberations on November 10. The not-guilty verdicts returned November 17 were as stunning as the events themselves.

Melvin had just finished a city council meeting and was waiting for news from the courtroom in an office at city hall. He and Tom Osborne had been talking about the day being a good one for a verdict—cold and rainy, the kind of night to keep people indoors—when a police officer alerted them to the jury's decision. Osborne slumped into a chair and uttered a curse; Melvin was virtually speechless.

Once again, the city went on alert. Melvin got on the phone and called his contacts around the city, especially in the black neighborhoods, and then made sure his family was safe. His wife, Susan, was on her way back to Greensboro, and the boys were at home with a babysitter. Mindful of the hate calls that his family had received a year earlier, he called the sitter and asked her to take his sons home with her. Then he got ready for a press conference. Reporters were not quite as hostile as they had been a year before. Some were more familiar with Melvin and Greensboro than they were in 1979. Melvin fielded the questions and at one point spoke of his own astonishment at the decision, a comment that drew some criticism from those who said he had no business de-claring his opinion. He returned to his office and began to prepare for two television appearances. The first was scheduled for that evening on ABC News's *Nightline* show with Ted Koppel. For better or worse, Mel-vin was going to be Greensboro for millions of people all around the globe who knew nothing about his hometown.

Melvin had appeared twice before on Koppel's show. This time would be a real test. Koppel asked how Melvin could have let such a verdict come from a court in his town. The question had been preceded by the news tape of armed Klansmen firing into the crowd at Morningside Homes. Koppel's disbelief at the verdict was evident. "That's a fast ball," Melvin said later. "I figured I was Casey at the bat and I had one swing, so I basically filibustered. I sort of gave a civics lecture about belief in the jury system, and if you do believe, you have to ask twelve people who saw the evidence, not me." He continued by telling Koppel, "I didn't see all the evidence, and I might have some personal views, but I don't think you want justice to be dealt out by one person's views." Koppel re-sponded, "Mr. Mayor, I apologize for asking that question."[23]

"Ninety-five percent of the people in Greensboro didn't know why that happened in Greensboro and had no part in it and wanted no part in it," said Melvin. "This community, unjustly, got unbelievable bad publicity it didn't deserve."

Susan joined him at the station, and the two finally got home around I AM. The phone did not stop ringing until after 2, when Melvin finally crawled into bed. He was up again at 6 AM for Lee Kinard's *Good Morn-ing* show at WFMY-TV. He knew this would go more easily. Later that day, the mayor did a live radio show on WEAL, a station with a black au-dience, where most of the callers were "pretty negative," as host Ty Miller later described them. "They were still in shock. I'd have to say Melvin did a good job of directly responding to their questions. He sounded like a mayor who felt his city would pull through. But he sugar-coated the city too much for that audience."[24]

A little more than a week later, the *Greensboro Daily News* began pub-lication of a series of articles about leadership in the city. The finding pronounced on the first day was that the city lacked leadership, and the writer lamented the missing "progressive buccaneers" like Julian Price who made their mark with grand gestures and reshaped the sky-line. What was required on the night of November 17, however, was not boldness, but understanding. No one was more qualified to talk about that before a national audience than Melvin, who performed with confidence, compassion, and integrity. The same newspaper series ranked Melvin as the most influential man in Greensboro.

Greensboro's ordeal was not over. The families of the dead had filed a $48 million civil suit against the city, Melvin, certain police officers, as well as Klansmen and neo-Nazis. A federal investigation also was mounted, and nine of the Klansmen and neo-Nazis were indicted on a series of charges that mainly revolved around their having violated the civil rights of the demonstrators. On April 15, 1984, the jury in the federal trial found the defendants not guilty. Six years after the shootings, on November 6, 1985, the civil suit was settled. A jury decided that the police commander on duty November 3, 1979, a Greensboro detective, his informant, and four Klansmen and neo-Nazis were liable in one death. All the other defendants, including Melvin and the city of Greensboro, were released from the suit. As part of the settlement, the city's insurance carrier agreed to pay $351,500 to the estate of Michael Nathan, one of those killed, as well as its share of the damages lodged against the police officer. The civil proceeding also produced no evidence of a conspiracy involving city officials and private corporate interests. For Melvin, the testimony and evidence reaffirmed his belief that the tragic affair was the result of radical political groups whose rhetoric escalated to violence with Greensboro suffering from the resulting conflict as much as any of the victims.

———

Years later, Melvin said that the turn of events shattered any plans he had for his final term. Any new initiatives were swept off the table: "We were just working to keep the doors open. It took a year out of this community's life."[25] He had agreed to run again in 1979 because of his involvement in projects such as the convention center that he had hoped would cap his career at city hall. That disappointment, followed by the strain of November 3 and its aftermath, left him more than ready to leave office at the end of his term. A friend, Florence Gatten, said she had never seen Melvin so low: "We had a confluence of the defeat of the convention center and the very aggressive attack by [mayoral candidate] Sol Jacobs that really hit Jim in his heart about questioning whether he did know what was best and did he make the wrong decision."[26]

When he announced his decision to leave office at the end of his term, Melvin had spent more time in office than any previous mayor—long enough to be the senior mayor among the state's largest cities. The city of Raleigh had been through four mayors while Melvin was in office. Charlotte was about to elect its third.

Ten years at city hall had changed Melvin. He compared the job to playing center on a professional football team: he was the man who was sure to take a hit on every play. "I had someone say to me one time," Melvin related later, "'Jim, you used to be a real nice fellow. Now, you go into a room and you've got your guns blazing.' In this business, if you are not prepared for that, then you get beat up so bad you can't get anything done."[27] Yet more than twelve years in public office had kept him trim: at forty-seven, he was a dozen pounds lighter than when he took office. There was a slight trace of gray in his hair, which he had finally allowed to grow beyond the buzz-cut length he wore when he left the army.

In spite of all the troubles, Melvin believed Greensboro was in good shape. The city's industrial base appeared strong, and new companies were moving in. The prospect of the new sewage treatment facility was enough to convince a major manufacturer, Procter and Gamble, to put a plant on the north side of the city. There also were stirrings of commercial development downtown around Southern Life Insurance Company's new office building on Elm Street, which adjoined a new luxury hotel. In a short time, downtown would have cranes lifting materials into the first new high-rise office buildings in nearly twenty years.

Yet the issue of how the members of the city council were to be elected lingered. It would not be easy to resolve.

Chapter 13

Restore the Luster

IM MELVIN was not even halfway through his first term as a member of the city council in 1969 when he declared that he would not run for reelection. By announcing his decision when he did, just prior to a referendum on a ward system vote in 1969, Melvin said, he was free to express his opposition to the proposed changes. More than a decade later, the question remained high on the public agenda, only now the lines were even more firmly drawn, and the urgency for change was creating deep divisions within the city.

In the intervening years, the city had tinkered with the charter. In 1972, it was adjusted to allow for the direct election of the mayor. In 1978, the citizens of Greensboro also voted in favor of the direct election of the city school board. However, each successive attempt to extend direct representation to districts or wards in the city was defeated. The tide was clearly running with those who favored change. With each referendum, the margin narrowed. The May 6, 1980, referendum for a plan with six districts and three members elected at large failed by only 304 votes out of more than 22,500 cast.

This 1980 referendum appeared to be the best effort to achieve a compromise. The ballot initiative had been proposed by the chamber of commerce, which had reopened the issue in the fall of 1979 just as George Simkins Jr. began collecting names on a new ballot petition for a seven-district plan. With sentiment clearly trending in Simkins's direction, chamber leaders met with the city's most influential black political leader to hammer out a 6-3 plan. In January 1980, the chamber board of directors endorsed the report of its study group and called for the council to schedule a referendum. It was set for May 6.

The coalition behind this effort was unlike any that had preceded it. The chamber leadership under president Harold O'Tuel, a Burlington Industries vice president, coordinated a campaign that included support from Simkins, the Citizens for Representative Government under neighborhood leader Carolyn Allen, and Sol Jacobs. There also were newcomers from neighborhoods on the city's south side, including Lonnie Revels, a small businessman and Lumbee Indian, and William J. Burckley, the president of the Glenwood Neighborhood Association.

Neighborhood groups like Burckley's were the outgrowth of a new political activism that had given rise to change in many American cities. Private citizens were coming together to challenge city hall on local issues, and coalitions of such groups already had reshaped how citizens elected their local leaders. In Charlotte, for example, citizen anger over a combination of school busing and a city decision to remove old trees along a shaded thoroughfare brought together citizens' groups that unseated an at-large city council.

Allied against the ward system in Greensboro, and in each of the cities, were the same interests: the business leaders and conservatives who had grown comfortable with their easy access to city hall. In Greensboro, Charlie Phillips Jr., a former councilman, led the opposition to the May 1980 referendum. His group was called Save Our City.

Melvin did not get out front in the 1980 campaign, but he clearly preferred the status quo, as did a majority of the council. Melvin prided himself on being able to talk to anybody, anywhere. He saw no reason for districts and told leaders in the black community he could represent them as well as anyone else in town, perhaps better.

On the eve of the election, Save Our City published a full-page advertisement in the *Greensboro Daily News* that read, in part, "With the proposed theoretical ward system, you only get to vote for half of the Greensboro city council. We know what the at-large system has done for the city of Greensboro. We don't know what the theoretical ward system will do."[1]

A map of returns from the election showed Greensboro was becoming increasingly divided between the haves and have-nots. It was a division that had long concerned Melvin, who had spoken out five years earlier in an effort to encourage citizens to become more involved in community affairs. District election of council members was not what he had in mind, however.

Melvin and those opposing change argued that Greensboro had enjoyed sound, clean government, and there was no need to "fix what isn't broken." That argument was heard most often among the slim majority

that was becoming increasingly isolated in the city's comfortable suburbs in the northwest. Those favoring change were blue-collar whites in
the southwest and northeast and blacks in the east and southeast. Both
groups argued that their voices were seldom heard and their needs went
unmet. The difference in sentiment was seen in the ballots cast at the
precinct on the A&T campus, where voters were twenty-to-one in favor
of the district plan, while voters at Irving Park School were five-to-one
against it.

The narrow margin of the May 1980 vote left both groups unhappy.
To punctuate his disgust with the chamber's role in promoting the
district election referendum, Jefferson-Pilot Corporation[2] CEO Roger
Soles pulled his company out of the chamber. The decision to withdraw
Jefferson's membership was announced on the afternoon of the voting,
before the polls closed but late enough in the day so as not to influence
the outcome. Carolina Steel Corporation and Guilford Mills Corporation followed the Jefferson example within two days. These high-profile
companies subsequently returned to the chamber, but the message had
been delivered: Greensboro's corporate leaders liked things the way they
were.

––––––

"If you liked Jim Melvin," lawyer Henry Isaacson said as Melvin's successor prepared to take office in November 1981, "you'll love John Forbis." As for Forbis himself, he cast the line a bit differently. "If you like
Greensboro like it is, I'm your man," he said.[3]

Indeed, Forbis and Melvin shared much in common. Both came
from families with deep roots in Greensboro. Forbis could trace his lin-
eage back nine generations to the colonial era, before there was even a
Greensboro. Both had come from modest circumstances and as teenagers had worked in their fathers' businesses. Forbis had succeeded his father in the funeral business. Both were likeable, eager civic workers who
had established their credentials with service in the Jaycees. Forbis had
chaired the GGO in 1972. And both were popular with voters. In Forbis's
first race for the city council in 1973, he placed third in the field of seven.
He later led the ticket and served two terms as mayor pro tem. Most important in the election of 1981, Forbis, like Melvin, was a champion of
the status quo.

Forbis declared his intention to run soon after Melvin announced
early in 1981 that he would not seek another term. Melvin's old nemesis,
Sol Jacobs, also declared his candidacy, but Forbis's most threatening

opponent was businessman Vic Nussbaum, another popular member of the council. The defining issue appeared to be Nussbaum's interest in bringing district elections to the city council. Nussbaum pitched a district plan to the council in the summer of 1981, but it was set aside in favor of one proposed by Melvin.

While Forbis's political track resembled Melvin's trek through the Jaycees, Nussbaum had come to power in the city by a different route. A steady, determined businessman who tried various ventures, he was a successful wholesale food distributor. He had a deep interest in Greensboro, his home for more than thirty years, and had invested time and money in organizations interested in the arts as well as social concerns. His base was decidedly within the groups that saw that change as inevitable or that had been ready for something new for years.

Melvin was in a quandary. He knew, and liked, both candidates. He was especially close to Nussbaum. Both Forbis and Nussbaum had been steady and supportive members of the city council. Melvin carefully kept his preferences to himself throughout the campaign; however, a number of his former allies, such as Isaacson, helped put the campaign together for Forbis.

The retiring mayor did make an attempt to find a compromise on district elections. After years of opposing a district plan, Melvin said he was willing to support what he called a "modified ward system" in an effort to resolve an issue that had become a drain on the council's energy and attention. "If you are going to spend half of your time on this issue," Melvin said later, "you are not going to get anything done for the city."[4] But Melvin's plan, the old 4-2 model that had been rejected before, satisfied no one. Melvin made speeches on behalf of his proposal, which was put on the November ballot, where it was overwhelmingly defeated. The *Greensboro Record* applauded Melvin's desire to settle the issue but concluded that his proposal had been salt rather than salve to the city's wounds.

—

As the election slate took shape, editorial writers said the city government Melvin was leaving to his successor would be an easy one to inherit. Those words were written before the fall municipal campaigns of 1981. The outcome left one of the victors—incumbent councilwoman Dorothy Bardolph—literally weeping for a city that had just elected an all-white city council, a majority of whose members, like Forbis, had campaigned on a pledge to keep city government as it was. Forbis, too, was troubled by the contentious campaign, and some years later he said that when the votes were counted, he realized he had been elected mayor of a city that was more racially divided than it had been at any time since Reconstruction.[5]

The outcome was the result of a white backlash against a new election strategy that had been adopted by Simkins, the Greensboro Citizens Association, and other political action groups. After failing in four attempts to persuade voters to approve a change in city government by referendum, Simkins decided in 1981 that the alternative was to elect a city council that would be more likely to make a change without calling for a vote of the people. Thus, in October 1981, Simkins directed that the endorsement of the influential Greensboro Citizens Association go to a slate of council candidates who favored change. With this organized support, the Simkins slate moved easily into the runoff election.

Simkins's efforts provoked a storm of response from white conservatives. Altogether, three organizations rose up to support an opposing slate of candidates who promised not to make any changes in the city's election format. Money seemed to be no object. The fever was high. Former mayor Jack Elam, who helped organize one group called Stand Up for Greensboro, said some years later he was appalled at the openly racist cheers he received from unidentified callers who telephoned his home.[6]

The status quo candidates succeeded in claiming four of the council's six seats in the November election and electing Forbis mayor over Nussbaum. The two candidates from Simkins's slate who survived were Bardolph and newcomer Jim Kirkpatrick, a stockbroker who was making his second bid for office. Both of them had worked to develop broad community support. "I felt alone," Bardolph, a college professor and neighborhood organizer, told the newspaper. "It was the dirty campaign that got me down."[7]

Simkins was equally upset. "Racism is alive, well and flourishing in Greensboro," he told a reporter. Nussbaum, a district plan champion, said, "Elam's committee ended up proving exactly the opposite of what they intended. They proved you need a district system."[8]

———

Attorney R. Cameron Cooke was one of the Stand Up for Greensboro candidates elected in 1981. A political newcomer, Cooke was in private practice and had been moderately active in the community. He was one of the early graduates of the Leadership Greensboro program, a chamber-sponsored tutorial aimed at producing new leaders of civic and community affairs. In the weeks after the municipal election, as Cooke began to get his feet on the ground with his new responsibilities, he talked about his concern for the city's racial health with a fellow Episcopalian, an African American named Charles Fairley, a Greensboro native who had returned to his hometown in 1980 to enjoy retirement. Fairley shared the conversation with one of his neighbors, Roy D. Moore, the chairman of the physical education department at A&T, whose connections within the community were considerably better than Fairley's. As the two talked, they agreed that it was time to get a group together to discuss Greensboro's deepening racial divide. They considered, and rejected, an informal, social setting. What was needed was something more substantial.

"The best way to solve a problem," Moore said some time later, "is to get the people who are involved to sit down and not sit just to decorate the mahogany, but make a contribution." He needed help, however, and he called upon Melvin, as well as Forbis, who agreed to help assemble an informal ad hoc committee. Melvin hoped the group could find a common ground on the representation issue: "Hopefully, they could come up with a recommendation that everybody could get behind and get this issue off the agenda."[9]

In February 1982, two dozen men and women, whites and blacks, gathered in a meeting room at the Greensboro Coliseum to talk. On hand to work with them was David DeVries of the Center for Creative Leadership and a colleague, Robert Kaplan. "We've got a problem in this community," Melvin told DeVries when he recruited him to facilitate the meetings on a pro bono basis. DeVries brought in Kaplan, who had experience in facilitating multiracial discussions.

The group was later described as a Noah's Ark of Greensboro. There were two ministers, the chancellors from the two state university campuses, two members with city council experience, two former presidents of the chamber of commerce, two senior corporate executives, two former members of the Human Relations Commission, and so on. Members' ages ranged from thirty-two to past sixty. Only Melvin had been publicly identified with any position on issues, such as district elections. All were committed to the community, however. Organizers bypassed the best-known personalities, whose participation was sure to draw attention. Simkins was not asked to join the group, nor was Elam or Jacobs. And Melvin withdrew after the first meeting because of his own high profile. "I was trying to play it straight," Melvin said later.

The early sessions were unusually polite, and DeVries said he realized, "One of the things we had to learn was how to put disagreement on the table." With help from Kaplan, the discussion moved more to the point. "There was a lot of suspicion about the motives [of the group]," recalled Cooke. As members talked, it became clear to him that a lot of the anger and resentment in the community was directly traceable to inequitable representation. "Blacks resented [the at-large election system] because they had to go to the whites and ask for votes."[10]

Earl Jones, a black man in his early thirties who worked with repeat criminal offenders, was among the most outspoken members. When he finally unleashed his anger, much of it sprang from the feeling among black citizens that they had no standing in making decisions about the future of the community. Sitting across the table from him was businessman William Hemphill, the CEO of United Guaranty Corporation, who absorbed what Jones and the others had to say. Quiet, deliberative, and thoughtful, Hemphill easily was the ranking corporate executive among the group. His credentials made him the most likely object of Jones's wrath, but if so, it was misplaced. Hemphill already favored a district plan and had privately given it support for some time. "I was looking at it from a very practical point of view," recalled Hemphill, who had grown up on the poor side of the tracks in south Greensboro. "If we didn't [do something], these things would fester. Imagine if you had been born black, and you lived down there, and you never had a chance of sending a representative to the city council. I expect over a period of time you would get madder and madder or say, 'To hell with it.' One of the things we have wrong with Greensboro now is we have too many people who say 'To hell with it' all over town."[11]

In time, the group became more comfortable, and discussions ranged across a number of issues, but district elections remained a primary focus. The consensus favored a district plan. Tendering ideas for the group to discuss was James Wright, the director of the city's Human Relations Commission, which had begun tinkering with various options. It was not until early summer, however, that the urgency of the discussion group's work began to increase. In mid-June 1982, the U.S. Justice Department rejected the city's plan to annex about ten square miles on the northern and western perimeter because, the agency said, the addition of nearly thirteen thousand new residents, most of whom were white, would dilute black voting strength.

The expansion of Greensboro's city limits was critical to the city's future. Without growth and new tax revenue, city budgets—and services

—would shrink, while taxes would continue to rise. The city council was faced with either finding a way to guarantee that the expansion would produce no loss of voting power to African Americans or challenging the Justice Department's decision in court. The latter option was not particularly attractive. Judicial sentiment had shifted in the 1970s, and decisions were falling in favor of those seeking direct representation. After more than a dozen years, the annexation decision became the checkmate that Simkins and the NAACP had hoped for when they had first proposed the district plan in 1968.

The work of the Dialogue Task Force, as the study group was now called, became critical. The group settled on a compromise plan that called for five districts, each of which would elect a representative, with three more council members elected at large. With five districts, at least two could have a majority black registration. In a nod to the sentiments of those favoring an at-large system, the plan specified that all the voters would have a hand in the election of at least one-half of the council. With agreement around the table, the members of the task force set out to sell it.

Cooke and Moore took the plan to Simkins. "He said he would agree," recalled Cooke, "if it was done by council and not referendum. I asked him if he wanted that in writing. He said my word was good enough for him." Cooke also went to Melvin, and others. The plan was not what Melvin would have preferred, but he went along. "Enough of us came to the conclusion that it is not worth the fight," Melvin said.

Cooke's toughest challenge was to persuade those who had won election with the ardent support of the Stand Up for Greensboro ticket. If they accepted his plan, they would be reneging on a campaign pledge. Before he approached those members, he signed on Dorothy Bardolph, who put aside her own support for a six-district plan to accept the alternative. Councilman Jim Kirkpatrick was an easier sell. He had not staked himself out, and he understood the difficult position the city was in: the annexation was more important, he concluded, than fighting the ward system. Cooke then went to the mayor. Forbis was wary, but he eventually came around. "Do you really think it is the thing to do?" Forbis asked Cooke. Assured it was, Forbis agreed to persuade others that the city might finally be able to settle one of the most divisive and longstanding issues in local affairs.

Agreement was not guaranteed among some enthusiasts of introducing a district system. There were those, like Bardolph and Carolyn Allen of the League of Women Voters, who favored six districts. They saw the plan as one designed to undermine their work. At a public hearing in mid-November, some of that frustration was expressed, but sentiment clearly ran in favor of the five-district option. The broad support for the new proposal, which came from everyone from former mayors Elam and Melvin to Simkins and the NAACP, was convincing. "You have the opportunity to do what is right simply because it's right," the chairman of the city's Human Relations Commission said. "You have the opportunity to restore the luster to the Gate City of the South."[12]

A month later, the council adopted the plan, changing nearly sixty years of electoral history. There was no outrage; there were no crowds of protest. Less than twenty people attended the meeting that Charles Fairley called "historic." One speaker, who insisted on being heard, reminded the council members they were breaking the pledge they had made a year ago. "Yes, ma'am," Kirkpatrick responded later. "We're fixing to break a promise that we made in the campaign. We've got to choose between a campaign promise and an oath we took up here with our hands on the Bible." The final vote was unanimous.[13]

In 1983, thirty-three candidates, the largest field ever, filed to run in the first election under the new district system. Most of the attention was focused on the districts where black voters were in the majority. In District 1, the competition was between Earl Jones and Cleveland Sellers, a veteran of the civil rights movement of the 1960s. Jones won that race, while in an adjoining district, Katie Dorsett, another black candidate and an active community worker, was elected. Lonnie Revels became the first council member from southwest Greensboro to be elected in decades. Voters elsewhere in the city seemed oblivious to the broken campaign promises of the incumbents. Every incumbent who ran for reelection was elected, and the decision to adopt the new election plan without a referendum never became an issue. Forbis was reelected for a second term.

The changes wrought by district representation were apparent from the start. There were new faces in public life. New voices were being heard at city hall. After the first blush of interest wore off, however, local electoral politics settled into a largely parochial pattern, with district issues often at the fore of debate. Longer-range problems, such as waste disposal and water needs, were shunted to the side. Those who lobbied the council on behalf of business interests as part of the good-old-boy network that had prevailed for years simply shifted strategies. Attorney Henry Isaacson, for example, who appeared frequently on behalf of developers and others, made sure he had the interested district representative on his side before he made his first appearance before the council.[14]

Before Simkins died in 2001, he saw the city council elect and re-elect black members. Some candidates became quite secure in their districts. Jones served nine terms before losing his seat to a challenger; he then went on to win election to the state House. In the year of Simkins's death, a black woman, Yvonne Johnson, led the ticket as an at-large candidate and was named mayor pro tem. Melvin "Skip" Alston, whose early community involvement was in the NAACP, was elected to the board of county commissioners, where he subsequently was named chairman. State representative Alma Adams, who started her political career on the city council, became the chair of the county's legislative delegation in 2003, which included a new state senator, Katie Dorsett, who had also held her first elective post on the city council.

Melvin spoke at Simkins's funeral. Despite their differences over the years, the two had remained friends. They had seen one another for the last time only a few weeks before Simkins's death at an annual banquet celebrating racial unity sponsored by the local chapter of the National Conference of Christians and Jews. Melvin was leaving his table at the end of the program when he caught Simkins's eye. "I love you, you old reprobate," Melvin told his friend. "I love you, too," Simkins replied.

Reflecting on the fifteen years that the city spent wrestling with the issue of representation, Melvin said, "We were probably wrong to stand our ground as long as we did. Maybe in hindsight I should have been more proactive, but back in those days, the feeling was so strong in the community that it would have cost you your political career. It may have been right, but it would have been dead right." Melvin said he had missed the essence of Simkins's argument that no matter how equitable the distribution of money and services, the lack of blacks in the decision-making process was the paramount concern. "I missed it," he said. "I admit that. I kept trying to convince him we were doing the right thing. He didn't care [about my arguments]."

Greensboro was the last major city in the state to discard at-large elections in favor of district representation.

Chapter 14

A Bolt out of the Blue

It WAS A LATE afternoon in October 1983—Halloween, to be exact —when Cone Mills Corporation's chairman and chief executive officer, Dewey Trogdon, got a call from Ceasar Cone III, who told him that his father, Ceasar II, had sold his 12 percent share in the business that carried the family name. Trogdon was stunned; it was a "bolt out of the blue," he would later say. He and Ceasar II had talked only a few days before, and the elder Cone had said nothing about plans to sell his birthright, much less turn over more than a tenth of the ownership of the company to a stranger.

The buyer who had picked up Ceasar II's 600,000-share stake in the company for $30 million—$50.00 a share—was Howard A. "Mickey" Newman of Western Pacific Industries. Trogdon knew Newman, at least in passing. The two had shared a table the year before at the Mother of the Year Awards dinner in New York City. While Newman's company bore the name of a well-known railroad, its profits came from investments, not transportation or the sale of goods. The railroad had long since passed into other hands. Trogdon suspected Newman wanted Cone Mills's assets to parcel out and sell for handsome profits. It was a strategy Trogdon soon confirmed through a mutual friend, who aptly described Newman's plans: Cone would "lose a leg, but keep the shoe."[1]

With textile stocks depressed in the early 1980s, Cone Mills was a likely target for speculators. Only months before, Greensboro's Blue Bell Corporation had fended off a hostile takeover at about the same time of Carl Icahn's raid on Dan River Incorporated of Greenville, South Carolina. Icahn failed, but he was just starting a career as a corporate raider that would make him one of America's richest men, known for the popular 1980s line, "In this business, if you want a friend, get a dog."

A year before Icahn's move, West Coast financier David Murdock had taken over Cannon Mills in a $413 million tender offer, a deal that eventually turned sour for Cannon's workers after Murdock used the company's pension funds to finance yet another corporate takeover.

The Dan River raid had been fair warning to Trogdon and his board. After Icahn made his move, the Cone Mills leadership had inserted language into the corporation's bylaws—several "poison pill" changes, such as staggered board terms and preferred stock—to frustrate anyone with ideas like Icahn's. It was prudent strategy, and timely. In the weeks before Ceasar III's telephone call, Trogdon had seen some movement in the company's stock price. Share prices had begun to rise after bumping along in the high teens.

Someone was buying, but Trogdon did not know who. When Newman's Western Pacific declared to the Securities and Exchange Commission its intention to take over the company four days after Trogdon got word that Ceasar II had sold his shares, Cone Mills stock was selling for around $46.00 a share. Before sales were suspended on November 4, 1983, the price jumped another $6.50. By that time, Newman had acquired 333,000 shares, and with Ceasar II's interest in his pocket, he was now Cone Mills's largest shareholder.

Like many old firms, Cone Mills held assets that were not reflected in the market price of its stock. There was $90 million in reserves on the books from cotton purchases. Perhaps most inviting was another $40 million in land and buildings. Timber sales and development of residential lots by the company's Cornwallis Development Corporation had proved to be a virtual gold mine. In Greensboro alone, New Irving Park homesites sold for tens of thousands of dollars on land purchased for fifty cents an acre a generation earlier.

New Irving Park had followed a high-end complex of attached homes called Fountain Manor that had been profitable and even brought Trogdon some amusement. The project had originally been named "Watergate" after a water gate that had once been on the property. Ceasar II retired his plaque with the Watergate name and logo to a bottom desk drawer after president Richard Nixon made Washington, D.C.'s Watergate complex famous in the scandal that brought down his presidency.

The manufacturing side of Cone Mills held little interest for Newman, but if he had cared to investigate it, he would have found a company that was well-run, up-to-date, and producing profits. Since 1979, Trogdon had completed nearly $400 million in plant improvements, and he was moving to diversify production in advance of anticipated changes in a challenging and competitive global market. He had adjusted the company's corduroy line after a trip abroad convinced him that Cone Mills could no longer compete with fabric coming off looms in Poland and China. One of the first plants to close was the Revolution Mill in Greensboro. The company's oldest, it sat just down the hill from the functional, nondescript corporate offices on Maple Street on the north side of the city.

Trogdon ran a tight, lean operation, just like Ceasar II, Ben, Herman, Bernard, Ceasar, and Moses Cone had before him. He had assumed leadership of the company in 1979 following the retirement of CEO Lewis S. Morris, who was the first non–family member to lead the company when he took over in the mid-1960s. Trogdon had cut his teeth as a cost accountant and knew where to find money. If a project did not add to the bottom line, it was earmarked for oblivion.

He kept the overhead basic, simple. There were no squadrons of airplanes like those in a hangar at the Greensboro airport for Burlington Industries, an outfit that Trogdon's management team called "the Battleship." Cone executives flew commercial or, when there was a crowd or some urgency, on charters. The company's ethos also did not allow for a fancy headquarters, although plans for new corporate offices were on the drawing board when Ceasar II put the company in play. Some talk held that Ceasar II had made his decision to sell because of his objections to the new building. Those closer to him said he was not *that* capricious. For the time being, Trogdon shelved the plans for the new building.

Western Pacific's run on Cone Mills cut right to the heart of Greensboro's economy. No company was more a part of the city's heritage or its culture, nor was any as important to its financial well-being. Over the years, jobs at the Cones' mills, and profits from the company, had helped transform Greensboro from a mill village into one of the state's leading cities. Half of Cone's ten thousand employees drew paychecks at plants located in Guilford County. When the community came up short in fund-raising campaigns, such as the annual United Way appeal, Ceasar II and Ben often made up the difference. Moreover, the company was an extended family. Fathers, sons, wives, and their cousins enjoyed relatively secure jobs. It was a place where workers signed on for life.

Trogdon and Ceasar II knew one another well. Earlier in Trogdon's career, his office had been near that of Ceasar II, who used vigorous debate on virtually any subject to test the resolve of young executives. One debate that stuck with Trogdon was Cone's insistence that fluoride belonged in milk, not in the city's drinking water. After Trogdon became CEO, he often cleared his plans in advance with Ceasar II, the company's largest single shareholder. In recent years, he had talked with Ceasar II and his brother Ben, the surviving sons of founder Ceasar Cone, about the future of the company. One of the options the brothers had considered was a plan drafted by corporate counsel Jack Elam that called for the brothers to sell their stock to Cone Mills employees. Elam prepared several drafts of an agreement to accomplish that, but nothing came of his work.

The accomplishment that assured Trogdon's rise to the top of the company hierarchy was the turnaround he had engineered at Otto B. May Company in New Jersey, a Cone Mills subsidiary that produced dye for the textile industry. It had taken four years to overcome incompetent and dishonest management, frightful violations of health and safety laws, a fierce strike that met him when he arrived on the job, and simple waste, such as millions of gallons of expensive violet-colored dye that had hardened in the vats. (He later pulverized the dried dye and mixed it with other colors to produce olive drab, which was used to dye uniforms for the American and Israeli armies. For years, Trogdon thought he could detect a violet hue in the uniforms that he saw on soldiers featured on the evening news.) After Cone Mills sold May in 1979 at a profit, Ceasar II told Lewis Morris that Trogdon was the man to succeed him.

All of this history made Ceasar II's decision all the more surprising. He was turning over stock he had received upon his father's death in 1917, when he was nine years old, to someone who planned to dismantle what his forebears had taken ninety years to build. Why this unilateral move? Trogdon suspected it was Cone's attempt to make his estate more manageable, a theory Ceasar II later confirmed in a newspaper interview. Cone was seventy-five years old and facing his own mortality. Whatever his reasons, Ceasar II was not one to explain his actions. His son was not aware of what his father had done until the deal was complete. A few minutes later, Ceasar III, whom everyone called "C.C.," put in the call to Trogdon.

By the time Western Pacific's intentions became public, Trogdon was already building defenses and preparing a tough response. He had been in the trenches before, including some real ones in Korea, but his challenge was far greater and more complicated than anything that had faced his predecessors. Ceasar II, for example, had never closed a plant or personally fired a worker. When it came time to close the Revolution Mill, which was then run by Herman Cone Jr., Morris and Ceasar II had de-tailed Trogdon to convince Herman to take retirement before the plant was actually shuttered.

Trogdon's first call from Newman reached him in the New York offices of Salomon Brothers, an investment banking firm. The firm had helped prepare the changes in the bylaws that had been put in place ear-lier. All were now girding for a fight. Bankers from J. P. Morgan were brought in, along with a New York law firm known for its experience in spoiling takeover attempts. Meanwhile, Trogdon started compiling a war chest. In the three weeks between Halloween and Thanksgiving, he lined up letters of credit for enough cash to not only meet Western Pacif-ic's bid but exceed it if need be. He found banks eager to do business.

Cone was a good risk; its debt was low. NCNB's CEO, Hugh McColl, called on Trogdon in Greensboro and told him his bank was good for half of whatever the company needed. Trogdon settled on support from ten banks, with the North Carolina banks—NCNB, First Union, Wacho-via, and Northwestern, where Trogdon was a director—taking the big-gest share.

At the same time, Trogdon put together a committee of directors to arrive at a fair market price for the company. If the company was on the block, then everyone needed to know what it was really worth. Fifty dol-lars a share was a higher composite value than anything Cone had seen in a while, but Trogdon believed that even that figure was low. When he talked to Newman, he bluntly told him that he would never get Cone for that. As the committee worked, the stock began trading higher and higher. When it reached $55 a share, other large shareholders put their holdings on the block.

Trogdon saw several options for the company, all of which promised changes, some more profound than others. Newman could succeed in his takeover bid. Or Trogdon might find another buyer, such as Cone Mills's own management, to enter the bidding. The company could be put up for auction, and there was a chance of a merger. If Cone was to be combined with another company, Trogdon's choice was Springs Mills, a closely held company that was known for its home products, such as sheets and bedspreads, not fabric for apparel, which was Cone's primary stock in trade. He sounded out the Springs management, but it was clear they were not interested in taking on the debt load that such a merger would require.

This deal was not just about share prices, however. For Trogdon, the company's value rested on its relationship with its employees and its customers. As the board's options came into focus, he flew to San Francisco to talk to the owners of the jean maker Levi Strauss, Cone's largest single customer. The signature brand consumed more than 40 percent of the millions of yards of denim that Cone produced each year. At one time, Levi had taken as much as 60 percent of Cone's denim. He found the management anxious about the prospect of Cone's ending up in the hands of people they did not know.

In March 1984, the Cone board met to consider its choices. The most attractive offer was a management proposal to take the company private at $70 a share—higher than Newman was willing to go. At a total exchange of $420 million in debt and $45 million in new stock, it was an obligation greater than anyone in the old company or the current administration could consider comfortably. Yet despite dour warnings from Ceasar II that the deal was "just plain dumb,"[2] Trogdon believed he and his management team could make it work. In a meeting on March 26 that lasted only fifteen minutes, Cone's board accepted the management bid, and Cone Mills Corporation ceased operation as a public company. The only family member left on the board was Jeanette Cone Kimmel, the daughter of Ben Cone and the namesake for the company's large reservoirs just north of Greensboro.

Newman walked away even richer than he was before. In six months, he had made $23 million just by buying an old man's stock. Ceasar II watched with no regrets, even though most shareholders enjoyed a 50 percent premium he never received. He told his son that what he was paid for his shares was fair. "The only thing he said," C.C. said some time later, "was, 'Nobody in the family [who cashed out at a higher stock price] ever thanked me.'"[3]

Ceasar II was like that. He didn't explain, and he made his own path. And he was right to be concerned about his health: in November 1986, he entered the hospital for surgery after his physician found spots on his lung. At the time, Cone was at odds with the management at Cone Hospital, and he asked his doctor if the procedure could be done safely at Greensboro's Wesley Long Hospital. Assured it could, Ceasar II had the surgery performed there and subsequently returned home to recuperate. During his recovery, his condition worsened, and his nurse called for help. He was unconscious when he was moved from his home to Cone Hospital, which was nearby. When he was revived, he demanded to be taken to Wesley Long, which would have been his choice had he been awake when the ambulance arrived at his home. He was finally transferred, but Ceasar III later said he believed the delay in treatment complicated his condition. He died on November 14, 1986, leaving an estate valued at nearly $40 million.

At the time of the transition of Cone Mills Corporation from a public to a private company, the changes did not create any particular alarm in Greensboro. For the moment, the initial fallout was minimal. Only about a hundred salaried employees, from secretaries to mid-level managers, were offered early retirement as Trogdon began to trim costs and streamline operations. Plans for the new building began gathering dust.

The entire affair had been watched closely, to be sure, but in the end the change was taken in stride and seen as a victory of local management over the out-of-towners. Yet the reshaping of the corporate structure at Cone and Blue Bell was the first troubling indicator of a shift in Greensboro's economic foundation. Textiles had been the bedrock of the city's economy and had remained solid for nearly a century through wars, good times, and financial upheaval. But the cracks that were beginning to appear were as inevitable as the flight of the textile industry from New England to the South that had created Cone Mills and the southern textile industry nearly a century before.

Chapter 15

A Different Era

As THE CONE Mills executives sorted out the future for their company, analysts from the Battelle Memorial Institute of Columbus, Ohio—the folks who pioneered digital recordings and photocopying—were completing a study of Greensboro's prospects in the increasingly competitive world of economic development. They found there was much to like about the city. Rand McNally's 1981 edition of the *Places Rated Almanac* ranked Greensboro first in the nation among medium-sized metropolitan areas. "The typical response of employers," the report said, "was 'we sometimes have trouble getting [employees to move] here, but once we get them here they don't want to leave.'"

There was more. Wages at local businesses and industries were good, although perhaps too good in comparison to labor costs in competing locations. Taxes were stable, municipal debt was low, and the city's central location made it a superb regional distribution center. In addition, the industrial base, anchored by Fortune 500 companies such as Cone Mills, Burlington Industries, Lorillard, Gilbarco, and Blue Bell, was to be envied. There also were divisional offices for Ciba-Geigy, a worldwide chemical firm; Volvo–White Truck Corporation, an expanding newcomer; and Western Electric and Bell Labs, whose laboratories brought high-paying jobs to the area.

Yet the negatives were unsettling, especially for those who had grown comfortable in the arms of the textile industry. Present conditions were good, but the future was cloudy. Greensboro was ill-prepared to generate replacement jobs for those that were beginning to disappear in manufacturing. This was especially true in the growing technology sector of the economy. Only one "high technology" business had chosen Greensboro in the previous three years, while fifteen had gone to the Raleigh-

Durham area and five had located in Charlotte. To further complicate matters, land costs were nearly twice those of competitors like Greenville, South Carolina, another textile center making some of the same hard choices. Furthermore, there were few large tracts of land available for sale.

Perhaps most disturbing was the realization that Greensboro's economic development was at a virtual dead stop, while competing cities like Raleigh and Charlotte were well on their way to improving their lot. Melvin had seen preliminary census figures that showed Greensboro's growth rate was the lowest in a century, largely because the city council under Melvin's leadership had imposed a moratorium on annexation.

Greensboro was losing in part because few beyond the city limits knew of the city's virtues. Even the state industrial recruiters in Raleigh had little information about opportunities in Greensboro. Old-time Jaycees like Melvin must have felt a twinge when they read that in the current market the Greater Greensboro Open added little to the city's reputation. "It is surprising that none of the respondents mentioned the golf tournament as a recognition factor for the community," the Battelle report said. The researchers also noted "a historic lack of business leaders' interest and commitment to the economic development of Greensboro."[1] In short, established employers did not appear to be eager to recruit new industry that would hire away their employees with better wages.

In early February 1984, Melvin was one of the first to receive a copy of the report, which had been commissioned by the Greensboro Development Corporation (GDC). This was a newly organized group of top businessmen and senior corporate executives that had grown out of informal breakfast meetings that Melvin had put together during his mayoralty to inform corporate leaders of developments at city hall. The seminal meetings had been held away from prying eyes at the company cafeteria in the Burlington headquarters on West Friendly Avenue. With Burlington CEO William Klopman as host, those who received Melvin's invitations responded without hesitation. Gathered for breakfast once every few months were Roger Soles, CEO of Jefferson-Pilot Corporation; Cone Mills's Dewey Trogdon; Blue Bell's Edward J. Bauman; William Hemphill, the head of United Guaranty Corporation; Stanley Frank, the chairman of the airport authority; Nat Hayes from Carolina Steel Corporation; William S. Jones of Boren Brick; and Charles Hayes, the brash and boisterous CEO at Guilford Mills.

There had been a time—in the 1950s especially—when organizing such a group would have been unnecessary. Then, the men running the largest corporations were closer to city hall, either in person or by proxy. Howard Holderness, Soles's predecessor, was a member of the school board. Burlington's Ed Zane was a member of the city council, and Ben Cone had been mayor. Ben's brother Ceasar II ran the airport authority, and he talked to city department heads whenever the spirit moved him. The city was smaller then, the pace was slower, and corporate executives often took their turn on the city council or at the helm of the chamber, which was the clearinghouse for politics, business, and civic affairs.

In the intervening years, these connections had withered as men like Holderness, the Cone brothers, Oscar Burnett, Orton Boren, and others had died or eased into retirement. By the late 1970s and early 1980s, the top executives at Greensboro's largest companies were largely absent from daily participation in local affairs. Their first allegiance was to their companies and stockholders, who were not paying premiums for civic participation. Roger Soles, for example, never set foot in city hall during his entire career at Jefferson.[2] Tim Burnett, who had succeeded his father at Bessemer Improvement Company, told a reporter in 1980, "We haven't had the people with vision who had clout and the people with the clout, if they had vision, didn't use it."[3]

Greensboro also had lost some of its political presence with the Republican victories in 1980. The county's state legislative delegation was fragmented, and losing six-term congressman Richardson Preyer was especially hard. Preyer, who was defeated by Republican businessman Gene Johnston, had gained tremendous respect during his twelve years in Washington. He had earned a national reputation for his steady and thorough management of the House investigation of the assassination of president John F. Kennedy. Some said if Preyer had not been defeated he would have had a shot at becoming Speaker.

In the early 1980s, the absence of leading business figures from visible participation in civic affairs was interpreted by some as sour grapes over the adoption of district representation on the city council. If the corporate bulls could no longer control the process, the reasoning went, then they would withdraw entirely. There was unhappiness among the old-timers over the change—and it would be voiced for years—but there was more at work than that.

The transition in civic involvement came as local companies were being absorbed into national or multinational operations. "That's almost a natural thing when companies grow and aren't local companies anymore," said United Guaranty's Hemphill, who found himself less attached to the city as he began spending more time in New York after his company became part of AIG, an international financial conglomerate. "When management shifts to professional management to a greater extent, then the people who are leading those companies come to think of Greensboro as just a bedroom community where they happen to live," Hemphill explained. "I can tell you this because that's exactly what I went through."[4]

During the 1970s, moreover, social issues had overtaken economic development as the primary emphasis at the chamber of commerce. It was a redirection that had alienated many corporate executives. Indeed, much of the success in economic growth during the 1970s had been by default. Ciba-Geigy, an important newcomer, had chosen Greensboro as the base for its textile and agricultural operations because Burlington's board chairman told Ciba-Geigy's board chairman that he had a building he wanted to sell, cheap. Had it not been for this offer, Ciba-Geigy and more than a thousand well-paid employees would have settled in Greenville, South Carolina, where a site for the new building had already been chosen. The growth at Western Electric and Bell Labs at an impressive new facility on Interstate 40-85 was due to the Cold War, which fattened defense contracts.

At first, Melvin's intentions in bringing the corporate leaders together had been purely informational, but he also hoped to rekindle some of the civic participation that the city had known before. More than once during his time at city hall, Melvin had said that Greensboro was not producing new leaders. One of his speeches had helped spawn a program called Leadership Greensboro, a leadership training institute that was one of the first in the state. Indeed, some of the young business and professional people who had completed this basic training in civic affairs and public responsibility had already entered the political stream.

"What was happening," Melvin recalled, "was a real change in public companies. CEOs couldn't be as obvious as before in leadership roles. Shareholders expected them to spend all their time on the company. The GDC gave them a way to do that without being public."[5] While Melvin did not expect Roger Soles to run for a seat on the city council, he knew that Soles and others could recruit and underwrite the campaigns of a new crop of civic leaders. The early efforts at such participation were not as successful as Melvin had hoped, however. The group's influence on local politics never really reached the level attributed to it by suspicious outsiders. "It was a politically naive group," said Hemphill. "They knew nothing about politics. I almost gave up in despair. They would say, 'Well we ought to have some people running for city council.' That is exactly right. Then, the people that somebody would come up with you couldn't elect to the presidency of a Sunday school class."[6]

In the spring of 1983, Melvin's informal corporate huddle was given a name, and the Greensboro Development Corporation was formally organized. The Battelle report, which cost the GDC fifty thousand dollars, came shortly thereafter. In incorporating and emerging from the shadows, the GDC was no different from similar groups that had come together in cities all across the state. In Winston-Salem, a similar group was called "Winston-Salem Business Incorporated." In High Point, it was "the CEO Roundtable." In Charlotte, it was simply called "the Group."

Melvin organized the GDC as a power center. Only the top executives were invited to join, and members were not allowed to send a subordinate to the meetings. The majority ruled, and the cost of approved projects was apportioned to members based on the size of their companies. It was implied that if members wished to protect their businesses' interests, then they had best attend the meetings. Melvin emphasized that the GDC was not designed to replace the chamber but to augment its work. He liked to compare it to the army's 82nd Airborne Division, whose members were well-trained, armed with sufficient resources, and motivated to take on special projects. The GDC was to support the work of the Greensboro Chamber of Commerce, which gave the new organization twenty-five thousand dollars in seed money. The group also was determined to work as closely as possible with other industry-hunting groups in Greensboro, Winston-Salem, and High Point—the three Piedmont cities known collectively as "the Triad."

When the GDC was incorporated, the membership included executives from the leading banks as well as relative newcomers like Philip Gelzer from Ciba-Geigy and Tagge Berggren, the top local executive for Volvo, whose North American heavy truck operation had recently consolidated its offices on the edge of Greensboro near the airport. The new membership brought broader viewpoints to the discussions than what Melvin heard in his earlier informal gathering of executives. Gelzer, for example, did not share the opinion about the evils of district representation held by many of the conservatives in the community. Mike Weaver, one of the most energetic of the new recruits, was more socially conscious and liberal in his politics than old-timers like Soles.

The one person the GDC never brought to the table was Joe Koury, the maverick builder who would eventually become the county's largest landowner. Melvin, Weaver, and another businessman, Jim Becher, paid a call on Koury and asked him to join, Melvin remembered. "We said, 'Look, the convention center thing is over. We are trying to make the economy of Greensboro better. You ought to be part of what we are about." Koury was cordial, but he never responded to the invitation.

Weaver was as much a Greensboro booster as Melvin. He had grown up trailing behind his father, Herman Weaver, as he made his way to various building sites around the city. When Mike was twelve, he gave his father the hundred dollars he had earned working odd jobs to buy a share in the family-owned Sunset Hills apartment project. The youngster then went out and planted trees around the units to improve their appearance. Weaver finished his undergraduate studies at Chapel Hill, where he had a passing acquaintance with Melvin, and then stayed on to earn a law degree and a graduate degree in business simultaneously. He never hung out his shingle but instead followed his father into the construction business after a stint in the air force.

Quiet, soft-spoken, even shy, Weaver embraced social issues as firmly as he did the conservative business principles he learned from his father, who took him on as a junior partner in the mid-sixties. Even before the city became embroiled in debate over open housing in 1968, Weaver approached his father about the discrimination that existed in their business, a condition Michael believed was wrong. How could he work beside a black laborer, brick mason, or carpenter and then tell him he could not bring his family to live in the very home he was building? Weaver remembers, "I said, 'Here are these guys, I knew by name, I knew their wife's name, and they can't rent an apartment. They are part of our team.'" [7]

Herman Weaver worried about the consequences for their business of ending housing discrimination. What if whites fled, emptying apartments when there were mortgages to pay off? What if whites and blacks turned violent? Father and son talked about the issue for some time. Finally, firmly convinced of the necessity of acting, Michael turned in his shares of family-owned units and told his father he would rather not own segregated housing. His father was impressed and agreed to the change.

They moved deliberately. While Herman Weaver contacted other owners and managers, Mike made plans to accommodate renters who might decide to move. The company announced its decision in the newspaper at the same time letters went to tenants offering them the option of canceling their leases and relocating with help from the property owners. "That was the program we worked out," Weaver said. "To try to be as fair as we could to our customers. We did it and none of those bad things happened."[8] Later, Weaver led the chamber's community unity division and found in Al Lineberry, home builder John R. Taylor, and others a kindred spirit to move the city beyond racial divisions.

If the GDC was the 82nd Airborne, Soles was the commanding general who detailed the legwork to younger men like Melvin and Weaver. While Klopman ran a larger company than Soles did and Trogdon had more employees, Jefferson-Pilot was the leading player in Greensboro, and Soles ran "The Jeff." He was gruff and disciplined, with an intimidating manner. His jowly face and broad paunch earned him the nickname of "Boss Hawg," although there were none who called him that to his face. Displays of humor were rare, although Soles could muster a pleasing smile when something amused him. Friends said he was most at ease with a fishing rod in his hand. As the successor to the easygoing, affable Howard Holderness, Soles had imposed the rigor of the investment side of the company on the business. Operations were well-planned, thoroughly grounded, and usually successful. He consolidated the Pilot Life and Jefferson Standard insurance operations into a single corporation and expanded the company when opportunities arose. By the mid-1980s, Jefferson-Pilot was a company with $4 billion in assets.

Soles had a strong allegiance to Greensboro, although he was no civic cheerleader. He did his share quietly, without fanfare. "I would see him make phone calls, make gifts, network on behalf of organizations," said Weaver. "He did the kind of things that greased the wheels and make things happen. Very positive things." Soles put Jefferson-Pilot money behind Melvin's plans for a downtown convention center, not because he thought Jefferson-Pilot ought to own a piece of a hotel but because he believed the project would be good for downtown.[9] In the late 1960s, he had helped plan and organize a downtown city club—one without the racial exclusion common in similar clubs elsewhere. In December 1984, Jefferson-Pilot and Melvin's First Home Federal announced a downtown residential project called Greensborough Court at Hamburger Square on South Elm Street. Plans called for rehabilitating a group of former warehouses and turn-of-the-century retail buildings and converting them into apartments and shops. A few years later, when Jefferson and Pilot combined offices, Soles made the decision to erect a $40 million addition to Jefferson's building at Elm and Market.

As the Battelle report began to circulate in the spring of 1984, Melvin also found himself back in the traces with Tom Osborne, who had retired from government work to become president of the chamber. Osborne replaced Larry Cohick, who before coming to Greensboro had worked for the state economic development office in Raleigh, where he was considered one of the hottest recruiters in the Southeast.

Cohick had been on the job for only a few years, and he was beginning to energize the economic development program. As a testament to his efforts, he had boosted by tenfold the amount of money the city devoted to industrial recruitment. He was drawing attention to Greensboro using many of the courtship techniques common to the business, but his personal style rubbed Melvin and others the wrong way. They could not understand a man who kept his office lights so dim it was hard to find a chair, who listened to Strauss waltzes, or who stationed a jar of moonshine whiskey on his sideboard. Many thought Cohick's lavish courting of corporate site selection specialists, which included expensive dinners, limousine service, and gifts, was too extravagant. They had never seen anything like that before. "He knew economic development," said Weaver, "but he did not present the kind of outward appearance you would want when you are meeting people." When Cohick left to be replaced by Osborne, however, he took with him a choice prospect. Time-Life Books was looking at Greensboro but opted instead to locate in Reston, Virginia.[10]

In the early days, the GDC functioned as Melvin hoped it would. At the top of its agenda was support for public education, including the universities; developing a reliable water supply; improving air service; and attracting more jobs. Development of new business opportunities took much of the group's time, and the first challenge came late in 1985 when officials at the Carolina-Virginia Fashion Exhibitors called mayor John Forbis and said they were considering a move out of Charlotte, where the group had been based for more than forty years.

The Carolina-Virginia Fashion Exhibitors was a confederation of representatives of fashion houses that held regular shows for small retailers around the region. More than six hundred members, most of whom lived in the Charlotte area, used the exhibition space to show new lines to customers in the Southeast who did not shop the major apparel markets. Landing the association's headquarters would be a significant boost to Greensboro's economy and its image. Not only would it give downtown a new tenant, but Greensboro boosters expected the sales personnel would be bringing their families to live in the city.

Municipal and private interests responded with plans for a $62 million project that included an office tower and adjoining exhibition hall on North Elm Street across from the new Southern Life Insurance

Building and Sheraton Hotel that had opened the year before. The GDC pledged $200,000 toward the project, and that amount was matched by $750,000 from Burlington, Cone Mills, Guilford Mills, and Blue Bell. Weaver's construction company put together the plans for the buildings.

In September 1986, the association's board of directors accepted the Greensboro offer and touted the city's virtues as a center for the textile industry. A month later, however, the full membership of the association voted nearly two to one to remain in Charlotte following an aggressive Charlotte campaign organized by NCNB's competitive CEO, Hugh McColl, and articles in the Charlotte newspapers complete with photographs of empty storefronts and deserted streets in downtown Greensboro.

"They should have followed us home," Melvin said some years later. "We put together a dynamite package." The tower building included parking and showrooms and was to house the headquarters of Blue Bell, the maker of Wrangler jeans and one of the country's largest apparel makers. Melvin was sitting beside Burlington's William Klopman at a Charlotte meeting with the apparel association when Klopman leaned over and said, "We are wasting our time. These people ain't going to move anywhere. They have done this to get Charlotte to put up some money."[11] And he was right.

At about the same time as the apparel market project, the GDC went to bat for improvements at the University of North Carolina at Greensboro, where chancellor William Moran was developing an aggressive new agenda for the school. When Moran arrived in 1979 to succeed retiring chancellor James Ferguson, UNCG was changed only in name from its prior incarnation as the "woman's college" of the consolidated state university system. The school had missed an opportunity in the 1960s to add graduate programs, expand its offerings, and become a full partner with the campuses at Chapel Hill and Raleigh. Rather than fully embrace its coeducational status, the campus had retained much of the style and attitude of its past. As a result, its future was as muddled as the confusing array of architectural styles of the campus buildings. Many senior faculty and trustees held fast to the traditions of "the W.C.," in spite of a growing male student population and thousands of commuter students returning to upgrade their academic credentials. By 1981, enrollment exceeded ten thousand, and the campus was ill-equipped to meet the demands on it.

Melvin eagerly embraced Moran's appointment as an opportunity to

FIG. 26. Ceasar Cone II was president of Cone Mills Corporation, the consolidated company that emerged after World War II, until he turned the company over to its first non-family chief executive, Lewis Morris, in 1965. *(Courtesy Greensboro Historical Museum)*

FIG. 27. Vance Chavis had a legendary following of his former students at Dudley High School when he was elected to the Greensboro City Council in the 1960s. *(Courtesy Greensboro Historical Museum)*

FIG. 28. The Jaycee leadership of the Greater Greensboro Open golf tournament broke ranks with leading tournament organizers and invited golfer Charlie Sifford, the first African American to become an approved tournament player through the Professional Golfers' Association, to participate in the 1961 tournament. Sifford returned for other tournaments. He is pictured here in 1967 with Bud Allin, a former GGO champion. (*Courtesy* Greensboro News & Record)

FIG. 29. Investment broker Oscar Burnett (center, flanked by GGO chairman Jim Melvin, left, and 1963 GGO champion Doug Sanders) turned the former military training base into one of the state's first industrial parks. In the 1960s, he helped negotiate racial tensions at the height of the civil rights movement. He was honorary chair of the GGO in 1963. *(Courtesy* Greensboro News & Record*)*

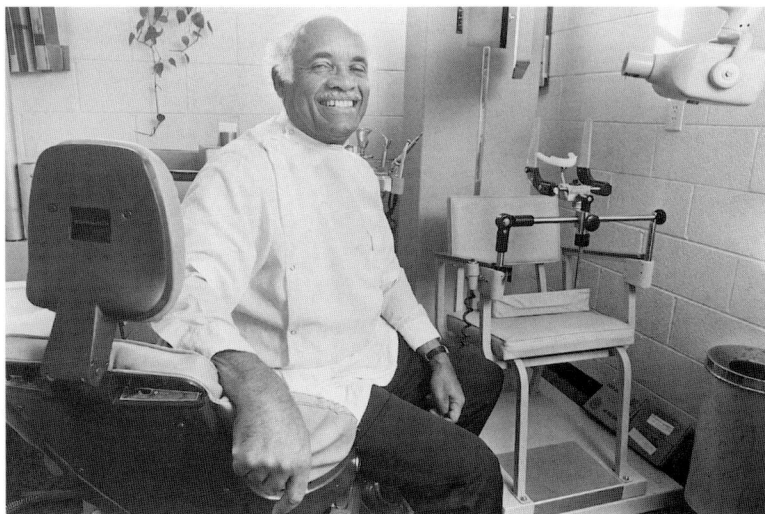

FIG. 30. Greensboro dentist George Simkins Jr. challenged the segregated world with determination and perseverance. His legal challenge to the racial segregation of Greensboro hospitals resulted in the removal of racial discrimination in medical facilities throughout the country. He later led the effort for district election of members of the city council. *(Courtesy* Greensboro News & Record*)*

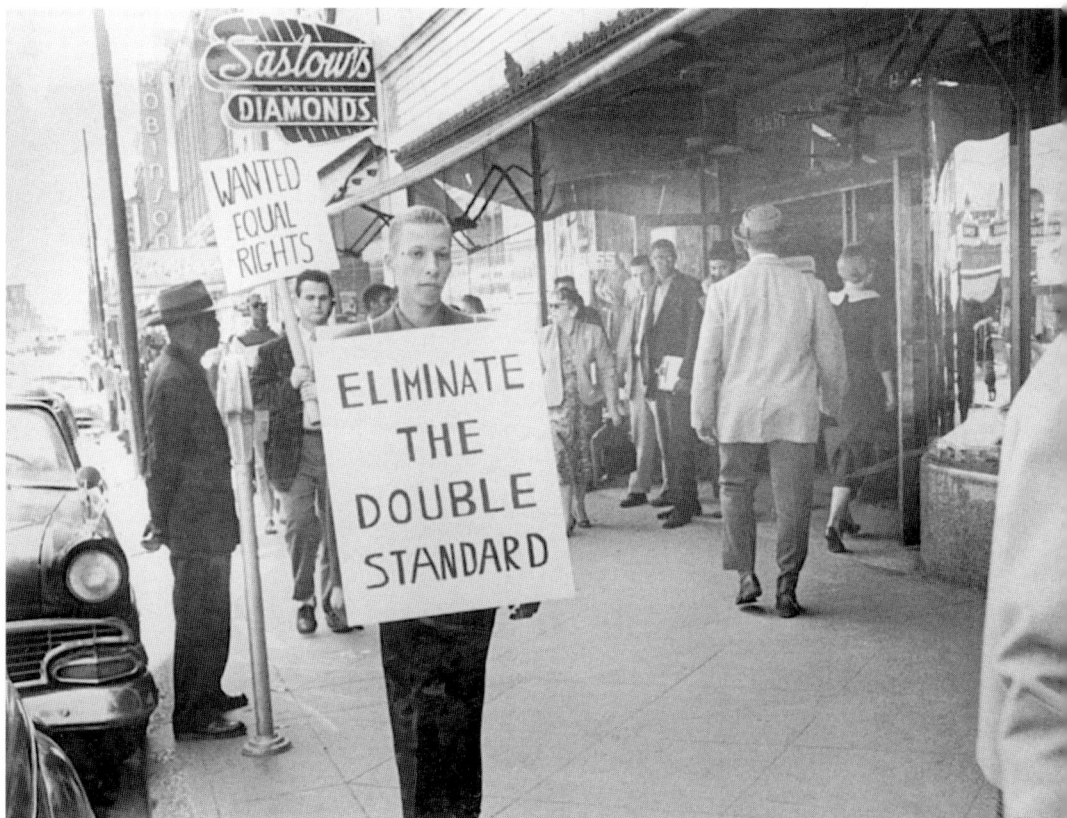

FIGS. 31 (above) and 32 (facing). The sit-in demonstrations at Greensboro's Woolworth store in February 1960 sparked a movement that led to similar demonstrations around the country. Later, African American demonstrators filled downtown in demonstrations that led to mass arrests. (Courtesy Greensboro News & Record)

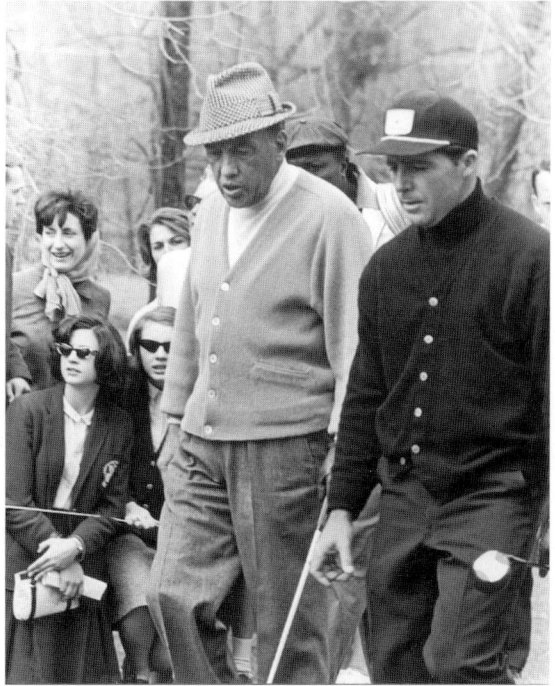

FIG. 33. Television's leading variety show host, Ed Sullivan, and South African golfer Gary Player played a round together at the 1965 GGO, where Sullivan hosted the tournament's annual banquet. *(Courtesy Greensboro News & Record)*

FIG. 34. Greensboro was selected as an All-America City by the National Civic League in 1966. Seated between L. Richardson Preyer (right) and his wife, Emily (left), at the celebratory dinner is businessman and civic leader Marion Follin. *(Photograph by Carol W. Martin)*

FIG. 35. Greensboro and Jim Melvin received nationwide attention in the late 1960s when a newspaper syndicate featured Melvin and the work of the state Jaycees' Partners of the Alliance project in Bolivia. Melvin traveled to South America with Greensboro businessman Hargrove "Skipper" Bowles, a major booster of the project. *(Courtesy Jim Melvin)*

FIG. 36. Jim Melvin watched returns on an early election with his wife, Susan. He was elected to a seat on the Greensboro City Council and, when reelected two years later, was chosen by council members as the mayor. He ran successfully for mayor four more times. *(Courtesy Jim Melvin)*

FIG. 37. Joseph M. Bryan adopted Greensboro as his hometown as if he had been born here. One of his favorite pastimes was hunting with his English spaniel, Jason. Jason's ashes are buried with those of his master at Bryan Park. *(Courtesy Joseph M. Bryan Foundation)*

FIG. 38. Gifts to the community from Joseph M. Bryan made possible the development of the award-winning park named in his honor on the banks of Lake Townsend north of the city. At the dedication with Bryan are his wife, Kathleen (seated left), and U.S. representative L. Richardson Preyer (at the podium). Behind and to the right is Greensboro mayor Jack Elam. *(Courtesy Greensboro News & Record)*

FIG. 39. Builder Joe Koury opened up new sections of residential development and then built the city's largest shopping mall, Four Seasons, which opened in 1975. He went on to develop the Grandover Resort and Conference Center. *(Courtesy Greensboro News & Record)*

FIG. 40. Greensboro's civic and business interests struggled to revive the center city after the major retail stores left Elm Street for the suburban shopping malls in the mid-1970s. The first major residential project was Greensborough Court, a joint development spearheaded by Jim Melvin of First Home Federal (left). With Melvin is Hugh North of Jefferson-Pilot Corporation, a partner in the venture that received a major setback when a fire destroyed a portion of the historic buildings included in the project. *(Courtesy Jim Melvin)*

FIG. 42. Mayor Jim Melvin's first campaign was powered by the slogan "Greensboro stinks." He and city manager Tom Osborne (center) worked for more than ten years to see the opening of a new sewage treatment plant that relieved south Greensboro of odors from an overworked facility. The groundbreaking celebrated by Melvin, Osborne, and Richard Howard preceded the 1984 dedication of the facility in Osborne's honor. *(Courtesy Jim Melvin)*

(facing, bottom) FIG. 41. The city council elected in 1983 included members elected from districts as well as from the community at large. The new method ended more than a decade of contentious debate. The new council included (left to right) council members Dorothy Bardolph, Jim Kirkpatrick, Earl Jones, and Joanne Bowie; mayor John Forbis, city manager Tom Osborne; and council members Lois McManus, Lonnie Revels, Katie Dorsett, and Cameron Cooke. *(Photograph by Carol W. Martin, Greensboro Historical Museum Collection)*

FIG. 43. On the morning of November 3, 1979, five demonstrators were killed after Ku Klux Klansmen and neo-Nazis descended on a group of communist labor organizers preparing for an anti-Klan march. A week later, marchers under heavy guard wound their way through Greensboro streets as the incident became embedded in the city's national reputation. *(Courtesy* Greensboro News & Record*)*

FIG. 44. Greensboro business leaders got behind a campaign to raise the level of sports competition at UNC Greensboro to Division I status. Leading the effort were (left to right) Stanley Frank, Michael Weaver, Charles Reid, Charles Hayes, and Jim Melvin. *(Courtesy Jim Melvin)*

FIG. 45. Sports became a major interest on the UNC Greensboro campus as the school's soccer team rolled up national championships under coach Michael Parker. The team celebrated its third NCAA Division III National Championship in Saint Louis in 1985. The Spartans won their third national title in four years with a 5-0 win over Washington University. *(Courtesy UNC Greensboro Sports Information)*

FIG. 46. Greensboro honored the contributions of Joseph M. Bryan to the city with the naming of a major thoroughfare in his honor following his death in 1995. At the unveiling of the signage for the new road were (left to right) Jim Melvin, Joseph M. Bryan Jr., N.C. secretary of transportation Garland Garrett, and the chairman of the state board of transportation, Douglas Galyon of Greensboro. *(Courtesy Jim Melvin)*

FIG. 47. One of the additions to downtown Greensboro came through the work of Action Greensboro, which spearheaded the development of Center City Park that formally opened in fall 2006. A signature of the park is a fountain with generous sprays of water. *(Courtesy* Greensboro News & Record*)*

FIG. 48. First Horizon Park replaced the city's aging War Memorial Stadium, which opened in 1927, as the home of the city's minor-league baseball team. In its first two years, the Greensboro team led the league with record-breaking attendance. *(Courtesy* Greensboro News & Record*)*

FIG. 49. Nothing symbolized the collapse of the textile manufacturing operations in Greensboro more than the demolition of the Burlington Industries headquarters building in 2005. *(Courtesy* Greensboro News & Record*)*

FIG. 50. The additions to the Greensboro Coliseum in the decades following its opening in 1959 created a facility capable of seating 23,500 in the arena and 2,400 in the adjoining auditorium. *(Courtesy* Greensboro News & Record*)*

FIG. 51. Downtown Greensboro began to enjoy a revival of businesses and entertainment venues. Elm Street is home to Triad Stage, a regional center for life performances; new eating establishments; and boutique businesses that took space in renovated buildings, some of which dated to the late nineteenth century. *(Courtesy* Greensboro News & Record*)*

move UNCG beyond its past. Melvin had long dreamed of a vibrant campus that offered all the trappings of university life, including a stronger sports program. He believed that intercollegiate athletics at a higher level would make the school more attractive to high school graduates selecting the site of their four-year college education. He had watched enviously when UNC–Charlotte, one of the youngest campuses in the UNC system, won national attention with its basketball program in the early 1970s.

Before Ferguson retired in 1979, Melvin had discovered just how tough effecting change would be. Melvin was a UNCG trustee and had access to the campus leadership's agenda when he proposed in 1977 that the school consider upgrading its sports program. At the time, UNCG's intercollegiate competition included a range of sports—golf, tennis, basketball, and fencing—but there were no full-time coaches on the staff, and there was no scholarship money to build competitive teams. Armed with a million dollars in pledges from Greensboro businessmen who were eager to start an athletic fund, Melvin made the pitch to Ferguson, who, in turn, passed the proposal on to the faculty. There, it was received as heresy. One senior faculty member, with her finger shaking under Melvin's nose, warned that such a change in the curriculum would turn UNCG into Ohio State, where football coach Woody Hayes had recently been fired for hitting a football player. Melvin was stunned, but he collected himself enough to respond. "I would hope so," he said. "Ohio State has eighty thousand students and some of the best academic credentials in the country." The scholarship fund was refused, but the school did hire full-time coaches for men's and women's basketball.

Chastened, Melvin retreated and waited until Moran had found his legs as chancellor. He then returned with the same proposition, which was more warmly received this time. Moran was cautious, but he saw the advantages of upgrading UNCG's sports program and understood the changes that were coming for the campus. UNCG was attracting a different student body, and students were looking for the full college experience, which included athletics.

A shift would take time, however. In 1983, Moran hired UNCG's first full-time athletic director, and two years later the athletic program was moved out of the department of health, physical education, recreation, and dance and put under student affairs, where the chancellor's office had more control over it. In 1987, after repeated winning seasons in men's soccer (five national championships) and women's volleyball and national rankings in the division for men's and women's basketball, the trustees voted to develop a Division I program by 1991. The university faculty council remained opposed, voting two to one against the change. Nonetheless, Moran moved ahead, armed with a commitment for $2 million in aid from the stalwarts of the GDC.

Moran and Melvin did disagree over the placement of the UNCG music building, a major addition to the campus in the 1990s. Early plans called for the $26 million building—at the time the largest academic structure at UNCG—to go on the south side of the campus. The three-story building would include a 350-seat recital hall and a 130-seat organ recital hall, plus rehearsal halls, library, studios, and faculty and student lounges. Melvin argued that the campus needed a public face on West Market Street, the main thoroughfare on its north side, where trees and old houses all but obscured the institution that lay beyond. Melvin told Moran the West Market Street location would help integrate the campus into the community and give it a public face. He marshaled support from other board members, who turned down the administration's plans for the southern site. After the building opened in the summer of 1999, a new campus entrance was added beside it.

Melvin also helped invigorate the UNCG trustees with new blood and members with bold ideas. One of those he brought on board was Charles Hayes, the CEO of Guilford Mills and one of the original GDC members. As Melvin was ending his term, he engineered Hayes's appointment, which brought a surprising response. When Melvin and Moran called on Hayes with an invitation to join the board, Hayes declined the offer. He argued that he was not qualified, since he had not even graduated from high school. Melvin and Moran insisted that he accept, and Hayes changed his mind. A few hours after their visit, Melvin was in his office when he got a call from Hayes, who asked where he could send a contribution to the school. Melvin gave him the address and a day or so later got a call from the school's development officer, who reported that Hayes's personal check had arrived and that it was for $25,000. It was the first of more than a $1 million in contributions that Hayes would make over the coming years.

Melvin knew Hayes would shake up the staid, tea party atmosphere of the trustee meetings. He was not disappointed. Hayes arrived late for his first meeting and pushed through the door with his tie loose, his face covered in sweat, with a huge cigar trailing smoke clinched in his teeth. Board members stared incredulously at this rough-hewn presence. Hayes made no secret that he was much more at home on the floor of his mill than he was in a meeting where the usual dress was a coat and tie.

Hayes later became chairman of the board and proved a valuable and steady ally for Moran. He was chairing the board when members became deadlocked over a site for a new art museum. As it looked like a stalemate, Hayes called for a recess. While others stretched their legs, Hayes called Moran aside and asked the chancellor which site he preferred. Moran told Hayes that he preferred the southwest corner of Tate and Spring Garden streets. When Hayes called the meeting back to order, he told the men to remove their jackets and suggested the women call their husbands to cancel dinner, because no one was leaving until the matter was settled. When the final vote was taken, the board followed the chancellor's lead.

Hayes, Melvin, Weaver, and others became champions for UNCG's cause in Raleigh as well. On one trip, with Moran waiting outside the Legislative Building in a van Weaver had outfitted as a traveling office, the group won a commitment from House and Senate leaders for a $10 million appropriation for capital construction, the largest amount the campus had received in years. Later that day, with the chancellor enjoying the glow of victory, Weaver and Melvin pressed for Moran's commitment to name UNCG's business school in honor of Joseph M. Bryan, who had already given $1 million for scholarships and endowed professorships. "Bill almost went white," recalled Weaver. "Here he is with his biggest group of supporters, he had just gotten money he didn't think he'd ever get, and we're asking him for the biggest favor he can give us. He stutters and stammers. And we say, 'This is what we want. Just think about it.' He goes to work and sells it. That is how the school came to be known as the Bryan School." Bryan subsequently donated $5 million for full scholarships to be given to selected students called Bryan Fellows. His money made up nearly three-fourths of the business school's total endowment.

The corporate effort also paid off for the Jaycees when they came to the GDC seeking help in keeping the Greater Greensboro Open golf tournament on network television after officials at the PGA announced the GGO would not be part of the 1989 broadcasts. The loss of television coverage would have made it difficult for the GGO to attract leading golfers and threatened to permanently sideline the tournament.

Melvin, Weaver, and a delegation arranged a meeting with PGA officials in Florida and were stunned by the cold reception they received. It was clear to the Greensboro men that despite the long history of the city's association with the PGA that PGA officials believed they had out-grown the Greensboro stop and were looking to shed an event that they considered a minor tournament on the tour. Melvin asked what Greens-boro could do to turn the situation around. The PGA's ultimatum was that the Jaycees secure a commitment for a million dollars in local ad-vertising for the open. It appeared to be an impossible demand; local firms gained little from advertising to a national television audience.

When the group returned to Greensboro, Melvin, Soles, and Weaver, who was a recent honorary chair of the GGO, agreed to contact eight or nine CEOs who might be willing to agree to underwrite the television time. Then they called a meeting of the GDC. When the subject of sup-porting the GGO with advertising was raised, Soles made his pledge, Weaver committed to a share of the television time, and in a few min-utes the entire guarantee was met. Melvin went to the bank and got a letter of credit that he shipped off to the PGA.

The GDC had called the PGA's bluff, but the deal was not sealed until after a top official at CBS, the network that carried the golf tournaments, got a call from one of his largest stockholders, Lawrence Tish, who also owned Lorillard, the cigarette maker on Greensboro's doorstep. Tish, meanwhile, had been briefed on the problems in Greensboro by J. Alex Spears, Lorillard's CEO and a member of the GDC. "The next day, I got a call from the president of CBS Sports," Melvin recalled. "'Don't you know,'" Melvin said he was told, "'we'd love to have you back in the pack-age and we'll see that it gets taken care of.'" A short time later, Melvin got a call from the PGA: "He was saying, 'We've got great news for you, and, by the way, do you know anybody at CBS?'"[12]

The GDC began flexing its muscle just as city hall was adjusting to the changes wrought by the new district election of council members. The first year of the district contests lifted voter turnout, but the results were relatively tame, despite the predictions of dire consequences. Incum-bent mayor John Forbis, who had staked his election two years before on maintaining the status quo, was returned for a second term. Joining him on the council were incumbents Dorothy Bardolph and stockbroker James Kirkpatrick, as well as those who had broken their 1981 campaign promises to maintain the at-large system.

The district campaigns ensured representation from black neighbor-hoods, as promised, but they also brought a new dimension of politics for the black community. The personalities of the sitting members were different from those of earlier council members. George Simkins Jr.'s protégé, Earl Jones, was a combative and outspoken proponent of black issues. He would be no Jimmie Barber, who seldom disagreed publicly with the white majority.

At the same time, there were unexpected consequences. Competition among black candidates generated divisions in the black community where none had appeared before. In the past, the political action committees selected candidates for their sample ballot, widely circulated just before Election Day, from among white candidates, choosing among "the lesser of evils," as one who participated put it. This time, black candidates faced off against one another, revealing a level of tension most had been eager to conceal in the past. This was particularly true in the district where Jones finished only one hundred votes ahead of Cleveland Sellers, who worked in the city personnel department.

Both Jones and Sellers were in their thirties and had been active in community affairs. Jones ran an offender rehabilitation program—he held a law degree but was not a practicing attorney—and had been a member of the dialogue task force that had formed following the 1981 elections. Sellers was a veteran of the civil rights movement of the 1960s. He was a student at South Carolina State College in Orangeburg in 1968 when three students were killed and twenty-seven others injured when police fired into a group of demonstrators. Sellers had earned a solid reputation in various positions at city hall, where he was involved with planning and job creation.

Jones got the nod of the committee. Sellers responded with an endorsement from Benjamin Hooks, the executive director of the NAACP. It was too late. Sellers said he was tainted by rumors that he was tied too closely to city hall, where he had worked for several years, while Jones was perceived to be more likely to pound the desk and be heard. Immediately after the election, the *Carolina Peacemaker* published an article that questioned the validity of the future of political action committees—an unthinkable position in previous years.

The new council members brought with them suspicions about how city decisions were made that stemmed from years of effective exclusion from the political process. Now, some asked questions that had never before been expressed in public in Greensboro. The answers were not always what they expected. For example, councilwoman Katie Dorsett's call for an accounting of the race and gender of citizens appointed to boards and commissions under the at-large system was prompted by the suspicion that African Americans had been slighted under that system.

When the report was produced, it revealed that minority appointments closely approximated the population: 26 percent of the appointees in recent years had gone to black citizens, who made up 32 percent of the city's population.

There also was a new mood at city council meetings. City staff hiring recommendations that once had been followed routinely were debated and often delayed. A plan to purchase the former Thalhimer's building on Elm Street for use as a downtown arts center ran into trouble, as did staff plans to sell surplus property around an outdated in-town water treatment plant. In time, the arts center died for lack of support, and the property around a holding pond was turned into a park.

Unanimous voting at council meetings became a thing of the past. Voting blocks emerged, and split decisions preceded by long and contentious arguments became common. Debate over whether the city should set aside a holiday for Dr. Martin Luther King Jr. went on for weeks, in public and in private. It was not settled until one day when the entire council happened to be in a van riding to the coliseum for an occasion. Discussion of the King holiday arose on the short trip from city hall, and the council members drove around the city until they reached consensus.

One of the first casualties of the new order was the city manager, Tom Osborne, who left about ninety days after the new council took office in 1983. Osborne had been manager for twelve years and a city employee since the 1950s. His departure ended the era of James R. Townsend, the legendary manager who had turned Greensboro city government into a model of efficiency in the years following World War II. Under Townsend and his protégés, taxes had remained stable, and the city's debt load, one of the highest in the state at the end of World War II, was reduced to a negligible level. At the time of Osborne's departure, Charlotte paid more in interest charges each year than the amount of Greensboro's entire debt. Osborne, like his mentor, had championed initiatives for infrastructure improvements, such as the building of a new waste treatment plant and the securing of an adequate water supply, but ventures beyond the day-to-day realm of city affairs were not for him or his followers. For example, the only plan for developing downtown Greensboro or planning the city's future that existed when Osborne retired was the one produced in the mid-1960s, before shopping centers had drained the city of retail business.

Osborne recommended that he be replaced by one of his assistants, but the council wanted a manager with no ties to the past. The selection was William Carstarphan, the city manager of Greenville, South Carolina. According to Councilman Revels, "We didn't want a manager with local ties to certain special interests who would have the ear of the manager more than others."[13]

All these changes, and others, complicated the life of Mayor Forbis, who later observed that district elections had turned his office into a "job" instead of a "position." His vote carried no more weight than that of any other council member, and he spent more time lobbying individual members than his predecessor did. "Jim Melvin didn't have to build consensus. It was already there," he said.[14]

The new districts, and the fresh representation that they produced, along with the new manager, marked a watershed in Greensboro. The comfortable arrangement that had prevailed for more than half a century, in which city hall managed affairs for the city's leading business interests, was over. In fact, the distance between economic interests and political interests in the city was wide and growing. Twenty years later, those who had lost their easy access to city hall would lament that the city had suffered as a result.

For some of those who had been watching from the sidelines for those same fifty years, however, the changes looked good. The new council was more democratic and reflected a broader range of the community. A new manager would bring a different kind of thinking to the city. To Herman Fox, who had fought alongside George Simkins Jr. in the fifteen-year battle for a district system, the city council demonstrated that the people, not the business interests of Greensboro, were the final authority in the city.

———

The lively atmosphere at city hall and the initiatives from the GDC produced a new energy in the city. By the mid-1980s, a three-hundred-room hotel and adjacent office building that were part of an $80 million project by Southern Life Insurance Company were nearing completion. A second, eighteen-story office building on North Elm was in the works. The Belk department store building, which had stood empty for more than a decade, got a facelift and a new tenant, BB&T, the eastern North Carolina banking firm, which was extending west. The capstone was an announcement by American Express in 1984 that it would locate a regional call service center on a corporate campus located near a new $65 million air passenger terminal that had opened in 1982. The first departure from the new airport was an Eastern Airlines flight to Atlanta. Eastern had first launched air service to the city in the 1930s.

The city was pushing outward. In the mid-1980s, more than nine thousand housing units were planned or under construction in northwest Greensboro, nine times the number that had been built in the first years of the decade. The housing boom was partly the result of the extension of a major sewer line that opened new areas of real estate to residential development in the west and northwest. The demand was due to a tight market plus the boost to the local economy provided by new businesses such as the American Express service center, where twenty-two hundred jobs were created, and Japan's Konishiroku Photo plant on the eastern side of the county in a new industrial park. More than a thousand jobs were added there.

Greensboro's population center was Friendly Shopping Center, whose owner, Starmount Company, had recently closed its Green Valley Golf Course and turned it into an office park with space for law firms, brokerage houses, and, in time, a new corporate headquarters for Lorillard Corporation.

The annexation of sections north and west of the city returned Greensboro to second place in size in the state. With a population of 176,000 in 1985, Greensboro was slightly larger than Raleigh. Much of the new housing was going up in the area served by a new, highly disputed route that extended Benjamin Parkway out to the airport. South of the city, work had begun on a 712-acre housing development called Adams Farm, where twenty-eight hundred homes were to be built. The development was only part of the infilling taking place between High Point and Greensboro. The open spaces around the new airport and along Interstate 40 midway to Winston-Salem were giving way to office parks. Eventually, ten thousand workers would commute to jobs in the area.

One of the most dramatic changes was to Wendover Avenue. The major crosstown thoroughfare that had opened in Melvin's early years as mayor was becoming one of the city's busiest commercial strips. Auto dealerships lined the road for more than a mile east of its intersection with Interstate 40. One of the early businesses to stake a claim there was Royce Reynolds's Crown Pontiac. When he moved a long-established dealership off Elm Street near downtown to Wendover in 1974, his competitors told him he was crazy to locate his dealership so far into the country.

At the time, Reynolds had his own doubts as well. In the first month at the new location, his sales went from about ninety cars a month to fifteen, a slump aggravated by the nation's growing energy crisis. Reynolds introduced himself to the mayor when he called Melvin one morning at the height of the gas shortage to ask him to stop riding the bus to work, a gesture Melvin had made to encourage citizens to save gasoline. Reynolds told Melvin his nod to conservation was not doing his business any good. In a few months, however, Reynolds's business rebounded when he secured a Honda dealership and customers started buying the Japanese automaker's new Civic models—"a tin can with a motor," Reynolds said—right off the truck. In time, he took command of the strip, with multiple dealerships that offered luxury BMWs from Germany, Hondas and Nissans from Japan, and Pontiacs and Dodge minivans from Detroit.

The folks at city hall had their hands full. The election of president Ronald Reagan in 1980 brought a new conservative agenda to Washington that was reshaping the way the federal government spent money. The easy cash of the 1970s that had built parks and playgrounds, tennis courts, and other amenities in Greensboro was gone. Between 1981 and 1985, the share of the city budget supplied by federal funds fell from 17 percent to 9 percent.

The most alarming change was the loss of federal support for flood-control projects such as the long-anticipated reservoir that Greensboro hoped to build near Randleman on the Deep River to supply the city with water into the twenty-first century. If Greensboro was to tap the Deep River, then the Randleman project would require far more local money than had been anticipated. One of the last projects Tom Osborne engineered before he left office was the creation of a new water authority that eventually would take on the building of the Randleman Dam and the filling of a reservoir to serve Greensboro, High Point, and other communities in the central Piedmont.

In succeeding years, the Randleman project also occupied Melvin's time. He accepted a six-year appointment to the state Environmental Management Commission largely to look after the interests of the Randleman project. "I tried to keep the porch light on for Randleman," Melvin said. Osborne's creativity in the establishment of a multi-jurisdictional water authority, linking together the needs of area governments, secured a reliable source of water for the future. Melvin said Osborne's vision and hard work should have been recognized in naming of the lake in Osborne's honor.

———

City manager William Carstarphan and mayor John Forbis ushered in a new dimension of citizen involvement with the Greensboro One Task

Force, which reached into the community for ideas. From that initiative came big-ticket items like a cultural arts center and a senior citizens' center downtown, as well as park improvements paid for by a bond program designed by citizens, not city hall. Also included were smaller projects important to individual neighborhoods. For example, residents on the east side asked for a pedestrian overpass at U.S. 29 to create a safe passage across a dangerous four-lane divided highway that had separated neighborhoods for thirty years.

The bond package included money to expand the Greensboro Coliseum, which was seeing competition from Winston-Salem and Charlotte, where a recently-constructed coliseum was home to the city's new professional basketball team, the Hornets. Voters rejected the coliseum bonds while passing other measures, such as a venture into low-income housing. The defeat came in the wake of revelations of discrepancies in the financial affairs of the coliseum under manager Jim Oshust. It would take two more bond proposals before voters would agree to borrow additional money to expand the hall.

On the heels of Greensboro One came Greensboro Visions, a cooperative effort between the city, the chamber of commerce, and the GDC that involved hundreds of people who participated in a two-year examination of the city and its needs. It was led by Philip Gelzer from Ciba-Geigy, a respected corporate leader with an avuncular nature who was as comfortable in the boardroom as he was with neighborhood volunteers. His career had been spent in corporate planning. His new job came quite naturally, and his bosses encouraged him to take the assignment. Even though he was one of the early members of the GDC, which put up one-third of the money to fund Visions, he was not identified with the old, established economic interests, and he moved easily among the corporate leadership and those long suspicious of such interests.

Visions extended the welcome mat to any citizen who wished to participate in determining the shape of a future Greensboro. Banks mailed flyers announcing the program to 100,000 customers. Five hundred people turned out for initial forums where ideas for the city were discussed. In all, about 175 people participated directly in the study and planning process. At the top of their list of concerns were issues like jobs, good roads, affordable housing, and improved planning.

"People started to recognize where there were holes that had never been admitted before," Gelzer said some years later. "Everybody said this is God's country. We had so many cheerleaders. . . . It helped [Melvin] and others to see that there are weaknesses in this town." In

1988, the city council made remedying two of the top issues identified in the Visions study—insufficient transportation and housing—its top priorities.

It was one of the first times that social issues had captured the total attention of city hall. Within a few years, the city launched an ambitious housing program under mayor Vic Nussbaum, who followed Forbis into office in 1989. Under Nussbaum, the council dedicated a penny of the tax rate—about a million dollars a year—to help build affordable homes. The city also assumed control of public transportation, which had deteriorated under its owner, Duke Power Company. Consolidation of the county's three school systems—one each in Greensboro and High Point and another for county residents—would eventually follow, but not for another five years, when it would be realized largely due to the leadership and campaign support of the GDC.

Despite the rise of neighborhood organizations and new leadership at city hall, the city's most prominent, and influential, businessman remained Jim Melvin. In 1988, the *News and Record*—the result of the merger of the city's afternoon daily, the *Greensboro Record*, and the morning *Greensboro Daily News*—reported at the conclusion of an exhaustive study that Melvin was "the person who wields the most power most often" in Greensboro. Melvin posed for a front-page photograph leaning on the railing at the headquarters of First Home Federal Savings and Loan, an institution he had joined in 1978 as CEO. Not since Greensboro insurance man Joe Hunt was Speaker of the House in the 1961 General Assembly and chaired the State Highway Commission under governor Dan Moore had any Greensboro political figure carried as much weight in Greensboro.

Melvin's critics said he wielded too much influence. Some complained that Greensboro in fact had two city halls: one was at the mayor's office downtown, and the other was at First Home. Melvin proudly declared his commitment to Greensboro and said he had not stopped working for the city just because he was no longer in elective office. But he said that when he left city hall he had left cleanly, with no regrets, and no lingering ties. "I really didn't have the time [to meddle]," Melvin explained some time later. "I had been a very active mayor. I had used the 'bully pulpit,' and I don't back off from that. The worst thing I could have done for John [Forbis] or Vic [Nussbaum] and the council was for me to keep trying to be the mayor. I always got accused of that, but I walked away from that. You can't build the kind of organization we were trying to build [at First Home] and be that heavily involved."[15]

Melvin's statements about his lack of involvement were weakened a bit, albeit unintentionally, a few months after his departure in 1981 when the city council voted to name the municipal building in his honor. The dedication of the Melvin Municipal Building was announced in February 1982 at a prime rib dinner that was followed by a lavish sound and picture retrospective of Melvin's life and career that left the honoree surprised, embarrassed, and fumbling for words. The honor recognized Melvin's role in city government and his part in bringing about the very structure that was to carry his name. He had worked for the successful 1968 bond campaign that raised money to build the Guilford Governmental Center, of which city hall was a part. He also was among those who worked with the architects as they designed the building that housed the police department and administrative offices of many city departments. When it opened in 1973, Melvin was mayor. Nonetheless, the honor was extraordinary. At the time, it was the first such facility in the state named for a living person.

———

Amid the economic growth and the welcome boom in the construction of downtown office buildings, there also were troubling signs that the city's corporate structure was changing. In July 1986, the management group that had taken Blue Bell Incorporated private two years earlier announced that the company had been sold to VF Corporation of Wyomissing, Pennsylvania. Blue Bell, the maker of popular Wrangler jeans and Jantzen swimwear, had been part of the city since 1904. Sales had topped a billion dollars in 1979, and the company was included among the Fortune 250 that year. After the announcement of the sale, operations continued without any significant change until November, when VF announced that Blue Bell was gone. Pink slips were passed around to secretaries and corporate staff. The company's offices downtown were reduced to one operating division of the world's largest apparel manufacturer.

At about the same time, Southern Life Insurance Company, which had not yet finished building its Elm Street hotel-and-office-building complex, was sold to the Liberty Corporation of Greenville, South Carolina. Like Blue Bell, Southern was a homegrown business born in the early years of the Depression. Sales had climbed dramatically following

World War II, and the company had done well. It was a closely held corporation, and the owners had not put it on the market, but Liberty's offer was too substantial for them to ignore. Liberty issued the standard notices saying that few changes would occur, but soon Southern Life, too, was gone. A casualty of the sale was the twenty-story office building that had been part of Southern's overall plan for its downtown property. Altogether, the sales of Blue Bell and Southern Life cost the city about three hundred white-collar jobs in downtown.[16]

Gone too was another chance at landing the headquarters of a statewide banking company. The loss was all the more bitter because many in Greensboro had already begun to make welcome the executives of Northwestern Bank. Northwestern CEO Ben Craig, along with about twenty of his top officers, had purchased homes in the city and were in the process of moving the bank's headquarters from North Wilkesboro to Greensboro when First Union Corporation of Charlotte acquired Northwestern. Corporate offices to accommodate the city's new resident had already been outfitted in the new Southern Life Insurance Building when board members were called to a special meeting. Mike Weaver, who had recently joined the Northwestern board, said one of the hardest votes he ever cast was in favor of the First Union merger. He knew the competitor's offer was the best deal for shareholders, but it pained him to see Greensboro's best opportunity at landing a major bank headquarters evaporate along with it.[17]

Shaken first by raids on textile firms, the region's economic underpinnings trembled again in 1985 when R.J. Reynolds Tobacco Company in Winston-Salem went through a leveraged buyout and the headquarters was summarily removed to Atlanta. At about the same time, the new Washington-based USAir Group purchased Piedmont Airlines, also based in Winston-Salem, casting doubt on the future of seventy-five hundred Piedmont employees.

More trouble was on the way. In April 1987, Canadian investor Asher Edelman began a run on Burlington Industries. As the world's largest textile firm, with $2.7 billion in sales, Burlington was Greensboro's—and North Carolina's—leading corporate citizen. More than twelve hundred employees reported daily to the company's modern headquarters building set on a sylvan campus west of downtown Greensboro. Designed by A. G. Odell, the headquarters building's unique exposed steel frame and glass skin made it a stop on tours of the city. North of the city was the company-owned Bur-Mil Club, a country park that was maintained for employees. It included a fishing lake, a swimming pool, a pitch-and-putt golf course, and a clubhouse where anyone on the payroll could enjoy Sunday brunch or Wednesday "chicken nights."

Edelman was the model for Gordon Gecko in the movie *Wall Street*, whose business school speech extolling the virtues of greed epitomized an era of rapacious business deals. Edelman and Dominion Textiles, which already had a stake in North Carolina textiles, put in a bid of $60 per share for Burlington stock, and Edelman launched a campaign to win over shareholders. He was a man known for extravagance in art and other fine things, but he told a reporter that Burlington suffered from "corporate excess." Edelman said he would ground the company's "executive air force," close what he called a "country club"—the Bur-Mil Club—and do away with the New York apartments reserved for executives working out of Burlington House, the company's office tower in midtown Manhattan. He would trim the New York staff and begin selling the company's assets, with the denim and yarn manufacturing most likely going to Dominion. No one was sure what would remain.

The battle for Burlington ranged across numerous venues, from Greensboro to Raleigh, Washington, New York, and Montreal. When rumors about Edelman's intentions were rampant, Burlington lobbyists in Raleigh sought company protection in new antitakeover measures. Protective legislation breezed through both chambers, with only eight dissenting votes. (The lobbyists later collected $200,000 for their work.) Similar bills were proposed in Congress.

Edelman took the company to court in Richmond to void the "poison pill" provisions, while Burlington filed suit in Canada and announced it was considering a takeover of Dominion. After two months of maneuvering, the battle finally ended when a federal district judge ruled in Burlington's favor in a case that argued Edelman had used insider information to his advantage. The Burlington directors ultimately accepted a bid of $78 a share, or $2.5 billion, from an investment group led by the company's management. The company headquarters remained in the city, but the new company was heavily burdened with debt.

The dire predictions of a dismantled Burlington did, in fact, come true, but at the hands of the same management that had opposed Edelman. The workforce at the corporate headquarters was reduced almost by half. Company plants went on the block, and the huge denim operations in Erwin, North Carolina, were sold to Dominion. Once a powerhouse with more than a 150 plants around the world, Burlington would eventually be reduced to one-third that number and would struggle mightily for five years before its stock returned to the open market.

As Burlington's future was being determined on Wall Street, Jim Melvin talked to a reporter at the *Charlotte Observer*. "The other day," Melvin said, "I walked by the Southern Life Center, and I couldn't help but think that at this time last year, I could walk by and say, 'Headquartered there are three of the largest corporations in our state.' Starting in June, I'll walk by and there won't be any corporate headquarters there."[18]

The losses were stunning, and they were not over.

Chapter 16

We Must Take Action

$\mathcal{J}$IM MELVIN watched the corporate landscape change in the summer of 1987 from his office at First Home Federal Savings and Loan at the edge of downtown where commercial Elm Street eased into the residential green of the turn-of-the-century Fisher Park neighborhood. If Greensboro could not attract the headquarters of a major bank, Melvin thought, then he would turn what was a successful, but very local, savings and loan into a statewide financial institution.

The building where Melvin had his office had once been the financial and regulatory hub for the S&L business in the Southeast. When it opened in 1970, the modern stone-and-glass structure housed the regional operations of the Federal Home Loan Bank Board. While Charlotte had landed the Federal Reserve Bank offices in the 1920s, Greensboro had become the center of the thrift industry from Virginia to Florida during one of the busiest times in the nation's home-building history.

The opening celebration of the new home loan bank offices included high school bands, and local officials made speeches. Then, eighteen months later, the regulators unexpectedly vacated the building, which had cost $1.8 million, and relocated to Atlanta. Subsequent investigations into the political shenanigans of the Nixon administration showed that the move was a political favor to a Georgia developer who had been generous to President Nixon and the Republican Party. The Greensboro building stood empty until Home Federal Savings and Loan, growing steadily and expanding its nest egg of residential lending, moved in and took over the Elm Street address.

Melvin became Home Federal's chief executive on February 1, 1978, nearly twenty years to the day after C. M. Vanstory had offered him his first bank job at Security National Bank. At the time, Home Federal was the largest of the state's nearly two hundred savings and loans. Melvin eagerly accepted the position, even though a friend told him he would be bored silly within six months. Running a savings and loan, whose bread and butter was home loans for growing families, was far different from working in the highly charged world of commercial banking, particularly at NCNB, which when Melvin left was within months of a bold expansion into Florida that made it an interstate bank.

Over the next ten years, the nation's financial industry would redistribute wealth and power, and no institution would be more aggressive in pushing the limits of change than NCNB. The bank would be transformed into first a regional and then a major national financial institution with offices from the Carolinas to Florida and west to Texas. Following close behind would be First Union National Bank, another Charlotte-based operation, with Winston-Salem's Wachovia, once the preeminent North Carolina bank, also in the hunt. By the early 1990s, the financial world would include Charlotte among the banking centers of the nation. Greensboro would fare considerably less well.

Melvin had an opportunity to be part of the explosive growth at NCNB just like his childhood chum from Asheboro Street, Jim Mims, who would run NCNB's Florida business before he retired and returned to Greensboro. During his time at NCNB, Melvin had turned down assignments to other cities. NCNB's tough-minded CEO, Thomas I. Storrs, who conceived the bank's interstate strategy, once told Melvin that he would have to choose between the role of a "public" banker who played a part in Greensboro and a "private" banker who knew how to make deals. "I had my fun in community building," Melvin said some time later. "It just happened that my vocation made it possible for me to have that fun."[1]

As he assumed his new duties at Home Federal, the federal government was relaxing restrictions on the range of business open to thrift institutions. For Melvin, these changes looked like opportunities to create a dynamic financial powerhouse that could compete with statewide banks for commercial loans, credit cards, and other forms of lending. In 1981, he arranged a merger with Winston-Salem Savings and created First Home Federal. A year later, Standard Savings of Winston-Salem was brought into the fold. By 1984, First Home was a $600 million institution with a commanding presence in two of the state's largest markets, Greensboro and Winston-Salem. "I had visions of First Home being that corporate headquarters bank that Greensboro so desperately needed," Melvin said.[2]

Melvin's first years in his new job coincided with his last years as mayor, and they brought him anything but the dull experience his friend had predicted. On his first day on the job, Melvin was faced with recovering what he could from the bankrupt $4 million Royal Villa convention hotel, a project that had been underwritten by his predecessor. Melvin ushered numerous prospective buyers through the building, which had been forced to close soon after it opened, but there were no takers, in part because the facility was located in a fading commercial section south of Greensboro with no compatible properties in sight. Melvin finally scored when he aroused some interest at the Greensboro Housing Authority, which agreed to take the building and convert it into an apartment complex for the elderly. Village Green, as it was renamed, got off to a rocky start, however, and would prove to be troublesome for months to come.

Far more vexing was a condition over which Melvin and his peers in the thrift industry had no control. By the early 1980s, First Home and other S&Ls all across the country were caught in a financial squeeze brought on by the highest interest rates in history. In order to have money available to compete in the marketplace, S&Ls were offering higher interest to attract deposits than they were earning on lower-interest loans made in preceding years. At a meeting of First Home shareholders at the end of his third year on the job, Melvin announced that First Home had lost $4 million the previous year, but for all the right reasons: the thrift's business was growing, he said, but not fast enough to offset the losses brought on by the spread in interest rates. Melvin's company was not alone. Not one of the federally insured S&Ls in Greensboro made a profit that year.

The answer, according to those Melvin listened to, was to package the old loans and sell them at a discounted value to produce cash that could then be reinvested at a higher rate of return. S&L regulators encouraged the move and even provided a new set of accounting rules that allowed First Home and others to write off the revenue lost from such sales over the next twenty years. In First Home's case, the transaction produced more than $230 million in cash that allowed the company to expand into new markets and serve new customers. The $57 million loss was considered tolerable under new regulations. After the sale, Melvin was ready to do business. "There really is a new bank in town," Melvin said in the summer of 1983.[3]

Calling First Home a "bank" rather than a "savings and loan" was important to Melvin and his directors. Melvin wanted to develop an image that projected energy as well as sound value but was not reminiscent of Depression-era S&Ls run by men like George Bailey, the character played by Jimmy Stewart in the film *It's a Wonderful Life*. Melvin suggested the name "Tri-Star Savings Bank"—with the three stars being Greensboro, Winston-Salem, and High Point—but didn't get very far with it. Another of his ideas was "Bankers Federal." Finally, the board decided to stick with First Home, but Melvin made it clear the company would be taking advantage of new regulations to expand into commercial ventures, retail checking accounts, and even automated teller machines.

One of Melvin's early and highly visible investments was in a downtown redevelopment project called Greensborough Court at Hamburger Square. The plans called for three partners—First Home and Jefferson-Pilot Corporation, along with builder J. M. Dixon Incorporated—to move Greensboro into the new market for downtown living. Early in 1985, work began on converting former warehouses, the old Dixie Belle textile plant, and other long-vacant buildings in the 300 block of South Davie Street into apartments and condominiums, a health club, and shops. The project complemented a new interest in downtown living and a modest revival of the south end of Elm Street, once the center of Greensboro's retail district. Others had already secured a historic site designation for the area, and the community was excited about the rehabilitation of the Carolina Theater. Downtown promoter Betty Cone and others envisioned a community of urban dwellers who would replace the drunks and transients often found sleeping on Elm Street doorsteps in the mornings.

The grand opening of Greensborough Court was only six weeks away when, on the night of April 13, 1985, firefighters arrived on South Davie Street to find a roaring fire in one of the Greensborough Court buildings. Within a short time, a two-block area, including all of the buildings under renovation, was ablaze. From a distance, it appeared as if all of downtown was burning. Flames leaped wildly into the sky, throwing off fist-sized embers that landed blocks away. A crowd of spectators, some of whom had just left an O. Henry festival at the Carolina Theater, was drawn to the sidelines to watch Davie Street burn. Standing with them was Jim Melvin, who began to feel sick as he watched his company's $2.5 million investment go up in smoke. Melvin telephoned his partner, Jefferson-Pilot CEO Roger Soles, to give him the news. Soles growled at Melvin about being disturbed late at night and told him they would take an accounting when the embers cooled.

The fire was a serious setback. Subsequent investigation determined that some of the buildings were simply too far gone to remain part of the project. To save the tax credits figured into the cost of the project, the usable buildings had to be returned to their original state, complete with the original brick. This sent rebuilding costs soaring.

The Lofts at Greensborough Court, a group of about a hundred apartments, opened six months behind schedule. They eventually proved popular, but the groundswell of interest was slow in building. The added expenses proved too much for Melvin, who sold First Home's interest to Jefferson-Pilot. In order to further cut their losses, the investors pulled the 1920s-era Greensboro National Bank building from the plan and gave it to Guilford County. (A decade later, the bank building proved to be a boon for businesses seeking high-speed Internet service: a subsequent owner discovered that the old building, which once held offices of AT&T, was one of the best-wired structures in the city.)

The fire at Greensborough Court was a rare disappointment in the days of First Home's expansion. The business was riding a growing swell in residential development greater than anything Guilford County had seen in years. By 1986, First Home had nearly four hundred and fifty employees working downtown, more than triple the number five years before. In addition to its banking offices on the east side of Elm Street, Melvin created First Home University, a comprehensive training program for new employees, and put the "school" in a four-story office building on the west side of Elm, where the company operated a large mortgage-loan servicing subsidiary.

"We were humming," Melvin said. First Home opened commercial loan offices in major markets in the Southeast, but Melvin's focus remained in the Triad, where he was a visible and active participant in building greater cooperation between Greensboro, Winston-Salem, and High Point, the leading cities of the region. Regional cooperation was inevitable, he said, and he predicted, "Regions that cooperate and do a good job . . . that really anticipate in planning and implementing their natural resources now, will be the successful regions of the twenty-first century."[4]

Melvin's regional emphasis made good business sense. First Home had more deposits than any financial institution in Greensboro and was in the top five in Winston-Salem, the home of Wachovia Bank. Melvin's board of directors included leading political and business figures from both communities. Among them were Greensboro mayor Vic Nussbaum, who had succeeded John Forbis in 1989, and Al Lineberry, who was an influential member of the state House. Winston-Salem board members included Colin Stokes, the top executive at R.J. Reynolds Tobacco Company, and Bert Bennett, an oil distributor and leading political figure.

Regionalism proved to be as hard a sell in the 1980s as it was in the 1950s, when Greensboro made an unsuccessful bid to build a regional water system. The region's two leading cities in banking, Greensboro and Winston-Salem, seemed content to compete rather than cooperate. Each had its own industrial base (Greensboro in textiles and Winston-Salem in tobacco) that appeared to be secure. For years, the two cities had operated competing airports that were located less than twenty miles apart. What looked easy on paper proved almost impossible in practice. Something as simple as coordinating the starting dates of the annual United Way fund drives was considered a major success.

That did not preclude Melvin from working to create the Piedmont Triad Development Corporation, which was formed with equal representation from Greensboro, Winston-Salem, and High Point. It, too, made little progress. A dozen years later, the only tangible result of this initiative was the renaming of the new Greensboro airport "Piedmont Triad International"—despite the fact that the only international landings were transports carrying goods between Wrangler's Greensboro base and its plants in Puerto Rico.

By the late 1980s, Melvin had opened First Home loan offices in Raleigh and Charlotte, two of the state's most vigorous markets, as well as Wilmington, North Carolina; Atlanta, Georgia; and Charleston, South Carolina. Raleigh's number-one home builder was an important customer. Much of the bank's growth came from $32 million in new capital that was brought into the business through its conversion to a stock-owned corporation in 1986. Melvin himself was among the 135 new shareholders; he had invested his entire life savings.

The conversion was required by the shifting positions of federal regulators. Two years after Melvin was told the bank's $57 million in losses could be charged off over twenty years, federal regulators reversed position and put First Home and a host of other S&Ls back on regular accounting methods. At that point, First Home was technically short of the required capital to remain in compliance with federal regulations. To return to a positive balance, First Home was put through a "supervised bankruptcy." In essence, the old business was discontinued, and the new stock-owned company took its place. The losses were carried forward on the books as "goodwill," an accounting decision that would come to haunt Melvin and thrift managers across the nation as a crisis in the industry began to build.

Excesses in the savings and loan business became national news in 1985 when institutions in Ohio and Maryland failed. In 1988, large institutions in the West and Southwest also went under. The federal government, which had increased federal guarantees for depositors, was left to clean up the mess, and the reserves set aside were not sufficient to cover the mountain of losses. Perhaps the most sensational case involved Charles Keating's Lincoln Savings and Loan in Arizona, whose failure cost taxpayers over $2 billion.

None of the lavish spending and corporate excess revealed in the Keating case or in similar cases in Texas and Florida was found in North Carolina, but First Home and other institutions were caught in the undertow of regulatory changes. "Congress was looking for someone to blame for almost the complete collapse of the financial industry. Not only thrifts, but banks too," Melvin said. "They found a few Keatings and painted everyone with the same brush."[5]

In response to the alarming losses, Congress passed new laws in 1989 that eliminated, among other things, the use of the goodwill provision that had carried First Home out of its conversion to a stock-owned company. Regulators told Melvin that First Home would have to come up with nearly $20 million in cash to be considered solvent. Just as Melvin was digesting this news, North Carolina began to feel the consequences of 1987 tax changes related to real estate investments. Within a year, real estate deals built on the old tax provisions were devalued by 10 to 20 percent, creating a desperate situation for lenders.

The new tax laws and a resulting recession in the real estate market exposed some significant problems at First Home. Projects that had looked golden before 1987 were in bankruptcy or foreclosure three years later. In 1990, First Home wrote off nearly $10 million in losses. Another $9 million was added in 1991. With each loan that federal examiners discounted as doubtful, the amount of cash required to meet reserve requirements increased. Rather than building a company, Melvin now found himself dismantling one to raise the cash necessary to satisfy the federal equity requirements.

"We had no court of appeal," Melvin said. "This examiner would come in with a team of people, he'd sit down with his calculator and appraise the loans." If the examiner determined First Home could only realize $800,000 on a $1 million loan, then another $200,000 was added to the amount that First Home was required to hold in cash reserves. Melvin told his management team: "Look, guys, this is going to be a dog-eat-dog battle. Our long-range plan is going to be to get through today. We are going to have to completely change our mode of operation."

The consequences were wrenching. Senior management was cut from fourteen to four. Melvin and Jim Mims, whom Melvin hired after Mims retired from NCNB to run First Home's banking operation, took pay cuts, and neither would ever again see a raise. The staff was cut by 20 percent. Some of the employees released were men and women Melvin had personally recruited, and he took their departure hard. Nonessential operations were closed. The company was prohibited from making any new loans. In some cases, real estate was repossessed and put on the market. "That was one of the most painful parts of this meltdown period," Melvin recalled. "We had to start downsizing and letting a lot of capable people go and not doing some things we were getting very good at." A second round of audits came in 1991, and this time the write-downs put First Home below the amount required for minimum reserves. "At that point," Melvin said, "they were telling us, 'You either sell this company or we're going to take it over.'"

Late in 1991, Melvin, along with First Home's chief financial officer, Larry Thompson, and a Washington, D.C., lawyer with expertise in S&L cases, reported to the newly created Office of Thrift Supervision (OTS) in Atlanta. They carried with them a recovery plan that called for undergirding First Home with new capital. If it succeeded, Melvin said, First Home would return to compliance in 1994. The proposal was rejected. Melvin said that Jack Ryan, the OTS executive in charge, told him, "We don't think you can do that. We are not going to let you do that. You have X number of months to do this, and if you don't then we will recommend that we take you over."

At one point in the negotiations, Melvin's frustration turned to anger, and he slammed his office keys onto Ryan's desk and told him that if he thought he could do a better job, he should take over First Home now. But if the government took control, Melvin said, it was going to cost taxpayers $100 million. Ryan shrugged off the offer, but Melvin's histrionics bought more time. Riding back to the airport on one of Atlanta's rapid transit trains, attorney Ray Tiernan told Melvin, "I don't think I would have said that."

Tiernan urged Melvin to resign and take measures to protect himself. He warned that the OTS usually went after the management of failed thrifts and that legal action could tie up Melvin's personal assets for years. "You could lose everything you own," said Tiernan. "They take everything you have. They will come in some afternoon at closing hours, put a lock on everything, put a lien against all personal assets, and they will ruin you. I would resign and let someone else liquidate this company." Melvin refused to quit. "We're going to fight this," Melvin told his associates. "We're going to stay the course, because we have too good of a company, and we have not done anything wrong other than get washed over by the real estate depression."

A certain amount of paranoia was inevitable. As the deadlines from the OTS approached, Melvin posted a lookout in a corner office on Friday afternoons, when federal examiners were most likely to arrive and execute takeover orders. The lookout was warned to be alert to the arrival of several cars in the parking lot just before closing time. "I don't know what we would have done if we had seen anyone," Melvin said later.[6]

As Melvin struggled with First Home's problems, he was hit by a deep personal loss in the death of Tom Osborne in December 1991. The two had been as close as brothers. Melvin had even saved Osborne's life while on a city trip. The episode produced a story both loved to tell: The two were in Washington on city business and were sharing a hotel room. When Osborne fell ill, they had quickly slipped on overcoats over their pajamas as they rushed to the hospital. On their return, other hotel guests gawked at two grown men returning to the hotel in the wee hours wearing their nightclothes.

Despite the troubles he was facing at First Home, Melvin remained active in civic projects. At the height of the thrift's negotiations with the OTS, Melvin and the Greensboro Development Corporation attempted to put together a science and engineering research center that would harness the faculties of UNCG and NC A&T. The GDC paid for an exhaustive study to justify the program and raised seed money to get it off the ground. After nearly two years of work, however, the UNC Board of Governors opted for another program, leaving the Greensboro interests disappointed once again.

After the OTS rejected his plan for refinancing First Home, Melvin knew the only answer was to sell the company, either as a whole or in pieces. If that was to be done, he was determined to remain to the end. He stayed on the job with the same stubborn determination he had exhibited in the face of the inevitable in his debates with George Simkins Jr. Melvin believed he owed his allegiance to investors, many of them good friends, who had put their money into First Home on his promises of future reward. He believed that his integrity, along with his life savings, was on the line. In addition, he was concerned about the fate of hundreds of employees, most of whom he knew by first name and whom he considered his corporate family. He was determined to execute a smooth transition, with as little harm to coworkers as possible and at no cost to the government.

Over the coming months, the negotiations with the OTS took their toll. Melvin experienced highs of relief when he thought he had a sale complete and depths of frustration when suitors backed away at the last minute. Bankers and other tire kickers from financial institutions around the country inspected various pieces of the company. Some were more eager than others. "Several banks went to the eleventh hour of merging with First Home," said Mike Weaver, who remained close to Melvin during the troubles. "Jim would do tremendous work. He would get his emotions wrapped up in it, and then it would fail. It happened two, three, or four times. Those were horrible letdowns for him. That took as much a toll on Jim as the federal government."[7]

The pressure was intense. Melvin released his anxieties at the end of the day at Bryan Park, where he littered the driving range with bucket after bucket of golf balls. But golf, his usual release, often was not enough. "I don't know how he held up," said Weaver. "It was really devastating. I remember one weekend we were supposed to play golf. He called one Friday late, and he sounded like he didn't have friend in the world. 'Mike, I am not going to play this weekend. I just want to stay home and do nothing. I just don't have it in me to go play.'"[8]

———

Melvin's faith sustained him. He attended West Market Street United Methodist Church, his spiritual home since he was a youngster. The working, generous faith he found there was the same one he had seen demonstrated over the years by his mother. "Even in her later years," said Jim, "she would spend half her day calling around to her friends and see if they were all right. She took people to buy groceries, waited on them at the doctor's office. I grew up watching her do that. My dad was pretty good at that too."[9]

After Jim and Susan married, their commitment spanned religions. Susan remained a Roman Catholic, while Jim continued his membership at West Market. "I am as comfortable at West Market as he is at St. Pius," Susan said. "We respect each other's place in that and try to make it work. Both of our boys were baptized in the Catholic Church and at West Market, too."[10]

Jim taught Sunday school for a group of teenagers. "Years ago, I got invited to speak to a lot of young people," said Melvin. "I told them, 'The first thing you have to do is have a faith.' I don't see how agnostics make it. You don't have anything to anchor to." He also played a pivotal role in church administration.[11]

Faith had helped the family through Jim's father's senseless death. Virgil and her sons did not blame God for taking Joe Melvin. Said Susan: "When his father was killed, he never came undone. He never carried any grudges. When those guys came up for parole, he didn't put up any roadblocks."[12]

Melvin did not withdraw from his involvement in the community. In fact, in an unintended way, he used an appearance as featured speaker at the graduation ceremonies for Greensboro College to reflect his own determination as he worked his way through the difficulties at First Home. Graduates, their parents, faculty, and visitors were all seated in chairs on the lawn of the campus just west of downtown for the event. Seated at the front with the college president and others of note, Melvin could not help noticing the rising unease of the crowd as the temperature turned cool and dark clouds pushed over the horizon. When William S. Jones, the chair of the college's board of trustees, finished his lengthy introduction, Melvin was fearful that raindrops would begin to fall at any minute. He stepped up to the podium without pulling his text from his jacket and paraphrased a quote from Winston Churchill, England's wartime leader: "My advice to you is never give up. Never, never give up," Melvin said, and then he sat down. The students applauded wildly.

The concern of the college's president was clearly evident on his face as he whispered to Melvin, "Is that all you are going to say?" Melvin allowed as the weather probably was not going to permit anything more, and the president dismissed the crowd. Later, the student newspaper at Melvin's alma mater wrote that perhaps University of North Carolina president C. D. Spangler Jr., the speaker at ceremonies on the Chapel Hill campus, should have used Melvin's speechwriter.

———

Duties beyond the bank helped relieve some of the strain, but the OTS was never far from Melvin's mind. One afternoon in the early summer of 1992, he got a call from a First Home customer who ran a pizza restaurant. Melvin's caller said he had just taken a large order for delivery to a Greensboro motel. The buyer was the Office of Thrift Supervision. The alert proved to be a false alarm. The OTS was not moving on First Home, but another troubled Greensboro institution, First American Savings Bank.

Melvin had become particularly hopeful about a sale of First Home to Southern National Bank, a growing regional bank with headquarters in Lumberton, North Carolina. It looked like the best deal for his investors and for Greensboro. Melvin hoped Southern National would buy First Home's Greensboro and Winston-Salem retail banking operations and make its headquarters in Greensboro. The deal fell through at the last minute, and Southern subsequently bought a Winston-Salem S&L and took its home offices there, only to merge in 1995 with BB&T, which was in the early stages of becoming a regional banking power.

Everyone was trying to buy time. One potential buyer of the First Home commercial loans literally pleaded with Ryan at the OTS in the spring of 1993 to hold off while his auditors examined the First Home portfolio. The company subsequently placed a successful bid for the commercial loans portion of the business, and the last piece of the puzzle that Melvin had been trying to construct for two years fell into place. The sale was complete.

On the Friday before Memorial Day weekend in 1993, Melvin and other officers at First Home took seats at the head of a long table in a conference room at a Greensboro law firm. For most of the day, they did nothing but sign their names as hundreds of documents were pushed in front of them by lawyers representing the array of buyers. At one point, as Melvin took a break, he looked at the gathering of nearly two dozen lawyers and federal regulators and said, "I think I now know how a pig feels at a pig picking." Nobody laughed. "The regulators were walking around beating their chests and thinking we have saved the taxpayers all of this money," Melvin recalled. "It was all I could do to be sane."[13]

A Rockville, Maryland, company bought First Home's $116 million commercial loan portfolio, while a Miami company took over the institution's 10,800 home mortgages valued at nearly $700 million. BB&T bought the Winston-Salem banking business, while Central Carolina Bank of Durham (CCB) added about $450 million in deposits with the purchase of First Home's Guilford County banking operations. The investments proved to be good deals: CCB recovered what it paid for First Home's business in less than two years. Out of nearly $1 billion in commercial and home loans, only one claim was filed against a reserve fund that First Home was required to post to cover bad debts, and it was for less than $15,000. "That meant our people were doing exactly as they were supposed to do," Melvin said.

The sale of First Home brought an end to a business that had been part of Greensboro for seventy-nine years. Through wars, depressions, and good times, First Home had built thousands of homes and helped hundreds of businesses. The thrift's management had made itself part of the community, and members of the board of directors were a who's who of the city. Gone, too, were Greensboro's chances of becoming the headquarters of a major state bank.

Melvin proved as good as his word. The closing was completed without the loss of a single dollar of taxpayers' money. The investors, on the other hand, forfeited all but about $4 million of the $32 million they had put up during the conversion in 1986. Melvin saw his life savings, as well as his retirement benefits, evaporate with the sale of the company. "We had no parachutes," Melvin said. "I lost all my retirement benefits. I walked away from there with nothing."[14]

During his negotiations to purchase the First Home Greensboro business, CCB chairman William Burns asked Melvin to remain on in Greensboro as a consultant, but Melvin was reluctant to do so. "I had had it. I was burned out," Melvin said. But as an unemployed fifty-nine-year-old, complete with the scars from a failed S&L, he realized he had few other options. He reconsidered Burns's offer.

Burns installed new management to run the day-to-day business and made Melvin part of the bank's management team and CCB's number-one ambassador in the community. Melvin moved into the former First Home operations building, which had housed the S&L's training program and mortgage servicing business. He and his assistant, Shirley McDevitt, who had been with him since his days at NCNB, worked in a space that was empty of people, although it remained outfitted with desks, chairs, and filing cabinets. The vast office was eerily silent. Melvin compared his own feelings to what he had heard about recurring nightmares experienced by war veterans. The battle over First Home had marked his life as indelibly as combat; the ghosts of the empty work areas remained with him for years. "Every desk was right like they left it the day they left. When I went in that building, I felt like the people were [still] sitting there," he said.[15]

———

First Home slipped from sight as further changes were altering Greensboro's economic landscape. During the S&L's waning days, Sears announced the closing of its huge mail-order center, a building that covered twenty-four acres and had provided jobs to more than eleven hundred workers for nearly fifty years. Countless numbers of refrigerators, hand tools, bicycles and sleds, and thousands of other items that appeared in Sears's thick, door-stopper catalogs had been shipped from the building on Greensboro's north side to homes all across the Southeast.

Sears customers were being drawn to competitors like Wal-Mart, Home Depot, K-Mart, and other big-box stores where prices were lower and the selection was just as broad. In fact, Greensboro developers were on their way to creating a retail city populated by such businesses just south of the intersection of Wendover Avenue and Interstate 40. The traffic jams that had once characterized downtown grew even more ferocious as virtually every major retailer opened a store within sight of the interchange.

The passing of Sears looked like the result of a shift in consumer preference, not a watershed. It came at about the same time as a modest uptick in the fortune of the textile companies, which offered some encouragement. Cone Mills Corporation and Burlington Industries emerged from private ownership with public stock offerings. In June 1992, Arthur Anderson and Company ranked Cone Mills as one of the top privately owned companies in North Carolina when it put six million shares on the market. In the intervening years, the company had closed eight plants, sold one, and converted one more to other uses. The reductions made it possible for Cone Mills to meet its debt obligations and maintain profitability. When Burlington issued stock in 1992, it was roughly half the size of the industry giant Asher Edelman had attempted to buy.

Yet there was no denying that the American textile industry was shrinking. Throughout the 1980s, import quotas had continued to grow despite appeals from industry executives like Dewey Trogdon, who became one of the leaders of the American Textile Manufacturers Institute. In the mid- and late 1980s, Cone Mills employees and family members wrote more than sixty-two thousand letters to president Ronald Reagan asking for his signature on a trade bill limiting imports. The president turned it down. In 1988, Trogdon had spent an hour with vice president George Bush appealing for help. Bush, too, refused to support legislation to aid the industry. Trogdon was disgusted with the lack of White House support, especially in light of the strong backing industry leaders had given Republicans, who had emerged as a potent political force in the South. "If we can get this kind of audience and you can't get anything done," Trogdon said some years later, "what can you do?"[16]

The changing look of his hometown bothered William Hemphill, now retired from United Guaranty, a company he had helped build from the ground up. In retirement, he had continued his civic work as a director of the Cemala Foundation. In the summer of 1999, Hemphill was to attend a meeting of the foundation's board of directors when, at the last minute, his plans changed. Priscilla Taylor, Cemala's president, asked Hemphill to videotape a message for the board.

Ceasar Cone II was a man of vision, Hemphill told Cone's children and grandchildren, who made up the foundation's board of directors, and the city was at a loss without someone like him. "He was a mover and a shaker. Look at the magnificent airport. It would not be what it is today if Ceasar had not been a SOB and gotten things done," Hemphill declared. Beneath Cone's gruff exterior and other eccentricities was someone who was devoted to his community. He seldom said no when Hemphill called on him to support one cause or the other.

As Hemphill finished his reminiscing, his tone changed, and he described what he saw as Greensboro's future for Ceasar II's family, none of whom lived in Greensboro. The textile industry was disappearing, he said. Tobacco was on the way out. Furniture factories would be gone next. The city's economic engine was sputtering. "There are forces working on Greensboro," he said, "that are going to make this a terrible place to live." He offered Cone's children and grandchildren a choice: they could continue with meaningful but modest projects or be bold. "If you want to have real clout," Hemphill announced, "you have to go after bigger things so that everybody can see that we must take action in Greensboro."[17]

Chapter 17

Action Greensboro

*O*n THE SUMMER of 2003, Schiffman's Jewelers remained tucked in the middle of the 200 block of Greensboro's South Elm Street in a modest building that had welcomed customers for seventy years. That's where Tony Schiffman was most often found. Tall, balding, with rimless glasses fixed tight in the middle of his nose, Schiffman was the senior member of the family and was casual, almost nonchalant, about the survival of Greensboro's oldest business enterprise, one that had supported three generations of Schiffmans for more than a hundred years.

Tony's grandfather, Simon, opened the family's first store in 1892, when Greensboro was on the cusp of entering the modern age. It was a time of great expectations, as well as deep disappointments. When Simon arrived, local investors were hopeful that the cash they had put into construction of a blast furnace north of town would turn Greensboro into a "little Pittsburgh." That hope never materialized, but a few years later two brothers named Cone guaranteed the city's future when they bought the steel mill land and outfitted their first textile mill.

Education also offered Greensboro some promise as Simon Schiffman surveyed the town. Local money had just secured the location of new state institutions—one to train white women to be teachers and a second to educate African Americans in agriculture and the trades—but students had yet to attend a single class. For the most part, higher education remained the province of church-sponsored institutions such as the Methodists' Greensboro and Bennett colleges situated on the fringe of downtown and the privately endowed Guilford College, long affiliated with the Society of Friends, whose campus was several miles out in the country.

Despite the uncertainty, Greensboro appeared to be a good place for a fresh start, so Schiffman ended his journey and opened a business. He chose the east side of Elm Street, where saloons were prohibited, so as to attract a high-class clientele who would be embarrassed to shop on the seedier west side.

More than a century later, Schiffman's was a surviving link to nineteenth-century Greensboro as well as a lingering reminder of the heyday of downtown, when Elm Street was the center of the area's retail business. At one time, three major department stores had been only a two-minute walk from Schiffman's front door. The street was lined with variety stores, shops offering men's and women's fashions, even a grocery store. Customers jammed the sidewalks throughout the year, not just during the busy holiday shopping season. At mid-century, Simon passed the business to his son, Tony's father, Arnold, or "Mr. A," as he was called, who in turn was succeeded by the next generation. By the 1970s, when Tony Schiffman's time came, the vibrancy of downtown was fading, and the jewelry store was on its way to becoming an island of commerce amid empty storefronts and occasional wig shops and record outlets specializing in soul music.

What had held Schiffman's in place through the years? The answer was simple, Tony Schiffman explained. When your inventory includes diamonds and fine jewelry equal in value to the annual take-home pay of a textile worker, reputation counts for more than location. The family never seriously considered leaving a building that was long paid for or forsaking a location that was familiar to the "carriage trade," said Tony, using an old-fashioned phrase. Despite the shifting character of downtown, the store remained convenient for "the locker rats playing poker at the Greensboro Country Club," he said, who could "leave the game and get to the store in less time than it takes to find a parking place at Friendly Shopping Center." In truth, Schiffman's had covered its bets with suburban locations, including a store at Friendly Shopping Center, and probably would have fled Elm Street had it been the location of the business's sole outlet. Altogether, the Schiffmans owned eight other locations spread out from Columbia, South Carolina, to San Francisco, California. Elm Street was a convenient, and inexpensive, home office where sales for the entire enterprise were coordinated.

Greensboro had almost come full circle in a hundred years. The city was again in transition, and the future was as uncertain as it had been when local boosters saw their dream of iron and steel mills evaporate. There were new stirrings in town. Outside Schiffman's store, a beefy fellow with tousled reddish-blond hair was slipping a sapling into a three-by-three-foot opening in the concrete sidewalk in front of the old Thalhimer's department store, just a few doors up from the jewelry store. That was Milton Kern, the man Schiffman called "the mayor of South Elm Street."

During the previous three years, Kern and his wife, Debby, had brought new life to downtown as they bought and overhauled long-forsaken buildings on South Elm. A new gallery had opened, and Triad Stage, an experiment in live theater, was in its third season. The latest project of the Kerns and their partners was the conversion of the former Thalhimer's department store, which had been the object of an earlier effort to create an arts center. It was to become the home of a comedy club and an elegant ballroom available for wedding receptions and large parties. Kern even had plans to flood a narrow alleyway and turn it into a water garden, complete with koi and a cascading waterfall. Other investors had renovated the old Kress store. The striking art deco building was home to a regional advertising agency, Bouvier Kelly, and the Hyatt Hammond architectural firm.

Nearby were new restaurants, a spa, renovated downtown residential space, and even a bakery whose front door opened onto an alley with murals on the walls and a decorative gate at the street. Greensborough Court, the forerunner of downtown living, had risen from the ashes of the disastrous 1984 fire. The apartments now were full of tenants, and the management had a waiting list. New condominiums were going up across the railroad tracks in the direction of Asheboro Street, now Martin Luther King Jr. Boulevard. Other condominiums had been built across from the Arts Center (the former offices of the *Greensboro Daily News* and *Greensboro Record*).

The old Southern Railway depot, largely unused since the company gave it to the city in 1979, had reopened as the city's public transportation hub. Local public transit—buses connecting Greensboro with High Point and Winston-Salem, as well as points in the city—flowed in and out of the place. Soon, Amtrak would close an embarrassment of a station that stood alongside the freight tracks west of the city, and rail passengers would return to the old depot after it was restored to its 1920s elegance. Nothing was more satisfying to Jim Melvin than the dedication of the depot in the name of his long-time friend and Jaycee ally, Doug Galyon. After years in local politics as a member of the city council and the county board of commissioners, Galyon had emerged as chair of the state transportation board, one of the top political appointments in the state. The naming of the station came as a surprise to Galyon, whose eyes filled with tears when the announcement was made at the grand-opening ceremony.

The anchor of downtown remained the Jefferson Building, now nearly twice the size it had been when it opened in 1927. Before Roger Soles retired in 1993 as CEO of the Jefferson-Pilot Corporation, he saw through the completion of a $40-million, twenty-story addition that complemented the old building's style and design. Soles said employees favored moving downtown, so he agreed to consolidate the company's operations there instead of building something new on the former Pilot Life Insurance Company campus south of Greensboro at Sedgefield. Of course, Soles could have put JP's headquarters anywhere he wanted. His decision to enhance the JP presence on Elm Street was a generous parting gesture to the city that had been the company's home for a century. It helped steady the number of downtown workers, which had hovered at around twenty thousand during the 1990s. Companies like United Guaranty and Wrangler remained on Elm Street, along with banks, law firms, and assorted small businesses.

One block north of the Jefferson Building, construction was under way on a downtown park that builders hoped would complement a cultural complex that included the Arts Center, the Greensboro Children's Museum, the YWCA, and a spacious, modern, Web-connected public library. One block south on Elm Street was the beginnings of a civil rights museum in the old F. W. Woolworth store. In a few months, bulldozers would begin the demolition of a county office building a few blocks west—it had once been the headquarters of Burlington Industries—to make way for a minor-league baseball stadium.

These changes had not sprung up overnight. Piece had built upon piece. Kern's confidence in investing in old buildings rose in 2001 when backers of Triad Stage began to convert a former department store into a three-hundred-seat performance hall. Proposals that had languished on the public agenda for years, such as the transportation center, were finally coming to fruition. Downtown Greensboro was not fully revived— far from it—but there was more activity afoot than anyone had been seen in decades.

Melvin was as enthusiastic about what was happening downtown as he had been about any change in the city landscape. His interest in the area had never flagged since the days when he was mayor. Only the scenery was different now, and more creativity was required, as demonstrated by the arrangement he brokered in 1998 for the Joseph M.

Bryan Foundation to help the Greensboro Children's Museum find a new home in space once occupied by an automobile dealership.

Melvin had taken an interest in the children's museum project after the museum's board of directors made an appeal to the foundation for help in a capital campaign. Most of the money was to pay for the renovation of a building on South Elm Street that had once been the Montgomery Ward department store. Melvin took a look at that space and decided there had to be a better place to put the museum. The Elm Street location offered only limited parking, and the building would require displays to be located on several levels. He approached David Brown, whose Gate City Motor Company had moved out of old buildings just across from the new library and historical museum. The car dealership had been empty for almost eight years.

Brown wanted to sell, but his price was higher than Melvin thought was reasonable. After some negotiation, they worked out a purchase price of $1.5 million for the property. The Bryan Foundation put up $1.2 million, while Brown donated $300,000 back to the nonprofit. Brown had a nice tax deduction, and the children's museum got three acres of land, a broad open area all on one level for its displays, and opportunities to expand outdoors.

Construction of the Randleman Dam also was under way south of Greensboro on the Randolph-Guilford county line. The $20-million dam—which made up less than a fifth of the project's total cost—would create a reservoir out of fifteen miles of the Deep River streambed. Once in service, it was designed to secure a water supply for Greensboro, High Point, Jamestown, Archdale, Randleman, and parts of Randolph County. The completion of the dam—water would begin to build by the spring of 2005—represented the end of more than twenty years of hard work. Backers had faced incredible obstacles, beginning with the decision in the early 1980s by President Reagan to scale back flood control efforts of the sort that had been the foundation of projects like the Randleman Dam for decades. A regional water authority was created, and it hammered together a joint initiative that overcame objections from many who questioned the quality of the water that would be collected and the simple economics of the plan.

These victories offered some welcome news in the face of the bad. By the fall of 2003, every major textile manufacturing firm in the city was trying to find new life in the bankruptcy court. Shifts in the world economy had reduced the mainstays of Greensboro's industrial base to shadows of what they had been in earlier decades. As Burlington Industries emerged from court protection, the company's new owner, New York financier Wilbur Ross, announced plans to empty the company's headquarters west of downtown, where more than twelve hundred had once reported to solid, well-paid jobs. The building had become excess space for a company that now had only five thousand workers at nine plants, two of those in Mexico.

Cone Mills was crippled too. In fact, Ross was preparing plans to bring Cone out of bankruptcy and combine the best of what was left of it with the remnants of Burlington. Cone's mighty White Oak Mill, where more denim had been made than under any other roof in the world, was still running, but another round of layoffs had just been announced. Across town, Guilford Mills's largest plant had been gone for a full year; the site was under excavation for construction of yet another shopping plaza at the crowded Wendover–Interstate 40 interchange, the center of the city's retail business. A second Guilford plant on West Market Street had a "For Sale" sign out front. It would later be demolished and the space developed as a shopping center.

Perhaps most troubling amid the news of layoffs and plant closings was the realization that the new jobs that were coming on line to replace those in textiles, tobacco, and furniture did not pay the same good wages. "As a result," one analyst wrote, "the typical Guilford [County] resident was poorer toward the end of the so-called 1990s boom than at the beginning."[1] The state employment office projected that for the balance of the twenty-first century's first decade, the demand would be for workers in retail sales, customer service, and fast food.

When Melvin had become mayor in 1971, Greensboro was the second largest city in the state, just behind Charlotte and well ahead of Raleigh. Thirty years later, Charlotte was a financial center, home to two of the nation's largest banks, with a vibrant center city, professional sports teams, and a diversified economy. Raleigh had prospered in the technology boom produced by the Research Triangle and the growth at North Carolina State University and in state government. It was home to SAS, one of the largest privately held technology firms in the nation. Its founder, James Goodnight, was North Carolina's richest man. The Raleigh airport had been chosen over Greensboro's as a regional hub for American Airlines. One resident described Greensboro as "pleasantly mediocre"[2] and losing momentum.

Greensboro's business community had been reshaped. The largest employer, with a staff of seven thousand, was Cone Health System, a multihospital medical care complex that had expanded from the Moses H. Cone Memorial Hospital. VF Corporation had moved Blue Bell from Greensboro in the mid-1980s, but the company had relocated its corporate headquarters to the city in 1998, adding more than a hundred well-paying corporate jobs. VF no longer manufactured apparel, but was the world's largest publicly held marketer of branded lines. During the 1990s, a local start-up, RF Micro Devices, had blossomed with the production of components for cell phones, creating a few millionaires as well as nearly two thousand jobs. United Healthcare, one of the largest health maintenance organizations in the country, was born and raised in the city. New Breed Incorporated applied new technology to an old chore—managing distribution systems—and produced a thousand jobs for the area's economy.

A rare jewel was found on the southern edge of Greensboro. It was Grandover Resort, a stunning complex that offered championship golf, a spa, office buildings, private homes, and a first-class hotel where president George W. Bush was entertained during a visit in August 2002. Grandover was the dream of the irrepressible Joe Koury, who had quietly gathered up the land that local boosters had hoped would become the home of Anheuser-Busch in the 1960s. Unfortunately, Koury never got to meet the president or see the completion of his dream, once billed as a $945 million investment. He died before construction was complete in 1998. He had seen through his promise of a convention center, however: the Joseph S. Koury Convention Center adjacent to his Four Seasons Mall had become one of the most successful privately owned facilities in the East.

These were all promising signs, but what of the future? Federal Express was moving ahead with plans for a $500 million shipping hub, a project that would be complete in 2009, once an endless track of court fights was concluded. As for the near term, no one would say. Even experienced hands like Melvin could do no more than hope for the best. The only certainty seemed to be that Greensboro was going to be different from the city that had been his home for nearly seventy years. He was resigned to big changes and lowered expectations. Old comparisons and ambitions of intercity competition were gone.

"What we have got to do—and there is some psychological adjustment for me—is we have got to work on being a better Greensboro," Jim Melvin said, resigned to facts that were not hopeful. "We have got to let Greensboro be what it is."

There was a note of "might have been" in Melvin's outlook. Perhaps Greensboro would have been a different place if North Carolina National

Bank had put its headquarters there instead of Charlotte in 1960. At the same time, there is no guarantee that the bank, which became NCNB, then NationsBank, and finally Bank of America, would have developed in Greensboro as it had in Charlotte. Neighbors in Winston-Salem, twenty-five miles away, could attest to the lack of guarantees. Winston-Salem's Wachovia Corporation, the leading North Carolina bank when NCNB was just being created, remained a local institution in name only after its merger with Charlotte's First Union. R.J. Reynolds Tobacco Company was also reduced in size and community stature.

"We need to expand our thinking and adjust our psyche," Melvin said. "If we can develop enough core recreational activities, we can attract a lot of people. They are not going to live here, a lot are not going to work here, but they might recreate here, educate here, entertain here, and look after health care needs here."[3]

Jim Melvin had retired from private business in 1996 but had never settled into the usual golf and grandchildren routine followed by many of his peers. He left banking for another full-time job: he was going to run the Joseph M. Bryan Foundation. It was an assignment that he accepted with a deep sense of obligation to a man who had loved Greensboro as much as he did. Melvin and Bryan had grown exceedingly close after their first meeting in 1968, when Melvin asked Bryan to increase his gift to the United Way. Neither would forget a poignant moment at Caldwell School, at the close of a program designed to show what his money had accomplished, when a youngster approached Bryan and asked to sing a song. As the ten-year-old sang "Jesus Loves Me," tears welled up in Bryan's eyes. Later, as Bryan and Melvin were driving away from the school, Bryan said, "Jim, I believe that was $25,000 well spent."

Over the years, the bond between the two had bordered on the familial: Melvin was Bryan's second son; Bryan became the father that Melvin had lost in 1972. In the later years of Bryan's life, he was an occasional dinner guest at the Melvins' home. Melvin regularly drove Bryan about the city to check on various projects in which Bryan's dollars were at work. The philanthropist was especially interested in anything with his name on it, such as the roadway dedicated in his honor that linked downtown to the airport. He wanted to be sure that such projects were the best they could be. Bryan would ask pointed questions about their progress; Melvin found the answers. Bryan's death in 1995—he was in his one hundredth year—bound Melvin even more firmly to his old friend's ambitions for Greensboro: in his will, Bryan named Melvin co-executor of his estate and put him in charge of the foundation.

Despite their close relationship, Melvin was unaware of the extent of Bryan's wealth until he assumed his new duties at the foundation Bryan had created in the mid-1980s. For its first ten years, the foundation had been a mere shell, with modest assets that produced an annual income of $25,000 or so that was distributed to local organizations. Bryan dispensed millions personally, however.

Melvin and the other directors had little to do at the annual meetings in Bryan's office other than share a pleasant time and listen to Bryan talk about his hopes for the future. Melvin was stunned when he learned that Bryan had left three-fourths of his $88 million estate—about $68 million in all—to the foundation. It was four times more than what Melvin was expecting. "Serious money," as Melvin said. For the community, it meant a minimum of $3.4 million a year would be available for distribution in grants.

Bryan's directions for the foundation were as explicit as they were broad. The foundation's first obligation was to support Bryan Park. Joe Bryan had an absolute love affair with the park's fifteen hundred acres north of Greensboro, a portion of which was bought and developed with his money. The park included deep woods, rolling hillsides, a soccer complex that would be expanded to seventeen playing fields and a stadium, as well as two championship golf courses that embraced the edge of Lake Townsend, the city's reservoir. In the years before his death, Bryan had visited the park almost daily and was on hand for the dedication of a life-size statue of him wearing his GGO blazer. It stood just outside the Bryan Enrichment Center, a gracious and modern public building whose construction he had monitored down to the smallest detail.

The center had been Bryan's idea. Melvin was in his fourth term as mayor when Bryan asked about planning a building to enhance the park opportunities for guests. Momentarily caught off guard, Melvin recalled that the city had recently built a community center for $600,000. He said the city could probably build something for that amount. "Let's build it," Bryan said. "I'll pay for it."

Melvin went straight to city manager Tom Osborne, and the two soon had in hand an architectural rendering from Hyatt Hammond for a modern, stylish building with broad windows and an atrium that opened the interior to the outside. When the construction bids were opened, however, the cost estimates were closer to $900,000, half again as much as Melvin had estimated. The mayor sheepishly reported the news to

Bryan and suggested cuts that would bring the building's cost down closer to his earlier estimate.

Bryan interrupted. "No," he told Melvin, "I like that building. Let's go on and build it." By the time the building opened in 1978, it had cost closer to $1.6 million, more than twice Melvin's initial estimate and nearly twice the amount of the bids. Bryan honored his commitment without complaint and contributed additional funds for furnishings. He personally selected the design for the flatware and linens purchased for meal service.

Once the special needs of Bryan Park were satisfied, the terms of Bryan's will left the board to make its own decisions about how to support projects that came under a broad umbrella of interests, from cultural to economic endeavors. Bryan's only restriction was that the foundation's money be used for the benefit of "the citizens of greater Greensboro." Just what that meant was not clear to Melvin and the other board members. During much of the first year after Bryan's death, while unhappy family members wrangled over Bryan's will in court, the directors sought advice on how to proceed. They asked for help from former University of North Carolina president William C. Friday and Tom Lambeth of the large Z. Smith Reynolds Foundation, as well as a wide range of community leaders.

The board ultimately decided to depend on its own understanding of the needs of the community rather than ask organizations to submit grant proposals. As a group, the Bryan board represented a broad spectrum of interests in the community, and each member drew on his or her own appreciation of community needs. Board member Shirley Frye had met Bryan when she went to him for financial help for NC A&T State University when she was implementing a new development program for the school. She was a former schoolteacher and community leader. Attorney Carole W. Bruce brought with her months of work with Bryan as he shaped each sentence in the foundation documents. Builder-developer Michael Weaver was a community leader whom Bryan had invited onto the board. Before his death, Bryan also had recruited Michael W. Haley, an enterprising businessman who had impressed Bryan with his efforts to bring a regional youth soccer program to Bryan Park. David L. DeVries was a management consultant and former staff member of the Center for Creative Leadership. He was the only board member who had not known Bryan personally.

Friday's visit to the board generated interest in a new style of educating youngsters called Paideia, which impressed upon students an appreciation for civility, character, and listening skills, as well as academic achievement. With a $1 million grant from the foundation, the National Paideia Center moved to Greensboro, and the Paideia instructional method was eventually incorporated into one-third of the schools in the system, producing profoundly positive results. The board also adopted an innovative program designed to develop the leadership potential of teachers and principals in the newly merged Guilford school system. In time, a $5 million grant paid for six hundred school leaders to undergo intensive training at the Center for Creative Leadership, which opened an ongoing partnership with the foundation.

The board also approved the disbursement of lesser amounts for community efforts. For example, Melvin took a fancy to plans for a Christmas parade of the sort that had once drawn tens of thousands to downtown Greensboro to kick off the holiday season. Thousands did return to see the parade after money from the Bryan Foundation allowed the Jaycees and other sponsors to bring to Greensboro huge cartoon balloons like those made famous by the Macy's parade in New York City.

Melvin and the other board members took a proprietary interest in the projects they launched. Rather than have grantees file perfunctory annual reports, school officials came in monthly to report in person on their progress. The board thought of the foundation as a true partner in the projects underwritten by Bryan money rather than simply a bank account. Accountability was a Bryan hallmark, and it continued under Melvin.

The ability to pick and choose projects gave Melvin and the board the flexibility to respond quickly to opportunities and needs without the encumbrance of grant deadlines and piles of applications to review. "We don't have to sit here and build a staff and look at hundreds of applications when you might do ten," Melvin explained. "In his wisdom Mr. Bryan wanted us to be proactive, not reactive."[4]

In 1999, Melvin and the Bryan board were beginning to see results from their investment in education. It was an encouraging sign at a time when the community's economic health was in decline. The city that had blessed Bryan with riches through his holdings of Jefferson-Pilot stock and other investments was falling behind others in the state that were experiencing galloping growth. The city's chamber of commerce was out of money and in disarray. A variety of economic development groups that had been created to boost the region's prosperity seemed impotent in the face of the challenge. Even the Greensboro Development Corporation was idle.

The city's reputation was further tainted by the constant public bickering of local officials, especially the members of the school board and the county commissioners, whose relationships to one another had been poisoned by deep distrust and insults. Voters were no longer surprised by news reports of fistfights, name-calling, and even lawsuits among members of public bodies. Municipal government seemed to be unable to take care of the basics. In 1998, the city suffered from a severe drought, and water restrictions were put in place. The sewage plant Melvin had worked on for ten years was nearing capacity. To Melvin's eye, city hall had lost its ability to deal with the city's needs.

Melvin had not been comfortable with the municipal leadership throughout much of the 1990s, when the city's mayor was Carolyn Allen, a soft-spoken retired college professor who was largely divorced from the economic establishment. "I'm the first mayor who doesn't play golf," she happily told an interviewer midway through her second term.[5] She had come to local politics through service with the YWCA and the League of Women Voters. Her steady pushing on behalf of the district system of election for the city council was a singular victory. "To this day," Allen said some years later, "I have an aversion to the phrase, 'If it ain't broke, don't fix it.'"[6] In 1989, she ran successfully for the council and announced as a candidate for mayor in 1993 at the end of Vic Nussbaum's term.

Allen confounded the business community in her first mayoral race and then was reelected in 1995 over another challenger who had its support. She owed much of her success to the strong support of the black precincts in southeast Greensboro, whose residents found her to be a mayor who paid close attention to their concerns. African American voters responded in a well-organized effort that operated under the name "the Underground Railroad."

Her victories fractured local politics. The business community, which had enjoyed control for generations, was totally bowed. During Allen's three terms in office, business-oriented members were in the minority on the council. By 1997, the mayoral contest had become so confused that a last-minute write-in candidate, *Rhinoceros Times* editor John Hammer, placed second behind Allen.

Allen's style was anathema to traditional leaders like Melvin. Quiet and unassuming, she sometimes appeared oblivious to her public persona. Once, when called on to say a few words to the state board of transportation, which was meeting in Greensboro on a special occasion, Allen passed on the chance to thump for the city's growing transportation needs before state officials with both clout and money. High Point mayor

Becky Smothers followed her to the podium and spent fifteen minutes talking about her own city.

Allen's forte was working in the neighborhoods and with groups that previously had little direct access to city hall. She labored quietly to promote long-range planning and land conservation. Forecast 2015, a look into the future of the community, came as a result of a partnership she forged with Wallace Harrelson, the chair of the Guilford County Board of Commissioners.

For Melvin, Allen's years were lost years. The city had slipped behind the curve on meeting essential needs. He was particularly unhappy that Allen had come late in her support of building the Randleman Dam and reservoir. She raised environmental concerns about the project, and it was only after she was convinced there was no other option that she got behind it.

In later years, Allen was bemused by her critics. Yes, she said, she had beaten the big boys. Why? They never could translate the ambitions for Greensboro that they hatched in private into action by the people, regardless of the potential benefit of their plans to the community. After leaving office, Allen had mellowed. "I learned a great deal from simply coming to know and understand more about the whole business process," she said. "To so many of my friends—God love them all—the corporate world is the demon."[7]

Melvin's deepest concern was for the city's economic health. Cone Mills, Burlington Industries, and Guilford Mills were all struggling. In 1998, Guilford and Burlington had pinned their hopes on new ventures, including heavy investment in Mexico, where Cone already had a plant making denim. Burlington's participation had been engineered in part by Charles M. Hayes of Guilford Mills, who hoped a Guilford-Burlington partnership would allow both firms to capitalize on the advantages offered to North American firms with the passage in 1993 of the North American Free Trade Act, or NAFTA. Guilford and Burlington announced plans to build an industrial park south of the border where workers would produce apparel from fabric that came from their mills in the states. If the plan succeeded, Hayes reasoned, his company's huge Greenberg plant on West Wendover Avenue could keep running. For Guilford Mills, the future of sixteen hundred local jobs was on the line.

Hayes had emerged as an unlikely leader in the textile industry, which was known as a cozy club dominated by conservative Southerners, many of whom claimed blood ties to the old cotton-mill barons. Hayes was a Yankee who had never graduated from high school, and he ran a warp knitting operation, a side of the industry not well understood by the older set. Moreover, Hayes was fond of bold gestures and bluster that he used to hide a deep shyness. He worked at a passionate, frenetic pace that would cut short his life in 2002. Through sheer determination and political savvy, Hayes reached the inner sanctum of the industry as president of the American Textile Manufacturers Institute largely through his prodigious efforts to bring the textile industry into line behind NAFTA.

Hayes's Mexican gamble was as important to Greensboro as it was to his own company. Guilford Mills was one of Greensboro's largest employers, and it added as much to the local tax base as any other firm, if not more, in part because it was the city's greatest single water user, buying more than two million gallons a day. Unlike Cone Mills, which had its own reservoirs, Guilford's water came straight out of the tap. Its water bill alone brought annual revenues of $2 million to the city.

In the early 1980s, as politics as usual under the cozy at-large system was disappearing from city hall, Hayes had dispatched Doug Galyon, one of his executives, to keep an eye on local affairs and issues that mattered to the company. Over the years, Galyon had won election to the city council, he had served a term on the county board of commissioners, and he brought Hayes, at the time a registered Republican, into the gubernatorial campaigns of leading Democrats such as lieutenant governor Bob Jordan and governor Jim Hunt. After Hunt took office in 1993, the governor put Galyon on the state highway commission. Hayes and Galyon also were paying close attention to Washington and the growing interest in dropping North American trade barriers. When president-elect Bill Clinton held an economic summit before his inauguration, Hayes had a seat at the table.

"The conclusion that Chuck came to," said Galyon, "was that we had repeatedly asked President Reagan for tariff protection, we had repeatedly asked President [George H. W.] Bush for tariff protection. They have repeatedly told us they are free traders and they weren't going to do it. Chuck said, 'Well, if you are not going to give us tariffs, the only alternative was to take all the tariffs off and level the playing field for all countries.' In theory, that is absolutely correct."[8]

Hayes thought he knew something about Mexico. Guilford Mills had owned a minority interest in a Mexican textile concern for twenty years. Before the passage of NAFTA, he had welcomed some of the country's leading political figures as his guests in Greensboro, where he introduced them to textile executives from across the South. With Asian textile operations cutting deeply into sales, the Mexican operation appeared to be an ideal option for Guilford, as well as Burlington. The two companies announced plans to build in Mexico. Guilford's initial ante was $60 million. Burlington said it would put up $80 million over three years.

The textile firms' joint Mexican venture was just getting under way in late June 1999 when Melvin got a visit from Priscilla Taylor, the president of the Cemala Foundation. She brought with her the taped message that William Hemphill had prepared for her board of directors. In Hemphill's words, Melvin found an encapsulated version of all the things that were troubling him. He was so impressed with Hemphill's concise analysis that he showed the videotape to the Bryan board members as soon as possible. When Mike Weaver saw it, he asked to be allowed to show it to the board members of his family foundation and dispatched Richard L. Moore, the chief executive of the Weaver Foundation, to talk to Melvin. At the time, Moore had his own concerns about the state of community leadership, which was a principal area of interest for the Weaver Foundation. Finally, all three foundation leaders—Melvin, Taylor, and Moore—gathered to talk about what they could do. Faced with a daunting task—jump-starting a city—the three did the only thing they knew to do at the time: they talked. Action would follow soon enough.

Chapter 18

Baseball

*J*IM MELVIN AND Priscilla Taylor were two people who probably would not have naturally gravitated to one another.

Melvin was impulsive, preferred action to contemplation, and liked to expedite his plans using the back channels of business and politics. He clearly missed the relative ease of an earlier era when he could appear at the office of some corporate bull, outline a problem, and be on his way to a solution in short order. Taylor was dedicated to a more open process and believed in bringing in as many people as possible to address problems. Her methods might take more time, but the results were more secure, she believed.

Taylor occasionally squirmed at Melvin's chauvinist manner, a product of his good-old-boy nature, but she could give as good as she got. In the 1980s, she had emerged as a community leader after stints as president of the Junior League and the YWCA. In addition to her enthusiasm, she brought to the table advanced degrees in business with a tilt toward the study of organizational behavior. She had won an appointment to the executive committee of the Greensboro Visions project—as one of three women on the board—and ended up as an enthusiastic cochair. Determined to make the grassroots process work, she virtually dragged reluctant citizens unaccustomed to public participation into neighborhood meetings, where they found they could talk about the city's future.

Through her civic involvement, she developed a coterie of neighborhood leaders who were dealing with pressing social needs, such as public transportation and low-cost housing. And she was not without political clout of her own. By the time she and Melvin became partners, she had served one five-year term on the University of North Carolina Board of Governors and was about to start another. A Cemala Foundation program she engineered for Guilford County preschoolers was later adapted by governor Jim Hunt and introduced statewide.

Melvin and Taylor's third collaborator, Richard Moore, had become immersed in the community through Greensboro Visions, where he had cochaired the task force on transportation. The Visions effort had led to the creation of a municipal transit system—as well as the upgrading of the city bus line—and Moore was named a member of Greensboro's first transportation board. When Moore met with Melvin, he was just beginning a new assignment as a foundation executive after a career in higher education. His last post at UNCG was in the development office, where he worked to upgrade the institution's program of annual giving. Moore had recently initiated a project to identify a new generation of leadership and support for Greensboro. During his first visit with Melvin, the two had talked about a Weaver Foundation proposal to organize a "roundtable" of emerging leaders.

Melvin, Taylor, and Moore had less experience in foundation management and philanthropy than most of their peers around the state. Taylor had been in her job only two years longer than Melvin. Moore had been at Weaver less than a year. In the end, their naiveté proved an asset. The three had not heard of an unwritten rule honored in the philanthropic world that foundations simply did not join together in support of a common goal. "We didn't have this long history to know we weren't supposed to do it," Taylor said.[1]

Despite their inexperience, their talents were impressive. All three knew the community, but, more importantly, they saw Greensboro from different perspectives. Melvin was well-connected to business and politics. Taylor had been working at the grassroots level for more than a dozen years. Moore understood the relationship between town and gown. Equally impressive was the $175 million in assets that they and their boards of directors could bring to bear on the problem once they could identify a solution. A common thread—and an important relationship for them all—was that the vast wealth in their care came from three successful entrepreneurs.

———

Probably the last thing on the minds of Melvin, Taylor, and Moore was the prospect that they were about to initiate a program that would put $37 million on the line for Greensboro's future. At the outset, they were simply trying to get a grasp on the problems and the challenges facing their community. Over a period of months, they met frequently and held lively discussions. Personalities clashed, as happens when head-strong, opinionated people get together. They brought in outsiders such as Greensboro city manager Ed Kitchen, a talented public administrator who had worked closely with Taylor on the Visions project. They talked to businessman Tim Burnett, whose father, Oscar, had helped lead an earlier industrial revival. His son was now president of the Greensboro Development Corporation. The head of the community's United Way program was invited in to offer ideas, as were clergymen and others from the African American community. For a time, Melvin, Taylor, and Moore held regular sessions with specialists from the Department of Urban and Regional Planning at the University of North Carolina at Chapel Hill.

Professionals were consulted, and Taylor pushed to hire a team from the Institute of Government in Chapel Hill that had helped turn around other communities. Moore balked at bringing in academics from out-side when Greensboro was home to two campuses of the consolidated university. As usual, Melvin was impatient with the process, which one proposal outlined as taking years to implement.

What the community needed, they all believed, was a "smoking gun," or clear, solid evidence that would awaken the people in Greensboro to the fact that the city was on the verge of becoming a third- or fourth-tier city like Salisbury, North Carolina, or Martinsville and Danville, Vir-ginia. Wilmington, North Carolina, which for years had been an also-ran in the municipal ratings, was closing in fast on Greensboro. Dur-ham was surging ahead.

"We were spoiled," Melvin said. "We had had it so good that we didn't realize we were spoiled. Then we got caught. What nobody could fore-see was the demise of the industry base." In fact, that was not altogether true. The Visions report had predicted more than a dozen years before that the city's economic base was going to change. Nonetheless, all three believed it was time to do something that was bold, decisive, and excit-ing. Melvin said often that Joe Bryan had not picked him to sit by and watch Greensboro die.

Nothing better described Melvin's approach than a framed quota-tion from General Omar Bradley hanging on his office wall. It read: "A second-best decision quickly made and vigorously carried out is better than the best decision too late arrived at and half-heartedly carried out. Every-day affairs are a battle. We are given one life to live and the deci-sion is ours whether to wait for circumstances to make up our mind or to act and in acting live." Melvin had liked the Bradley quote the moment he first saw it in Bill Hemphill's office some years before. He believed it now applied, in spades.

After several months of talking, meeting with outsiders, and ruminating on their own, the foundation heads agreed to underwrite a baseline study they hoped would define Greensboro's condition. McKinsey and Company, a nationally recognized name with credibility in many sectors, had recently completed such a study in Winston-Salem. Perhaps the firm would take on Greensboro as well. McKinsey accepted, with some encouragement from David Stonecipher, Roger Soles's successor as CEO of Jefferson-Pilot Corporation, which was once a McKinsey client. The McKinsey report arrived in November 2000, just as Guilford Mills announced a second round of layoffs, bringing the total number of jobs that Guilford had eliminated in that year alone to a thousand. When cuts at Burlington and the Pillowtex plants in neighboring Rockingham County were counted, the total number of local textile jobs eliminated in 2000 topped three thousand.

The McKinsey and Company analysts said that Greensboro was better off than what they called "peer cities" around the Southeast, but Greensboro's economic base was declining, and there was no focused, cohesive local effort to reverse the trend. Moreover, the community was aging. Though the area had nearly fifty thousand students attending colleges and universities, graduates were leaving as soon as they got their degrees. Most often, they were headed to places like Raleigh, Charlotte, or Atlanta that offered better pay, better jobs, and a livelier social life.

"Greensboro now faces a future in which continuing with business as usual could lead to a gradual erosion in its standard of living and quality of life," the report said. "The community can maximize its ability to shape its long-term economic prospects by building consensus around a few critical initiatives and focusing its collective efforts in those places. Those discussions will not be easy, but they will be essential. The sooner the community begins this process, the sooner it can expect to begin changing Greensboro's long-term outlook."[2]

All in all, the report contained some of the same commentary that leaders like Melvin had heard more than a decade before in the Greensboro Visions report. Side-by-side comparison of the two reports revealed a stunning level of agreement. Declining industrial base, flight of corporate structure, unfocused economic development efforts: Visions had raised all these flags. Priscilla Taylor noticed the similarities and explained that in the late 1980s it was social issues that had captured the most attention. Now, she said, quoting a mantra that helped put Bill Clinton in the White House, "It's the economy, stupid."[3]

By the time McKinsey and Company finished its work and delivered its report, Melvin, Taylor, and Moore had expanded their base of support by bringing on board the Community Foundation of Greater Greensboro, the Moses Cone–Wesley Long Community Health Foundation, and the Tannenbaum-Sternberger Foundation, all of which had chipped in to help pay McKinsey's $250,000 fee. The contributions of these additional sources would help pay some of the bills, but Melvin, Taylor, and Moore brought them in primarily because they wanted to cultivate as broad a base of cooperation as possible before moving ahead.

Melvin, Taylor, and Moore had hoped that once they collected evidence of the problems that needed attention, their job would largely be over. They planned to stand ready to support initiatives to turn Greensboro around, but nothing more. Taylor recalled hoping that "the story would be so compelling that [city leaders] would have to do something."[4]

The three toured the community delivering the details of the report to virtually any group of two or more that would hear them. To their astonishment, no person or group volunteered to take on the job of identifying the next steps and moving forward. Moore recalled the response from city officials this way: "We did the study, got the report, and started talking about it. Nobody stepped forward. We had two or three breakfast meetings with city council and county commissioners (most of whom did not show up). After we gave them the report, one of the council members raised their hand and said, 'This is all fine, but who is going to provide the leadership?'"

She continued, "Well, we were thinking they were all going to get up and say, 'We have to do something.' And they are saying, 'Who is going to be the leader?' Duh. How about you?"[5]

Failing to arouse the political sector, the three convened a gathering of corporate leaders and community activists in a group they called the Core Committee. Included in the group were the heads of Greensboro's largest businesses, who, Melvin discovered, barely knew one another. Melvin, Taylor, and Moore asked these corporate volunteers to lead and participate in focus groups to look at the key interrelated areas highlighted by McKinsey. The challenges included attracting and retaining young professionals, enhancing existing businesses, fostering business development, improving education, and developing and marketing Greensboro's image.

At about the time that this effort was getting under way, Melvin was traveling to Sea Island, Georgia, with JP's David Stonecipher. Melvin had joined the JP board in the 1980s and had been a member of the search committee that had nominated Stonecipher as Roger Soles's replacement. He had personally taken Stonecipher on a tour of the city when the executive came to Greensboro to look the place over. "I call him Mr. Greensboro," Stonecipher said. "Jim said, 'I am going to do whatever it takes to convince you to come to Greensboro, even if it means standing on the hood of this car.' He is such a salesman. He was convinced he was going to get the close."[6]

As the two headed to Georgia, Melvin shared with Stonecipher a news clipping that told the story of how private interests had built a minor-league baseball stadium in Chattanooga, Tennessee. It was an idea the owners of the Greensboro Bats, Melvin among them, had been kicking around for some months. Stonecipher told Melvin he was traveling to Chattanooga the following week and invited him along to learn about the city's new ballpark firsthand.

Melvin discovered that the ballpark was only one piece of a transformation that was under way in Chattanooga. He found a city that was re-shaping itself after experiencing problems that had been even more severe than those in Greensboro. In the 1980s, Chattanooga's industrial base had disappeared and left behind a city that was racially divided and worn into ugliness by industrial pollution and neglect. The condition led to a crisis of confidence before concerned citizens finally mobilized to bring about change. Much of the support for the rebuilding had come from the Lyndhurst Foundation, which, Melvin learned, bore a striking similarity to the Bryan Foundation.

The Lyndhurst Foundation was supported by the wealth of Cartter Lupton, a pioneer in the Coca-Cola bottling business who had been as devoted to Chattanooga as Joe Bryan was to Greensboro. The size of the foundation had grown considerably following Lupton's death in 1977 and in the 1980s was under the direction of Lupton's son, John. Wanting to go beyond the normal routine of reading applications and making grants, John Lupton challenged the foundation's top executive, Rick Montague, as well as another top staff member, Jack Murrah, to look beyond the traditional approach to see what the foundation could do to help not just individual institutions but the community at large.

The result was a community-wide discussion of issues and goals that brought people together to consider what they wanted the city to be in the future. It was not all that different from Greensboro Visions, which was taking place about the same time. Approximately fifteen hundred people participated, and the result was a list of forty concrete objectives. People set about to achieve them, and during the next ten years, Chattanooga began to change. One of the most striking improvements was the creation of a new park along the Tennessee River that was built after the community convinced the state to leave standing a highway bridge that was unsafe for cars but could easily carry pedestrian traffic. The bridge became the centerpiece for Riverwalk, a large riverside park that in time spawned residential and commercial development in an area that had once been written off as uninhabitable.

After learning about Lyndhurst, Melvin called Jack Murrah, who had succeeded Montague as foundation president. The two talked by phone, and within a few weeks, Melvin and Taylor were on their way to Chattanooga to hear the story in person. Murrah told them the lessons that the Lyndhurst Foundation board had learned: Think beyond the traditional grant-making approach of foundations, open the process to include participation from the entire community, be prepared to make significant investment, and follow through.

"Confidence spurs investment," Murrah said, and Lyndhurst had led by example. The foundation picked from the list of goals generated by community meetings one of the most audacious projects and agreed to build the world's largest freshwater aquarium. The project drew scoffs until Lyndhurst put its money to work, raised additional funds, and opened the $40 million Tennessee Aquarium in 1992 as the anchor for a major redevelopment on the banks of the Tennessee River. The striking twelve-story facility, with tanks and exhibits holding up to four hundred thousand gallons of water, was expected to draw about six hundred thousand visitors annually. Nearly a decade later, when Melvin and the others arrived, more than a million visitors were enjoying it each year, and a new IMAX theater had opened as a companion center.

While Melvin, Taylor, and Moore had been unsuccessful in rousing public officials to take on the job they saw ahead, they had gathered the names of hundreds of volunteers who had offered to help. People had come forward in such numbers that Taylor grew concerned and anxious: volunteers want to have their offers accepted, and she had nothing to give them to do. Finally, the three foundation leaders decided to take a group to Chattanooga, and in March 2001, a chartered 727 lifted off from Piedmont Triad International Airport carrying about 180 of those who had said they wanted to help. On the return trip, after the group had heard the local story and seen the aquarium, the riverfront, and the new minor-league ballpark, they were asked to suggest a signature project for Greensboro. Overwhelmingly, they recommended the construction of a new ballpark.

By the late spring of 2001, with momentum beginning to build, Melvin, Taylor, and Moore decided that if no established institution or organization was willing to take on the task of transforming Greensboro for the future, they would do it themselves. Thus was born Action Greensboro. Thirty corporate sponsors, along with foundations (Bryan, Cemala, and Weaver, plus the Community Foundation of Greater Greensboro, the Toleo Foundation, and the Tannenbaum-Sternberger Foundation), organized to underwrite the initial program of work. Six task forces were organized to concentrate on the key areas identified as most urgently needing attention. A full-time director, Susan Schwartz, went on the payroll. Schwartz had held a similar position in Greensboro Visions.

Other trips followed to Columbus, Ohio, and Oklahoma City, where aroused residents had approved a $350 million bond package to add vitality and life to the city, especially its downtown. In the middle of the flat plains, far from any significant body of water, the city had built a canal, as well as a new library, a twenty-thousand-seat sports arena, and a minor-league ballpark.

As one idea flowed into another, Action Greensboro commissioned a study by the Center for Connective Architecture, a division of Cooper Carry Incorporated of Atlanta, one of the leading land-planning firms in the nation. In the late fall of 2001, Cooper Carry presented a plan for downtown Greensboro that gave shape and definition to dreams of a revitalized city. The plan divided downtown into districts, with distinctive features attached to each. It envisioned a museum district and a market district, with residential, entertainment, and retail woven into the mix. A new park might accompany a concert hall. Greensboro's downtown would be a place for living, working, and playing. Anchoring the south end in a blighted corner of downtown would be a minor-league ballpark.

———

"Have you ever been to a minor-league baseball game?" Melvin would ask those curious about his enthusiasm for a ballpark. "Nobody pays attention to the score. It's just good family fun." He would embellish his description with such color and personality that it became a virtual Rockwellian illustration: Mom and Dad with the kids on a summer evening enjoying hot dogs and sodas and the crack of the bat as a ball heads to the outfield. His musing suggested a man who had grown up tagging along behind his father to Memorial Stadium to watch the old Greensboro Patriots. Nothing could be further from the truth. Joe Melvin did not take in baseball with his boys. Jim Melvin would learn more about the sport as he approached seventy than he had when he was seven.

Golf was Melvin's sport. He had played basketball and football as a youngster, but on weekends he could be found at the old Gillespie Park Golf Course. One childhood chum said Melvin slept with a string tied to his toe, the other end out the window, so his buddy could awaken him early for a few holes before the paying customers arrived. As an adult, he played wherever and whenever he was given the chance, including at some exalted courses in the British Isles and Italy. His score hovered around eighty. In later years, his regular haunt was the Greensboro Country Club or the courses at Bryan Park.

He had attended perhaps one minor-league baseball game in the ten years the team had been playing at Greensboro's War Memorial Stadium when he got a call in the summer of 1999 from UNCG athletic director Nelson Bobb. Melvin and Bobb had come to know one another over the years through Melvin's efforts to upgrade the university's athletic program to Division I competition. In this phone call, Bobb told Melvin he had someone he wanted him to meet, and at Bobb's office Melvin was introduced to John Horshock, the manger of the Greensboro Bats. The team owners were interested in selling, Bobb told Melvin, and he thought it was time for a local group to try its hand at running the team.

Melvin was intrigued. He had signed on as a potential investor in the gamble to get a major-league team in the Triad, but he had never paid much attention to the Bats. He was intrigued enough about Bobb's proposition that he huddled with attorney Cooper Brantley and businessman Len White, two men who owned a small part of the team and who were interested in pursuing local ownership. Together, they compiled a list of thirty-eight people whom they planned to ask to put up $100,000 each to meet the $3.8 million asking price for the team.

"We ran out of $100,000 investors right quick," Melvin said later.[7] They revamped their strategy, lowered the threshold for investors, and finally borrowed enough cash to make the deal. When Melvin announced the purchase in September 1999, he told a newspaper reporter, "It's sort of like a dog chasing cars. We've caught it, and now what do we do with it?"[8]

Melvin took a close look at War Memorial Stadium after the group purchased the team, and he quickly understood why previous owners said they could not make a profit in the city's antiquated facility. He was appalled at the sorry condition of the place. The locker rooms were small, cluttered, and unheated. The ceiling in the front office was collapsing. An adjoining bathroom was a public health hazard. The sewer lines backed up, and the public toilets became unusable whenever there was a rainstorm. Most distressing was the limited space for food concessions, which were an important moneymaker for any owner. Before the next season, Melvin and the new owners put $300,000 into renovations, mainly to make the place sanitary and functional. Major changes in the seating and main structure were out of the question because of the cost, although the need was clear.

The Cooper Carry plans for downtown Greensboro included a surprise for Melvin. He suspected a ball stadium would be included in the plan, but he had not anticipated where the designers would put it. As a managing director of the Bats, Melvin had investigated alternative sites to the aging city-owned facility. One was on the east side of downtown on a compact wedge of land between the railroad tracks and the children's museum. Another site was on the west side of downtown where the county's social services offices were housed in a building that had opened in 1935 as the headquarters of Burlington Industries.

Cooper Carry proposed a new location right in the center of one of the most depressed areas in the city. The intersection of South Elm and Lee streets had once been a major crossroads, but lately it was known for rundown buildings and the day laborers who congregated at the edge of a public housing project. Auto garages, a bakery, a coal yard, and other businesses that had once inhabited the area were long gone. Left behind were vacant lots and aging structures, weeds, and soil tainted by motor oil, chemicals, and the other hazardous residue of commerce. It was an environmental brownfield that would have to be cleaned up before construction could be allowed.

Melvin was energized. If the Lyndhurst Foundation could give Chattanooga an aquarium, then Bryan could help Greensboro get a new ballpark. Over the next few weeks, a private group quietly obtained options on twenty-one of the twenty-three pieces of land included in the two square blocks that would be needed for the stadium. Melvin also began talking with city manager Ed Kitchen about a plan. He proposed that the foundation purchase the land and give it to the city, which would then lease it to a private entity created by the foundation that would build the stadium. At the end of twenty years, when the stadium was paid for, the entire facility would be given to the city. The plan showed considerable promise, and Kitchen privately polled the members of the city council for their reactions. A comfortable majority said they would support the project.

The deal was no less ambitious than what another civic entrepreneur, Julian Price, had accomplished sixty years earlier. After the county's board of commissioners expressed reluctance to build a courthouse for High Point, Price arranged for the private purchase of the land and a loan from Jefferson Standard to build a structure that was then leased to the county.[9]

Once Melvin's plan became public, however, those who had counted on using the federal money that Kitchen had earmarked to clean up the site for their own projects raised a howl. The NAACP objected, neighborhood groups protested, and leading the opposition was a former council member, Bill Burckley, who quickly made the opposition personal. Burckley claimed that Melvin personified the behind-the-scenes manipulation that had long characterized how things were done in Greensboro. He aroused opposition with the exaggerated claim that federal funds that had been intended for low-income housing were being used to line the pockets of the big boys. The comfortable majority on the council quickly dissolved. Melvin was left with only two solid votes.

As the deal with the city began to fall apart, Melvin began looking elsewhere. He talked to Duke Power about the land on the east side of town. He decided it was too small a plot for a stadium and that siting a stadium there would probably be detrimental to the future development of the nearby children's museum. He then switched to his alternative, the land where the county building was located. If the foundation could find another location for the county offices, then the downtown property would be available. He explored this option with county manager Roger Cotton, who had long been eager to find more suitable quarters for the social services and health department housed in the seventy-year-old building. Cotton was receptive.

Melvin quickly shifted gears. The county could not easily give up land and a building, as inadequate as it was, without receiving something to replace it. He scouted several locations to find a new home for the offices and clinics of the health department and social services. One possibility was the former Carolina Circle Mall, which had closed a few years earlier. Portions of it were being developed as a health and sports complex, but there was plenty of space available and ample parking. Certain features that came with the space proved to be unsuitable for the county, however. Melvin kept looking.

Along the way, he learned that the former site of Cone Mills Corporation's headquarters might be available. The land was optioned for a new Home Depot store, but when that deal fell through, Melvin put in a call to Cone officials, who agreed to give him an option on the land. With that in hand, Melvin went back to talk to Cotton. Cotton liked the new location: it was convenient to another social services building a few blocks away on Wendover and would be a welcome replacement for the crowded offices the county had downtown. Melvin and his allies began to put together a package. In exchange for the downtown property, he proposed that the Bryan Foundation would build the county a 120,000-square-foot, $10-million office building. It appeared to be a win-win deal.

The county commissioners ultimately agreed, but not without dissent. Further roadblocks were also put up at city hall, where Burckley and others objected to the closing of a street that ran through the proposed outfield. Finally, after city approval was given, a petition drive was mounted to reverse the council's decision, and yard signs appealing for the city to save the old stadium went up in some neighborhoods.

———

Greensboro had long had an ambivalent attitude toward professional baseball. When War Memorial Stadium opened in 1927, it was to be for amateur sporting events exclusively. The city's minor-league baseball team played its games at Cone Field, a simple affair on Summit Avenue with wooden bleachers. That changed in 1930, when the Saint Louis Cardinals, the parent team of the minor-league Greensboro Patriots, paid the city of Greensboro $23,000 to install lights at War Memorial Stadium, improve the grandstand, and reconfigure the playing field for baseball. (It had been designed for football and track competition.) Play at the stadium lasted for only five years. Saint Louis pulled out before the 1935 season after Greensboro voters overwhelmingly approved Sunday blue laws that closed movie theaters and banned professional sports.

A professional minor-league team returned to the stadium after World War II, when the blue laws had been removed, and over the years the Patriots gave way to the Hornets, who opened in the city in 1978 after ten years in which Greensboro had no local baseball team. The Hornets proved to be one of the most successful teams in the Class A South Atlantic League. They were eventually succeeded by the Bats.

While the name of the team had changed over the decades, the home field the city leased to team owners had not. By the 1990s, the Greensboro park was the second oldest in the nation, and it looked its age. The classic style—two towers at the entrance topped by flagpoles—engendered nostalgia but did little for the team owners, who said the limited seating and parking, as well as the sorry condition of the building, discouraged attendance. After years of complaints from team owners, the city council finally included $2 million for renovations in a 1996 bond package. Voters turned it down.

A year before the bond referendum, public attention suddenly shifted from the minor-league Bats to the prospect of luring a major-league organization to the Triad. A group of investors led by Stonecipher and Walter McDowell of Winston-Salem, the head of North Carolina banking for Wachovia Corporation, surprised most everyone in the summer of 1995 by beginning a campaign to bring major-league baseball to the Triad. The pair represented the two largest financial institutions in the area and made a formidable combination. Their plan was to raise $180 million to build a forty-thousand-seat stadium on a site near Kernersville, midway between Greensboro and Winston-Salem.

It was a bold move, and the team was among the first to propose putting big money down on a regional project. The project seemed a natural fit to Stonecipher. "We had the population," he said. "If you take Winston-Salem, Greensboro, and High Point, the metro area adds up to more than Charlotte. We felt like North Carolina, the home of so many minor-league teams, was a good combination to try to do something, to step out of the box."[10]

McDowell also was an enthusiastic salesman for a regional venture. He had just stepped down as the chair of the Piedmont Triad Partnership, a twelve-county economic development effort. When the plans for major-league baseball were announced, he was eager to put Wachovia on par with banking competitors First Union and NationsBank, which had helped bring pro basketball (First Union) and pro football (NationsBank) to Charlotte. He called Wachovia the "designated hitter" for major-league baseball in the Triad.[11]

Many in Greensboro had been waiting for Stonecipher to step into the public arena and lead a major public venture. While his decision to do so as the leader of an initiative to attract a baseball team surprised others, it was a natural one for him. He believed baseball was just the thing for him to take up in the wake of a visit earlier in the year by his friend Billy Payne, the man who organized the campaign to bring the

1996 Olympics to Atlanta. On Stonecipher's invitation, Payne had spoken to the Greensboro Chamber of Commerce, where he asked, "Where are the risk takers willing to make things happen?"[12] Confident, upbeat, and resourceful, Stonecipher stepped up to the plate. "I think we need an energy in our community that's missing," Stonecipher would later say. "We so oftentimes sell ourselves short. We need to dream big dreams."[13]

The project gathered momentum with the help of a wealthy Hickory businessman, Don Beaver, who owned minor-league teams in Winston-Salem, Charlotte, and Hickory. Beaver opened negotiations with the owner of the Minnesota Twins, who was bargaining with Minneapolis officials over a new stadium. In the summer of 1996, Stonecipher, McDowell, and others attended the major league's all-star game in Philadelphia, where they made a pitch to acting commissioner Bud Selig, who gave his nod of approval. Enabling legislation to permit a referendum on a local option sales tax on restaurant meals passed the legislature in 1997, and the vote was set for May 1998. By that time, however, the multicounty effort had been reduced to just two, Guilford and Forsyth.

The vision of major-league baseball under the lights in a handsome new stadium pulled together corporate interests who had never before been harnessed in such a way. Investors included businessmen from Winston-Salem, High Point, and beyond. There were executives of the leading furniture companies, bankers, real estate developers, and attorneys. The chambers of commerce from area communities fell in behind the project. The daily newspapers supported it with editorials. The News and Record compared the stadium to Greensboro's "vision" in earlier years that had resulted in the construction of the coliseum and the creation of Bryan Park. Governor Jim Hunt endorsed the project. So did state treasurer Harlan Boyles, whose word was considered solid gold.

Ken Conrad of Greensboro was not impressed. He owned fourteen seafood restaurants, most of them in the Triad, and he was incensed that influential business interests were asking voters to approve a special tax that would increase the cost of meals in his restaurants. He was not against the stadium, he said, but he believed it was wrong to put the tax on a single segment of the community. Conrad rallied other opponents, who scraped together $33,000 to finance a campaign against the tax. It looked hopeless; nearly $900,000 was being spent to put the measure over. Nonetheless, in May 1998, the opponents of the new tax won in a landslide. The tax was crushed by a vote of 96,433 to 55,262.[14]

Stonecipher was stunned by the vote—not by the loss so much, as he was prepared for that, but by the absolute, overwhelming rejection of the tax. Why had it happened? Perhaps it was a result of growing public discomfort with the outrageous salaries being paid to sports figures. Perhaps it was a consequence of the perception that the owner of the Twins was playing his friends in the South to leverage a better deal in Minneapolis. Or it may have been that the Triad was reaching too far. The venture seemed unrealistic to people who just did not see their hometown in the same league as the major metro regions of the nation.

––––

Melvin's plan was nowhere near as far-reaching as the one voters rejected in 1998, but four years later, the idea of building a baseball stadium—even one financed with private money—still aroused resentment. Residents in the Aycock neighborhood adjacent to War Memorial devised a plan to rehabilitate the stadium and use it as the centerpiece for the continued improvement of the neighborhood, but they had no one to pay for it. In Fisher Park, another downtown neighborhood, homeowners said that traffic and lights from the new stadium would disturb their tranquility. In doing so, they failed to mention a large auto dealership even closer to private homes than the ballpark would be that kept its car lot illuminated through the night. A petition was circulated and lawsuits were filed to stop city officials from awarding the proper zoning to the new stadium. After the city council voted to close a street that would run through the center of the outfield, the city was forced into a referendum on whether a stadium of any kind could be built downtown.

Outsiders in Charlotte and Raleigh looked on in amazement at Greensboro's apparent reluctance to accept a plan for a privately financed stadium. Usually plans like this one faltered on the use of public money to build them. The ensuing campaign got personal, especially in the overheated pages of John Hammer's nagging weekly newspaper, the *Rhinoceros Times*, which lived up to its motto, "All the rumors fit to print," in every edition. This episode in the city's history was reminiscent of the public debate fifty years earlier over the siting of the coliseum. Once again, Greensboro took the long, hard way around to making up its mind.

Melvin argued that the important thing about the stadium initiative had little to do with baseball or with supplying a new home for the Greensboro Bats, a farm team for the Florida Marlins, who won the 2003 World Series champions. Rather, the new stadium would be a symbol that Greensboro was turning the corner and making progress, not slipping into stagnation and decline. Like the step-by-step overhaul that was taking place on Elm Street, the stadium would be a tangible, positive move forward that would eventually create momentum for other developments. "Tipping point," Melvin said, repeating the phrase over and over as he talked about the project.

Melvin did not slow his efforts. His lawyers told him that regardless of the outcome of the referendum, the project could proceed. Work commenced on the county's new building, and Melvin and the stadium builders made a show at the site downtown. A fence went up around a small construction building, and a modest groundbreaking for the stadium was held on May 16, 2003. As a handful of protesters lined the sidelines, Greensboro mayor Keith Holliday tossed a shovelful of dirt and said, "It's not the complete answer for downtown revitalization, but it's the flagship."[15]

Throughout the public debate, Melvin drew criticism from virtually all quarters. His bullish nature only irritated the opposition. He was accused of using his influence at city hall to get his way. Even some of his allies began to get anxious. "I warned them," Melvin said, "there are some storm clouds out there. Everybody ain't going to love you."

Overshadowed in the political turmoil over the stadium was the solid work of Action Greensboro, which was beginning to give a new focus to economic development and assist emerging companies in a small-business incubator. There was even a new slogan—"Greensboro Connects"—that played on the city's superb location at the intersection of electronic as well as concrete highways.

Out of the early initiative came a hefty private investment in the Guilford County schools. Including the early efforts by the Bryan and Cemala foundations, private contributions totaled nearly $3 million from fifty local companies. The money was used to create for incentives for students, teachers, and administrators to improve themselves and raise standards. Melissa Nixon, the principal at Faust Elementary School, said, "This private investment shows that businesses understand the importance of lifelong learning that is critical to our success. It is making a positive difference."[16]

In the spring of 2003, ground was broken for a one-and-a-half-acre downtown park, another idea incorporated into the Cooper Carry plan that Melvin and others, including a group of downtown promoters led by Betty Cone, had been musing about for more than five years. Two years before Action Greensboro was created, Melvin had been playing golf in Ireland with Mike Weaver and other friends. One morning, Melvin and Weaver set off from their Dublin hotel for a walk about town. Melvin spied a small park and commented to Weaver that Greensboro needed someplace downtown like that park where visitors could find relief from the concrete and steel. When Melvin returned to Greensboro, he asked landscape designer Chip Callaway to capture the feel and style of the park he had seen in Dublin. Callaway complied and produced a plan for a park that Melvin promoted to whoever appeared interested.

Action Greensboro turned the planning of the new park into a creative exercise. During the first year of work on the park, after the existing buildings had been removed from the land designated for the park and the site graded, moveable benches and light canopies were installed for use by a growing downtown contingent that could enjoy the space and muse about what should go where. Within a short time, downtown workers were eating lunch outdoors, and on several evenings during the summer bluegrass and beach music concerts drew hundreds of spectators. As Melvin had done with the ballpark, Priscilla Taylor took the lead in bringing the center-city park to life. A plan was adopted, and the park began to take shape, rising from the ashes of a defeated bond referendum in 2000, when voters refused to fund either a downtown park or the civil rights museum struggling to emerge from the F. W. Woolworth store.

The stadium referendum was a cloud over Action Greensboro through the summer of 2003. Some public officials, especially incumbent city council members eyeing reelection, remained uneasy about the mood. Even with an organized campaign on behalf of the stadium project, those closest to the project were unsure how voters would respond. Melvin had promised to move ahead with the stadium regardless, leaving Taylor anxious about the divisions such a determined move would create in the community. Everyone was relieved—elated is a better term—when voters overwhelmingly rejected the stadium prohibition in early October. It was one of the largest turnouts in municipal voting history. A few weeks later, voters also approved a $300 million school bond issue.

"For this town to approve a tax increase on themselves for $300 million in bonds is historic," Melvin said a few days after the election. "That is historic."

Making a Difference

*A*BOUT TWO hundred Action Greensboro volunteers turned out late in the afternoon of March 23, 2005, for hot dogs and soft drinks and a preview of the new minor-league baseball stadium that their work had helped bring to life. Some of those wandering about the concourse had been part of the trip to Chattanooga five years earlier that had led to the creation of Action Greensboro.

This night, the children of some of the younger adults who had backed the effort raced around the infield, leaving footprints in the neat red dirt. A handful of the city's political and corporate leaders were on hand, but mainly this was a night for those who had believed that a refocused effort in Greensboro could make a difference.

Jim Melvin moved with purpose about the crowd as he encouraged all to enjoy the treats and see what their work had wrought. A storm was brewing on the city's northern perimeter, and as the sky darkened, a stiffening wind fluffed Melvin's hair into a modest bouffant. As the tempest increased, he cautioned any standing exposed to the weather to move back under the eave of the grandstand.

Melvin nursed the crowd through the evening just as he had nursed the city through the construction of the stadium. The construction site was only a short ride from his office on the edge of downtown, and with little encouragement, he had often escorted his visitors to see what was going on as the stadium began to take shape. Together, they would wander through the unfinished corridors and onto the field, where he pointed out the features before they had come to life. In early winter, when the playing field was first illuminated with lights, he had invited the board of directors of Jefferson-Pilot Corporation to a cocktail party on the concourse.

The first season of the Greensboro Grasshoppers, renamed for the new era of minor-league ball in the city, was just days away from beginning in late March 2005. As the Action Greensboro crowd roamed about the stadium and toured the paneled locker rooms and the other well-appointed spaces in the interior, Melvin bent over to retrieve a loose napkin or paper plate that skittered by, carried by the ever-increasing blow. He told any who stopped to chat that he was most proud of the new social services building that had been part of the creative construction package that had produced a ballpark in downtown Greensboro. It was clear, however, that while the new social services building satisfied his deep sense of civic responsibility, the ballpark was going to be just plain fun.

As the evening's preview crowd began to drift off and head for home, Melvin thanked those who remained and reminded them that what they had started was just the beginning. The new stadium was the product of their efforts, but Greensboro's future was in their hands, and they would continue to shape the city. These were words he had used before and undoubtedly would use again.

The opening game on April 3, 2005, at First Horizon Park—naming rights were sold to an out-of-state bank—was an exhibition game between the Grasshoppers and its major-league parent, the Florida Marlins. The day was perfect. There were clear skies, a warming sun, hot dogs, and a capacity crowd of 8,540 spectators. Melvin and architect Ken Mayer had created a playground for the entire city. By the end of 2005, First Horizon Park had been the scene of outdoor concerts, a couple of weddings, and even a funeral.

It also was a work of art. For Mayer, the ballpark was a dream come true, literally. He had always wanted to design a structure like this. The result was a combination of ideas—a bit of Camden Yards and even Churchill Downs—with an emphasis on ease of use. The wide concourses allowed spectators to leave their seats, pick up a hot dog and a beer, and return without losing sight of home plate.

The stadium also was a showcase of local talent. Local sculptors and artists had turned the functional into the beautiful. The gates at the stadium's plaza were made from 162 aluminum bats that stood at a high polish. Roger Halligan had created six oversized baseballs from cement and white sand. At three thousand pounds each, they anchored a small plaza at the corner of the property. Sculptor Brad Spencer of nearby Reidsville created a sequence of baseball in motion with a batter and pitcher in brick relief on the inside wall.

Baseball proved more popular than ever in Greensboro. The team's 2005 season set an all-time attendance record. Moreover, the Grasshoppers drew more spectators than any team in the league—more than 406,000. The superlatives for the opening year even included a favorable review of the concourse cuisine by the *News and Record*'s food writer.

The opening of First Horizon Park was a welcome relief as Greensboro's old economy continued to fade away. The new stadium was built on land where the headquarters of Burlington Industries had stood during the days of company founder Spencer Love. A few miles west on Friendly Avenue, the modern Burlington headquarters building, a striking rendition of glass and steel that had opened in the early 1970s, had been empty since the company had gone into bankruptcy. Wilbur Ross, the financier who had gathered up the remains of Burlington and Cone Mills, signed its eventual death warrant and returned it to the landowners, the Starmount Company. In midsummer, after the interior had been stripped bare, a series of well-placed explosive charges brought the building down in a heap of twisted metal. The Starmount Company gathered up the rubble and began clearing the site for an expansion of its Friendly Shopping Center.

Another blow to the community psyche came when Guilford Mills, a home-grown company, moved its headquarters to Wilmington, North Carolina, after closing its Greensboro plants. And by the end of the year, the deepest cut of all came with news that Jefferson-Pilot was engaged in a merger with Lincoln Financial Group of Philadelphia. There were the usual declarations to soothe Greensboro's fears over the loss of one of its few remaining corporate leaders. Yet there was no mistaking that a door had closed on an era.

There was some good news. Greensboro would certainly share in the jobs created by the opening of a Dell computer manufacturing plant just across the county line in Forsyth County. Work was progressing on a major reconfiguration of the Piedmont Triad International Airport and on the new regional handling facility for Federal Express that was due to open in a few years. Unemployment was coming down, and there was a major addition for downtown: in January 2004, Elon University, whose main campus was about twenty miles east of Greensboro in Alamance County, announced that it planned to open a law school in downtown Greensboro.

Jim Melvin had never set foot on the Elon University campus before he got a call early in 2003 from a top assistant to Elon president Leo

Lambert, who told him the president hoped he would visit. Melvin issued his usual defense against requests for money from those outside of Guilford County, but he agreed to meet with Lambert and tour the campus of what most considered a small, church-affiliated liberal arts college, despite its new status as a university.

Melvin had last been to Elon nearly thirty years earlier, when he had accompanied Sixth District congressman Richardson Preyer to a political meeting at the home of Reid Maynard, who was one of the leading textile men in the county and a leader in the southern textile industry. Maynard had gathered many of his peers to meet congressman Wilbur Mills of Arkansas, who was planning a bid for the Democratic Party's nomination for president in 1972. Mills promised tariff protections, but his campaign dissolved virtually overnight a few months later after the District of Columbia police fished him and a stripper named Fanne Foxe out of Washington's Tidal Basin.

Melvin related the Mills story to Lambert as they enjoyed lunch at the Maynard home, which had become the university president's residence. Since Mills's visit, Lambert and former Elon president Fred Young had entertained a far more illustrious crowd of guests, including president George H. W. Bush, former British prime minister Margaret Thatcher, former Polish president Lech Walesa, and Pakistan's former prime minister Benazir Bhutto. Most of these distinguished guests had come to the campus to speak and meet students as part of an ambitious public affairs program underwritten by the school's alumni.

During his luncheon with Lambert, Melvin learned that these high-profile visitors were just the more-public evidence of Elon's emergence as a robust campus with more than four thousand students, including a growing and expanding graduate program. It was a national leader among schools of comparable size and a serious competitor for quality students from across the nation.

"Leo has a golf cart," Melvin recalled, "and he drove me around the campus. As we were riding around, he said, 'Jim, we have been studying the feasibility of starting a law school, and we are discussing whether we ought to put it on campus or in an urban setting. We have looked at putting it at Charlotte, but I have been watching and reading all the things that you are doing with Action Greensboro, and I wonder if there is something that might have some interest to you and to us about putting it in downtown Greensboro.'"[1]

The conversation reminded Melvin of another day, when he and Joe

Bryan were standing beside Lake Townsend and the opportunity to buy additional land for the park arose in casual conversation. Melvin heard Bryan say quietly, "Get it." This time, it was Melvin's decision to take the discussion a step further. He asked Lambert for details, and two weeks later he had a proposal on his desk. Elon was interested in opening its new law school in Greensboro if suitable space could be located and if the community could raise nearly $10 million to help the school bring the $13 million project to fruition. Melvin told Lambert he would give it a try.

With encouragement from Melvin, Lambert brought his site team to Greensboro to look at possible locations for the school. Downtown office space was plentiful at the time, and Melvin walked his guests through an unfinished portion of the Jefferson-Pilot building, as well as a couple of floors of the adjacent Bank of America building. As the group was leaving the Bank of America building, Lambert mentioned that one of the school's needs would be an auditorium.

Lambert had no more than finished the sentence when Melvin looked a half-block away at a building that had once housed the Greensboro Public Library. Melvin turned the entourage toward the old library and headed across the street. The building had been put to other uses by city government since the opening of a new library several blocks away, and Melvin surprised some city employees as he steered his group through a tour. He assured those he saw that he was only showing off the details of the building's interesting architecture and design.

The library site was perfect. The 165-seat auditorium was large enough to suit the law school's needs, and after a tour around the block, Lambert was satisfied that the building would be just right. In the coming months, Melvin raised the needed $10 million and successfully negotiated the purchase of the former library building from the city. The 115 members of the charter class of the Elon University Law School began their work on August 10, 2006.

Other changes were taking place nearby. Just a block away, Center City Park, another signature piece of Action Greensboro's plan for downtown, was nearing completion. The new green space included a distinctive fountain, as well as open areas for seating and strolling. In between these two sites, work had finally begun on bringing new life to the long-empty Wachovia Building, which was being converted into condominiums.

The space in the Bank of America building that Melvin had first showed Lambert as a possible location for his law school did not stay empty long. In January 2006, the American Judicature Society (AJS), a nonpartisan organization dedicated to better judicial administration, opened its new Institute of Forensic Science and Public Policy in the Bank of America building. Once again, the Bryan Foundation and Melvin had taken the lead in raising the $750,000 needed to secure the AJS's new institute for Greensboro, but much of the heavy lifting that went into securing the commitment was done by Henry Frye and his wife, Shirley. Frye, a former chief justice of the Supreme Court of North Carolina, received the AJS Justice Award along with his wife for their contributions to the administration of justice on the national level.

There was a new momentum in downtown Greensboro. By the end of 2006, more people were living, eating, learning, and working downtown than anyone had thought possible just a few years before. In fact, more new businesses had opened on Elm Street and nearby than at any time since the 1940s. There was even a need for something downtown had lacked for decades: a grocery store to serve the new residents.

Greensboro's future certainly looked brighter than it had before Action Greensboro started to work. It remained uncertain, however. The loss of Jefferson-Pilot—whose corporate logo and name had disappeared from the company's office tower downtown—was further confirmation that Greensboro was the satellite rather than the sun; corporate decisions were being made elsewhere.

On some levels, the city seemed stuck massaging old problems. Local government remained in turmoil, with infighting among the county commissioners. In the late spring of 2006, a small but vocal group called the Greensboro Truth and Reconciliation Commission released its report on the tragic events of November 3, 1979, when Klansmen and neo-Nazis clashed with communist organizers and five people were killed. The lengthy report revived the insistent efforts of people who had been close to those killed that day to keep November 3 on the public agenda. It provided no new insight into what had happened, but it did stir another round of debate, led by some African American members of the city council, over whether Greensboro remained a racially divided city.

Action Greensboro also was in transition. After five years of intense work, the foundations were considering their own limits. Melvin worried about what could come in its wake. "We funded [Action Greensboro] on blind faith, and a lot of good things happened," he said in 2005. "We are at a critical stage. There are questions that we still don't have answers to, but we need to hold this thing together. I can't tell you where

[Greensboro] is going, but I can tell you where it ain't going if we aren't here. We'd be in deep yogurt."[2]

Melvin was approaching his seventy-third birthday at the end of 2006. He looked a full decade younger. A regimen of golf and exercise, along with a busy schedule, helped keep him trim. The streaks of gray in his dark brown hair were becoming more noticeable. Eyeglasses were carried but not worn, at the ready when he needed them. He was beginning to turn over some of his duties to Ed Kitchen, the former Greensboro city manager who had retired from his municipal duties in 2005 and joined the Bryan Foundation as Melvin's heir apparent earlier in the year.

Greensboro had been Melvin's home from the day he was born. He lived in the same house that he and Susan had built nearly thirty-five years earlier, when he was a young bank executive and she a community volunteer. Their sons had graduated from public schools. One had become an investment banker in New York; the other was in the construction business in Greensboro. Jim had left Asheboro Street fifty years before, but he still believed what his father had told him: put in a hard day's work and the future will take care of itself. At least, he believed the part about hard work. Over the years, he had learned to do a little more planning.

The depth of Melvin's energy and imagination was a marvel to his friends. "To understand Jim, you have to realize that this is a guy who gets up every morning and thinks up ten great ideas of things to do for Greensboro," city council member Florence Gatten said one day. "Now, by the end of the day, he knows nine of them were not good ideas, but there is one that he is still working on."[3]

His old friend Mike Weaver, who toiled beside Melvin on community ventures for more than twenty years, said, "He is a miniature George Washington. I have never seen anybody who has the compass he has got to do things for the right reasons and the belief that things can be accomplished. I can't tell you how many times if I have a decision to make I say, 'What would Jim Melvin do?'"

Melvin said he was inspired by the words of George Bernard Shaw, who wrote, "I am of the opinion that my life belongs to the whole community. And for as long as I live, it is my privilege to do for it whatever I can. I want to be thoroughly used up when I die. For the harder I work, the more I live."

"You are a dreamer," retired minister Joe Mullin wrote Melvin on New Year's Day, 2004. Mullin and Melvin had become close following the death of Melvin's father in 1972. Mullin was new in town at the time, and when he heard about the shooting, he called and offered the comfort of prayer, as well as his condolences. A few years later, Mullin became the spiritual leader of a small private prayer group that met regularly in the mayor's office. "You have vision," Mullin told Melvin in 2004, "and the tenacity to match it. And in God's Providence and the love of Joe Bryan for you, now you are being given unusual opportunities to touch and change the lives of children, youth and adults in our city. Did you ever dream it would work out like this?"[4]

What Mullin had in mind was the kind of imagination that was alert and alive when Melvin heard a news account of a man laid off from his job after twenty-one years with his company. The man's wife, who herself had devoted twelve years to the same company, also had received a pink slip. They were the parents of five children. The situation was stark. Economic numbers about layoffs and plant closings that Melvin had at his fingertips now had a face and a story. The next day, he called Neil Belenky, president of the United Way of Greater Greensboro, and asked where people like this could go for help.

Over the next six weeks, Melvin and Belenky met with contacts from more than a dozen agencies, from Employment Security to faith-based programs. The usual stories were told, and often with the same ending: there were programs in place to assist those laid off, and in two to four years a person could be retrained for a new career. But the family Melvin heard about needed help now.

"I asked them, 'Come up with something that works,'" Melvin recalled. Casting about for ideas, the group found a model in a program created two years earlier in Greenville, South Carolina, another textile center hit hard by the global shift in manufacturing. There, sixty-four companies had laid off more than 13,800 workers in just a few years. Greenville agencies had gone to work, and in a period of two years more than 4,000 former textile workers had been retrained, sometimes within ninety days, for new jobs in industries that were short of employees. It was not for everyone, but it was a start.[5]

Ninety days after Melvin's call to Belenky, Guilford Technical Community College (GTCC) announced a new program called "Quick Jobs with a Future." Training sessions would last ninety days or less and would focus on skills suitable for jobs in health care, construction, distribution, and warehousing. All were businesses that needed workers now. Starting pay in these industries was low, from seven to eleven dollars an hour, but it was a new start for those laid off from textile jobs who had few transferable skills. Action Greensboro underwrote the nearly $400,000 needed to get the program up and running. When classes began, a thousand people turned up for the four hundred training slots that had been planned for. GTCC officials said additional classes would be organized as soon as possible.

Melvin and the Bryan Foundation jump-started another program at Goodwill Industries, where Bryan board member Mike Haley was active. After Melvin saw a news report about a welfare-to-work program in New York, he talked with the board, which made a $500,000 grant to Goodwill to help increase training and job placement for the unemployed.

For Melvin, his response was not extraordinary. He was simply doing what Joe Bryan asked him to do—and nothing less than the old man himself had done when he learned the city could not continue a summer jobs program for teens. "How much does it cost?" Bryan had asked then-mayor Melvin, who quoted a figure. "Go ahead," Bryan had said. "The check's in the mail." Problem. Solution.

Melvin enjoyed using his clout and the foundation's checkbook to cut through the fog. He was practical. For example, after paying for an expensive annual report for the Bryan Foundation, Melvin scrubbed the entire idea. Instead, the foundation began sponsoring an annual luncheon, with guests invited from all the agencies that received support. College administrators sat with disabled workers and recovering drug addicts. Schoolteachers and principals were at the same table with county commissioners and city council members. Sports enthusiasts from Bryan's favorite venue, Bryan Park, broke bread with sponsors of downtown projects and young people looking for a second chance. Each year, speakers from three or four programs that had received aid during the previous year were asked to offer testimonials about their work.

In 2006, the president of Elon University and the dean of the new law school shared the podium with a passionate defender of homeless teenagers who had taken shelter at Joseph's House, a new nonprofit that received important start-up funding from the foundation. Accompanying the Reverend Nancy McLean was one of her charges, Patrick, whose life was renewed through the intervention of Joseph's House. He was due to start training as a Greensboro police officer the next morning. They were followed by a presentation on the newly opened Center City Park, a showcase for downtown. One of the quotations chiseled into the stone at the park was from an early-twentieth-century observer who said Greensboro stood for the best of the Old South with its hospitality and culture, and also for the energy and progress of the New South. "Mr. Bryan would be proud," Melvin said at the 2006 luncheon. "We have taken his resources and put them to work. In this room is enough horsepower that we can do whatever we want to do."[6]

"One of the things we heard in Chattanooga," Melvin later observed, "was, 'Break ground and move on.' Break ground and move on. The naysayers, the NIMBYs (Not In My Back Yard), the CAVES (Citizens Against Virtually Everything), they are going to be against everything you do. But if you break ground and move on, they will break off that project and start moving to another. But just keep on breaking ground."[7]

Throughout the twentieth century, no other person was longer involved in or more passionate about Greensboro than Jim Melvin. His tenure at city hall eclipsed that of the legendary General Townsend, whose planning and careful administration of postwar Greensboro profoundly shaped the city in ways that were still having an impact a half-century later. After leaving public office, Melvin used the private sector to influence the direction of his hometown. He was successful at that for more years than Jefferson's storied leader, Julian Price. Even in his "retirement" years, Melvin proved more productive than those who were years younger.

There probably would not be another Melvin, anymore than there would be leaders like Price or Townsend. The era in which Melvin thrived was over. There was a new model emerging, however. Action Greensboro showed that civic leadership could come from private, nonprofit foundations if they continued their commitment.

"The town has been good to me," Jim Melvin said. "The system has been good to me. And I'd like to think young people will have the same opportunity I did. I chose to stay [in my hometown] and see if I could make a difference."[8]

Melvin was an optimist. "Tipping point," he had called it that chilly morning as the first shovels of dirt were moved to create the new county office building. It had been just a step in the process, and months would pass before the results would be in. More than likely, it was just one point of departure for the city that Greensboro was on its way to becoming in the new century. There was no way to tell what would emerge from the old textile and manufacturing economy. It would be different, but that was also true of Charlotte, which had become a financial center, and even Durham, where technology had overtaken manufacturing.

Greensboro's future included a wider range of possibilities. While the textile manufacturing jobs that had built the city were disappearing, Greensboro remained the headquarters of VF Corporation, one of the world's largest apparel companies, whose brands include old denim favorites like Wrangler and Lee as well as outdoor clothing such as North Face and Nautica sportswear. Some saw the city as a distribution center, with the pending Federal Express facility serving as one of the hubs not only for its worldwide operations but for the area as well. Businesses that depended on fast, efficient delivery service were expected to find their way to the perimeter of the Federal Express operation. Others suggested that Greensboro would emerge as a center for higher education, with the new law school enhancing the existing mix of liberal arts colleges and research universities. Nearly fifty thousand students were in post–high school classrooms in the Triad.

There was no way to predict what would happen in the city's third century. In 1955, when the last history of the city was published, the writer compiled an inventory of the city's assets and reported that Greensboro had "accomplished a well-rounded development of enviable proportions,"[9] largely overlooking the city's dependence on manufacturing and the seismic shifts that would take place when the bottom fell out of textile manufacturing in the United States. The author's "well-rounded" assessment was based upon the city's expansion in spending on public schools, the increasing number of flights landing at what was then called the Greensboro–High Point Airport, a water system that would serve communities within a fifty-mile radius, and the "large business potentiality for Greensboro as a livestock marketing center." The chamber of commerce at the time had an ambitious agenda and a new slogan, "Keep Greensboro Ahead."[10]

A half-century later, the sons and daughters of the farmers of the 1950s were building computers at the Dell manufacturing plant built on the land that had once been pastures and cornfields. Others were producing microchips and components for makers of cell phones and communication devices whose headquarters were half a world away in Scandinavia. The city's largest employer was a health-care complex.

Well into the first decade of the twenty-first century, Greensboro was gathering itself for a new era, as it had a century earlier when the manufacturing base upon which the modern Greensboro was built was just beginning to take shape. It was a city in transition then, as it was once again in the first decade of the new century. There were plenty of challenges ahead.

"I really do believe in that speech by Winston Churchill," Melvin mused one day, reflecting on the stout determination of the British prime minister in the darkest days of World War II. "You never give up. No matter what happens, you get up off the canvas, dust yourself off, and go again."

Greensboro certainly had a new, growing base of twenty-first-century businesses, from transportation and logistics to technology development. From them, and from the community, would rise a new generation of leaders as the years passed. Others would succeed Melvin and his contemporaries, just as they had filled in the places vacated by those who had made Greensboro what it was in the twentieth century.

Chapter 1. The Pivot of the Piedmont

1. Jacquelyn Dowd Hall, James Leloudis, Robert Korstad, Mary Murphy, Lu Ann Jones, and Christopher B. Daly, *Like A Family: The Making of a Southern Cotton Mill Village* (Chapel Hill: University of North Carolina Press, 1987), p. 197.
2. Gayle Hicks Fripp, John Harden, and Dewitt Carroll, *Greensboro: A Chosen Center* (Woodland Hills, CA: Windsor Publications, 1982), p. 101.
3. "United Bank Opens Its Doors This Morning," *Greensboro Daily News*, July 1, 1932.
4. "Is Now Doubtful That City Can Meet Its Bills April 1," *Greensboro Daily News*, March 28, 1932.
5. "Price Optimistic over Future Events," *Greensboro Daily News*, March 5, 1933.
6. Howard Holderness, interview by Pamela Dean, April 14, 1985, Southern Oral History Program Collection (hereafter SOHP), Southern Historical Collection, Manuscripts Department, Wilson Library, University of North Carolina at Chapel Hill (hereafter SHC).
7. "Scrip Corporation Can Act with Promptness," *Greensboro Daily News*, March 14, 1933.
8. *Greensboro Daily News*, March 28, 1933.
9. "Hoboes Rest in Pomona 'Jungle,'" *Greensboro Daily News*, March 19, 1933.
10. George Bradham, "A Company That Serves the Carolinas and the South," *Greensboro Daily News*, November 19, 1933.
11. John Van Lindley, interview by the author, April 20, 1989, SHC.
12. "Business Much Better Than Any Holiday since 1931," *Greensboro Daily News*, December 21, 1933.
13. Huger King, interview, Greensboro Oral History Project, Greensboro Public Library (hereafter GOHP).
14. Clara Layton, interview by Ida L. Moore, Federal Writers Project no. 669, SHC.
15. "No Textile Plants in Guilford County Involved in Strike," *Greensboro Daily News*, September 4, 1934.
16. "Peace Offer Made by Labor Leaders in Textile Strike," *Greensboro Daily News*, September 9, 1934.
17. "Textile Plants Here Are All in Operation," *Greensboro Daily News*, September 11, 1934.

18. Allen Tullos, *Habits of Industry: White Culture and the Transformation of the Carolina Piedmont* (Chapel Hill: University of North Carolina Press, 1989).
19. King, interview.

Chapter 2. Army Town

1. Mose Kiser Jr., interview by the author, June 26, 2002, Bryan Foundation archives (hereafter BF).
2. Huger King, interview, GOHP.
3. Alexander R. Stoessen, *The Elixir of War: Greensboro as an 'Army Town,' 1942–1946*, Greensboro Historical Museum archives.
4. Julia Burnett Davis, interview, September 16, 1982, GOHP.
5. Ibid.
6. "Greensboro ORD: Its Past and Present," Headquarters, Public Relations Office, AAF Overseas Replacement Depot, Greensboro, North Carolina, Greensboro Historical Museum archives.
7. Gayle Hicks Fripp, *Greensboro: A Chosen Center* (Sun Valley, CA: American Historical Press, 2001).
8. "Quakers Urged to Weep over Dead Rather Than Rejoice over Victory," *Greensboro Daily News*, August 11, 1945.
9. "ORDS Transfer," *Greensboro Daily News*, August 2, 1946.

Chapter 3. Building a City

1. Michael Weaver, interview by the author, September 2, 2002, BF.
2. "Cone Mills to Alter Village," *Greensboro Daily News*, November 9, 1949.
3. Ethel Stephens Arnett, *Greensboro, North Carolina* (Chapel Hill: University of North Carolina Press, 1955), p. 355.
4. Robert Jamieson, interview, May 1, 1978, GOHP.
5. John R. Foster, undated interview, GOHP.
6. "Radio Recreation Is Being Planned," *Greensboro Daily News*, July 17, 1948.
7. Jim Schlosser, "Polio," *Greensboro Record*, August 2, 1975.
8. "Plans Discussed for Building Semipermanent Polio Hospital," *Greensboro Daily News*, June 26, 1948.
9. Foster, interview.
10. "Wallace Showered with Eggs Here," *Greensboro Daily News*, August 30, 1948.
11. Foster, interview.
12. Arnett, *Greensboro, North Carolina*, p. 356.

Chapter 4. Honor City of America

1. Julia Burnett Davis, interview, September 16, 1982, GOHP.
2. "Voice of the People," *Greensboro Record*, August 19, 1946.
3. Fred Williams, interview by the author, March 17, 2003, BF.
4. "City Planning Commission Again Snubs ORD Proposal," *Greensboro Daily News*, September 28, 1948.
5. "Closed Sunday Advocates for Council Action," *Greensboro Daily News*, August 28, 1946; "Evangelistic Crusade Ended," *Greensboro Daily News*, November 25, 1951.

Chapter 5. The General

1. Ben Cone, interview, June 23, 1977, GOHP.
2. "Catastrophe Is the Word," *Greensboro Daily News*, October 1, 1954.
3. Horace Kornegay, interview by the author, June 25, 2002, BF.
4. "Residents of City Hunt New Ways to Save Water," *Greensboro Daily News*, October 11, 1954.
5. "Fluoridated Water Inspires No Complaints of Bad Taste," *Greensboro Record*, October 15, 1952.
6. Walter Johnson Jr., interview by the author, November 4, 2002, BF.
7. William Little, interview by the author, September 27, 2002, BF.
8. Stanley Frank, interview by the author, December 29, 2002, BF.
9. Thomas W. Hanchett, *Sorting Out the New South City* (Chapel Hill: University of North Carolina Press, 1998), p. 226.
10. William Jones, interview by the author, October 2, 2002, BF.
11. Ben Cone, interview, June 23, 1977, GOHP.
12. Ceasar Cone II, interview, June 28, 1981, SOHP, SHC.
13. Ibid.
14. William Chafe, *Civilities and Civil Rights* (New York: Oxford University Press, 1980).
15. Jim Melvin, interview by the author, July 18, 2002, BF.
16. JSL to MEL, December 10, 1960, James Spencer Love Papers, SHC.
17. Weddie Huffman, interview by the author, December 2, 2002, BF.
18. JSL to Messrs. Upson, Rauch, Myers, and Zane, October 26, 1960, James Spencer Love Papers, SHC.
19. JSL to MEL, December 10, 1960, James Spencer Love Papers, SHC.
20. Little, interview.
21. Howard E. Covington Jr., *Belk, Inc.: The Company and the Family That Built It* (Charlotte, NC: Belk, 2002), p. 125.
22. Greensboro Chamber of Commerce, *Glimpses of Greensboro* 6, no. 8 (November 1958).

Chapter 6. Elephants with Ears Flapping

1. Charles T. Hagan Jr., interview by the author, July 18, 2002, BF.
2. Ibid.
3. "The Coliseum, the Heart of a City," *Greensboro Daily News*, April 16, 1971.
4. Jim Melvin, interview by the author, May 16, 2002, BF.
5. Ibid.
6. "Brown Demands Probe into Real Estate Deals," *Greensboro Daily News*, September 30, 1948.

Chapter 7. Best in the Nation

1. Irwin Smallwood, "A Part of Our History," *Greensboro Daily News*, May 24, 2002.
2. John Cathey, "Snead Says Remarks on Course Made in Interest of Tourney," *Greensboro Record*, April 21, 1960.
3. Carson Bain, interview, June 30, 1977, GOHP.

4. Smith Barrier, *GGO: The First Forty-Four Years* (Greensboro: Greensboro Jaycees, 1982).

5. Laurence Leonard, "It's a Great Game," *Greensboro Daily News*, September 27, 1938.

6. Ibid.

7. William Burns Jr., interview by the author, July 8, 2002, BF.

8. Charlie Sifford, *Just Let Me Play* (Latham, NY: British American Publishing, 1992).

9. Ibid, p. 111.

10. Henry Frye, interview by the author, April 24, 2003, BF.

11. Sifford, *Just Let Me Play*.

12. Ibid.

13. Jim Melvin, interview by the author, May 23, 2003, BF.

14. Ibid.

Chapter 8. Changing Times

1. John Harden, *Greensboro Daily News*, November 12, 1963.

2. William Little, interview by the author, September 27, 2002, BF.

3. C. A. Paul, "Central District Needs Cleanup," *Greensboro Daily News*, March 3, 1959.

4. Roy Thompson, "Observer Thinks Greensboro Being Beset by Populationitis," *Greensboro Daily News*, December 1, 1963.

5. Lewis Mumford, *The City in History* (New York: Harcourt Brace and World, 1961).

6. Abe Jones Jr., *Greensboro 27* (Bassett, VA: Bassett, 1976), p. 42.

7. C. A. Paul, "Downtown Greensboro," *Greensboro Daily News*, December 6, 1961.

8. C. A. Paul, "Plans for Redevelopment Offered," *Greensboro Daily News*, January 13, 1963.

9. Van King, "City's Downtown Redefines Mission," *Greensboro Daily News*, February 11, 1979.

10. Jim Melvin, interview by the author, May 16, 2002, BF.

11. Ibid.

12. Doug Galyon, interview by the author, October 8, 2002, BF.

13. Jim Melvin, interview by the author, July 10, 2002, BF.

14. Ibid.

Chapter 9. Greensboro Stinks

1. David H. Shelton, "Greensboro '70: An Essay on the City and Its Economy," School of Business and Economics, University of North Carolina at Greensboro.

2. Jack Elam, interview by the author, August 12, 2002, BF.

3. Ibid.

4. Ibid.

5. "Disorders Blamed on Inequality," *Greensboro Daily News*, March 21, 1970.

6. H. J. Elam III, "View of Chamber from Mayor's Chair," Greensboro Chamber of Commerce, December 8, 1969.

7. Ken Irons, "Jim Melvin: Local Boy Makes Good," *Greensboro Record*, May 11, 1971.

8. "Townsend Dam Dedicated," *Greensboro Daily News*, April 15, 1971.

9. "Bryan Park Dedicated," *Greensboro Record*, May 21, 1971.
10. Roger Soles, interview by the author, January 23, 2003, BF.
11. Shelton, "Greensboro '70," p. 65.
12. Ibid.
13. C. A. Paul, "What's Wrong with Downtown?" *Greensboro Daily News*, December 7, 1961.
14. Jim Melvin, interview by the author, July 10, 2002, BF.
15. Lee Kinard, interview by the author, August 8, 2002, BF.
16. Jim Betts, interview by the author, June 11, 2002, BF.
17. Melvin, interview, July 10, 2002.
18. Ibid., August 8, 2002.
19. Ibid., July 10, 2002.
20. Mike Forte, "Two Gunmen Kill Mayor's Father," *Greensboro Record*, October 25, 1972.
21. J. A. C. Dunn, "Greensboro," *Winston-Salem Journal*.

Chapter 10. From Camelot to Dodge City

1. "Metro Funds Exhausted," *Greensboro Daily News*, April 3, 1976.
2. Jim Melvin, interview by the author, July 18, 2002, BF.
3. Ibid., August 1, 2002.
4. Justin Catanoso, "The Man behind the Vision," *Greensboro News & Record*, January 29, 1995.
5. Charles L. Weill Jr., interview by the author, October 7, 2002, BF.
6. Winston Cavin, "Southern Life Will Develop O. Henry," *Greensboro Daily News*, October 27, 1978.
7. Thomas Hines, "Center Foe Explains Why He's Fighting," *Greensboro Record*, September 26, 1979.
8. "For Mayor: Melvin," *Greensboro Daily News*, November 4, 1979.

Chapter 11. They Don't Give a Thing

1. Jim Melvin, interview by the author, July 18, 2002, BF.
2. "Four Die in Shootout," *Greensboro Daily News*, November 4, 1979.
3. Ned Cline, *Adding Value: The Joseph M. Bryan Story from Poverty to Philanthropy* (Asheboro, NC: Down Home Press, 2001).
4. Walter Johnson Jr., interview by the author, July 16, 2002, BF.
5. "George Simkins: A Lifelong Struggle for Civil Rights," *Greensboro News & Record*, February 4, 1990.
6. Ibid.
7. Ibid.
8. George Simkins, interview by Karen Kruse Thomas, April 6, 1997, SOHP, SHC.
9. "George Simkins," *Greensboro News & Record*, February 4, 1990.
10. Ibid.

Chapter 12. Casey at the Bat

1. Joe Knox, "Greensboro Race Crisis," *Greensboro Daily News*, September 15, 1963.
2. Boyd Morris, undated interview, GOHP.

3. David Schenck Jr., undated interview by William Chafe, Special Collections, Perkins Library, Duke University.

4. "Greensboro, Head Start on Becoming Great Metropolitan Area," *Greensboro Daily News*, November 12, 1963.

5. William Little, interview by the author, June 20, 2002, BF.

6. Mike Weaver, interview by the author, March 10, 2004, BF.

7. Greensboro Chamber of Commerce, *Greensboro Business*, Summer 1968.

8. Jo Spivey, "Four-Zone Council Election Is Approved in Chamber Study," *Greensboro Record*, October 3, 1968.

9. Vance Chavis, undated interview, GOHP.

10. Ibid.

11. Jack Elam, interview by the author, January 2, 2003, BF.

12. Jim Melvin, interview by the author, August 1, 2002, BF.

13. Kelso Gilenwater, "Race Relations Inadequate," *Greensboro Daily News*, October 5, 1969.

14. Joe Knox, "Plan B Cuts City into Twelve Political Pieces," *Greensboro Daily News*, December 10, 1968.

15. Henry Frye, interview by the author, April 20, 2003, BF.

16. Lindsey Gruson, "After Violence, Community Leaders Ask for Calm," *Greensboro Daily News*, November 4, 1979.

17. Nelson Johnson, interview by the author, August 6, 2003, BF.

18. Reverend Howard Chubbs, interview by the author, November 18, 2002, BF.

19. Jim Melvin, interview by the author, September 26, 2002, BF.

20. Jo Spivey, "Webb Lends Support to March," *Greensboro Record*, January 26, 1980.

21. Melvin, interview, September 26, 2002.

22. Ibid.

23. Ibid., August 1, 2002.

24. William March, "For a Day, Melvin Was Greensboro," *Greensboro Daily News*, November 23, 1980.

25. Jim Melvin, interview by the author, September 19, 2002, BF.

26. Florence Gatten, interview by the author, November 11, 2002, BF.

27. Melvin, interview, September 26, 2002.

Chapter 13. Restore the Luster

1. "Before You Vote on Tuesday," advertisement, *Greensboro Daily News*, May 4, 1980.

2. Jefferson Standard Life Insurance Company and Pilot Life Insurance Company became components of Jefferson-Pilot Corporation in 1968.

3. "Forbis, Council Hold First Meeting," *Greensboro Record*, November 4, 1981.

4. Jim Melvin, interview by the author, November 7, 2002, BF.

5. John Forbis, interview by the author, August 8, 2003, BF.

6. Jack Elam, interview by the author, August 12, 2002, BF.

7. Jim Schlosser, "Conservative Grip on City Is Firm," *Greensboro Record*, November 5, 1981.

8. Ibid.

9. Roy Moore, interview by the author, February 18, 2002, BF; Jim Melvin, interview by the author, January 22, 2003, BF.

10. Cameron Cooke, interview by the author, January 6, 2003, BF.

11. William Hemphill, interview by the author, August 20, 2002, BF.
12. Cole C. Campbell, "Opposing Sides Now Agree on Wards, Urge Council Vote," *Greensboro Daily News*, November 16, 1982.
13. Cole C. Campbell, "Council Adopts District Rule in Greensboro," *Greensboro Daily News*, December 17, 1982.
14. Henry Isaacson, interview by the author, April 17, 2003, BF.
15. Jim Melvin, interview by the author, November 14, 2002, BF.

Chapter 14. Bolt out of the Blue

1. Dewey Trogdon, interview by the author, September 4, 2003, BF.
2. Ibid.
3. Ceasar Cone III, interview by the author, August 27, 2003, BF.

Chapter 15. Different Era

1. Battelle Memorial Institute, "Greensboro, North Carolina Economic Development Program," February 1984.
2. Roger Soles, interview by the author, January 23, 2003, BF.
3. Jack Scism, "City Drifting from Lack of Dominant Leadership," November 23, 1980, *Greensboro Daily News*.
4. William Hemphill, interview by the author, August 20, 2002, BF.
5. Jim Melvin, interview by the author, April 11, 2003, BF.
6. William Hemphill, interview by the author, December 12, 2002, BF.
7. Michael Weaver, interview by the author, September 2, 2002, BF.
8. Ibid.
9. Roger Soles, interview by the author, January 23, 2003, BF.
10. Florence Gatten, interview by the author, November 11, 2002, BF.
11. Jim Melvin, interview by the author, August 15, 2002, BF.
12. Ibid.
13. Thomas A. Barstow, "City Manager in Saddle; Mayor Still a Burr," *Greensboro News & Record*, December 23, 1992.
14. John Forbis, interview by the author, October 16, 2002, BF.
15. Jim Melvin, interview by the author, November 14, 2002, BF.
16. Jeri Fischer and John Cleghorn, "Greensboro Fighting Merger Tide; City Leaders Look on Helplessly," *Charlotte Observer*, April 13, 1987.
17. Michael Weaver, interview by the author, October 14, 2002, BF.
18. Fischer and Cleghorn, "Greensboro Fighting Merger Tide."

Chapter 16. We Must Take Action

1. Jim Melvin, interview by the author, August 8, 2002, BF.
2. Ibid., November 14, 2002.
3. "First Home Federal Takes S&L Plunge in Banking Strategy," *Greensboro News & Record*, June 5, 1983.
4. Bob Garsson, "Jim Melvin on Regionalism," *Carolina Piedmont*, May 1988.
5. Jim Melvin, interview by the author, September 11, 2003, BF.
6. Ibid.
7. Mike Weaver, interview by the author, October 14, 2002, BF.

8. Ibid.

9. Jim Melvin, interview by the author, May 23, 2002, BF.

10. Susan Melvin, interview by the author, September 30, 2002, BF.

11. Jim Melvin, interview, May 23, 2002.

12. Susan Melvin, interview.

13. Jim Melvin, interview, August 8, 2002.

14. Ibid.

15. Jim Melvin, interview, September 11, 2003.

16. Dewey Trogdon, interview by the author, September 4, 2003, BF.

17. William Hemphill, recorded message for Cemala Foundation Board of Directors, June 1999, Cemala Foundation archives.

Chapter 17. Action Greensboro

1. Alan Tonelson, "When the Dinosaurs Die," American Economic Alert, March 6, 2001, http://www.americaneconomicalert.org/view_art.asp?Prod_ID=175.

2. William Hemphill, interview by the author, August 20, 2002, BF.

3. Jim Melvin, interview by the author, January 23, 2003, BF.

4. Ibid., November 13, 2003.

5. Carolyn Allen, interview by Kathryn Hass, December 6, 1994, SOHP, SHC.

6. Carolyn Allen, interview by the author, October 8, 2003, BF.

7. "A Conversation with the Mayors of Greensboro," Greensboro News & Record, February 25, 2001.

8. Doug Galyon, interview by the author, October 8, 2002, BF.

Chapter 18. Baseball

1. Priscilla Taylor, interview by the author, January 21, 2003, BF.

2. "Building Consensus for Greensboro's Future," McKinsey and Company, November 2000, BF.

3. Priscilla Taylor, interview by the author, November 17, 2003, BF.

4. Ibid.

5. Richard Moore, interview by the author, January 6, 2003, BF.

6. David Stonecipher, interview by the author, December 11, 2002, BF.

7. Jim Melvin, interview by the author, November 21, 2002, BF.

8. Bill Hass, "Local Group Buys Greensboro Bats," Greensboro News & Record, September 8, 1999.

9. Jack Scism, "City Drifting from Lack of Dominant Leadership," November 23, 1980, Greensboro Daily News/Record.

10. Stonecipher, interview, December 11, 2002.

11. Justin Catanoso, "Some Triad Business Stalwarts Are Making Major-League Play," Greensboro News & Record, August 30, 1995.

12. Justin Catanoso, "Will Bats Get Field of Dreams?" Greensboro News & Record, May 13, 1995.

13. John Nagy, "Triad CEOs Committed to Baseball Efforts," Greensboro News & Record, May 1, 1998.

14. Jim Schlosser, "One Year Later, Opinions Remain Firm on Stadium," Greensboro News & Record, May 4, 1999.

15. Mark Binker, "Controversy Continues," *Greensboro News & Record*, May 17, 2003.
16. "Private Investment in Public Schools," undated report, Joseph M. Bryan Foundation, BF.

Conclusion

1. Jim Melvin, interview by the author, November 2, 2004, BF.
2. Ibid., April 8, 2004, BF.
3. Florence Gatten, interview by the author, November 11, 2003, BF.
4. Joseph B. Mullin to Jim Melvin, January 1, 2004, personal collection of Jim Melvin.
5. Melvin, interview, April 8, 204.
6. Jim Melvin, remarks at Bryan Foundation annual luncheon, February 7, 2006, BF.
7. Jim Melvin, interview by the author, September 3, 2006, BF.
8. Ibid.
9. Ethel Stephens Arnett, *Greensboro, North Carolina* (Chapel Hill: University of North Carolina Press, 1955), p. 415.
10. Ibid., p. 417.

election system of for city officials, 151–52

expansion of the city limits and fair voting districts, 185–88, 208

federal aid to, 4, 9, 134, 213

finances of, 16–17, 210

fluoridation of the water system in, 65–66

future of, 276–78

garbage strike in, 121

as the "Gate City," 12

geographical location of, 61–62

as the "Honor City of America," 57

housing growth in, 13, 19–20; (post–World War II), 39–43; (1980s), 211–12

Human Rights Commission of, 109

industry and industrial development in, 54–56, 73–75, 196, 240–42

integration of schools in, 80–81, 91, 128

lack of financial services in, 15–16

manufacturing strength of, 2, 11–12, 116

as the "Pivot of the Piedmont," 12

population of: (1948), 42; (1960), 85; (1969), 115; (1970), 4; (1985), 212

prosperity and growth of (1900–1940), 12–14

public debt of, 57–58

referendum on the city's charter (1980), 179–81

rent strike in, 121

resistance to change in, 9–10

retail business expansion in, 74

sewage system of, 135, 138–39

subdivisions of, 14, 42

suburban development of, 134–35

thoroughfare/roadway systems in, 3, 12, 60–61, 137

water supply/system of, 61–65, 123, 124, 135, 139–40, 213

zoning and planning commission of, 55

Greensboro, downtown area of, 1, 12–13, 23, 45, 51, 78, 125–27, 133–35, 142–43, 223, 237–39, 257. See also Action Greensboro, downtown development plan of

Cooper Carry plan for development of, 257, 259, 265

decline of, 103–5

post–Great Depression growth of, 25–27

Greensboro, economic development and growth in, 199–200, 211–12, 250–53, 269 (see also Greensboro Development Corporation [GDC])

economic competition of with Charlotte, 3–4, 197

economic report concerning (1984 [Battelle Report]), 196–97, 200

economic report concerning (2000 [McKinsey Report]), 7, 253, 254

post–World War II, 39–43

Greensboro, minor league baseball in, 26, 36

Greensboro Bats, 255, 258

Greensboro Hornets, 261

Greensboro Patriots, 36, 261

history of, 261

multiple uses for the new stadium (First Horizon Park), 268

purchase of land for new stadium, 259–61

stadium development, 8–10, 264–65

success of new team (Greensboro Grasshoppers), 267–69

Greensboro, racial issues in, 51, 72, 150–51, 153–58, 159–60, 182–83, 272. See also Greensboro Chamber of Commerce, progressiveness of in race relations; Morningside, shootings at

civil rights demonstrations in (1963), 31, 32, 102, 106, 109

community civil rights committee of, 160–61

and the desegregation of hospitals, 157–58

and the desegregation of restaurants, 159–60

Greensboro, textile industry in, 2–3, 4, 5–6, 22, 43, 195, 196, 233. See also individually listed mills

decline of, 239–40

and the labor strike of 1934, 22–24

and the North American Free Trade Agreement (NAFTA), 247–49

Greensboro, and World War II, 8, 29–37

and the Basic Training Unit Number 10 Army Base, 7, 9, 31–34

effect of on local businesses, 30–31

housing shortage during, 34

industrial war effort of, 30

local war heroes, 35

and the Overseas Replacement Depot (ORD), 34, 35, 36, 37, 41, 52–54, 55

U.S. Army expenditures in Greensboro, 33, 35, 36

Greensboro Association of Poor People, 170–71